Lying, Cheating, Bullying, and Narcissism

This vibrant book examines individual and societal factors contributing to the rise of lying, cheating, bullying, and narcissism, with emphasis on the influence of Trumpism and the valuing of "getting things done" over the importance of self-discipline and issues of morality.

George Bear explores individual and environmental factors that influence the development of self-discipline. He examines reasons for the growing prevalence of lying, cheating, bullying, and narcissism and their underlying factors, and the role of parenting and peer relationships in their development. The volume highlights the critical roles that moral reasoning, moral emotions, and mechanisms of moral disengagement play in dishonest and harmful behavior.

Lying, Cheating, Bullying, and Narcissism is for students and scholars of child development, parenting, psychopathology, and criminology; professionals in psychology, mental health, and education; as well as others interested in the prevalence and roots of lying, cheating, bullying, and narcissism in America.

George Bear, Ph.D. (University of Virginia), is an internationally recognized expert on children's behavior problems, self-discipline, school discipline, and school climate. He is a Professor Emeritus of school psychology at the University of Delaware. In addition to publishing nine books, he has authored over 100 journal articles and book chapters. He is a Fulbright Specialist and recipient of the 2017 Lifetime Achievement Award of the National Association of School Psychologists.

Lying, Cheating, Bullying, and Narcissism

The Development of Self-Discipline and the Influence of Trumpism

George G. Bear

Routledge
Taylor & Francis Group

NEW YORK AND LONDON

Designed cover image: © GettyImages/Fanatic Studio/Gary Waters

First published 2024
by Routledge
605 Third Avenue, New York, NY 10158

and by Routledge
4 Park Square, Milton Park, Abingdon, Oxon, OX14 4RN

Routledge is an imprint of the Taylor & Francis Group, an informa business

© 2024 George Bear

ISBN: 978-1-032-51134-4 (hbk)
ISBN: 978-1-032-49858-4 (pbk)
ISBN: 978-1-003-40127-8 (ebk)

DOI: 10.4324/9781003401278

Typeset in Galliard
by MPS Limited, Dehradun

To my wife and best friend, Patti.
To the grandkids: Jackson, Madison, Susan, and Reagan.

Contents

1 Getting Things Done
Trumpism and the New Normal

Presidential Moral Character

Millions of Americans watched news reports, press conferences, and a daily flood of Twitter (now known as X) in which the president of the United States, Donald J. Trump, demonstrated how lying, cheating, and bullying "gets things done." Whereas 81 million voters ended up firing him, almost as many, 74 million, wanted to rehire him. Votes were based on the economy, abortion, gun rights, the coronavirus pandemic, health care, immigration, racial injustice, and the environment, but many also were based on the moral character of Trump. For many voters, moral character did not matter but for many others it did.

Moral character refers to one's personality and more specifically to moral qualities such as honesty, trustworthiness, empathy, and acceptance of responsibility for one's actions. In grade school children are taught of presidents who were role models of traits of moral character. Upon being elected, George Washington said "Integrity and firmness is all I can promise." He also said, "Ninety-nine percent of failures come from people who make excuses." Thomas Jefferson asserted that "Honesty is the first chapter of the book wisdom." Abraham Lincoln's nickname was "Honest Abe." Teddy Roosevelt asserted "The one thing I want to leave my children is an honorable name." While leading our nation during World War II, Franklin Roosevelt noted that the presidency is "a place of moral leadership." In modeling responsibility for one's behavior, Harry Truman famously said "the buck stops here."

In contrast to lessons learned from those presidents, Trump is likely to be remembered for his leadership in promoting a culture in which lying, cheating, bullying, and narcissism are normal; viewed as acceptable, if not admirable, character traits. Instead of quotes from presidents presented above that largely defined their moral character, historians are likely to cite the following quotes of Trump when writing about his moral character:

- "Sometimes you don't have time to be totally, as you would say, 'presidential.' You have to get things done."[1]

DOI: 10.4324/9781003401278-1

- "When someone crosses you, my advice is 'Get even!' That is not typical advice, but it is real-life advice. If you do not get even, you are just a schmuck! ... Always fight back and get even."[2]
- "Part of the beauty of me is that I am very rich."[3]
- "And when you're a star, they let you do it. You can do anything ... Grab'em by the pussy. You can do anything."[4]
- "For the most part, you can't respect people because most people aren't worthy of respect."[5]
- "You're fired."
- "I WON THE ELECTION!"[6]

As noted by Peter Wehner, a political writer, Evangelical Christian, vice president at the Ethics and Public Policy Center (a conservative think tank), and former speech writer for presidents Ronal Reagan, George H. W. Bush, and George W. Bush: "We've never had a president who takes psychic delight in shattering moral norms, or discrediting morality as a concept." Wehner adds "Asking Trump to understand morality is like asking a person born blind to understand color."[7] More bluntly, President Joe Biden commented "This guy just isn't really an American president."[8]

It is quite likely that at one time or another everyone reading this book has lied and cheated. As either a child or adult, most also have engaged in bullying behaviors, such as teasing, excluding others, and even pushing, shoving, or hitting a sibling or someone else. Many also have thought that they were the greatest person on earth and announced this to others. Exhibiting those behaviors every now and then, and especially in childhood, is normal. Fortunately, due largely to good childrearing and children's maturing ability to consider the impact of their behavior on others, most children do not become full-fledged liars, cheaters, bullies, and narcissists. Most learn and appreciate that moral character matters, and that dishonesty and self-promotion are neither highly valued character traits nor normative in *most* of America.

Of course, there always have been children, and adults, who fail to value moral character and who frequently violate societal norms. What has largely held the number of those individuals in check have been moral norms against dishonest and harmful behavior. Children quickly learn which behaviors are normal and valued by society and which ones are deviant and frowned upon, often leading to social rejection or outright punishment. In shattering moral norms and discrediting morality as a concept, Trump has cultivated a new normal among many Americans, one in which children learn that lying, cheating, and bullying are no longer viewed as deviant or immoral but as behaviors that one should feel proud if they lead to greater wealth, fame, and power. Indeed, many children are learning not only that moral character really does not matter but that often it is an obstacle to success—an obstacle to be avoided.

Changing American Values: What Matters More Than Moral Character Is Getting Things Done

During Trump's presidency, a 2018 national poll showed that although 90% of Americans thought it was important that a president be a good role model, 67% agreed that Trump was *not* a good role model.[9] The same poll also found that an astounding 72% of Republicans believed that Trump *was* a good role model for children. Revealing a cultural divide, only 1% of Democrats agreed. Moreover, 84% of Republicans (5% of Democrats) found Trump to be honest. Most Republicans also saw Trump as "someone who shares your values" and who made them feel proud.[10] The viewpoint that Trump is of sound moral character and a good role model for our children was held by most Republicans but particularly those who frequently watched *Fox News* (those referred to in polls as "Fox News Republicans"). One poll in 2017 found that whereas most Americans (63%) believed that Trump had damaged the dignity of the presidency, only 9% of Fox News Republicans agreed (compared to 27% of Republicans in general and 36% of White evangelical Protestants). Another national poll in late 2019 reported that about half (53%) of Republicans viewed Trump as a greater president than Abraham Lincoln. Lincoln is almost always rated as the greatest American president by historians, political scientists, and the public. Most historians rank Trump among the worst presidents. A survey of 142 presidential historians taken in June 2021 ranked only three other presidents lower (i.e., Franklin Pierce, Andrew Johnson, and James Buchanan).[11]

As it became clear to nearly everyone during Trump's presidency, including Fox News Republicans, that Trump lied, cheated, and bullied, many of his supporters experienced what is called *cognitive dissonance*. That is, their beliefs about the importance of honesty and other moral character traits no longer aligned with their actual behavior—they said they valued honesty and integrity but supported a dishonest president. When cognitive dissonance occurs, individuals experience emotional discomfort. To relieve such discomfort, they must change either their behavior or their beliefs. For example, one can either quit enabling and supporting a liar, cheat, and bully or no longer believe that those behaviors are bad. Whereas a few Trump supporters chose the former, most chose the latter.

Polls conducted throughout Trump's presidency revealed a seismic shift in attitudes toward Trump and perceptions of his character. Largely in response to cognitive dissonance experienced by about half of Americans, a new normal in America emerged. In polls taken early in his presidency, his supporters denied that Trump was dishonest. By the end of his presidency, they acknowledged that he was dishonest and lacked moral character, but now excused and accepted it. During the last year of his presidency, the 2020 *PRRI*'s American Values Survey found that only 21% of Americans agreed that Trump was honest and trustworthy, 24% that he "cares about people like you," 25% that he "has the right temperament and personality to be president," and 18% that he "has strong religious beliefs." Despite the low percentage of Americans who found him possessing those personal qualities (and ones that most people desire to be presidential qualities), almost half supported and voted for him in the 2020 election.

Trump's support among voters diminished a bit after his second impeachment for inciting the insurrection at the US Capitol; however, a large number of Republicans, including many governors and members of Congress, continued to support, if not adore, him. A *Suffolk University/USA TODAY* poll taken almost two months after the 2020 insurrection found that half of those polled believed that the Republican party should become "more loyal to Trump," even if it meant losing support among establishment Republicans.[12] The poll also found that 46% would abandon the Republican party and join a Trump party if the former president decided to create one. Being a Trumphite was more important to them than being a Republican or holding traditional moral values.

After being indicted in late March 2023 for criminal offenses related to his alleged role in hush money payment to porn star Stormy Daniels (see Chapter 5), Trump's poll numbers diminished a bit in May and June of that year. Still, the majority of Republicans continued to view him favorably: *CNN* polls found that 77% of Republicans viewed him favorably in May and 67% in June.[13] Support among his base continued after a federal grand jury indicted him in late May 2023 for 37 counts relating to taking national defense documents from the White House and retaining them illegally at his Mar-A-Lago resort (see Chapter 3). An NPR/PBS NewsHour/Marist national poll showed an increase in support, with 76% of Republicans and Republican-leaning independents having a favorable opinion of Trump (the same poll found 68% in February).[14] Another poll, conducted July 2023, found that 71% of Republicans planned to vote for him.[15]

Some people supported Trump throughout his presidency and continue to do so—despite being the first president impeached twice and charged with federal crimes (with indictments from four grand juries)—because they believe he is Christ-like, or the chosen one. The *PPPR* 2020 American Values Survey found that about one in five Republicans (19%) agreed that Trump "Is being called by God to lead during this critical time in our country." The percentage is much higher among Republican White evangelical Protestants, with an astounding 72% believing that Trump, regardless of his character flaws, has been called by God to lead. In justifying their support (and reducing cognitive dissonance), many cite King David in the Bible as also being someone chosen by God as a leader of a nation (Israel) despite his immoral behavior. David murdered Goliath and those he believed to be traitors. Like Trump, David also committed adultery.

Other than someone being called by God to lead a nation, why might someone view a president, or anyone else widely known to be dishonest, as a good role model for children? The answer lies in responses to a statement in the *PRRI* survey: Many Americans dismiss the importance of a president and other national leaders being moral. This was best seen in responses to the statement "an elected official who personally behaves in an immoral way can still be effective in their public and professional life." That statement was included in *PRRI's* 2011 and 2020 American Values Survey.[16] Almost twice as many Republicans agreed to the statement in 2020 as they did in 2011. In 2020, 71% of Republicans (47% of Democrats, 57% of Independents) agreed. The greatest shift in American values about a president's moral behavior was seen in responses by evangelical Protestants: 30% agreed in 2011 and 68% in 2020 that an elected official who acts immorally can still be effective.

For many Americans, honesty and moral character are not important in leaders who are successfully accomplishing their shared agendas. The agendas of many Trump supporters are driven by a moral concern about abortion, or life, but for many others, they are driven by fear, realistic or not, and fear that is centered on oneself and not on the rights or needs of others. Common fears are losing their guns, religious rights, jobs, and the right to private health insurance; immigration; crime; people of color; paying higher taxes; socialism; and the government telling them what to do (e.g., having to wear a mask to or be vaccinated to help prevent the deaths of others). To them, achieving self-centered agendas is what matters most. How it is done is irrelevant or of much less importance than a person's moral character. As will be seen in Chapter 7 on Trump's bullying, another fear more common among Republican politicians, others close to Trump, and those who question or challenge him, is the fear of being a target of his public insults, shaming, and lawsuits. As true with most other of his supporters, it is fear rather than moral values that motivates their behavior.

The Machiavellian perspective among Trump and many of his supporters that the means justifies the ends was seen in a survey in which respondents were asked over 16-time points in 2017 to select the personal characteristics and qualities that apply to the president.[17] Among the top three characteristics and qualities selected by Republicans (including "those leaning Republican") was "can get things done." On average across time points, 70% of Republicans selected that characteristic (vs. 8% of Democrats). The other two characteristics and qualities selected by the greatest number of Republicans were "Stands up for what he believes" (71% vs. 14% of Democrats) and "Tough enough for the job" (68% vs. 7% of Democrats). Interestingly, in contrast to polls in which the majority of Republicans agreed that Trump was honest and trustworthy, over the course of those surveys the characteristic chosen the *least* by Republicans to describe Trump was "Honest and trustworthy" (28% vs. 2% of Democrats).

In sum, during the Trump presidency, a rapidly growing number of Americans came to value getting things done over the traditional moral values of honesty and trustworthiness. As argued forcefully by Steven Hassan in *The Cult of Trump* and by John Dean and Bob Altemeyer in *Authoritarian Nightmare: Trump and His Followers*,[18] valuing "tough" authoritarian leaders who get things done over morality is a common characteristic of members of cults—most of whom have authoritarian personalities themselves.

The most authoritarian voting bloc in America is evangelical Christians[19]—Trump's political base. To authoritarians, obedience to authority, law, order, and standing up for one's beliefs (whether they are moral or not) are greater American values and virtues than honesty and integrity: Being tough and getting things done are viewed as values and virtues that will Make America Great Again (MAGA).

Trump's Character: Moral, Immoral, or Amoral?

Which of the following best describes the values and behavior our children are learning and the new normal, or culture, that exists in many areas of the country, and particularly those areas of Trump's political base: Is it moral, immoral, or amoral? Let's look at each.

Trump as a Role Model of Morality?

Most people agree that a person of sound moral character is truthful and trustworthy, kind, respectful, and follows the Golden Rule of treating others as you want them to treat you. With the exceptions of Trump himself, his close family members, and many evangelical Christians that constitute Trump's political base, it is very difficult to find individuals who honestly believe that Trump is a moral person and agree with Jerry Falwell, Jr., a popular Christian leader and past-president of Liberty University, who emphatically stated, "He's a moral person."[20]

To be sure, nearly all his supporters would give examples of Trump acting in a way they would consider highly moral, such as supporting laws against abortion, placing hundreds of pro-life judges on federal courts, protecting gun rights, and building a wall on the Mexican border. It is difficult, however, to find public figures, except those lacking in moral character themselves, who actually describe Trump as a person of fine moral character.

Trump as a Role Model of Immorality?

Although it might sound rather harsh, might Trump's character and that of many of his friends and enablers best be described as immoral rather than amoral? As with moral, it is difficult to find prominent public figures, especially Republicans, who refer to Trump's character and the culture he has fostered as immoral. Exceptions, however, as revealed in polls mentioned previously, are most Democrats. My guess is that the term immoral is rarely used among Republicans because it is perceived as a bit too harsh, connoting a sense of evil. It certainly isn't what should describe a true Christian, much less someone believed to be Christ-like.

Whether evil or not, immoral refers to behavior that violates common standards of morality. Someone who is immoral deliberately and repeatedly violates those standards. As seen in the following chapters on lying, cheating, bullying, and narcissism, Trump has a long history of frequently acting in an immoral manner. But is that enough to refer to his character and the culture he has fostered as immoral? Not only do most Democrats believe so, but so do some leaders among Trump's strong evangelical Christian base. Among them is Mark Galli, editor-in-chief of the magazine *Christianity Today*, which was founded by Billy Graham. In a 2020 editorial, Galli concluded that Trump was immoral, or at least often acted that way. Writing about Trump being impeached for bribing the president of Ukraine, Galli called for Trump's removal from office while stating:

> That [the bribery] is not only a violation of the Constitution; more importantly, it is profoundly immoral ... The reason many are not shocked about this is that this president has dumbed down the idea of morality in his administration. He has hired and fired those who are now convicted criminals. He himself has admitted to immoral actions in business and his relationship with women, about which he remains proud. His Twitter feed alone—with its habitual string of mischaracterizations, lies, and slanders— is a near perfect example of a human being who is morally lost and confused.[21]

As one might predict from a bully who highly values retribution, Trump responded to Galli with several tweets in which he attacked *Christianity Today* calling it "A far left magazine, or very 'progressive,' as some would call it, which has been doing poorly." Stoking fear among his Christian base, he added that Galli "knows nothing about reading a perfect transcript of a routine phone call and would rather have a Radical Left nonbeliever, who wants to take your religion & your guns, than Donald Trump as your President." He further tweeted: "No President has done more for the Evangelical community, and it's not even close," ... . "You'll not get anything from those Dems on stage. I won't be reading ET [sic] again!"[22]

Trump's response reveals a key element to his immoral behavior and how he "dumbed down the idea of morality in his administration." That key element is immature moral reasoning, as discussed in Chapter 10. Immature moral reasoning is grounded in maximizing rewards and avoiding punishment. Reciprocity, retribution, retaliation, and invoking fear in others are highly valued: Might is right. As taught and practiced by Trump: "When someone attacks me, I always attack back ... except 100x more. This has nothing to do with a tirade but rather, a way of life!"[23]

Ten Commandments as a Litmus Test of Morality

I grew up in Virginia as a southern Baptist, married in a Baptist church, and was baptized as a young adult in a Presbyterian church. As a child I was taught that one's guiding moral code was the Bible and that the most straightforward litmus test for determining if one is moral or immoral is the Ten Commandments. For centuries the Ten Commandments have been of fundamental importance in Christianity and Judaism for guiding moral behavior, and they continue to be the foundation of many of our laws. In Sunday school and summer Bible camp I had to memorize the Ten Commandments and I learned at church and home that if I failed to follow them, I would burn in hell with other sinners and the devil. For years, the fear of burning in hell, and the fear of St. Peter not accepting me into heaven, guided my moral behavior. Members of Trump's strongest political base, evangelical Christians, are raised the same.

If one were to apply the Ten Commandments to decide if Trump is best characterized as moral or immoral, how might he do? Might he go to heaven or hell? Let's check off the commandments that he has repeatedly violated.

- *Has strange gods or graven images before God?* As seen in Chapter 9 on Trump's narcissism, he worships himself. Nearly all his properties are adorned with TRUMP in golden capital letters and with portraits, pictures, and even statues of himself. He has gravened his name or image on bottled water, steaks, coffee, wine, vodka, menswear, perfume, deodorant, eyeglasses, the Monopoly game, mattresses, home décor, and more recently trading cards (at $99 each). Trump also has had a great fondness for young and beautiful women, and images thereof. He once pronounced: "It doesn't really matter what [the media] write as long as you've got a young and beautiful piece of ass."[24] He has had more images of himself and young and beautiful women around him than images of God or anything else in the Bible.
- *Uses God's name in vain.* In addition to GD (I was taught never to say God's name in vain, or I would go to hell), Trump frequently says fuck, motherfucker, shit, bullshit, and all other curse words my mother, a single parent, punished me for saying (because my mother was blind, however, I was rarely punished by writing those words). Such language was routine in the White House. It also was endorsed by many Trump supporters, as seen in the standing ovations he receives when cursing at his campaign rallies. As noted by Winsor Mann in *The Week*, "His supporters regard his cussing with the same esteem as the national anthem."[25]
- *Fails to keep holy the Sabbath day.* Trump rarely attends church (attending it only 14 times while president, including for photo-ops[26]) and generally spends the Sabbath playing golf. As noted by his niece, Mary Trump, her uncle views church as a photo opportunity. An infamous example was Trump standing in front of Saint John's Episcopal Church in Washington, DC, smiling and awkwardly holding the Bible while peaceful protesters nearby were dispersed with teargas and hurricane force winds by a National Guard helicopter. Trump thought that this behavior set a good Christian example as to how "liberal" governors should react to protesters in their states.
- *Fails to honor father and mother.* Trump has seldom spoken about his parents. When he has done so he has almost always spoken fondly about them. However, Trump has admitted, and bragged, that he often did not

listen to his parents; that he was rebellious as a child, which was why his father sent him off to military school. Trump failed to honor his mother and father in additional ways. Noting that his mother immigrated from Scotland to the United States and worked as a domestic servant, Rabbi David Paskin wrote in *The Times of Israel* that Trump "dishonors her memory when he attempts to shut down immigration, belittle and bully those who clean and cook for his hotels and withhold wages from those who perform vital work for his projects."[27]

In the Bible, Matthew 19:19 tells the story of a rich man who seeks guidance from Jesus, asking him what he must do to go to heaven. Jesus responds that he is to obey the Ten Commandments and says to "honor your father and mother, and love your neighbor as yourself." If Trump has not violated this commandment by failing to honor his father and mother, he has certainly broken it by not loving his neighbor as he loves himself. In loving your neighbor, I don't think Jesus was referring to adultery and coveting your neighbor's wife and goods or to loving a "young and beautiful piece of ass."

Jesus also advised the rich man that "If you want to be perfect, go sell your possessions and give to the poor, and you will have treasure in heaven. Then come, follow Me." To Trump, being perfect means having great wealth and power on earth and only sharing with others if it helps getting him what he wants, which is greater wealth, power, and fame.

- *Kills (or "murders" depending on one's interpretation of the Bible).* This is the toughest one to check off, as I don't know of Trump personally killing or murdering anyone. He is too wise to do so. As seen in Chapter 7, Trump has harmed others in other ways, particularly by bullying others with verbal insults, lawsuits, and social exclusion. He also is famous for bragging "I could stand in the middle of Fifth Avenue and shoot somebody, okay, and I wouldn't lose any voters, okay?" If one also considers turning his back on our allies, the Kurds, in fighting ISIS in northern Syria, which resulted in the murdering of hundreds of Kurds (and prompted the resignation of Secretary of Defense Jim Mattis), then he violated this commandment. One might also well argue that his failure to restrict guns, including among those who are mentally ill, resulted in many murders and mass shootings, and that his refusal to sell arms to Ukraine unless they investigated Joe Biden's son increased the number of deaths in that country during Russia's invasion. Trump also incited the mob that stormed the Capitol, which resulted in five deaths.[28]
- *Commits adultery.* It is widely reported that Trump committed adultery in his first two marriages and very likely did so in his third (see Chapter 5 on Trump's cheating). He often bragged about it, once stating that adultery is not a sin.[29]
- *Steals.* Just look at his business dealings, especially not paying employees and taxes. As seen in Chapter 5, he was even found guilty of stealing

from his own charitable foundation and was indicted for stealing national defense documents from the White House and retaining them illegally at Mar-A-Lago.

- *Bears false witness against your neighbor (lying).* Trump made more than 30,573 false or misleading claims during his presidency.[30] As seen in Chapter 3, many were BIG lies, like lying that he lies. He still lies, with his biggest lie being that he won the 2020 presidential election (which he lost by over 7 million votes).
- *Covets thy neighbor's wife.* In the infamous *Access Hollywood* tape in which he bragged about his many sexual affairs, Trump told television host Billy Bush that "I did try and fuck her. She was married ... I moved on her like a bitch. But I couldn't get there. And she was married."[31]
- *Covets thy neighbor's goods.* Trump has a long history of coveting his neighbor's goods, especially properties he desires. He threatened and filed countless lawsuits to obtain many of his properties.[32] A classic example was his legal battles and dirty tricks in trying to acquire a farmer's land in Scotland to build a golf resort.[33]

So, if following the Ten Commandments is the litmus test for morality, as believed by Trump's evangelical Christian base, Trump fails miserably, and it is evident that the culture he has fostered is best characterized as immoral instead of moral. Indeed, one may well argue, as argued by the American politics researcher and writer Ben Pryor in *Newsweek*, that in light of the above, as well in denouncing Christians as "fools," "idiots," and "schmucks;" never asking for forgiveness (while denying that he has sinned, and believing more in retribution than forgiveness); and in manipulating Christians, especially his evangelical Christian base, to his political advantage, Trump might be considered "America's first atheist president."[34] Our children have been watching and learning, and not someone modeling what most people recognize as the values of Christianity and other major religions.

Trump as a Role Model of Amorality?

Instead of moral and immoral, *amoral* is most often used to characterize Trump and the culture he has promoted. As defined by Merriam-Webster dictionary, amoral refers to "(a) having or showing no concern about whether behavior is morally right or wrong (e.g., amoral politicians; an amoral, selfish person)" and (b) "being neither moral nor immoral." Given this definition, it is likely that amoral is what Secretary of Defense General James Mattis had in mind when characterizing Trump as having "no moral compass" and thus being "dangerous" and "unfit,"[35] and when Trump's sister characterized him as having "no principles."[36] For persons who are amoral, moral character doesn't matter. It doesn't matter if one lies or tells the truth, cheats or is trustworthy, is kind or mean: What matters is getting what one wants, or getting things done.

In shattering moral norms and discrediting morality as a concept, it makes little difference if one is amoral or immoral—one's actions are the same. A major difference between amoral and immoral is the motivation and reasoning (or lack thereof) underlying the behavior. Those who are immoral *intend* to harm others, whereas those who are amoral simply don't care about the impact of their behavior on others or how their actions are viewed by others—morality doesn't matter. As will be seen in later chapters, especially Chapter 7 on Trump's bullying, at times Trump has made it very clear that his behavior is intended to harm others (and otherwise violate the Ten Commandments), and thus such behavior is immoral. However, it also is quite clear that more often than not the intention of his behavior is simply to get what he wants, guided by immature moral reasoning and the Machiavellian perspective that the means, whether moral or immoral, always justify the end. In this sense, most of his behavior is amoral—it really doesn't matter to him how his behavior affects others.

Amoral not only best describes Trump's character but also the likely character of many of his enablers and followers. A 2019 national survey found that the majority (64%) of White evangelical Christians believed that it is necessary to believe in God (and assumingly God's Ten Commandments) to be a moral person.[37] Yet, the same survey revealed that almost half (47%) thought that Trump's personal conduct makes no difference to them. Moreover, 16% responded that Trump's personal conduct made them *more likely* to support him. To them, it appears that morality doesn't matter. Only 36% responded that Trump's personal conduct made them less likely to support him. Almost a third (31%) responded that there was "almost nothing Trump could do to lose approval." Perhaps Trump was correct in once saying that he could shoot someone on Times Square and not lose many of his voters.

Interestingly, the same 2019 survey revealed that those affiliating as *non-Christian* viewed Trump's behavior differently than evangelical Protestant Christians: Nearly twice as many (70% vs. 36% of evangelical Protestant Christians) responded that Trump's personal conduct made it *less* likely to support him.

As noted in Chapter 8 when discussing narcissism, an amoral and self-centered perspective toward decision-making and behavior has its advantages, as it serves to protect one's self-esteem and narcissistic self. It allows one to think: "If lying, cheating, and bullying are neither bad or good, immoral or moral, then engaging in those behaviors does not make me a bad or immoral person. All that truly matters is whether the outcome is good for me." This is what our children are learning in the new normal.

Learning Lying, Cheating, Bullying, and Narcissism: Beyond Modeling and Reinforcement

How do children learn moral behavior from others? Three powerful environmental determinants are (1) observing others (i.e., observational learning), (2) positive reinforcement, and (3) punishment. Quite simply, children learn new behaviors mostly by watching others. They listen to and observe their parents, siblings, peers, and others in-person or via various forms of media (e.g., TikTok, YouTube, video games, television). Observing others is especially a powerful means of learning when the person being observed is someone the observer is taught to respect and desires to be like, which might be a parent, peer, media star, or the president of the United States. Common sense and a century of research in psychology tells us that if the observed behavior leads to a positive outcome—that is, the behavior is positively reinforced—the observer is more likely to display the same behavior. Conversely, if the observed behavior is followed by a negative or aversive outcome, or punishment, replication is much less likely. This applies to both the behavior exhibited by the model and the behavior repeated by the observer. That is, behavior is more likely to be copied and repeated if the person modeling the behavior is reinforced, not punished, and if the observer is positively reinforced and not punished for copying the behavior. For example, when children see someone lie and successfully get what they want, which includes avoiding getting caught and punished, they learn to do the same. When lying works for them too, it often becomes habitual and a character trait. This applies to such moral character traits as honesty, trustworthiness, and caring, as well to immoral character traits of lying, cheating, bullying, and narcissism. Children watch and learn.

As with many diseases, many behaviors are contagious, especially among children. This holds true for both moral and immoral behavior. The more often a behavior is seen and reinforced, the more likely it spreads among the population. When most people exhibit, accept, and support the behavior, it is considered normative in that environment. The norm might exist at home, school, within a political religious group, or throughout society.

Of course, not all behavior evolves simply from observing others or is dependent on positive reinforcement and punishment. People often *choose* not to copy the behavior of others, especially if the behavior is inconsistent with their values and beliefs. Moreover, children often come up with new behaviors on their own, without having observed the behavior in others, while developing values and beliefs that underlie and maintain their behavior. As discussed briefly below and more thoroughly in a chapter on moral reasoning, moral emotions, and mechanisms of moral disengagement, those three cognitive and emotional processes, as well as additional factors, greatly influence learning and behavior. Nevertheless, much behavior can be explained by observing others and basic principles of positive reinforcement and punishment. This holds true for lying, cheating, bullying, and narcissistic behavior. As seen in chapters that follow, by modeling each of those behaviors Trump and many of his enablers and supporters have fostered a new normal in many parts of our country in which lying, cheating, bullying, and narcissism are common and accepted, if not highly valued, if they get things done.

Although modeling, positive reinforcement, and punishment are powerful forces determining moral behavior, they often fall short. Most of us do not watch others lie, cheat, and bully (and often get away with it) and do the same. One of the greatest challenges in psychology has been explaining why some people are much more likely than others to harm others or otherwise act in an immoral manner: Why are some prone to violate rules, commit crimes, and harm others while others are more prone to help? Why do many people exhibit both antisocial and prosocial behavior? Why do some students, but not all, cheat when a teacher leaves the classroom? Why do some cheat frequently, while others not at all? Why do some adults cheat on their taxes? Why do some kids bully others on the playground and adults bully at the workplace while others defend the victim even when risking harm to themselves? Why are lying, cheating, and bullying found at all levels of education and income, as well as within all religious and ethnic groups? In sum, beyond environmental factors such as salience of rewards and punishment and peer pressure, what is it *within* individuals that account for differences in moral behavior? Relatedly, and perhaps most intriguing, what best explains hypocrisy: how nearly all of us, including supposedly moral leaders such as priests, police, teachers, and those in the highest positions of government engage in immoral behavior that is clearly inconsistent with our values and beliefs and with what we want and teach others to do?

Answers to those questions lie largely in three cognitive and emotional processes: (1) moral reasoning, (2) moral emotions, and (2) mechanisms of moral disengagement. Understanding how those processes develop is the key to understanding how children become liars, cheats, bullies, and narcissists in the new normal. Those processes are described briefly below and more thoroughly in the following chapters.

Moral Reasoning: Looking Out for Oneself versus the Needs and Welfare of Others

Undoubtedly, at times children (and adults) fail to think before they act, and this occurs much more often among some than others. Some are more impulsive, acting without reflecting upon the consequences of their behavior on others or to themselves or otherwise thinking about what is right or wrong. For most of us, however, determining right vs. wrong and what one *ought* to do is one of the first steps, and arguably the most important, in guiding moral behavior (another very important step, however, is the awareness, recognition, and understanding that a moral issue or problem exists, as opposed to being oblivious or simply having the amoral perspective that morality doesn't matter). Typically, we want to do what is right, at least what we think is right, and the right thing is not to blindly copy or approve the behavior of others. At least momentarily, we reflect, or reason, about the morality of our behavior and decide to do what we think is right. To do otherwise is counter to our moral values and what we were taught.

How one reasons and determines what is "right," or what one ought to do, evolves with maturity. Moral reasoning of young children is quite simple: *Good* behavior is that which is rewarded and *bad* behavior is that which is punished. As such, moral reasoning and behavior is self-centered and hedonistic. You do what it takes to get what you want, which means to gain rewards and avoid punishment. In early childhood (and for some also in adulthood) throwing tantrums helps get you what you want. Of course, it also helps, especially after childhood, to be not only physically stronger than others but to possess other sources of power that enables one to strike fear in others in many other ways such as verbal insults via social media and with lawsuits. Being nice to others is contingent upon them praising or rewarding you or not punishing you. Thus, lying, cheating, and bullying are viewed as good or moral if they help achieve self-centered aims of greater rewards and power.

Self-centered, hedonistic moral reasoning is developmentally normal until about early elementary school when it tends to be replaced by moral reasoning that focuses increasingly on the needs of others, laws that are best for society, and principles of justice. However, this does not happen automatically nor for everyone. Some children become fixated in their self-centered, hedonistic moral reasoning and learn that if one's aim is to get things done, or what one wants, then moral reasoning that focuses on others, and not oneself, is often more of an impediment than something to be valued.

Moral Emotions Also Determine Behavior, but Only When Felt

Inextricably linked to moral reasoning and moral behavior are the moral emotions of empathy (and sympathy), guilt, and shame. Empathy refers to the ability to share the perspective of others, which triggers caring or feeling sorry about them (i.e., sympathy). Although empathy is not the only basis of guilt and shame, it is the most common. Guilt and shame are closely related; thus, the two terms are often used interchangeably. There is an important difference between the two, however: The negative feeling associated with guilt is directed to a specific action ("What I did was wrong and I feel badly for doing it"), whereas with shame the feeling is more global, or pervasive, focusing not just on a specific action but also on the self per se ("I am a bad person for doing that"). In addition to guilt and shame often occurring out of empathy, both also can occur when one violates self-imposed moral standards—when one believes what he or she has done is wrong, irrespective of any harm caused to others. Regardless of the source of guilt and shame, those emotions, either experienced or anticipated, provoke self-condemnation and feelings of negative self-worth.

As discussed in Chapter 10, guilt and shame play major roles in the self-regulation of human behavior, causing most of us to assume responsibility for our actions. They often provide the spark that motivates us to act in a manner consistent with our moral reasoning, moral standards, and religious beliefs.

When I ask students in my classes "Why do you inhibit immoral behavior and act morally?", the most common response is that they would feel bad about themselves if they didn't. That response is often linked to their religion, whether it is Catholic, Protestant, Jewish, Muslim, or other. Grounded in religion or not, it is empathy, guilt, and shame that regulates much of our behavior. On the flipside, it is the *lack* of empathy, guilt, and shame that makes it much easier to engage in dishonest and harmful behavior. As also true with immature moral reasoning, the lack of empathy, guilt, and shame is a common characteristic of individuals who lie,cheat, and bully.

Mechanisms of Moral Disengagement: Absolving Oneself of Responsibility for Harming Others

Hedonistic moral reasoning and the lack of moral emotions largely account for much of immoral behavior. Those two traits characterize the most cold and callous criminals.[38] As will be seen in later chapters, they also are common among individuals who are prone to more everyday acts of immorality and incivility, including lying, cheating, and bullying. As is true with modeling and principles of positive reinforcement and punishment, moral reasoning and emotions do not always explain harmful behavior. Many people who behave in harmful ways are not necessarily lacking in mature moral reasoning or the ability to experience empathy, guilt, and shame: They are quite capable of those self-regulatory processes but simply deactivate, or disengage, them when it best serves them. Thoughts and emotions concerning right or wrong and moral character traits such as honesty, trustworthiness, caring, and integrity consume their time and cognitive and emotional energy. Too often moral reasoning and emotions interfere with achieving their aims, diverting time and energy away from thinking about getting what they want or getting things done. More disruptive to their aims, however, is that moral reasoning and emotions make them feel responsible, and thus badly, about their harmful behavior. From this perspective, it helps to avoid thinking about the impact of one's behavior on others and issues of morality, but if that can't be avoided then an alternative to absolving oneself of responsibility is to come up with self-convincing reasons to excuse or justify one's harmful behavior.

Dr. Albert Bandura, professor of psychology at Stanford University, identified eight such *mechanisms of moral disengagement* that people use to deactivate moral reasoning and moral emotions and exonerate themselves of a sense of responsibility.[39] As described in Chapter 11, those mechanisms of moral disengagement are denial, distortion, or disregard of harmful effects (e.g., "I didn't do it." "I didn't lose the election. I won it!"); blaming others (which include three types identified by Bandura, as seen in "He started it." "The election was rigged." "They made me do."); advantageous comparison (e.g., "The Democrats are far worse." "David also was an adulterer and murderer and was chosen by God to be King of Jerusalem."); moral, social, or economic justification ("I lied and cheated to get things done."

"Morality doesn't matter because I'm saving our religion, guns, economy, and America from the socialists."); euphemistic labeling ("It was only a joke." "It was only locker room talk."); and dehumanization ("They aren't even humans." "She's a dog.").

Some individuals are more prone than others in the use of mechanisms of moral disengagement and thus are more inclined to act in dishonest and antisocial ways.[40] However, at one time or another nearly everyone employs mechanisms of moral disengagement to avoid assumption of responsibility for their harmful behavior. This includes lying, cheating, and bullying.[41] As discussed by Bandura, it also includes some of the most repulsive acts by mankind, such as the holocaust, the Mai Lai massacre in Vietnam, the 9/11 attack on the Twin Towers in New York and other acts of terrorism, and child abuse in the Catholic Church.

Bullying, Lying, Cheating, and Narcissism: A New Normal?

As noted previously, at one time or another nearly everyone lies and cheats. White lies and cheating in school and at work (e.g., leaving work early or calling in sick when one is not) are quite common, especially when the culprit believes no harm is caused. Fewer engage in bullying, especially when bullying is defined as it is in Chapter 6; nevertheless, verbal and social bullying behaviors are fairly common, particularly hurtful teasing and social exclusion. The same holds true with narcissism: at one time or another nearly everyone conveys that they are the greatest, yet few think of themselves as braggards or narcissists.

Until recently, lying, cheating, bullying, and narcissistic behaviors were frowned upon, especially when viewed as harming others or when such behaviors are frequent and severe enough to be considered character traits. But norms are changing. As revealed in poll results presented earlier in this chapter, a large percentage of Americans are just fine with immoral behavior if it gets things done. To them, morality doesn't matter and it doesn't seem to matter what children are observing and learning.

What children are learning, and particularly with respect to hurtful behavior, was shown in a study published in the prestigious scientific journal, *Educational Researcher.* In that study, Professors Francis Huang and Dewey Cornell at the University of Virginia reported a significant increase in general bullying and especially in hurtful teasing about race and ethnicity following Trump's election in 2016. The increase was strongest in areas of the country with many Trump supporters. The researchers attributed the increase in verbal bullying to Trump supporters repeating racial slurs and adopting hateful attitudes toward minorities that were modeled by parents and in the right-wing conservative media.

In many cases the hatred that Trump and his supporters espoused and modeled to our youth was criminal. An FBI report found that hate crimes increased 20% during his presidency, reaching the highest rate in 28 years.[42]

Increases in hate crimes were particularly high in counties in which Trump held a campaign rally, where they increased over 200% in 2019.[43] Most hate crimes were motivated by bias based on the victim's race/ethnicity/ancestry (57.6%), religion (20.1%), or sexual orientation (16.7%). Most of the offenders were White males, whereas most of the victims were Black, Latino, Asian, Jewish, Muslim, or gay. Other hate crimes were motivated by politics, with the perpetrators being White MAGA Republican males and their victims White Democrats. Three examples that captured national attention were the 2017 Unite the Right rally in Charlottesville, VA, in which protesting White supremacists (including neo-Nazis, neo-fascists, White nationalists, Klansmen, and far-right militias) resulted in the murder of a White female counter-protester and the injuries to 35 others; the domestic terror plot by a paramilitary militia group to kidnap of Michigan's Democratic Governor Gretchen Whitmer; and the brutal beating of the husband of Democratic Congresswoman, and then Speaker of the House, Nancy Pelosi.

After Trump began calling the coronavirus the "Chinese virus," people of Asian descent were particular targets of hate crime, with many of the attackers shouting to their victims "go back to China" or "you are the virus."[44] Although Trump often insisted that he was not to blame for the increase in hate crimes, a report by *ABC News* showed that in a large number of hate crime cases the attackers invoked Trump's name during the crime, such as saying "This is for Trump."[45]

Trump's name also was often cited by individuals refusing to follow city, state, and federal laws requiring the wearing of masks on airplanes. The Federal Aviation Administration reported 5,981 incidents of unruly airplane passengers in the United States in 2021, which was by far the highest number recorded. Of those incidents, over 4,000 involved the wearing of masks. During that same year, a survey of flight attendants revealed that 85% of them had dealt with unruly behavior on airplanes that concerned the wearing of masks, with 61% reporting that passengers had used sexist, racist, and/or homophobic slurs, and 17% reporting physical incidents such as hitting, shoving, and throwing trash at them.[46]

Trump as a Role Model

The new normal with respect to the acceptance and modeling of dishonesty, bullying, and narcissism began before Trump's election as president in 2016. As argued by many others, greater acceptance coincided with the rise of authoritarianism.[47] Authoritarianism in the United States began to take hold in the 1960s, spearheaded by conservative populists in the media and politics such as Rush Limbaugh, Newt Gingrich, Pat Buchanan, and Ronald Reagan, and promoted on the Fox News network. This was long before ultra-conservative Fox television hosts Sean Hannity, Tucker Carlson, Laura Ingraham, and Lou Dobbs elevated authoritarianism to the new normal among many in America. Their authoritarianism was grounded in conservative

Republicans' concerns about moral decay and threats to social order and safety, which they attributed to increasingly liberal policies and laws, especially ones relating to race (school integration, voting rights), sexual orientation, women's rights (e.g., equal pay and feminism), and religion (e.g., abortion).

In telling 30,573 false and misleading statements in his four years as president, Trump's lying is pathological. As seen in Chapter 3, it is not just the number of his lies that are pathological but also their degree of falsehood and repetition. In a firehose of falsehoods, his lies often are completely void of fact and repeated over and over, with Trump aware that this propaganda technique, perfected by the Russians, creates an alternative reality for his followers[48]—it gets things done. Millions believe, and thus reinforce, his lies. Multiple polls conducted in 2021 and 2022 reported that about 70% of Republicans continued to believe that Trump won the 2020 election, despite no solid evidence supporting this big lie.[49] A national poll conducted in March 2023 found that 79% of Republicans supported Trump's MAGA movement.[50]

As seen in Chapter 5, cheating is well documented in Trump's businesses (with Trump University being a classic example of fraud), taxes, marriages, throughout the White House (including bribery, nepotism, and cronyism), and even in golf. Trump will long be remembered in history as the only president impeached twice and who threatened our very democracy by cheating to win reelection while precipitating an insurrection.

As seen in Chapter 7, Trump meets all criteria commonly used to define bullying: his aggressive behaviors are intentionally hurtful, have continued overtime, and occur in the context of an imbalance of power. They occur verbally, socially, physically, and electronically (i.e., cyberbullying). Undoubtedly if Trump were a student in school today, he certainly would be suspended, if not expelled, for bullying.

Finally, as discussed in Chapter 9, Trump is an exemplary narcissist. Although mental health experts may debate whether he meets all formal criteria for the psychiatric diagnosis of narcissistic personality disorder (and particularly the criterion that his narcissism is associated with significant distress or disability in important life activities), few, if any, deny that he *is* a classic narcissist. Indeed, he demonstrates all nine behavioral symptoms of narcissism. Among them is that he believes he is superior to others and others are inferior to him (while claiming to be a "very stable genius" who knows more than others about almost everything).

Children Are Watching and Learning the New Normal

The greater number of role models that children observe of dishonest and harmful behavior, the more likely they will behave the same. Trump isn't the only governmental role model to our youth for lying, cheating, bullying, and general incivility. There are many other role models. Recent examples are Representative Marjorie Greene falsely claiming that President Obama was

Muslim, President Clinton had John F. Kennedy murdered, 9/11 was a hoax, supporters of Black Lives Matter were terrorists, and several mass school shootings were staged by the government to garner support of anti-gun legislation.[51] She verbally abused fellow members of Congress, calling them terrorists, cowards, liars, and pathetic, and endorsed their execution.[52] On national television, Greene heckled President Biden throughout his presidential address to Congress[53] (her heckling was joined by Representative Lauren Boebert, whom Greene reportedly called a "little bitch" on the floor of Congress for copying her articles of impeachment for President Biden[54]). For asking him to follow rules in Congress to wear a mask during the peak of the pandemic, Representative Hal Rogers poked fellow Representative Joyce Beatty and told her to "kiss my ass."[55]

With respect to cheating, in recent years multiple members of Congress were investigated and reprimanded by the House Ethics Committee for insider stock trading, misusing campaign funds, and improper awarding of contracts to relatives of members of their staff.[56] Among the cases in the national spotlight were freshman Congressman George Santos, who lied on his vita about his education and career, falsely claimed he was Jewish, and allegedly cheated by violating campaign contribution laws.[57] As will be seen in Chapter 5 on Trump's cheating, throughout his presidency multiple members of his cabinet cheated in various ways, ranging from insider stock trading to flying on luxury private jets for government business at taxpayers' expense.

In a classic case of bullying, Governor Ron DeSantis berated a group of high school students for wearing masks (as required by their school) while they shared a stage with him at an indoor news conference, telling them "You do not have to wear those masks. I mean, please take them off."[58] Both male and female members of Congress bullying others during televised congressional hearings has become a standard practice, as modeled best by MAGA extremists Marjorie Taylor Greene and Jim Jordan (Chairman of the House Judiciary Committee). In investigating almost anything that might help Trump, and while insulting and ridiculing others, Greene and Jordan have demonstrated how bullying is effective in getting things done. Out of fear, no one wants to be added to their list of victims.

While watching government leaders and their supporters disobey laws by lying, cheating, bullying, and disrespecting others, many are bound to ask, "Why shouldn't I do the same?" Many also surely wonder, "What is the difference between cheating or stealing from the government by not paying taxes and stealing from an individual or store?" As Trump once stated during a televised presidential debate, one must be "stupid" not to cheat when paying taxes. Are children, as well as robbers and thieves, also "stupid" for not stealing when they believe they won't get caught? In addition to teaching others that one must be stupid not to cheat and steal, Trump and his supporters have taught children that government institutions, including the Federal Bureau of Investigation, the Department of Justice, the Central Intelligence Agency, the Center for Disease Control, and even the Pentagon, are not to be respected, nor are laws to be followed that interfere with one's self-centered goals. As stated by New York mayor and 2020 presidential candidate, Michael Bloomberg, "He lies. He bullies. He gets away with it. Our kids are watching Donald Trump. Is this the lesson we want them to learn?"[59]

Children also are learning that hypocrisy is justified and normal—that there is no problem vilifying others who are liars, cheats, bullies, and narcissists while engaging in the same behaviors themselves. Hypocrisy *should* cause cognitive dissonance and coinciding negative feelings of anxiety, guilt, and shame. As seen in later chapters, those negative feelings can be avoided or greatly minimized, however, with immature moral reasoning; the stifling of moral emotions of empathy, guilt, and shame; and use of various mechanisms of moral disengagement. With Trump and his political base modeling those processes, a new normal has emerged wherein children learn how they can lie, cheat, bully, and be narcissistic while damning others who do the same and all the while feeling good about themselves. How that learning occurs and how Trump models those behaviors are the focus of the following chapters.

Notes

1 Charlie Spiering, 2020. "Trump: Getting Things Done More Important Than Being 'Presidential.'" *News Break*, September 16. https://www.newsbreak.com/news/2061637965325/trump-getting-things-done-more-important-than-being-presidential

2 Donald J. Trump and Bill Zanker, 2007. *Think BIG and Kick Ass in Business and Life*. New York: Collins.

3 *Neil King Jr., 2011.* "Trump on 2012: 'Part of Beauty of Me Is I'm Very Rich.'" *Wall Street Journal, March 17.* https://www.wsj.com/articles/BL-WB-29144

4 Danielle Paquette, 2016. "Why the Most Outrageous Part of Donald Trump's 'Hot Mic' Comments Isn't the Vulgar Language." *The Washington Post*, October 7. https://www.washingtonpost.com/news/wonk/wp/2016/10/07/the-real-issue-with-donald-trump-saying-a-man-can-do-anything-to-a-woman/

5 Michael D'Antonio, 2016. *The Truth about Trump*. New York: Thomas Dunne Books, 1.

6 Donald J. Trump (@realDonaldTrump), 2020. "I Won the Election." *Twitter*. https://twitter.com/realDonaldTrump/status/1328200072987893762?lang=en

7 John Harwood, 2020. "Trump's Historical Place Defined by His Amorality." *CNN*, February 12. https://www.cnn.com/2020/02/12/politics/amorality-presidency-donald-trump/index.html

8 Bob Woodward and Robert Costa, 2021. *Peril*. New York: Simon & Schuster, 33.

9 "Trump Is No Role Model for Children, U.S. Voters Say 2-1; Quinnipiac University National Poll Finds; He Does Not Provide Moral Leadership, Voters Say," 2018. *Quinnipiac University Poll*, January 25. https://poll.qu.edu/national/release-detail?ReleaseID=2516

10 McClatchy-Marist Poll, February 2017. https://assets.documentcloud.org/documents/3472775/McClatchy-Marist-Poll-National-Nature-of-the.pdf

11 Gillian Brockell, 2021. "Historians Just Ranked the Presidents. Trump Wasn't Last." *The Washington Post*, June 30. https://www.washingtonpost.com/history/2021/06/30/presidential-rankings-2021-cspan-historians/

12 "Suffolk Poll Shows Trump Voters Would Favor New Trump Party More Than GOP," 2021. *Suffolk University News*, February 22. https://www.suffolk.edu/news-features/news/2021/02/22/01/51/suffolk-poll-shows-trump-voters-would-favor-new-trump-party-more-than-gop

13 Jennifer Agiesta and Ariel Edwards-Levy, 2023. "CNN Poll: Trump's GOP Support Appears to Soften Post-Indictment, But He Holds Lead in Primary Field." *CNN*, June 20. https://www.cnn.com/2023/06/20/politics/cnn-poll-trump-indictment-republicans-2024/index.html

14 NPR/PBS NewsHour/Marist National Poll, 2023. "The 2024 Presidential Candidates." Retrieved July 17, 2023, from https://maristpoll.marist.edu/polls/the-2024-presidential-candidates/

15 Mark Murray, 2023. "Poll: 71% of GOP Voters Stand with Trump Amid Investigations." *NBC News*, July 31. https://www.nbcnews.com/meet-the-press/meetthepressblog/poll-71-gop-voters-stand-trump-investigations-rcna97305

16 PRRI Staff, 2020. "Dueling Realities: Amid Multiple Crises, Trump and Biden Supporters See Different Priorities and Futures for the Nation." *PRRI*, October 19. https://www.prri.org/research/amid-multiple-crises-trump-and-biden-supporters-see-different-realities-and-futures-for-the-nation/

17 Mark Blumenthal, N.D. "Thirteen Charts Explain the 2018 Trump Approval Uptick." *SurveyMonkey.com*. https://www.surveymonkey.com/curiosity/explaining-trump-approval-uptick/

18 John W. Dean and Bob Altemeyer, 2020. *Authoritarian Nightmare: Trump and His Followers*. New York: Melville House. Steven Hassan, 2019. *The Cult of Trump*. New York: Free Press.

19 Marc J. Hetherington and Jonathan D. Weiler, 2009. *Authoritarianism & Polarization in American Politics* New York: Cambridge University Press.

20 Harriet Sherwood, 2018. "Christian Leader Jerry Falwell Urges Trump Support: 'He's a Moral Person.'" *The Guardian*, October 9. https://www.theguardian.com/us-news/2018/oct/09/christian-leader-jerry-falwell-urges-trump-support-hes-a-moral-person

21 Mark Galli, 2019. "Trump Should Be Removed from Office." *Christianity Today*, Dec. 19. https://www.christianitytoday.com/ct/2019/december-web-only/trump-should-be-removed-from-office.html

22 Aaron Rupar, 2019. "Christianity Today Made a Moral Case That Trump Needs to Go. He Responded by Proving Its Point." *Vox*, December 20. https://www.vox.com/2019/12/20/21031611/christianity-today-trump-removal-editorial-response-mark-galli

23 Donald J. Trump, (@realDonaldTrump), 2012. "When Someone Attacks Me, I Always Attack Back … " November 11. https://twitter.com/realdonaldtrump/status/267626951097868289?lang=pl

24 Alan Rappeport, 2016. "Donald Trump's Trail of Comments About Women." *The New York Times*, March 25. https://www.nytimes.com/2016/03/26/us/politics/donald-trump-women.html

25 Winsor Mann, 2019. "The Cursing President." *The Week*, November 7. https://theweek.com/articles/875118/cursing-president

26 Emily Singer, 2020, "Trump Has Attended Church 14 Times Since Taking Office—Including Photo-Ops," June 02. https://americanindependent.com/donald-trump-church-attendance-photo-ops-st-johns-religion-white-house/

27 David Paskin, 2017. "Donald Trump Has Already Broken All 10," *Times of Israel*, February 17. https://blogs.timesofisrael.com/how-donald-trump-has-already-broken-all-10-commandments/

28 U.S. House of Representatives, Select Committee to Investigate the January 6th Attack on the United Capitol, 2022. *Final Report of the Select Committee to Investigate*

the January 6th Attack on the United States Capitol. House Report 117-663, December 22. https://www.govinfo.gov/app/details/GPO-J6-REPORT/

29 Gideon Resnick, 2017. "Donald Trump in 1990: Adultery Is Not a Sin," *The Daily Beast*, July 12. https://www.thedailybeast.com/donald-trump-in-1990-adultery-is-not-a-sin

30 Glenn Kessler, Salvador Rizzo, and Meg Kelly, 2021. "Trump's False or Misleading Claims Total 30,573 over 4 Years." *The Washington Post*, January 24. https://www.washingtonpost.com/politics/2021/01/24/trumps-false-or-mis-leading-claims-total-30573-over-four-years/

31 "Transcript: Donald Trump's Taped Comments about Women," 2016. *New York Times*, October 8. https://www.nytimes.com/2016/10/08/us/donald-trump-tape-transcript.html

32 James D. Zirin, 2020. *Plaintiff in Chief: A Portrait of Donald Trump in 3,500 Lawsuits.* New York: All Points Books.

33 Yohana Desta, 2017. "Meet the Defiant Scottish Farmer Who's Been Feuding with Trump for a Decade." *Vanity Fair*, February 9. https://www.vanityfair.com/hollywood/2017/02/donald-trump-scotland-sam-bee

34 Ben Pryor, 2022. "Was Donald Trump America's First Atheist President?" *Newseek*, March 8. https://www.newsweek.com/was-donald-trump-americas-first-atheist-president-opinion-1685586

35 Bob Woodward, 2020. *Rage.* New York: Simon & Schuster, 166.

36 Michael Kranish, 2020. "In Secretly Recorded Audio, President Trump's Sister Says He Has 'No Principles' and 'You Can't Trust Him.'" *The Washington Post*, August 22, https://www.washingtonpost.com/politics/maryanne-trump-barry-secret-recordings/2020/08/22/30d457f4-e334-11ea-ade1-28dafla5e919_story.html

37 PRRI Staff, 2019. "Fractured Nation: Widening Partisan Polarization and Key Issues in 2020 Presidential Elections." *PPRI*, October 20. https://www.prri.org/research/fractured-nation-widening-partisan-polarization-and-key-issues-in-2020-presidential-elections/

38 Paul J. Frick and Stuart F. White, 2008. "Research Review: The Importance of Callous–Unemotional Traits for Developmental Models of Aggressive and Antisocial Behavior." *Journal of Child Psychology and Psychiatry* 49, no. 4: 359–375. https://doi: 10.1111/j.1469-7610.2007.01862.x
    Darrick Jolliffe and David P. Farrington, 2004. "Empathy and Offending: A Systematic Review and Meta-Analysis." *Aggression and Violent Behavior* 9, no. 5: 441–476. https://doi.org/10.1016/j.avb.2003.03.001

39 Albert Bandura, 2016. *Moral Disengagement: How People Do Harm and Live with Themselves.* New York: Worth Publishers.

40 Ibid.Gianluca Gini, Tiziana Pozzoli, and Shelley Hymel, 2014. "Moral Disengagement Among Children and Youth: A Meta-Analytic Review of Links to Aggressive Behavior." *Aggressive Behavior* 40: 56–68. https://doi.org/10.1002/ab.21502

41 Frances Lee Doyle and Kay Bussey, 2018. "Moral Disengagement and Children's Propensity to Tell Coached Lies." *Journal of Moral Education*, 47, no. 1: 91–103. https://doi.org/10.1080/03057240.2017. 1380611 Tamera B. Murdock and Jason M. Stephens, 2007. "*Is Cheating Wrong? Students' Reasoning about Academic Dishonesty,*" in *Psychology of Academic Cheating* edited by Eric M. Anderman & Tamera B. Murdock. New York: Elsevier Academic Press, 229–251. Zhaojun Teng, George G. Bear, Chunyan Yang, Qian Nie, and Cheng Guo, 2020. "Moral Disengagement and Bullying Perpetration: A Longitudinal Study of the Moderating Effect of School Climate." *School Psychology* 35, no. 1: 99–109. https://doi: /10.1037/spq0000348

42 Daniel Villarreal, 2020. "Hate Crimes Under Trump Surged Nearly 20 Percent Says FBI Report." *Newsweek*, November 16. https://www.newsweek.com/hate-crimes-under-trump-surged-nearly-20-percent-says-fbi-report-1547870U. S. Department of Justice, Federal Bureau of Investigation, 2019. "2019 Hate Crime Statistics." https://ucr.fbi.gov/hate-crime/2019/hate-crime

43 Amanda Sakuma, 2019. "Hate Crimes Reportedly Jumped By 226 Percent In Counties That Hosted Trump Campaign Rallies." *Vox*, March 24. https://www.vox.com/2019/3/24/18279807/trump-hate-crimes-study-white-nationalism

44 Weiyi Cai, Audra D.S. Burch, and Jagal K. Patel, 2021. "Swelling Anti-Asian Violence: Who Is Being Attacked Where." *The New York Times*, April 3. https://www.nytimes.com/interactive/2021/04/03/us/anti-asian-attacks.html?action=click&pgtype=Article&state=default&module=styln-atlanta-massage-parlor-shootings&region=MAIN_CONTENT_1&context=storylines-godeep

45 Mike Levine, 2020. "No Blame?' ABC News Finds 54 Cases Invoking 'Trump' in Connection with Violence, Threats, Alleged Assaults." *ABC News*, May 30. https://abcnews.go.com/Politics/blame-abc-news-finds-17-cases-invoking-trump/story?id=58912889

46 Maggie Jones, 2022. "See the Worst People in the World!" *New York Times*, February 16. https://www.nytimes.com/2022/02/16/magazine/flight-attendants-covid.html

47 Marc J. Hetherington and Jonathan D. Weiler, 2009. *Authoritarianism & Polarization in American Politics*. New York, Cambridge University Press.

48 Christopher Paul and Miriam Matthews, 2023. *"The Russian 'Firehose of Falsehood' Propaganda Model: Why It Might Work and Options to Counter It."* Retrieved April 17 from https://www.rand.org/pubs/perspectives/PE198.html

49 Jon Greenberg, 2022. "Most Republicans Still Falsely Believe Trump's Stolen Election Claims." *PolitiFact*, June 14. https://www.politifact.com/article/2022/jun/14/most-republicans-falsely-believe-trumps-stolen-ele/

50 "Mixed Signals on Trump: Majority Says Criminal Charges Should Disqualify '24 Run, Popularity Is Unchanged, Leads DeSantis by Double Digits," 2023. *Quinnipiac University Poll*, March 29. https://poll.qu.edu/poll-release?releaseid=3870

51 Em Steck and Andrew Kaczynski, 2021. "Marjorie Taylor Greene's History of Dangerous Conspiracy Theories and Comments." *CNN*, February 4. https://www.cnn.com/2021/02/04/politics/kfile-marjorie-taylor-greene-history-of-conspiracies/index.html

52 Ibid.

53 Catie Edmondson, 2021. "Marjorie Taylor Greene's Controversies Are Piling Up. Republicans Are Quiet." *The New York Times*, January 29. https://www.nytimes.com/2021/01/29/us/politics/marjorie-taylor-greene-.republicans.htmlJordan Mendoza, 2022. "Lauren Boebert and Marjorie Taylor Greene Heckle Biden During State of the Union." *USA Today*, March 2. https://www.usatoday.com/story/news/politics/2022/03/01/state-union-heckle-lauren-boebert-marjorie-taylor-greene/9337266002/

54 David Moye, 2023. "Marjorie Taylor Greene Reportedly Calls Another Republican A 'Little B***h' On House Floor." *Huffington Post*, June 22. https://www.huffingtonpost.co.uk/entry/marjorie-taylor-greene-republican-impeachment-us_uk_6493fb98e4b007604cf6f08b

55 Paul LeBlanc, Manu Raju, and Morgan Rimmer, 2022. "Rep. Joyce Beatty Says Rep. Hal Rogers Poked Her and Said 'Kiss My a**' After She Asked Him to Put on a Mask," *CNN*, February 9. https://www.cnn.com/2022/02/08/politics/joyce-beatty-hal-rogers-poke-mask-dispute/index.html

56 Catie Edmondson and Luke Broadwater, 2021. "House Ethics Committee Details Accusations against 4 Lawmakers." *The New York Times*, October 21. https://www.nytimes.com/2021/10/21/us/politics/house-ethics-kelly-malinowski-mooney-hagendorn.html?

57 Brian Mann, 2023. "The House Ethics Committee Is Investigating Rep. George Santos." *NPR*, March 2. https://www.npr.org/2023/03/02/1160682985/george-santos-ethics-investigation

58 Andrew Atterbury, 2022. "DeSantis Called a 'Bully' After He Scolds Students for Wearing Masks." *Politico*, March 2. https://www.politico.com/news/2022/03/02/desantis-bully-masks-students-00013348

59 Michael Bloomberg (@MikeBloomberg), 2020. "He Lies. He Bullies. He Gets Away with It." *Twitter*, February 15. https://twitter.com/MikeBloomberg/status/1228755924115955712

2   Lying

Good and Bad Lies

"Did you take the cookies off the table?" asks Angela's mother. Angela, age four responds "I didn't eat them. BoBo (her dog) ate them!" Angela's mother then asks, "Why do you have cookie crumbs on your lips?" to which Angela blurts out "We both ate them!"

"We had no homework tonight because our teacher was absent and we had a substitute," Alfonzo, age 15, lied when his father asked why he was playing videogames all evening. Believing his son, no further questions were asked, and Alfonzo continued playing.

"Thanks so much for the birthday gift, Granny. I love the green sweater you gave me," Kadisha, age ten, said upon opening the gift and concealing her disappointment and dislike of the sweater.

All three of these children lied. They voiced a false statement, knowing that the information was false and intending to mislead or deceive the target of their lie. Although all three lied, their lying differed in several important ways. Angela's and Alfonso's lies were *antisocial* lies—"bad" lies that are generally frowned upon by others, causing them to lose trust in the lie teller. Antisocial lies are self-serving, motivated to conceal transgressions; to avoid blame, punishment, or an obligation; to get a reward; to manipulate the behavior or beliefs of others; or otherwise to get what one wants.[1] Angela lied to avoid being punished for taking the cookies and Alfonzo lied to get out of the obligation of doing his homework and to avoid likely punishment if he told the truth.

Because Angela is only four years old and Alfonzo is 15, most people would consider Alfonzo's lie much worse (and many of us would laugh about Angela's lie). Still, the purpose of both lies was the same. Although not evident in the examples above, many antisocial lies are intended to hurt or cause harm, such as when a bully tells a victim she is ugly and stupid or spreads false rumors about her. Antisocial lies are the kind of lies that cause one to lose trust in the lie teller, especially when lying is habitual; liars cannot be trusted.

DOI: 10.4324/9781003401278-2

Most lies are not bad or antisocial; they don't harm social relationships or cause the lie-teller to be called a liar. Those lies are generally called *White* lies. White lies are "light" lies that are inconsequential and harmless, such as saying "I'll be ready in 5 minutes" while knowing it is likely to be 10 minutes or more. White lies also include lies told to entertain others, such as when one jokes or exaggerates (e.g., "The fish was too big to get into the boat."). Rarely is someone accused of being "a liar" for telling only White lies.

White lies are harmless, and some are helpful or at least intended to be so. Thus, researchers often distinguish helpful lies, called *prosocial lies*, from other types of lies. When telling a prosocial lie, both the target of the lie and the lie-teller are better for having the lie rather than the truth told. That is, the prosocial lie avoids harming or hurting the target's feelings and makes the lie-teller feel good for doing so. Some prosocial lies are even altruistic—an unselfish moral act that is performed out of concern about the welfare of others while running the risk of harming oneself. For example, to protect the target of the bully a child might lie to the bully "I'm the one who said that" while risking bodily harm. A classic example of an altruistic lie was both Germans and non-Germans risking that own lives by lying to the Nazis in World War II about the whereabouts of Jews to save them from the holocaust.

Kadisha's lie that she liked her grandmother's gift could be considered either a White lie or a prosocial lie. Not causing any harm, it would clearly qualify as a White lie. Because her motive is unknown, however, one can only guess that it was a prosocial lie; that she lied about liking the gift so that her grandmother would not feel hurt, embarrassed, or disappointed. If she had told her mother that was her intention, then we would know it was a prosocial lie. However, her motive might not have been prosocial. She might have lied not thinking about her grandmother's feelings but instead thinking about the negative consequences to herself if she had told the truth (e.g., being reprimanded by her mother).

One other type of lie is often distinguished from antisocial lies: *self-protecting* and *self-enhancing* lies. Those lies are intended to neither hurt nor help others, but to benefit oneself. Examples of self-protecting lies are a socially rejected child lying to peers that he has plenty of friends; a homeless child lying that she lives in an apartment rather than in a van; and a teenage boy falsely telling others that it was him and not his girl-friend who broke off their relationship. Also included in this type of lie are lies that go beyond protecting one's sense of self to enhancing one's positive or superior self-image. Lies that serve this purpose are a form of self-deception. Examples of self-enhancing and self-deceptive lies are when individuals lie about their wealth, education, and achievements (and fail-ures) to impress others while also enhancing their own sense of superiority (e.g., "I'm a true genius." "I know more than anyone about [anything]."). As will be seen later in Chapters 8 and 9 on narcissism, self-enhancing lies are common among narcissists. Narcissists often lie to deceive others *and* themselves.

Nearly Everyone Lies, and a Few Are BIG Liars

The average person reports telling one to two lies daily,[2] and believes others lie more.[3] Although lying once or twice daily is average, this "average" is a bit misleading. There are a lot of people who report no lies on a given day and a few who report a very large number. In a national sample of adults who were asked to report the number of lies they told during the past 24 hours, Serota and colleagues replicated the findings of several earlier (and smaller) studies reporting that the average person tells one to two lies daily (average = 1.65). Intriguingly, they also found that one-half of all lies were told by only 5.3% of the study's participants and that almost one-fourth (22.7%) were told by just 1%. No lies were told on a given day by over half of the participants (59.9%). Those findings led the researchers to conclude that "the majority of lies are told by a few prolific liars."[4]

An average of one to two lies daily is misleading not only because a small number of people lie a lot while most people lie infrequently but also because there is much variability over time in the number of lies told by both big liars and little liars. This was shown in a more recent 2022 study by Serota and colleagues in which 632 college students recorded their lies daily over a period of three months.[5] In general, the study replicated their earlier findings with respect to the average number of lies told daily, finding an average of 2.03. They also replicated the finding that most lies are told by a few prolific liars: 75% of the participants told an average of 0–2 lies daily, and a few prolific liars (5.7% of the participants) were responsible for a large number of lies told (i.e., 28%).

A major contribution to research on lying was Serota and colleagues demonstrating both stability and variability in lying. Over the three-month period of the study, the big and little liars tended to remain the same. Approximately 75% of the participants were consistent in telling only 0–2 day-to-day. However, an appreciable amount of day-to-day variability in lying also was found: There were some days when the big liars—the chronic or prolific ones—told few if any lies, and there were some days when the little or normal liars told more than the average one or two lies.

Lying Is Normal and Adaptive, but Not Always

For most people, lying a couple of times daily is normative, socially acceptable, and viewed by psychologists as adaptive, or healthy, for social relationships and mental health. It is not only the small number of lies that the average person tells that makes lying acceptable and adaptive, but more importantly the type of lies. Of all lies told, 90% are White lies or prosocial lies that are unlikely to hurt or harm others. Indeed, White lies and prosocial lies are necessary or essential for positive social interactions and relationships. They are more likely to benefit the liar psychologically than materialistically.[6] The other 10% of lies are antisocial lies, or big lies, that *are* hurtful and harmful, and often maladaptive. Fortunately, antisocial lies are relatively rare, constituting only about 1% of total communication.[7]

White lies and prosocial lies rarely create life problems and often help avoid them. They are generally perceived favorably by others who witness and are aware of the lie. Likewise, seldom do people regret telling a White lie or prosocial lie. Indeed, there are times when being honest and not telling a lie is viewed by most people as socially inappropriate, impolite, or rude, such as telling a spouse, date, or friend who prepared their favorite dish "I think you over-cooked it, and I'll pass" or "It's okay but I've had much better."

In addition to playing an important role in healthy social relationships, White lies and prosocial lies serve the adaptive function of self-preservation.[8] In the above example, telling a prosocial lie not only protects the target of the lie from negative feelings but also protects the lie-teller from embarrassing oneself and from likely social rejection. Thus, there are situations in which telling a lie instead of the truth helps maintain a positive sense of self-worth and does so by supporting a self-identity as a kind and moral person. Another adaptive function of White lies and prosocial lies is that they often help with emotion regulation.[9] A little lie can avoid, reduce, or mask anger and disappointment, such as in falsely stating "No, I'm not upset that you broke the vase, as it was an accident."

To whom do people lie? During childhood and adolescence, the most common targets of lying are family and friends. About 82% of adolescents and young adults admit lying to their parents about friends, money, alcohol/drugs, dating, parties, or sex.[10] While in college, friends are twice as likely as family members to be the targets of lying. In a large sample of college students, Serota and colleagues found that 50.6% of lies were told to friends, 20.8% to family, 11.3% to school/business colleagues, 8.9% to strangers, and 8.5% to casual acquaintances.[11]

When Lying Is Maladaptive

Telling White lies and prosocial lies, and an occasional antisocial lie, is normal and adaptive. Rarely does it lead to being viewed by others as dishonest, untrustworthy, or "a liar." For some individuals, antisocial lies are adaptive even when told often, causing them little or no psychological or social harm. Indeed, some people are in the business of lying (and cheating)—think of the classic conman, snake-oil salesperson, and used-car dealer; those who promote unproven and unhelpful vitamin supplements and healthcare products; and the thousands of rip-off artists and scammers over the telephone and internet. Gang members are another example of adaptive lying. They lie to protect themselves and others in the gang. As seen in the next chapter, adaptive lying is found among many popular individuals who have built their wealth and political careers largely upon lying. Lying helped them get things done.

Although chronic lying can be adaptive, such as in reaping big financial (and political) gains while causing little psychological or social harm to the liar, for most chronic liars their lying is maladaptive. As reported by both parents and teachers, about 3% of children are chronic liars,[12] and as noted previously, only about 5% of adults are responsible for one-half of all lies. Thus, few children and adults are chronic liars.

Lying is maladaptive and detrimental to mental health when it interferes with everyday life functioning and particularly social relationships.[13] Chronic and big liars are generally viewed by others as dishonest and untrustworthy and are socially condemned (there are many exceptions, however, as seen in the following chapter). Peer rejection of chronic liars begins as early as late childhood, as few children befriend or continue friendships with those whom they cannot trust, as their promises are worthless, and opinions and views lack credibility.[14]

For lying to negatively impact social relationships, the liar must be caught lying and the person lied to must view lying unfavorably. Social relationships are not harmed if the person lied to believes that the liar is truthful or uses various mechanisms of moral disengagement to excuse or justify the lying. Those mechanisms, as discussed in Chapter 10, are often the same ones used by the liar such as "Everyone lies," "The lies are for good reasons," or "They aren't lies but alternative facts."

For most people, antisocial lying negatively impacts how they are viewed by others and perhaps more importantly how they view themselves, which is as a liar—someone who is untrustworthy and dishonest. Lying, especially telling lies that harm others and relationships with others, is typically associated with feelings of guilt or shame and with a negative self-image. When this occurs, it negatively impacts the person's mental health. Individuals who devalue the importance of a moral identity and who lack guilt and shame are able to avoid the negative impact of their lying on their mental health. To them, being honest and trustworthy matters much less than getting things done. They are quite skilled in disregarding or dismissing the importance of how their behavior is viewed by others, especially others whose opinions they do not value or deem important. For most people, however, dismissing the importance of social relationships and the harm caused to others does not come easily. Thus, among most people, guilt and shame serve as powerful self-sanctions and deterrents of antisocial lying.

When Lying Is Maladaptive and Pathological

Chronic antisocial lying can be a sign of psychopathology, particularly when it coexists with other antisocial behaviors. Chronic lying alone is not pathological, at least not in the formal sense. Although "pathological liar" is commonly used by the public in reference to chronic lying, there is no such psychiatric diagnosis. However, chronic lying is one of 15 antisocial behaviors that meet the criteria for psychiatric diagnosis of *conduct disorder* in the American Psychiatric Association's *Diagnostic and Statistical Manual of Mental Disorders, Fifth Edition, Text Revision* (*DSM–V–TR*).[15] The 15 antisocial behaviors fall into one of four general categories: (1) aggression to people and animals, (2) deceitfulness or theft, (3) destruction of property, and

(4) serious violations of rules (e.g., staying out late at night, is truant from school). Lying is among the behaviors under the category of deceitfulness or theft, with the specific behavior being "Often lies to obtain goods or to avoid obligations (i.e., 'cons others')."[16] What the behaviors in those four categories have in common is that they "violate the basic rights of others or major age-appropriate societal norms or rules."[17]

Note that not all children who are chronic liars have a conduct disorder, as lying is only one of its symptoms. Likewise, not all children with a conduct disorder are chronic liars, although about two-thirds are.[18] Their lying serves to avoid being caught and punished for antisocial behaviors that deceive, manipulate, and hurt others. To meet the diagnostic criteria for conduct disorder at least three of the 15 behaviors listed in *DSM-V-TR* must be prevalent during the past 12 months (and at least one must have been present in the past six months). As one might guess, children meeting those criteria are likely to have poor relationships with peers, teachers, siblings, parents, and others. They also are at great risk for poor academic achievement, substance abuse, juvenile delinquency, and various psychiatric disorders in adulthood.[19] Although the diagnosis of a conduct disorder can be made at any age, it is used mostly with children and adolescents under the age of 18. Prevalence estimates range from 2% to over 10%, with a median of 3–4%.[20]

When a pattern of behavior constituting conduct disorder exists before the age of 15 and continues after age 18, the adult is likely to meet the diagnostic criteria for *antisocial personality disorder*. As noted in *DSM-V-TR*, "Persons with this disorder disregard the wishes, rights, or feelings of others. They are frequently deceitful and manipulative in order to gain personal profit or pleasure (e.g., to obtain money, sex, or power)."[21] Upon adulthood, about 40% of children and adolescents diagnosed with conduct disorder meet the diagnostic criteria for antisocial personality disorder.[22] Thus, for a sizable percentage of adults, the behaviors comprising a conduct disorder, which includes lying, are a precursor to antisocial personality disorder.

As with conduct disorder, deceitfulness is among the defining characteristics of antisocial personality disorder. As described in *DSM-V-TR*, deceitfulness is indicated by "repeated lying, use of aliases, or conning others for personal profit or pleasure."[23] Deceitfulness is one of seven behaviors representing a pervasive pattern of disregard for and violation of the rights of others. The other six behaviors are a failure to conform to social norms with respect to lawful behavior, impulsivity or failure to plan ahead, irritability and aggressiveness, reckless disregard for safety of self or others, consistent irresponsibility, and lack of remorse. For the diagnosis of antisocial personality disorder, three or more of those behaviors must be present.

In addition to individuals with conduct disorder and antisocial personality disorder, lying is common among those diagnosed with narcissistic personality disorder, with most narcissists being liars.[24] However, lying is not listed among the criteria for that diagnosis (see Chapter 8 for the criteria).

A fundamental difference in the lies of individuals with conduct disorder or antisocial personality disorder and those with narcissistic personality disorder is that the lies of the former are told to conceal violations of rules, crimes, and other moral offenses, whereas the lies of narcissists are typically exaggerations told to convince others, and themselves, that they are the greatest. Often, there is a thin line between exaggerations and antisocial lies; exaggerations become antisocial lies when they harm others, which includes relationships. Likewise, an exaggeration is an antisocial lie when it entails a crime, such as fraud. For example, claiming to a bank that one's property is worth ten times its actual value to obtain a greater loan is an exaggeration *and* an antisocial lie. A person whose chronic lies are antisocial and narcissistic is likely to meet the behavioral criteria for the diagnoses of antisocial personality disorder *and* narcissistic personality disorder. It is important to note, however, that meeting the behavioral criteria may not be sufficient for the diagnosis of those two or any other mental disorder, as *DSM-V-TR* states "the disturbance causes clinically significant distress or impairment in social, occupational, or other important areas of functioning."[25] This issue is discussed in greater depth in Chapter 9.

Development of Lying and Deceit

Except for some strict religious fundamentalists, few people believe that children are born wicked and speaking lies. As discussed below, genetics certainly influences behavior, especially antisocial behavior, but so too does the environment.

Genetic and Environmental Effects

Genetics places some children at greater risk than others for antisocial behavior, which includes the risk of conduct disorder and antisocial personality disorder (and most other psychiatric disorders).[26] The influence of genetics is stronger for overtly aggressive antisocial behaviors such as fighting, bullying, and assault than for more covert antisocial behaviors such as lying and stealing. Although no specific gene, or combination of genes, is known to predict lying per se, it makes sense that lying is influenced by the same genes that underlie other antisocial behaviors, both overt and covert. This includes differences in impulsivity, emotional regulation, executive functioning, empathy, and intelligence—differences manifested in children's temperament, personality, and behavior often observed shortly after birth.

In a comprehensive meta-analytic review of over 100 research studies, many of which included children of twins and siblings who were adopted and raised apart, Dr. Alexandra Burt found that genetic influences were significant for both aggressive behaviors and non-aggressive rule-breaking behaviors (e.g., lying, cheating, stealing, vandalism).[27] Perhaps more intriguingly, was the finding that genetic influences were much greater for aggressive antisocial behaviors than for non-aggressive rule-breaking behaviors, whereas the opposite was found for environmental effects. Genetics explained 65% and 48% of the variance in aggressive antisocial behaviors and non-aggressive rule-breaking behaviors, respectively. In contrast, environmental effects accounted for 35% and 52%, respectively, of the variance in the same behaviors.

Burt examined both *shared* and *non-shared* environmental effects. Shared environmental effects refer to features of the environment that are similar for siblings such as parenting style, parental education and income, and crime in the community. Nonshared environmental effects refer to those features of the environment that differ between siblings such as having different peers, different treatment by parents, and attending different schools. Environmental effects, but particularly shared environmental effects, were greater for non-aggressive rule-breaking than aggressive antisocial behaviors. Shared environmental effects accounted for 18% of the variance in non-aggressive rule-breaking behaviors and only 5% of the variance in aggressive behaviors. Non-shared environmental effects also were greater for non-aggressive rule-breaking behaviors than for aggressive behaviors, but the difference was much smaller (34% vs. 30%).

With respect to lying, cheating, and other non-aggressive rule-breaking antisocial behaviors, genetics accounted for about half of those behaviors. Environmental effects accounted for the other half, with non-shared environmental effects (e.g., different parenting styles, peers, different schools) being more significant than shared environmental effects (e.g., same parenting style, parental education). With respect to physical bullying and other aggressive antisocial behaviors, genetics played a greater role, accounting for two-thirds of the behaviors. Environmental effects explain the other third, with non-shared environmental effects explaining 30% of antisocial behaviors and shared environmental effects explaining only 5%.

Learning to Lie

Although children are not born liars, they start telling lies as early as age three. Initially, young children lie to conceal wrongdoing and avoid negative consequences, but quickly discover that lying also can reap tangible rewards.[28] Lying that you didn't eat the cookies not only avoids punishment but also just might gain you another cookie. Children quickly learn that at times they can benefit more from lying successfully (i.e., not getting caught) than from telling the truth. Young children lie mostly for self-centered and hedonistic reasons, which are to avoid punishment and gain rewards. This applies to antisocial lies, White lies, and prosocial lies alike.[29] With age and development, moral reasoning becomes less self-centered and centered more on the needs and perspectives of others.

Learning and development does not occur in a vacuum: The environment has a powerful impact on children's lying. This is true regardless of a person's genetic makeup. However, genes place some individuals at greater risk than others for antisocial behavior. For example, children who are impulsive and lacking in emotion regulation, which includes most children with attention-deficit/hyperactivity disorder (ADHD), are more prone than others to break rules. This includes rules against lying and cheating. ADHD has a genetic basis, with heritability of about 74%;[30] however, environmental factors, and particularly parenting in early childhood, largely determine the extent to which children, including those with ADHD, become "normal" liars who tell mostly White and prosocial lies and occasionally antisocial lies, or become big liars who tell antisocial lies and a lot of them.

Environmental factors determine the expression of genetic effects. Developmental, familial, cultural, interpersonal, and contextual factors interact with genetics in determining antisocial behavior. Regardless of one's genetic composition, harsh parenting, delinquent peers, and disadvantaged neighborhoods are particularly strong predictors of antisocial behavior and conduct disorder.[31]

Most influential in the teaching and learning of lying are significant others in a child's home, school, and neighborhood. This includes parents (or guardians), siblings, other relatives, neighbors, playmates, classmates, teachers, coaches, close friends, and peers. In general, parents have the earliest and most lasting effects on children's behavior. Their effects are both direct and indirect. Directly, parents teach children lying, cheating, bullying, and other antisocial behaviors primarily by modeling and reinforcing those behaviors, not confronting and correcting them when they occur, and failing to model and reinforce moral behavior. Indirectly, they teach children antisocial behavior primarily by exposing them to those who model, and often reinforce, the same antisocial behaviors such as in television shows, movies, books, games, and social media.

Children learn much about lying from their parents and others who they observe benefit from their lying. They learn that if not caught, lying is very effective in attaining what you want and especially avoiding punishment. In many homes, parents often preach that lying is wrong, if not sinful, but nevertheless teach and promote lying by providing their children with ample models and lessons that demonstrate its benefits. For example, children learn to lie by watching their parents lie about being sick to avoid going to work, their siblings lie about having completed homework, and their friends lie to their parents about where they are going or have been. Likewise, in admiring chronic and big liars in the popular media and highest positions of government, parents teach their children that lying not only avoids punishment but also leads to positive outcomes, including greater fame, wealth, and power. They observe that lying gets things done. Of course, positive reinforcement and punishment also largely explain lying.[32] Thus, when their own lying is reinforced, and not punished, those watching others lie successfully often become just like the models they observe.

Social Cognitive Processes That Promote or Deter Lying

With age and development, cognitive processes become more complex and sophisticated, and children become more successful in their deceitfulness. Their behavior becomes less impulsive and more reflective: They think more about whether to lie, and why; when best to do so; and how to avoid detection. Primary among the more complex and sophisticated social cognitive skills that children develop that are related to lying and other forms of deceitfulness are *executive functioning*, *social perspective taking*, and *moral reasoning*, with moral reasoning closely linked with moral emotions.

Executive Functioning and Social Perspective Taking

Executive functioning refers to cognitive skills that enable a person to focus and stay focused in attaining a goal—skills that underlie self-regulation of behavior. Whether telling the truth or a successful lie, one needs to control the impulse to do the first thing that comes to mind, which too often is to attain one's immediate and self-centered goal and without consideration of the negative consequences of the impulsive behavior to the self and others. Conducting a cost-benefit analysis before acting is a great challenge for impulsive individuals, which includes most young children. It also includes children and adults with ADHD, most of whom have deficits in executive functioning.

A second major aspect of executive functioning related to lying is the regulation of emotions. When telling a good lie, whether antisocial or prosocial, one needs to conceal emotions, thoughts, and physical signs that might reveal that one is lying. This means keeping a straight face, not saying something that suggests one is lying, and perhaps faking certain emotions (e.g., smiling when you're disappointed, acting sad when delighted, or demonstrating anger to arouse the emotions of others). Such deceptive behaviors are difficult for very young children, as was seen earlier in Angela having crumbs on her face and blurting that Bobo ate a cookie. With age, deceptive behaviors come more easily.

In addition to inhibiting or controlling the expression of impulses and emotions that might provoke or reveal lying, executive functioning includes goal-oriented planning (e.g., planning to lie for a given purpose), adaptive and flexible thinking (e.g., the ability to think of different demands and of alternative responses and their consequences to lying), and good working memory (i.e., the ability to remember and manipulate important pieces of information while telling the lie). Although not yet fully developed, by middle childhood those skills are developed enough to make children much better liars. They come in handy for telling a lie that others are likely to believe and for avoiding getting caught telling the lie.

Developing simultaneously with executive functioning is the ability to assume the perspectives of others, or *social perspective taking*. Similar to what is called Theory of Mind, this ability entails reading the minds of others—thinking about what others might be thinking and feeling, and how their thoughts and feelings might impact and be impacted by one's behavior. Social perspective taking is invaluable for manipulating others through deceit, either for antisocial or prosocial purposes.

Although both executive functioning and social perspective-taking skills can foster deceit, they also can foster honesty and truth-telling. Hence, more complex and sophisticated executive functioning and social perspective-taking skills are a two-edged sword with respect to deceitful behavior. They are found among both saints and sinners. On the one hand, those skills are seen in greater impulse control, self-regulation of emotions, and understanding why lying is bad (beyond being punished and rewarded). When reasons and emotions for honesty are internalized and valued, they serve as powerful motivators in curtailing antisocial lies and successfully navigating the social environment.[33]

On the other hand, when equipped with more complex and sophisticated executive functioning and social perspective-taking skills, one can lie more successfully, if so desired and motivated to do so. The same skills that underlie self-discipline and prosocial behavior are used by skilled liars to manipulate others through deceit to attain self-serving goals. Skilled liars know their targets, or audience: who is less knowledgeable, more gullible, and less likely to question and challenge the accuracy of their lies. They understand that some people can be manipulated more easily than others; recognize that deceit is more effective in certain situations than others; are more aware when the costs of lying outweigh the likely benefits, and vice versa; and are better at avoiding detection. To avoid detection, skilled liars embed lies into truthful information, keep false statements clear and simple, and provide plausible accounts of the false statements.[34]

The development of executive functioning and social perspective-taking skills does not guarantee greater moral behavior, including less antisocial lying, but it does help. That is, the two sets of skills are related to less antisocial lying and more prosocial lying, although the associations are not particularly strong. This makes much sense, as executive functioning skills are related to the sophistication of lies but not to the decision to lie.[35]

Moral Reasoning (and Emotions)

With respect to deciding to lie, what often matters much more than executive functioning skills is one's goal in a given situation. As with other moral behavior, decision-making and personal goals are highly influenced by moral reasoning and moral emotions. For example, two children may possess the same executive functioning and social perspective-taking skills, but one decides to lie with the goal of avoiding punishment whereas the other decides to tell the truth to maintain the self-image of an honest person, out of concern about the harm the lying causes others (i.e., empathy), or to avoid the negative emotions of guilt and shame. In this case, and many others, executive functioning and social perspective-taking skills alone fail to predict honesty from dishonest behavior.

As discussed more thoroughly in Chapter 10, with increasing maturity, children's moral reasoning becomes less self-centered and focused more on the perspectives of others. Children recognize that whereas prosocial lies foster positive relationships with others, antisocial lies harm them.[36] By middle childhood, or about age nine, this is seen in children telling more prosocial than antisocial lies, with the reasons underlying the prosocial lies centered less on obeying authorities and the personal consequences of their actions and more on an understanding and concern about others.[37] They understand that trust is essential for effective communication and positive social relationships, and that most people do not like liars—liars cannot be trusted. They come to anticipate, and experience, guilt or shame about their moral transgressions.

However, they also understand that not all lies harm relationships, and some help. They recognize that depending on the social context, a low or moderate degree of antisocial lying is socially acceptable and often effective in maintaining social relationships. For example, the social acceptance and effectiveness of a lying largely depends on the amount of harm caused, the number of lies told, and the motives for lying. By middle to late children, children have learned to evaluate the badness of a lie based on such considerations. They recognize that antisocial lies can range from being a little bit bad to morally reprehensible. They understand that not all lies are the same and that the worst lies are those that cause others the greatest harm and are punished the harshest.[38]

From early to middle childhood, children also come to understand that although violating rules or harming others is wrong, lying about it is worse. It is worse not only because they are likely to get into greater trouble, but also because others are likely to view them more negatively. Their behavior is now twice as wrong: They harmed their brother *and* lied about it! The views of others become increasingly important and especially the views of those highly respected and valued. More so than in earlier years, and through the gradual process of socialization, the moral standards of important others become internalized. Internalization of moral standards translates into children understanding and valuing that a "good" person is one who is honest and trustworthy. Persons who are honest and trustworthy do not tell antisocial lies even when they are confident that their lies will go undetected. As such, self-evaluations and self-sanctions play a greater role in determining honesty and other moral behaviors.[39]

As noted previously, and discussed more thoroughly in Chapter 10, as children grow older and internalize moral standards, doing the "right" thing no longer means simply obeying authority, avoiding punishment, and garnering praise and rewards. For sure, those factors are still important but what now matters more is that one is a good or moral person, as evaluated by oneself and significant others. Unfortunately, as seen in the following chapter, not all children, adolescents, and adults come to value a moral identity, or experience negative moral emotions when their lying harms others. Just as most children learn and internalize prosocial moral values held by their parents and others, so too do some learn and internalize antisocial values and behaviors. Those who internalize antisocial values learn that lying, cheating, and bullying get things done. For them, self-sanctions are deterrents to lying and to getting things done, and thus are to be avoided.

With Development, More Lies?

One might think that with greater executive functioning and the teaching of social and moral values and behavior, that children's lying decreases in later childhood and adolescence. Unfortunately, the opposite is more common. Despite greater internalization, executive functioning, and social perspective taking skills, lying often increases rather than decreases.[40] This paradox can largely be explained by older children viewing many rule-violating behaviors, including lying, as excusable or justifiable, and particularly rule-violating behaviors that are normative and acceptable among their peers. Lying is now excused or justified because it is understood that not all lies are equally bad, and many issues that they lie about are *not* moral issues. As discussed in Chapter 10, violating rules pertaining to issues not viewed as being moral, and lying about it, is not perceived to be morally wrong. This includes common issues that parents and their teenagers often battle over such as physical appearance, schoolwork, friends, dating, alcohol and drug use, and consensual sex.

Especially during adolescence, in many situational contexts, peers are more influential than their parents in determining their behavior. Peer pressure and peer approval are powerful determinants of prosocial and antisocial behavior, with lying much more likely occurring in situations with which others are doing the same.[41] Peer influences often extend beyond the situational context. Antisocial behavior, including lying, is more common among adolescents who affiliate with antisocial peers. Fortunately, peer influences also can be powerful deterrents of antisocial behavior: Adolescents who affiliate with prosocial peers are much more likely to exhibit prosocial behavior and inhibit non-aggressive rule-breaking behavior.[42] This holds true even among adolescents who are at greater genetic risk for such behavior, which indicates that exposure to prosocial peers promotes resilience to genetic risk for antisocial behavior.[43]

After peaking in adolescence, lying declines in early adulthood. There are exceptions and primary among them are individuals whose immature self-centered moral reasoning and lack of moral emotions continue beyond their childhood. Although this encompasses adults with antisocial personality disorder and narcissistic personality disorder, it also includes others who do not meet diagnostic criteria for those disorders but nevertheless share many of the same characteristics. Among those individuals, chronic lying (as well as cheating and bullying) continues and increases, as it is an effective means of attaining their self-serving goals and avoiding negative consequences.

A person does not have to be hedonistic and self-centered or lacking in moral emotions to lie, cheat, or bully others, although it helps. There are many people who possess the opposite of each of those characteristics—who hold high moral principles, care about others, and experience feelings of guilt and shame—and still lie, cheat, and bully others while viewing themselves as moral. They do so by disengaging, or neutralizing, their dishonest and harmful behavior, absolving themselves of feelings of responsibility by using common mechanisms of moral disengagement. For example, they lie that they did not lie, assert that the lie is not a lie but an "alternative fact" or "truthful hyperbole," blame others for their lying, or otherwise justify their behavior or the harm caused. Mechanisms of moral disengagement are discussed in Chapter 10, with examples of their Trump's use presented in Chapter 11.

Parenting That Contributes to Lying (and Other Antisocial Behavior)

Among environmental determinants of antisocial behavior, none is stronger and more enduring than parenting.[44] Parenting effects are strongest in early childhood, when parental guidance and supervision are more present, and children have less autonomy. Although weaker, the effects continue into adolescence and adulthood.

Some parents are much more effective than others in deterring antisocial behavior and promoting prosocial behavior, with a large body of research having identified the styles of parenting that characterize the most and least effective parents. The research has been replicated with classroom teachers, showing that the most effective teachers share the same characteristics as the most effective parents.[45] Much of this research has been guided by theory and research of Dr. Dianne Baumrind that began over half a century ago, in the 1960s. Baumrind identified four styles of parenting: *authoritative, permissive, authoritarian,* and *disengaged* (also often referred to as *uninvolved/neglectful*).[46] They differ along two basic dimensions: *responsiveness* and *demandingness.* As described by Baumrind, responsiveness refers to parents providing warmth, guidance, and support that meets their children's individual needs and promotes their cognitive, social, emotional, and moral development. Demandingness refers to parents presenting clear and high behavioral expectations; providing necessary supervision and monitoring of behavior; and having fair rules, while enforcing them consistently and fairly.

Authoritative parenting is high in both responsiveness and demandingness; disengaged parenting is low in both dimensions; authoritarian parenting is high in demandingness and low in responsiveness, and permissive parenting is low in demandingness and high in responsiveness. Deficits in either the responsiveness or demandingness dimensions, as found in disengaged, authoritarian, and permissive parenting, are associated with a number of negative outcomes, including greater antisocial behavior, less prosocial behavior, and lower academic achievement.[47]

Greater negative outcomes among children of disengaged and permissive parents are due to their parents' lack of demandingness. Their parents often fail to monitor, supervise, and correct misbehavior. Whereas permissive parents overlook or ignore their children's lies, disengaged parents simply aren't around. Thus, children's lying often goes undetected and when detected it is seldom confronted. Worse yet, many permissive parents are overly indulgent and over-protective: pampering their children, fostering their narcissistic sense of entitlement, and believing or defending their lies. To them, their children can do no harm and others are to blame for their children's misbehavior. Common examples are when parents falsely believe their children's failure in school is because the teachers are "mean" or that their lack of playtime in a sport is because the coach is "unfair" (when neither is true). Generally, overindulgence and overprotection are less common among disengaged parents than permissive parents since the former are less involved and often not present. There is a subset of disengaged parents, however, for which overindulgence and overprotection is quite common—the wealthy who have others care and pamper their entitled children. Researchers often distinguish this parenting style from the other styles, referring to it as uninvolved/overindulgent parenting.

In contrast to disengaged and permissive parents who lack in demandingness, authoritarian parents are overly controlling and coercive. Control is either psychological (e.g., threats of love withdrawal, personally demeaning insults such as "loser," "stupid," etc.) or physical and harsh (e.g., spankings). Their children learn that lying and other behaviors are wrong *if* you get caught and are punished; a successful lie is one that goes undetected and achieves what you want: Telling a lie just might avoid the wrath of a parent, including a spanking. Authoritarian parents fail to teach reasons for telling the truth beyond "obey authority" and "fear punishment." They fail to provide necessary guidance and support for the development of cognitive, social, moral, and emotional processes that underlie self-discipline. Moreover, they fail to teach their children differences between White lies, prosocial lies, and antisocial lies; when the former is socially appropriate; and of alternatives to lying for attaining one's goals.

Whereas overly harsh punishment is associated with greater lying, this might not be the foremost feature of the authoritarian approach that contributes to lying. Some researchers argue that it is the lack of warmth among authoritarian parents, more so than their harshness and power assertion, that contributes to lying and other antisocial behavior.[48] It is likely both.

Characterized by a healthy balance of responsiveness and demandingness, authoritative parents are the most effective parents when it comes to deterring their children's antisocial behavior,[49] which includes deterring lying.[50] Responsiveness is seen in authoritative parents establishing and maintaining warm, close, and trusting relationships; addressing children's social and emotional needs; and developing and social-cognitive and emotional processes that underlie moral behavior. Primary among those processes, and as discussed in Chapter 10, are other-oriented moral reasoning and the moral emotions of empathy, guilt, and shame.

Authoritative parents are also high in demandingness. As found among authoritarian parents, authoritative parents have high behavioral expectations, closely monitor their children's behavior, and set and enforce rules and consequences. They differ from authoritarian parents, however, in that they are not overly controlling, neither physically nor psychologically. Their long-term aim is not to manage and control their children's behavior but for their children to manage their behavior themselves. Although authoritative parents don't hesitate to correct misbehavior, their methods are less controlling and harsh than those of authoritarian parents. To be sure, mild forms of punishment are often used (e.g., taking away privileges, time-out, verbal reprimand), but harsh forms of punishment are rare. A combination of guiding persuasion and reasoning is preferred.

Consistent with research on children's lying, authoritative parents recognize that the best way to prevent lying is not by threats of punishment but by modeling and reinforcing truth-telling and developing and appealing to their children's self-evaluations and motivations for telling the truth.[51] When their children are caught telling antisocial lies, authoritative parents are quick to tactfully confront the lying while focusing on *why* lying is wrong. Instead of teaching that lying is wrong solely because it leads to punishment (if one is caught), the focus is on the harm it causes to relationships and the importance of how one is viewed by others (i.e., as "honest and trustworthy" vs. "a liar").

Of course, tactfully confronting children's lying requires close supervision and monitoring and catching the lie. This is often a great challenge. As noted earlier, in later childhood and adolescence children become more successful liars, with their lies often avoiding detection. Additionally, it is during this time that children experience greater autonomy and spend more time with friends, peers, and others outside of the home and in the use of social media. Generally, there is less parental monitoring and supervision of children's behavior; thus, the influence of others, particularly peers, increases. Indeed, this is when lying peaks. And having undesirable peers is a very good predictor of lying, with the influence increasing from grade 4 to grade 12.[52] This does not mean that authoritative parenting is no longer influential. It is, but less so. That is, in both the short-term and the long-term (adulthood) children of authoritative parents exhibit less antisocial behavior compared to children raised by permissive, disengaged, and authoritarian parents.[53]

Whereas parenting is a major determinant of lying and other antisocial behavior, it is certainly not the only one. Genetics and multiple environmental factors beyond parenting, and especially the situational context (e.g., salience of rewards or punishment, peer pressure), also determine behavior. Ultimately, however, it is a combination of individual characteristics, influenced by genetics and the situational context, that determines whether a person decides to lie or tell the truth. Primary among those individual characteristics are moral reasoning, moral emotions, and mechanisms of moral disengagement, as will be discussed in greater depth in Chapter 10.

Notes

1 Jan N. Hughes and Crystal R. Hill, 2006. "Lying," in *Children's Needs III: Understanding and Addressing the Developmental Needs of Children*, edited by George G. Bear and Kathleen Minke. Silver Springs, MD: National Association of School Psychologists, 159–170.
2 Bella M. DePaulo, Debroah A. Kashy, Susan E. Kirkendol, Melissa M. Wyer, and Jennifer A. Epstein, 1996. "Lying in Everyday Life." *Journal of Personality and Social Psychology* 70, no. 5: 979–995. https://doi.org/10.1037/0022-3514.70.5.979

   Kim B. Serota, Timothy R. Levine, and Franklin J. Boster, 2010. "The Prevalence of Lying in America: Three Studies of Self-Reported Lies." *Human Communication Research* 36, no. 1: 2–25. https://doi.org/10.1111/j.1468-2958.2009.01366.x

   Kim B. Serota, Timothy R. Levine, and Tony Docan-Morgan, 2022. "Unpacking Variation in Lie Prevalence: Prolific Liars, Bad Lie Days, or Both?" *Communication Monographs* 89, no. 3: 307–331. https://doi.org/10.1080/03637751.2021.1985153
3 DePaulo et al.
4 Serota et al., "The Prevalence." 12.
5 Serota et al., "Unpacking."
6 Ibid.
7 Ibid.
8 Ibid.
9 DePaulo et al.
10 Lene A. Jensen, Jeffrey J. Arnett, J., S. Shirley Feldman, and Elizabeth Cauffman, 2004. "The Right to Do Wrong: Lying to Parents Among Adolescents and Emerging Adults." *Journal of Youth and Adolescence* 33 no. 2: 101–112. https://doi.org/10.1023/B:JOYO.0000013422.48100.5a
11 Serota et al., "Unpacking."
12 Magda Stouthamer-Loeber, 1986. "Lying as a Problem Behavior in Children: A Review." *Clinical Psychology Review* 6 no. 4: 267–289. https://doi.org/10.1016/0272-7358(86)90002-4
13 Talwar and Angela Crossman, 2011. "From Little White Lies to Filthy Liars: The Evolution of Honesty and Deception in Young Children." *Advances in Child Development and Behavior* 40: 139–179. https://doi.org/10.1016/b978-0-12-386491-8.00004-9
14 Talwar and Crossman.
15 American Psychiatric Association, 2022. *Diagnostic and Statistical Manual of Mental Disorders, Fifth Edition, Text Revision*. Washington, DC: American Psychiatric Association.
16 Ibid., 531.
17 Ibid., 530.
18 Talwar and Crossman.

19 American Psychiatric Association.
20 Ibid.
21 Ibid., 749.
22 American Psychiatric Association.
23 Ibid., 748.
24 Nicole Atkinson Azizli, Breanna E. Baughman, Holly M. Chin, Kristi Vernon, Philip A. Harris, and Elizabeth L. Veselka, 2016. "Lies and Crimes: Dark Triad, Misconduct, and High-Stakes Deception." *Personality and Individual Differences* 89: 34–39. https://doi.org/10.1016/j.paid.2015.09.034
25 American Psychiatric Association, 23.
26 American Psychiatric Association.
27 Alexandra S. Burt, 2009. "Are There Meaningful Etiological Differences within Antisocial Behavior? Results of a Meta-Analysis." *Clinical Psychology Review* 29, no. 2: 163–178. https://doi.org/10.1016/j.cpr.2008.12.004
28 Magda Stouthamer-Loeber, 1986. "Lying as a Problem Behavior in Children: A Review." *Clinical Psychology Review* 6 no. 4: 267–289. https://doi.org/10.1016/0272-7358(86)90002-4
29 Jia Ying Sarah Lee and Kana Imuta, 2021. "Lying and Theory of Mind: A Meta-analysis," *Child Development* 92, no. 2: 536–553. https://doi.org/10.1111/cdev.13535
30 American Psychiatric Association, 70.
31 Alexandra S. Burt, 2022. "The Genetic, Environmental, and Cultural Forces Influencing Youth Antisocial Behavior Are Tightly Intertwined." *Annual Review of Clinical Psychology* 18: 155–178. https://doi.org/10.1146/annurev-clinpsy-072220-015507
32 Margarita Leib, Nils Köbis, Ivan Soraperra, Ori Weisel, and Shaul Shalvi, 2021. "Collaborative Dishonesty: A Meta-Analytic Review. *Psychological Bulletin* 147 no. 12: 1241–1268. https://doi.org/10.1037/bul0000349
33 Lee and Imuta.
   Victoria Lee Talwar and Kang Lee, 2008. "Social and Cognitive Correlates of Children's Lying Behavior." *Child Development* 79, no. 4: 866–881. https://doi.org/10.1111/j.1467-8624.2008.01164.x
34 Brianna L. Verigin, Ewout H. Meijer, Glynis Gobaard, and Aldert Vrij, 2019. "Lie Prevalence, Lie Characteristics and Strategies of Self-Reported Good Liars." *Plus One* 3, no. 14. https://doi.org/10.1371/journal.pone.0225566
35 Angela D. Evans and Kang Lee, 2011. "Verbal Deception from Late Childhood to Middle Adolescence and Its Relation to Executive Functioning Skills." *Developmental Psychology* 47, no. 4: 1108–1116. https://doi.org/10.1037/a0023425
36 Talwar and Crossman.
37 Jennifer Lavoie, Karissa Leduc, Cindy Arruda, Angela M. Crossman, and Victoria Talwar, 2017. "Developmental Profiles of Children's Spontaneous Lie-Telling Behavior." *Cognitive Development* 41: 33–45. https://doi.org/10.1016/j.cogdev.2016.12.002
38 Talwar and Crossman.
39 Albert Bandura, 1986. *Social Foundations of Thought and Action: A Social Cognitive Theory.* Englewood Cliffs, N.J.: Prentice-Hall.
40 Evelyne Debey, Maarten De Schryver, Godon D. Logan, Kristina Suchotzke, and Bruno Verschuere, 2015. "From Junior to Senior Pinocchio: A Cross-Sectional Lifespan Investigation of Deception." *Acta Psychologica* 160: 58–68. https://www.sciencedirect.com/science/article/abs/pii/S0001691815300184
41 Margarita Leib, Nils Köbis, Ivan Soraperra, Ori Weisel, and Shaul Shalvi, 2021. "Collaborative Dishonesty: A Meta-Analytic Review," *Psychological Bulletin* 147, no. 12: 1241–1268. https://doi.org/10.1037/bul0000349

42 Nancy Eisenberg, Tracy L. Spinrad, and Ariel Knafo-Noam, 2015. "Prosocial Development," in *Handbook of Child Psychology and Developmental Science. Vol. 3: Socioemotional Processes*, edited by Michael E. Lamb and Richard M. Lerner. New York: John Wiley, 610–656.

43 Alexandra S. Burt and Kelly L. Klump, 2014. "Prosocial Peer Affiliation Suppresses Genetic Influences on Non-Aggressive Antisocial Behaviors During Childhood." *Psychological Medicine* 44, no. 4: 821–830. https://doi.org:10.1017/S0033291 713000974

44 Manuel P. Eisner and Tina Malti, 2015. "Aggressive and Violent Behavior." In *Handbook of Child Psychology and Developmental Science. Vol. 3: Socioemotional Processes*, edited by Michael E. Lamb and Richard M. Lerner. New York: John Wiley, 794–841.

45 George G. Bear, 2020. *Improving School Climate: Practical Strategies to Reduce Behavior Problems and Promote Social and Emotional Learning*. New York: Taylor & Francis.

46 Diana Baumrind, 2013. "Authoritative Parenting Revisited: History and Current Status," in *Authoritative Parenting: Synthesizing Nurturance and Discipline for Optimal Child Development*, edited by Robert E. Larzelere, Amanda S. Morris, and Amanda W. Harrist. Washington, DC: American Psychological Association, 11–34, 26.

47 Robert E. Larzelere, Amanda S. Morris, and Amanda. W. Harrist (Eds.), 2013. *Authoritative Parenting: Synthesizing Nurturance and Discipline for Optimal Child Development*. Washington, DC: American Psychological Association.

48 Fengling Ma, Angela D. Evans, Ying Liu, Xianming Luo, and Fen Xu, 2015. "To Lie or Not to Lie? The Influence of Parenting and Theory-of-Mind Understanding on Three-Year-Old Children's Honesty." *Journal of Moral* Education 44, no. 2: 198–212. https://doi.org/10.1080/03057240.2015.1023182

49 Ibid.

50 Victoria Talwar, Jennifer Lavoie, Carlos Gomez-Garibello, and Angela M. Crossman, 2017. "Influence of Social Factors on the Relation Between Lie-Telling and Children's Cognitive Abilities." *Journal of Experimental Child Psychology* 159: 185–198. https://doi.org/10.1016/j.jecp.2017.02.009

51 Victoria Talwar, Cindy Arruda, and Sarah Yachison, 2015. "The Effects of Punishment and Appeals for Honesty on Children's Truth-Telling Behavior." *Journal of Experimental Child Psychology* 130: 209–217. https://doi.org/10.1016/j.jecp.2014.09.011

52 Stouthamer-Loeber, 293.

53 Baumrind.

3 Trump

A Role Model for Lying

It's Not the Number of His Lies That Is Abnormal but Also Their Meanness

As discussed in the previous chapter, about one-half of all lies are told by 5% of adults and almost one-fourth are told by only 1% of adults. If not for the few prolific liars, the average number of lies in our society would be cut in about half. Perhaps foremost among the few prolific liars is Trump. Trump told a whopping 30,573 false or misleading statements during his four years as president,[1] for an average of 21 false statements or lies every day, which is 10 to 20 times the average of one to two lies daily that others tell. In one month alone he made nearly 4,000 false or misleading statements and lies, with an average of 150 daily. On a single day, Trump made 503 false or misleading statements. That day was November 2, the day before the 2020 election, during which he spoke at multiple campaign rallies.[2] Those counts are likely underestimates of his lying, as they reflect only the false or misleading statements and lies he told publicly. Even without counting those lies, however, it is apparent that Trump's lying falls at the 99th percentile. Perhaps his biggest lie has been: "But one thing I can promise you is this: I will always tell you the truth."[3]

Trump is not the only president known for his lying. Richard Nixon notoriously said "I am not a crook" after spearheading the Watergate break-in. His dishonesty led to his resignation from office. Reflecting a belief system shared by Trump, Nixon once said "If you can't lie, you'll never go anywhere." Bill Clinton lied under oath "I did not have sexual relations with that woman, Miss Lewinsky." He was impeached for lying and obstruction of justice (which included telling others to lie about his affair).

Trump, Clinton, and Nixon will long be remembered for their big lies and moral ineptitude, but with over 30,000 lies it is likely that Trump will be the only American president to be remembered as a pathological liar. It is not just the number and chronicity of Trump's lies that are deviant or pathological, but also the type of lies. In an article entitled "I Study Liars. I've Never Seen One Like President Trump," Professor Bella DePaulo analyzed a sample of 400 of Trump's lies.[4] DePaulo is the author of one of the major studies of

DOI: 10.4324/9781003401278-3

lying cited in the previous chapter. She found that Trump's lies were like those told by the college students and community members in her earlier study, but with some noteworthy exceptions. In the earlier study, DePaulo found that about half of adult lies were self-serving antisocial lies and about a quarter were prosocial lies. For Trump, 65% of his lies were self-serving and about 10% were prosocial. Trump told 6.6 times as many self-serving lies as prosocial ones. That ratio is three times greater than what DePaulo found for the average adult.

DePaulo also found that many of Trump's lies did not fit clearly into the self-serving or prosocial categories but fell into a category she called "Other," consisting of a combination of lies that were uncommon and not of any one type. Close examination of those lies revealed that most were "mean" lies—"cruel lies, told to hurt or disparage others." In her earlier study, DePaulo found that only 0.8% of the lies of college students and 2.4% of the lies of community members were of this type. In comparison, she found that 50% of Trump's lies were mean lies, with many of them being "more malicious than ordinary people's." DePaulo also found that many of Trump's lies served dual purposes, which she rarely found in her earlier study: They served to both belittle others and to enhance himself.

Trump's First Big Lies

Very little is known about Trump's lying in childhood and adolescence. However, Trump once told his biographer, Michael D'Antonio: "I don't think people change very much. When I look at myself in the first grade and I look at myself now, I'm basically the same."[5] Thus, unless Trump was then lying, he has always been a big liar (as well as cheater, bully, and narcissist). For both genetic and environmental reasons, it is likely that Trump lied more than others as a child. As discussed in the previous chapter, antisocial rule-breaking behavior, which includes lying and cheating, has both genetic and environmental bases, with the environment playing a greater role. Trump often credits his father for being the person he is. It is well documented that Trump's father, Fred Trump, a billionaire real estate developer in New York City, was repeatedly accused, charged, and sued by the city and federal government for various forms of fraud and tax evasion (i.e., for lying and cheating).[6] Foretelling a practice later followed by his son, Fred even lied about his name and about his family descent: He assumed the fake persona of Mr. Green to mislead others when inquiring about purchasing property and when renting properties to Jews, claiming he was Swedish rather than German.

Genetically and via parenting, Fred passed his authoritarian personality traits, self-centeredness, lack of empathy, and skills of lying and cheating on to his son. He also passed much of his wealth. Trump clearly lied when bragging repeatedly "I built what I built myself."[7]

Lying in Business: Avoiding Taxes and Exaggerating Wealth

Among Trump's first big lies as a businessman and real estate developer was lying about discriminating against Blacks. In 1973, when Trump was 27, the United States Justice Department sued Trump Management for racial discrimination in its housing projects. Trump was the company's president and his father was the chairman. Both defendants denied the charges, but it was clearly shown that discrimination occurred.[8] Thus began Trump's long history of lies in his businesses.

Starting early in his business career, Trump lied about the value of his properties. Both Fred and his son undervalued their properties to avoid taxes—they lied. But being more of a narcissist than his father, and also to obtain more favorable loans, Trump also frequently *overvalued* his assets, claiming he was much wealthier than he was. When author Timothy O'Brien revealed in his 2005 book *TrumpNation: The Art of Being the Donald*[9] that Trump was worth $150 to $250 million, which was far less than Trump bragged, Trump sued for defamation and libel, seeking $5 billion in compensatory and punitive damages. During the 2007 trial, and under oath, Trump was repeatedly caught lying. He admitted 30 times that over the years he lied about his wealth, his debt, the money he borrowed from his father to avoid bankruptcy, the size of his buildings and real estate projects, and about doing business with career criminals.[10] Trump lost his lawsuit.

Among Trump's biggest business failures, and lies, were those concerning the hotels and casinos he built in Atlantic City. One year after opening his prized hotel and casino, the Taj Mahal, Trump was $1.1 billion behind on loan payments across his businesses and properties. Trump's Taj Mahal filed for bankruptcy, and his two other casinos did the same shortly thereafter. Trump claimed success. In a 2016 interview with *The Washington Post,* he bragged "The Taj Mahal was a very successful job for me" and "I got out great." *The Washington Post* thought otherwise about his business acumen. As found earlier by O'Brien, as well by *Forbes* and the New Jersey State Casino Commission, the newspaper found that Trump greatly exaggerated, or lied about, his personal wealth.[11]

After the bankruptcies, Trump continued to fraudulently inflate the value of his properties to obtain loans from banks and to claim he was richer than he truly was, while simultaneously undervaluing his properties to avoid paying fair taxes.[12] In 2022 this double lie led to New York Attorney General Letitia James filing a lawsuit against Trump, his two sons, his daughter Ivanka, and the Trump Organization. The lawsuit alleged over 200 instances of fraud over ten years. As noted by James, the defendants often made fraudulent and misleading statements (i.e., lied) "in both their composition and their presentation."[13]

Given the long history of fraudulent schemes used by Trump and his father to avoid taxes and Trump's exaggerations of his wealth, it is not surprising that Trump lied during the 2016 election that he would release his tax returns.[14] Trump released his tax returns to neither the public nor a Congressional Committee that had sought them for over three years while fighting his delays and multiple court battles. It was not until after courts ruled that he had to release them, and the Supreme Court refused to intercede, that in November 2022 the Committee was given his 2015–2020 tax returns.[15] The returns revealed that Trump, a billionaire, paid only $1.1 million in federal income taxes during the first three years of his presidency.[16] During the first year of his presidency (2017), and claiming major business losses, he paid only $750 in federal taxes. He paid no federal taxes in 2020.[17] He also claimed $0 in charitable giving in 2020, despite promising that he would donate to charity his $400,000 annual salary as president.

Lying as a Business: Trump University

Trump lied, and cheated, not only in business, but also *as* a business. In his businesses, he was proud of being a master of the use of what he called "truthful hyperbole" in his 1987 book, *The Art of the* Deal. He defined truthful hyperbole as "an innocent form of exaggeration—and a very effective form of promotion" and defended its use by stating "I play to people's fantasies."[18] Examples of his truthful hyperbole are Trump claiming that Trump Steaks were "the world's greatest steaks, and I mean that in every sense of the word .... Trump Steaks are by far the best-tasting, most flavorful beef you've ever had—truly in a league of their own."[19]

Trump University is perhaps the foremost example of a Trump business that was built upon what Trump called truthful hyperbole, and others might call blatant lying. It also is an excellent example of cheating, and one of the rare instances in which he got caught for his deceitfulness *and* experienced punitive damages. Trump University defrauded thousands of students out of their money. As noted by New York's Attorney General Eric Schneiderman in that state's lawsuit against Trump, the "university" was never a real university but "a fraud from beginning to end" that resulted in "swindling thousands of innocent Americans out of millions of dollars."[20] The core of the scam was offering students a free introductory seminar about investing in real estate during which they were highly pressured by salespersons who used detailed "playbooks" to upgrade to a three-day seminar for $1,495, then to an "elite" package costly over $10,000, and finally to a "gold" mentorship program for $35,000.

The scam led to two class action lawsuits in federal court for fraud and another lawsuit by the state of New York for fraud and operating an unlicensed and illegal education/training institution. During testimony in the three lawsuits, including dispositions from salespeople and Trump himself, multiple false claims and promises in advertising were revealed.[21] Advertisements claimed that the instructors and mentors were successful real estate professionals personally selected by Trump and who followed a curricular program that he designed. None of that was true. In late 2016, and shortly before assuming the presidency, Trump agreed to a $25 million settlement to end the three lawsuits against him, with much of the settlement money going to over 6,000 victims of the scam.

Lies during 2016 Presidential Campaign

On June 16, 2015, Trump formally launched his 2016 presidential campaign at Trump Tower in New York City by descending an escalator to a cheering crowd that included actors he paid to help fill the room.[22] Pulitzer Prize winner *PolitiFact*, a nonprofit project of the Poynter Institute in St. Petersburg, FL, tracked the false statements made by Trump that year and throughout his presidency. For the year 2015, *PolitiFact* awarded Trump the Lie of the Year. Typically, the award goes to someone who told the biggest lie, but for 2015 it was for "various statements" that Trump made during his campaign.[23] *PolitiFact* found that 76% of his campaign statements were "Mostly False," "False" or "Pants on Fire." Among Trump's "Pants on Fire" lies were:

- That he watched the World Trade Center collapse on 9/11/2009 when he was in Jersey City, NJ, where, according to Trump, "thousands and thousands of people were cheering as that building was coming down" (while adding that the people celebrating were Muslims).[24]
- That the Mexican government was behind criminals entering the United States illegally, stating that "The Mexican government … they send the bad ones over." When he was making this false claim, illegal immigration from Mexico had declined greatly and there was no evidence that the Mexican government was sending "the bad ones over."
- That the murder rate in the United States in 2015 was the highest in 45 years. At that time the murder rate had declined 42% since 1993.[25] Trump also falsely claimed that most Whites are murdered by Blacks.
- Repeatedly calling climate warming a hoax (and later denying he said it). From 2012 to 2016, he called it a hoax and "bullshit," claiming it was "created by and for the Chinese" to make US manufacturing less competitive due to increased regulations and was perpetrated by "scientists [who] are having a lot of fun."[26] When Hilary Clinton challenged him during a 2016 presidential debate about calling climate warming a hoax he lied by denying that he had said it.[27]

Throughout Trump's presidency, *PolitiFact* tracked 100 promises that Trump made during the 2016 campaign. He broke over half of them (53%), kept less than a quarter (23%), and compromised on 22%. Among the campaign promises he often repeated, while arousing his political base, but never kept, were that he would build a wall and make Mexico pay for it, remove all undocumented immigrants, establish a ban on Muslims entering the United States, expand the right to carry a gun to all 50 states, eliminate gun-free zones at schools and military bases, repeal Obamacare, release his tax returns, bring back manufacturing to the United States (there was no overall improvement), grow the economy by 4% a year (it never did grow at that rate even before the coronavirus recession), eliminate the federal debt in eight years (it went up, not down), and dramatically scale back the US Education Department.[28]

Big Lies during His Presidency

As reported by the Fact Checker project of *The Washington Post*, the longer Trump was in office the more he lied.[29] Nearly half of his 30,573 false statements and lies were made in his final year. Trump averaged six false claims daily in year one, 16 in year two, 22 in year three, and 39 in year four. Fact Checker discovered that "Trump made false claims about just about everything, big and small." For example, in his first address to the nation as president, which was his inauguration, he greatly exaggerated, or lied, about winning by a "landslide" and about a host of other things. Repeating his earlier lies, he lied that the country was suffering with rapidly increasing crime, a weakening military, a great loss of manufacturing jobs, and a declining economy.

Strangely, later that day he lied about what everyone could see while watching the inauguration—about the weather. He falsely claimed that the sun shined on his main event and that the rain "just never came."[30] It poured. His White House press secretary, Sean Spicer, whose job was to communicate to the public what the president wanted reported, even lied about the size of crowd, telling the news media "This was the largest audience to ever witness an inauguration—period—both in person and around the globe." That same week a government photographer doctored photos of the crowd to make it look larger. Trump and his aides also falsely claimed that he had written his inaugural address, while providing as evidence a staged photo of him at his desk writing it (with a Sharpie pen).[31]

Perhaps the greatest lie he told on the first day of his presidency was one made under oath—that he would "preserve, protect and defend the Constitution of the United States." As seen later in this chapter, his presidency ended with multiple lies designed to keep him in power, which including lies that disregarded the Constitution and incited an insurrection.

Trump's presidency got off to a bad start, and it got worse. The number of lies increased, with many of them really big ones. Foremost among them were ones he repeated over and over about immigration, the economy, and the coronavirus; lies involving the Mueller investigation; and the biggest lie of all—that he won the 2020 election. As discussed below, each of those lies are excellent examples of self-serving, and often harmful, pathological lying.

The "Incredible" Economy

Perhaps trying to prove his business acumen to his supporters and the world, one-fifth of Trump's nearly 2,500 falsehoods or lies were about him creating the greatest economy in American history. As noted by Fact Checker, economies were much stronger under other presidents. This did not stop Trump from repeating some version of this lie 493 times, which was more than any other of his many lies.[32] Trump repeated hundreds of times that he passed the largest tax cut in history, which was a lie; his tax cut was the eighth largest in 100 years, with tax cuts by Obama, Bush, Clinton, and Reagan being greater. He often repeated that he had the greatest employment rate in history. In truth, Trump was the first president since World War II to have fewer people employed at the end of his presidency than at the beginning. He repeated that under his watch that the "incredible" US economy outperformed all others in the world. As again found by Fact Checker, this too was false, especially during the pandemic when China's growth in the Gross Domestic Product (GDP) was 11.5 whereas the US's was minus 9, and unemployment in the US reached 7.9% compared to an average of 7.4 for other developed countries. He also lied when stating that "For the first time in many, many years, wages are going up." In fact, wages have been rising steadily since 2014.

Immigration: Building a "Big Beautiful Wall" to Protect Americans from Mexican "Animals" and "Rapists," and Muslim "Terrorists"

Trump repeatedly warned of a rapidly rising flood of immigrants illegally entering the country, especially from Mexico, with many of them being hardcore criminals that included "animals" and "rapists."[33] He also promised to reform the immigration system, which never happened. The one promise regarding immigration that he repeated most often was that he would build a "big beautiful wall" and Mexico would pay for it. As pointed out by *PolitiFact*, the number of illegal immigrants entering the United States declined from 2000 to 2017 and spiked in the second half of Trump's term. *PolitiFact* also found no evidence to support Trump's fearmongering claim "We've arrested nearly 500,000 illegal aliens with criminal records, some with very serious criminal records of the type you don't want to know about, like murder."

Despite Trump's promises and claims to the contrary, his "big beautiful wall" across the Mexican border was never built. Only 80 miles of new barriers, which included 33 miles of secondary wall built to reinforce existing barriers, were constructed along the 1,954 miles of the US-Mexico border. Mexico did not pay for it.[34]

Another Lie of the Year Award: The Mueller Investigation

In the spring of Trump's first year as president, a Special Counsel led by special prosecutor Robert Mueller began its nearly two-year investigation of (a) Russian interference in the 2016 elections, (b) the extent to which Trump and his associates conspired with the Russians, and (c) obstruction of justice by Trump and members of his presidential campaign and administration. Although Trump repeatedly stated "No Collusion. No Obstruction,"[35] the final report concluded that Russia clearly interfered with the elections, and that such interference was welcomed by the Trump campaign.[36] However, it also concluded that there was insufficient evidence linking Trump to criminal conspiracy. Multiple indictments for criminal offenses were made, with 13 Russian nationals and three companies indicted for fraud and deceit to interfere in the election and 12 Russian intelligence officers indicted for hacking the Democratic National Committee and Hillary Clinton's presidential campaign. Individuals close to Trump also were indicted, including Paul Manafort, Trump's former campaign manager, and Manafort's business partner Rick Gates. The two were charged with money laundering, tax evasion, and foreign lobbying. Gates also pleaded guilty to lying to the FBI.

Others were indicted for obstructing justice, which largely entailed lying. George Papadopoulos, Trump's former campaign foreign policy adviser, and Michael Flynn, Trump's former national security advisor, both pleaded guilty of lying to the FBI. Michael Cohen, Trump's former personal attorney pleaded guilty of lying to Congress about Trump's real estate deal in Moscow. And Roger Stone, a longtime political adviser to Trump was indicted on five counts of lying and for witness tampering.[37]

As seen in the indictments above, lying was common among Trump's associates, with Trump often directing officials in his administration and others to lie. Mueller reported to Congress that rampant lying was a major impediment in his investigation, noting that "I think there are probably a spectrum of witnesses in terms of those who are not telling the full truth and those that are outright liars."[38]

Regarding obstruction of justice, the report did not rule out that Trump was guilty, stating that the investigation "does not exonerate" Trump. Based on the Office of Legal Counsel's opinion prohibiting the federal indictment of a sitting president, the investigation did not attempt to determine if Trump obstructed justice. However, the report noted that Congress had the authority to pursue the legal case of obstruction of justice after Trump left office and offered ten episodes in which Trump likely obstructed justice.

In recognition of all their lies about the Mueller investigation, Trump and his associates were awarded the 2017 Lie of the Year by *PolitiFact*.[39]

Another Lie of the Year Award: Trump's First Impeachment and Lies about Ukraine

Trump is among only three American presidents to be impeached, and the only one to be impeached twice. Plenty of his lies led up to both impeachments, and plenty have been made since. The first impeachment evolved around Trump coercing Ukraine to commit, or at least support, two major lies that might have helped him in his 2020 re-election: (1) that Ukraine, not Russia, interfered in the 2016 elections, and (2) that Joe Biden, his

Democratic opponent for the 2020 election, and his son, Hunter, were corrupt. The House of Representatives, which at the time was controlled by Democrats, impeached him for abuse of power and obstruction of Congress. The Senate, which was controlled by Republicans, acquitted him.

As revealed in the impeachment proceedings, Trump made multiple efforts to force Ukraine to promote a fully discredited conspiracy theory (i.e., lies) that Ukraine, not Russia, possessed a hacked computer server belonging to the Democratic National Committee (DNC) and that Ukraine used information from the server to interfere in the 2016 elections. If found to be true, information in the server would have been a big embarrassment to the Democratic Congress and possibly Joe Biden. Locating the hacked DNC server in Ukraine also would have countered findings of the Mueller's investigation which had concluded that Russia, not Ukraine, was responsible for using information from a hacked DNC server to attack Hilary Clinton and support Trump in the 2016 election. No evidence was found to support the conspiracy theory, promoted by Russia, that Ukraine possessed the server. Evidence was presented, however, that Trump and his surrogates (primarily Trump's personal lawyer Rudy Guiliani) attempted to interfere in the 2020 elections.[40]

Trump's claim that the Bidens were corrupt was behind his infamous telephone call with Ukrainian President Volodymyr Zelenskyy. Before the call, Trump had blocked the release of $400 million to Ukraine that Congress had mandated for military aid (the funds were later released). It was alleged during the impeachment that Trump withheld the funds and a visit by Zelenskyy to the White House to obtain quid pro quo cooperation from Zelenskyy in support of the investigations of the conspiracy theory, and of the Bidens.

As in the Mueller trial, the second impeachment trial disclosed multiple efforts by Trump to obstruct Congressional investigations. In checking the facts, *CNN* reporter Daniel Dale listed 65 ways that Trump was dishonest about Ukraine and the impeachment, reporting that "relentless deceit has seemed to be Trump's primary defense strategy in the court of public opinion. He has made false claims about almost every separate component of the story, from his July phone call with Ukrainian President Volodymyr Zelensky, to the whistleblower [Lt. Col. Vindman] who complained about the call, to Democratic presidential candidate Joe Biden's own relations with Ukraine."[41] Fact Checker recorded over 1,000 false and misleading claims Trump made about the phone call in just four months. Recognized by *Politifact* as the biggest of those lies was Trump's lying that Vindman was "almost completely wrong." For that lie, Trump was given *Politifact*'s 2019 Lie of the Year Award.[42]

Coronavirus: Magical Disappearance

Few of Trump's lies led to deaths. An exception was Trump repeatedly lying to the public about the coronavirus, also called COVID-19. The virus was the cause of over 386,00 deaths during the first year of the pandemic and over 400,000 deaths by the end of his presidency. Many of those deaths could have been prevented if he had been truthful to the public. *The Washington Post's* Fact Checker found that Trump made over 2,500 misleading or false claims about the coronavirus in 2020. Many of those lies were about wearing masks. Despite scientific evidence that wearing masks helps prevent the virus, Trump refused to wear them and lied to the public about masks being ineffective, even falsely stating that research by the Centers for Disease Control and Prevention (CDC) had demonstrated that they did not work.[43]

If Trump did not believe that wearing masks would stop the coronavirus, what did he believe and tell the public would stop it? He gave mixed messages to his supporters about vaccines. After being booed at campaign rallies for endorsing the vaccine, Trump changed his tune and emphasized that taking the vaccine was a matter of personal choice (and not public safety). Trump's solution was magic or a miracle, wrapped with more lies about the virus being under control. After contracting the virus and being released from the hospital and while standing on the White House balcony on October 10, 2020, he declared "It's going to disappear, it is disappearing."[44] Despite rising hospitalizations and deaths, Trump also suggested that sunlight and ingesting disinfectants (which are known to be poisoning and causing death) could help cure the virus.[45]

As revealed in interviews with Bob Woodward for his book *Rage*, Trump knew he was lying when he made such claims as "When it gets a little warmer, it miraculously goes away." "We have it very much under control" and "This is a flu. This is like a flu."[46] When Woodward asked Trump why he misled the public, Trump responded that he wanted to avoid "panic," and show "calm," "confidence," "strength," and "leadership." Millions of his supporters followed his "leadership," and many of them and others died refusing to wear masks, to social distance, and to be vaccinated.

Election "Bullshit" and the Second Impeachment

"I won the election" is widely recognized as "The Big Lie" (except among Trump and his supporters who believe "the Big Lie" is Trump *losing* the election). Trump lost decisively to Biden by 7 million votes, with Biden earning 306 electoral votes to Trump's 232, which is the same margin he defeated Hillary Clinton in 2016 and repeatedly called a "landslide."

Trailing Biden in most polls and laying the groundwork for challenging the outcome, Trump began his big lie and false claims about the election well before it was even held. His telling of the big lie greatly increased after he lost. It was a calculated lie that he was confident his followers would believe (and wanted to hear) and would help him maintain their support, which included financial donations and future votes. *The Washington Post's* Fact Tracker found that from November 3, 2020, to his last day in office, Trump told over 800 lies, falsehoods, or misleading claims about election fraud.[47] Those claims continued even after they were rejected by judges in over 60 court cases. Courts sided with the findings of the government's Cybersecurity and Infrastructure Security Agency which concluded that the 2020 election was the "most secure in American history" and that there was "no evidence that any voting system deleted or lost votes, changed votes or was in any way compromised."[48]

In a speech at the Ellipse in Washington, DC on January 6, 2023, Trump made 107 false or misleading claims about the "rigged" election. Inciting his supporters to storm the Capitol, Trump told them "if you don't fight like hell you're not going to have a country anymore."[49] The insurrection led to five deaths and hundreds of arrests, and Trump's second impeachment. It also resulted in the House of Representatives creating a bipartisan *Select Committee to Investigate the January 6th Attack on the United States Capitol.* In hearings of that committee, clear evidence was presented that Trump was well aware that "I won the election" was a big lie.[50] Trump's own attorney general, William Barr, testified to the committee "I made it clear I did not agree with the idea of saying the election was stolen and putting out this stuff, which I told the President was bullshit." Barr called claims by Trump that the election was rigged and a hoax "idiotic," "disturbing," and "without basis."[51] He told the committee that "There was never an indication of interest in what the actual facts were" and that "I was somewhat demoralized because I thought, boy, if he really believes this stuff he has, you know, lost contact with—with—he's become detached from reality if he really believes this stuff." Other attorneys in the administration shared Barr's concerns, testifying that they informed Trump that the multiple conspiracy theories that he, his friends, advisers, and allies were spreading about the election were false, but Trump did not listen.

For lies related to the January 6 attack on the Capitol, including the Big Lie that he had won the election, Trump and his allies earned *Politifact*'s 2021 Lie of the Year Award.[52]

The final report of the Select Committee, published in December 2022, concluded that Trump's lying and fraud, and particularly the lie that he had won the election, precipitated the attack on the Capitol. His lies were accompanied by acts of cheating, bullying, and unlawful behavior, including likely witness tampering and obstruction of justice.[53]

Most Republicans in the House of Representatives rejected the committee's findings and produced a counter-report blaming the insurrection on the security failures of the Democratic leadership and law enforcement.[54] Some Republicans, however, agreed that Trump's lies led to the insurrection and that Trump was responsible. Among them was GOP leader of the Senate, Mitch McConnell, who stated that "the mob" that staged the "failed insurrection" was "fed lies;" that "Trump's actions that preceded the riot were a disgraceful, disgraceful dereliction of duty;" and that Trump was "practically and morally responsible for provoking the event of that day."[55] (Despite those words, McConnell voted to acquit Trump of inciting the insurrection.)

The conclusion in the select committees report that Trump repeatedly lied about winning the 2020 election and McConnell's own conclusion that the mob was fed lies were confirmed in the US Justice Department's investigation, led by special counsel Jack Smith, into the actions of Trump and co-conspirators to subvert the election. As described in Chapter 5 on Trump's cheating, the investigation led to Trump being indicted on August 1, 2023, on four counts, with each entailing lying and cheating. Special counsel Smith stated that the January 6th insurrection was "fueled by lies—lies that the defendant targeted at obstructing a bedrock function of the US government: the nation's process of collecting, counting, and certifying the results of the presidential election."[56] Among the lies Trump repeatedly told the public, which were supported by evidence that Trump understood they were lies, were:[57]

- Thousands of ballots were cast in Georgia in the names of dead people and by out-of-state voters.
- Election workers in Georgia engaged in "ballot stuffing."
- Pennsylvania had 205,000 more votes than voters.
- A suspicious "dump" of votes occurred in Detroit, Michigan.
- Nevada had tens of thousands of double votes.
- Substantial voter fraud occurred in Wisconsin.
- In addition to dead people voting, over 30,000 non-citizens voted in Arizona.
- Voting machines switched votes from Trump to Biden.
- Trump won every state by hundreds of thousands of votes.
- The Justice Department had identified significant concerns about the legitimacy of the election results.
- Vice President Pence had the power to reject Biden's electoral votes (and that Pence agreed to such).

Despite substantial evidence that the election was fair, and Trump had lost, Trump made the big lie that he had lost the election the centerpiece of his 2024 reelection campaign. He repeated his lies and various conspiracy theories about the Democrats and Big Tech working together to steal the election from him. He even proposed the termination of the Constitution to restore him to power, posting the following on the social network Truth Social (which he formed after being banned from Twitter for multiple lies and other postings inciting violence):

"Do you throw the Presidential Election Results of 2020 OUT and declare the RIGHTFUL WINNER, or do you have a NEW ELECTION? A Massive Fraud of this type and magnitude allows for the termination of all rules, regulations, and articles, even those found in the Constitution" …. "Our great 'Founders' did not want, and would not condone, False & Fraudulent Elections!" Two days later, and after considerable backlash including from Republicans, he denied (lied?) that he wanted to terminate the constitution.[58]

More "Bullshit": Lies about Documents Taken to Mar-a-Lago

On multiple occasions, after Trump left office in early 2021, the National Archives and Records Administration (NARA) informed him that he was illegally holding documents at his Mar-a-Lago resort in Florida, including classified and top-secret records that belonged not to him but to the American people. After refusing on multiple occasions to return all the records for safe storage with NARA, and at times lying that all had been returned, a judge approved a search warrant for the FBI to search Mar-a-Lago and reclaim the records taken.

Trump responded to the FBI's search and recovery of the stolen documents the same as he had responded to other investigations before—by denying (i.e., lying) that he had done anything wrong, attacking the FBI and others, and suing to delay or overturn the investigation. Not only did Trump repeatedly lie about the documents but he directed others in his administration, including White House attorneys, to do the same (some refused to do so).[59] Trump claimed that many of the documents were his rightful souvenirs and possessions and that the records were not classified because "I declassified everything." Trump argued (and lied) that no formal declassification process was necessary because as president "you can declassify just by saying 'it's declassified'—even by thinking about it."[60] Multiple national security legal specialists challenged such claims, viewing them as "preposterous," "idiotic and dumb," "utter baloney," "ludicrous," "ridiculous," and "bullshit."[61]

Trump told many more false statements, or lies, related to the documents, including that the FBI planted the documents at Mar-a-Lago and that Presidents Clinton, G. W. Bush, G. H. W. Bush, and Obama did the same as he had done—that they had personally taken "millions" of presidential documents from the White House.

In November 2022, Attorney General Merrick Garland appointed special council Jack Smith to investigate Trump's alleged mishandling of classified documents (as well as actions by Trump to overturn the 2020 election results).[62] This resulted in a grand jury indicting Trump in June 2023 on 37 counts: 31 counts of violating the Espionage Act that bars the willful and unauthorized retention of national defense documents (which included 30 documents marked "Top Secret") and failing to turn them over under court order to do so; three counts of withholding or concealing documents in a federal investigation; two counts of making false statements in the investigation; and one count of conspiring to obstruct justice.[63] The latter three counts of indictment pertained to Trump lying to the FBI and grand jury and directing his aide and attorneys to do the same and to conceal or destroy documents that were found in his Mar-a-Lago resort.

Liar, Liar, Pants on Fire

The above or just a few of the lies for which Trump will be remembered and are among his biggest ones. Additional lies that captured media attention follow:

- Stating: "They say [windmills] noise causes cancer."[64] (Note: Here and often at other times Trump uses "They say" when telling a lie and without revealing who "they" are).
- Insisting that he did not know that his attorney Michael Cohen paid $130,000 to porn star Stormy Daniels. He continued this lie even after being indicted by a grand jury on 34 felony charges related to the hush money. (The trail is expected to begin in early 2024.)[65]
- Accusing the Obama administration of planting a spy inside his 2016 presidential campaign to help Hilary Clinton win the election.[66]
- Insisting that the National Weather Service predicted that hurricane Dorian would hit Alabama. It did not make that prediction. To prove that he was correct, he showed the media a weather map of Hurricane Dorian that he had redrawn using a Sharpie pen (thus, this became known as "Sharpiegate").[67]
- Accusing Congresswoman Ilhan Omar, the nation's first Muslim in Congress, of marrying her brother, committing "large-scale immigration and election fraud," and having wished "death to Israel."[68]
- Claiming that he had "done more for the Black community than any president."[69] (Nearly all prominent historians say that Lincoln, who abolished slavery, did the most, and that presidents Grant, Truman, Franklin Roosevelt, Kennedy, Johnson, and Obama did much more than Trump.)[70]
- Claiming that he was top of his class in college (he didn't even appear on the dean's list), that he was Michigan's Man of Year (a false claim made at a campaign rally in Michigan), and he won 18 golf club championships (as revealed in *Rick Reilly's Commander in Cheat: How Golf Explains Trump*, not only did Trump not win the championships, but he wasn't even present during some of them).[71]

Firehose of Falsehood

Likely being at the 99th percentile with respect to lying, and with his lies being markedly more hateful and hurtful than those of most other people, Trump qualifies as what is commonly considered a pathological liar, and a mean one. There is no formal psychiatric diagnosis specifically for liars, including pathological liars. However, several psychiatric disorders include lying or deceitfulness as one of its major symptoms. The two disorders most often mentioned as applying to Trump are narcissistic personality disorder and antisocial personality disorder. Those two disorders, and whether Trump meets their diagnostic criteria, are discussed in Chapter 9. As discussed in that chapter, Trump fails to meet all official diagnostic criteria for either of the two disorders; nevertheless, he *is* a narcissist, pathological liar, and "crazy as a fox." Crazy as a fox refers to his lying (cheating and bullying) not being "crazy" as in constituting a psychiatric disorder, but in being calculating, manipulating, and self-serving.

As noted by Jonathan Rauch, a senior fellow at the Brookings Institution, Trump's Big Lie is a perfect example of a contemporary information-warfare technique used by Russian President Putin in his invasions of Ukraine called the "firehose of falsehood."[72] Although Rauch was addressing Trump's lying at that time, or the Big Lie, many of Trump's other repetitive lies can be viewed as classic examples of the information warfare technique. As described by researchers at the RAND Corporation, a nonprofit and nonpartisan policy think tank, this form of propaganda has two distinctive features: "high numbers of channels and messages and a shameless willingness to disseminate partial truths or outright fictions."[73] Popular channels used to disseminate lies are television, radio, printed press, campaign rallies, podcasts, and especially multiple social media platforms on the internet. Disinformation is disseminated in a rapid, continuous, and repetitive fashion. There is no commitment to either objective reality or consistency. The intent is to entertain, confuse, and overwhelm the audience and ultimately have them believe the disinformation.

As revealed by *The Washington Post's* Fact Checker, during his presidency there were about 750 instances in which Trump repeated a variation of the same falsehood. Many of them were big "Three or Four Pinocchio Lies" about the 2020 election. They included that Dominion voting machines were manipulated, GOP poll watchers were denied access to the counting of votes, and the election otherwise was rigged—many of the same lies detailed in Special Counsel Smith's 45-page indictment of Trump on four counts.

As reviewed by RAND, research in experimental psychology shows that such flooding of dissemination from multiple sources is highly effective, with consumers often paying little attention to the credibility of those spreading the false information. The popularity and appearance of persons spreading the disinformation is often more important than their actual knowledge of the topic, particularly if the liars are individuals whom the consumer admires, are viewed as sharing their own values and beliefs, and who espouse what the listener wants to hear (e.g., masks don't work so you don't need to wear them, and people who wear them are stupid; Trump won the election). Thus, followers of Trump are prone to watch *Fox News, Newsmax*, and other ultra-right networks and are more likely to believe the hosts of their programs. The number, or flood, of supporting arguments matter more than their validity. Moreover, the lies are more likely to be believed when those telling the truth are constantly accused of lacking credibility and trustworthiness. Disseminating a lot of false information using multiple sources also is effective because it drowns out the dissemination of the truth.

Based on their analysis of the research in psychology on persuasion and propaganda, RAND found that much of the findings on the firehose of falsehood "flies in the face of intuition and conventional wisdom, which can be paraphrased as 'The truth always wins.'" They attribute the effectiveness of disseminating disinformation and lies to consumers often being "cognitively lazy," believing the first thing they hear on a topic (and what they want to hear), especially if the information is repeated by multiple sources. They are too lazy or unwilling to check the validity of what they are being told, regardless of the source and quality of the information, or to listen to counterarguments. They also are poor at discerning truth from falsehood. In telling a big lie it often helps to insert a little bit of truth or factual evidence, but that might be all it takes to persuade others of the much bigger lie. For example, Trump supporters were told on *Fox News* and other conservative networks that dead people voted in the election. There is some truth in this, as it is not uncommon for some to cast a vote by mail and die before election day. For many Trump supporters, this was all the proof they needed to believe the election was rigged and that Trump really won.

Another factor that often comes into play with respect to the firehose of falsehood is what is called *confirmatory bias*, which is the tendency for people to seek information and interpret it in a manner that confirms their existing values, attitudes, and beliefs, as well those shared by groups of which they are members. Confirmatory bias is seen in Republicans watching *Fox News* and *Newsmax* while Democrats watch *CNN* and *MSNBC*. Those networks are biased, and their biases are exactly what their viewers want to hear—confirmation of their existing beliefs. As also found by RAND, disinformation, which includes conspiracies and other lies, is especially likely to be accepted as valid when presented in a manner or event that is emotionally arousing: angry audiences are easily persuaded by angry messages. This is why Trump and Fox talk show hosts often appear angry.

Throughout his presidency, Trump orchestrated a very effective firehose of falsehoods. To be sure, campaign rallies, Twitter, and Facebook were instrumental in disseminating propaganda, lies, and his self-proclaimed "truthful hyperbole" that plays "to people's fantasies."[74] Trump had over 80 million followers on Twitter and 34 million on Facebook. As noted by *CNN* senior political analyst Kirsten Powers: "Without Twitter, there would be no Donald Trump presidency, and I think he knows that."[75] However, Trump's firehose of falsehood would not have been anywhere as successful if not for Fox and his GOP friends reinforcing his lying and helping spread the lies. As revealed in multiple emails, text messages, and other sources in a $1.6 billion lawsuit against Fox by Dominion (which was settled before trail, with Fox paying Dominion $787.5 million[76]), the television's hosts and others at Fox understood they were spreading lies. They also understood that their viewers would likely believe whatever they said (and wanted to hear). Many of them admitted that spreading lies was good for their ratings.[77] It also was good for Trump. Almost a year after he lost the election, and with no solid evidence to support that he had won, a *CNN* survey found that 78% of Republicans and over a third of Americans (36%) did not believe that Biden legitimately won the election.[78] Another poll in July 2023, three years after the election, found largely the same, with 71% of Republicans continuing to support Trump and believing that he committed no serious crimes.[79] As with Trump's many other self-serving lies, Trump's firehose of falsehood about having won the election worked—it got things done.

Notes

1 Glenn Kessler, 2021. "Trump Made 30,573 False or Misleading Claims as President. Nearly Half Came in His Final Year." *The Washington Post*, January 23. https://www.washingtonpost.com/politics/how-fact-checker-tracked-trump-claims/2021/01/23/ad04b69a-5c1d-11eb-a976-bad6431e03e2_story.html

2 Ibid.

3 Politico Staff, 2016. "Full Text: Donald Trump's Remarks in Charlotte." *Politico*, August 18. https://www.politico.com/story/2016/08/donald-trump-never-lie-227183

4 Bella DePaulo, 2017. "I Study Liars. I've Never Seen One Like President Trump." *The Washington Post*, December 8. http://wapo.st/2iDBdSh?tid=ss_mail

5 Michael D'Antonio, 2016. *The Truth about Trump*. New York: Thomas Dunne Books.

6 David Barstow, Susanne Craig, and Russ Buettner, 2018. "Trump Engaged in Suspect Tax Schemes as He Reaped Riches from His Father." *The New York Times*, October 2. https://www.nytimes.com/interactive/2018/10/02/us/politics/donald-trump-tax-schemes-fred-trump.html

7 Ibid.

8 Jonathan Mahler and Steve Eder, 2016. "No Vacancies' for Blacks: How Donald Trump Got His Start, and Was First Accused of Bias." *The New York Times*, August 27. https://www.nytimes.com/2016/08/28/us/politics/donald-trump-housing-race.html

9 Timothy L. O'Brien, 2005. *TrumpNation: The Art of Being the Donald*. New York: Warner Business Books.

10 Timothy L. O'Brien, 2018. "I've Watched Trump Testify Under Oath. It Isn't Pretty." *Bloomberg*, January 25. https://www.bloomberg.com/opinion/articles/2018-01-25/i-ve-watched-trump-testify-under-oath-it-isn-t-pretty

11 One might argue that Trump was not lying when he told *The Washington Post* "I got out great." As reported by *The New York Times*, Trump "declared a $916 million loss on his 1995 income tax returns, a tax deduction so substantial it could have allowed him to legally avoid paying any federal income taxes for up to 18 years."

12 Jim Zarroli, 2017. "As Trump Built His Real Estate Empire, Tax Breaks Played a Pivotal Role." *NPR*, May 18. https://www.npr.org/2017/05/18/528998663/as-trump-built-his-real-estate-empire-tax-breaks-played-a-pivotal-role

13 Summer Concepcion and Tom Winter, 2022. "New York AG Sues Trump, 3 of His Children and Their Company, Charging Large-Scale Business Fraud." *NBC News*, September 21. https://www.nbcnews.com/politics/donald-trump/new-york-ag-sues-trump-children-company-charges-large-scale-business-f-rcna48668

14 Katie Rogers, 2020. "Trump on Releasing His Tax Returns: From 'Absolutely' to 'Political Prosecution.'" *The New York Times*, July 9. https://www.nytimes.com/2020/07/09/us/politics/trump-taxes.html?

15 Robert Barnes, 2022. "Supreme Court Clears Way for Trump Tax Returns to Go to Congress." *The Washington Post*, November 23. https://www.washingtonpost.com/politics/2022/11/22/supreme-court-trump-taxes/

16 Jim Tankersley, Susanne Craig and Russ Buettner, 2022. "Key Takeaways from Trump's Tax Returns." *The New York Times*, December 30, https://www.nytimes.com/2022/12/30/us/politics/trump-tax-returns-takeaways.html

17 Ibid.

18 Donald J. Trump (with Tony Schwartz), 1987. *The Art of the Deal*. New York: Ballentine.

19 Colin Campell, 2016. "Anderson Cooper Grills Donald Trump about the 'Trump Steaks' Piled Up at Trump's Press Conference." *Business Insider*, March 10. https://www.businessinsider.com/anderson-cooper-donald-trump-steaks-interview-2016-3

20 Rosalind S. Helderman, 2016. "Trump Agrees to $25 Million Settlement in Trump University Fraud Cases." *The Washington Post*, November 18. https://www.washingtonpost.com/politics/source-trump-nearing-settlement-in-trump-university-fraud-cases/2016/11/18/8dc047c0-ada0-11e6-a31b-4b6397e625d0_story.html

21 William D. Cohan, 2013. "Big Hair on Campus." *Vanity Fair*, December 3. https://www.vanityfair.com/news/2014/01/trump-university-fraud-scandal

22 Phillip Bump, 2017. "Even the Firm That Hired Actors to Cheer Trump's Campaign Launch Had to Wait to Be Paid." The *Washington Post*, January 20. https://www.washingtonpost.com/news/the-fix/wp/2017/01/20/even-the-firm-that-hired-actors-to-cheer-trumps-campaign-launch-had-to-wait-to-be-paid/

23 Angie Drobnic Holan and Linda Qiu, 2015. "2015 Lie of the Year: The Campaign Misstatements of Donald Trump." *PolitiFact*, December 21. https://www.politifact.com/article/2015/dec/21/2015-lie-year-donald-trump-campaign-misstatements/

24 Glenn Kessler, 2015. "Trump's Outrageous Claim That 'Thousands' of New Jersey Muslims Celebrated the 9/11 Attacks." *The Washington Post*, November 22. https://www.washingtonpost.com/news/fact-checker/wp/2015/11/22/donald-trumps-outrageous-claim-that-thousands-of-new-jersey-muslims-celebrated-the-911-attacks/

25 Trump-O-Meter, 2023. *politifact.com, retrieved April 18.* https://www.politifact.com/truth-o-meter/promises/trumpometer/?ruling=true

26 Jeremy Schulman, 2018. "Every Insane Thing Donald Trump Has Said about Global Warming." *Mother Jones*, December 12. https://www.motherjones.com/environment/2016/12/trump-climate-timeline/

27 Louis Jacobson, 2016. "PolitiFact–Yes, Donald Trump Did Call Climate Change a Chinese Hoax." *PolitiFact*, June 3. https://www.politifact.com/factchecks/2016/jun/03/hillary-clinton/yes-donald-trump-did-call-climate-change-chinese-h/

28 Trump-O-Meter, 2023. *politifact.com, retrieved April 18.* https://www.politifact.com/truth-o-meter/promises/trumpometer/?ruling=true

29 Kessler. 2021.

30 Daniel Dale, 2021. "The 15 Most Notable Lies of Donald Trump's Presidency." *CNN*, January 16. https://www.cnn.com/2021/01/16/politics/fact-check-dale-top-15-donald-trump-lies/index.html

31 Megan Garber, 2019. "The First Lie of the Trump Presidency." *The Atlantic*, January 13. https://www.theatlantic.com/politics/archive/2019/01/the-absurdity-of-donald-trumps-lies/579622/

32 Glenn Kessler and Joe Fox, 2021. "The False Claims That Trump Keeps Repeating," *The Washington Post*, January 20. https://www.washingtonpost.com/graphics/politics/fact-checker-most-repeated-disinformation/

33 Amber Phillips, 2017. "'They're Rapists.' President Trump's Campaign Launch Speech Two Years later, Annotated." *The Washington Post*, June 16. https://www.washingtonpost.com/news/the-fix/wp/2017/06/16/theyre-rapists-presidents-trump-campaign-launch-speech-two-years-later-annotated/

34 Christopher Giles, "Trump's Wall: How Much Has Been Built during His Term?" *BBC*, January 12. https://www.bbc.com/news/world-us-canada-46748492

35 Jonathan Lemire and Jill Colvin, 2019. "WATCH: 'No Collusion, No Obstruction,' Trump Declares at Wounded Warrior Event." *PBS News Hour*, April 18. https://www.pbs.org/newshour/politics/watch-live-trump-speaks-at-wounded-warrior-projects-soldier-ride

36 Special Counsel Robert S. Mueller, III, 2019. *Report on the Investigation into Russian Interference in the 2016 Presidential Election*. Washington, DC: U.S. Government Printing Office. https://www.govinfo.gov/app/details/GPO-SCREPORT-MUELLER

37 Abby Johnston and Leila Miller, 2019. "The Mueller Investigation, Explained." *PBS*, March 25. https://www.pbs.org/wgbh/frontline/article/the-mueller-investigation-explained-2/

38 Brett Samuels, 2019. "Mueller Agrees Lies by Trump Officials Impeded His Investigation," *The Hill*, July 24. https://thehill.com/homenews/house/454519-mueller-agrees-lies-by-trump-officials-impeded-his-investigation/

39 Angie Drobnic Holan, 2017. "2017 Lie of the Year: Russian Election Interference Is a 'Made-up Story." *Politifact*, December 12. https://www.politifact.com/article/2017/dec/12/2017-lie-year-russian-election-interference-made-s/

40 House Permanent Select Committee on Intelligence, 2019. *The Trump-Ukraine Impeachment Inquiry Report*. Washington, DC: U.S. Government Printing Office. https://context-cdn.washingtonpost.com/notes/prod/default/documents/ac8c9c61-bf69-4714-a683-0a6e0a86f80b/note/05e7033d-329b-445a-bf6e-093a0d4c7c7c.pdf

41 Daniel Dale, 2020. "Fact Check: A List Of 65 Ways Trump Has Been Dishonest about Ukraine and Impeachment." *CNN*, January 20. https://www.cnn.com/2020/01/20/politics/65-ways-trump-dishonest-impeachment-ukraine/index.html

42 Katie Sanders, 2019. "Lie of the Year 2019: Donald Trump's Claim Whistleblower Got Ukraine Call 'Almost Completely Wrong.'" *PolitiFact*, December 19. https://www.politifact.com/article/2019/dec/16/lie-of-the-year-donald-trump-whistleblower-wrong/

43 Daniel Dale, 2020. "Fact Check: Digging into Trump's False Claim That CDC Found That 85% of People Who Wear Masks Get the Coronavirus." *CNN*, October 16. https://www.cnn.com/2020/10/16/politics/fact-check-trump-cdc-masks-85-percent/index.html

44 Daniel Wolfe and Daniel Dale, 2020. "'It's Going to Disappear'": A Timeline Of Trump's Claims That Covid-19 Will Vanish." *CNN*, October 31. https://edition.cnn.com/interactive/2020/10/politics/covid-disappearing-trump-comment-tracker/

45 Reality Check Team, 2020. "Coronavirus: Trump's Disinfectant and Sunlight Claims Fact-Checked." *BBC*, April 24. https://www.bbc.com/news/world-us-canada-52399464

46 Bob Woodward, 2021. *Rage*. New York: Simon & Schuster, 244–252.

47 Kessler, 2021.

48 Cybersecurity & Infrastructure Security Agency, 2020. "Joint Statement from Elections Infrastructure Government Coordinating Council & the Election Infrastructure Sector Coordinating Executive Committees." November 12. https://www.cisa.gov/news/2020/11/12/joint-statement-elections-infrastructure-government-coordinating-council-election

49 Georgia Wells, Rebecca Ballhaus, and Keach Hagey, 2021. "Proud Boys, Seizing Trump's Call to Washington, Helped Lead Capitol Attack." *The Wall Street Journal*, January 17. https://www.wsj.com/articles/proud-boys-seizing-trumps-call-to-washington-helped-lead-capitol-attack-11610911596?st=yth6m520hdi8j4d&reflink=article_gmail_share

50 Daniel Dale, 2022. "10 Trump Election Lies His Own Officials Called False." *CNN*, June 16. https://www.cnn.com/2022/06/16/politics/fact-check-trump-officials-testimony-debunking-election-lies

51 Ibid.

52 Angise Holan, Bill McCarthy, and Amy Sherman, 2021. "The 2021 Lie of the Year: Lies About the Jan. 6 Capitol Attack and Its Significance," *PolitiFact*, December 15. https://www.politifact.com/article/2021/dec/15/2021-lie-year-lies-about-jan-6-capitol-attack-and-/

53 Select Committee to Investigate the January 6th Attack on the United States Capitol, 2020. *Final Report of the Select Committee to Investigate the January 6th Attack on the United States Capitol*. Washington, DC: U.S. Government Printing Office. https://january6th.house.gov/final-report

54 Chris Pandolfo, 2022. "House Republicans Release Counter Report on Jan. 6 Security Failures at Capitol." *FOX News*, December 22. https://www.foxnews.com/politics/house-republicans-release-counter-report-jan-6-security-failures-capitol

55 Alex Rogers and Manu Raju, 2021. "McConnell Blames Trump but Voted Not Guilty Anyway," *CNN*, February 13. https://www.cnn.com/2021/02/13/politics/mitch-mcconnell-acquit-trump/index.html

56 Alan Feuer and Maggie Haberman, 2023. "Riot was 'Fueled by Lies' from Trump, Special Counsel Says." *The New York Times*, August 1. https://www.nytimes.com/live/2023/08/01/us/trump-indictment-jan-6

57 United States District Court, District of Columbia, 2023. United States of America v. Donald J. Trump. Retrieved August 2, 2023 from https://www.justice.gov/storage/US_v_Trump_23_cr_257.pdf

58 Olivia Olander, 2022. "Trump Denies He Suggested 'Termination' of Constitution, without Deleting Post." *Politico*, December 05. https://www.politico.com/news/2022/12/05/trump-terminate-constitution-00072230

59 Maggie Haberman and Michael S. Schmidt, 2022. "Lawyer Declined Trump Request to Tell Archives All Material Was Returned." *The New York Times*, October 3. https://www.nytimes.com/2022/10/03/us/politics/trump-alex-cannon-archives.html

60 Charlie Savage, 2022. "Presidential Power to Declassify Information, Explained. *The New York Times*, August 14. https://www.nytimes.com/2022/08/14/us/politics/trump-classified-documents.html

61 Katie Kedian, 2022. "The Classification Status of Trump's Mar-a-Lago Document." *LAWFARE*, August 18. https://www.lawfareblog.com/classification-status-trumps-mar-lago-documents
  Jamie Gangel, Elizabeth Stuart, and Jeremy Herb, 2022. "CNN Exclusive: 'Ludicrous.' 'Ridiculous.' 'A Complete Fiction.': Former Trump Officials Say His Claim of 'Standing Order' to Declassify Is Nonsense." *CNN*, August 18. https://www.cnn.com/2022/08/18/politics/trump-claim-standing-order-declassify-nonsense-patently-false-former-officials/index.html

62 Devlin Barrett and Perry Stein, 2022. "From Europe, Trump Special Counsel Takes Over Mar-a-Lago, Jan. 6 Probes." *The New York Times*, November 21. https://www.washingtonpost.com/national-security/2022/11/21/trump-investigations-jack-smith/

63 Rachel Weinger, 2023. "Here Are the 37 Charges against Trump and What They Mean." *The Washington Post*, June 9. https://www.washingtonpost.com/dc-md-va/2023/06/09/trump-charges-classified-documents/
  United States District Court, Southern District of Florida, 2023. United States of America v. Donald J. Trump and Waltine Nauta. Retrieved July 14 2023 from https://www.washingtonpost.com/documents/e6276c02-dfd0-428d-9731-8594c1f7261d.pdf?itid=lk_inline_manual_4

64   Brad Plumer, 2019. "We Fact-Checked President Trump's Dubious Claims on the Perils of Wind Power." *The New York Times*, April 3. https://www.nytimes.com/2019/04/03/climate/fact-check-trump-windmills.html

65   Dareh Gregorian, 2023. "Stormy Daniels, the Doorman and a 2024 Trial: The Trump Indictment Top Takeaways." *NBC News*, April 4. https://www.nbcnews.com/politics/donald-trump/stormy-daniels-doorman-2024-trial-trump-indictment-top-takeaways-rcna78221

66   Julie Hirschfeld Davis and Maggie Haberman, 2018. "With 'Spygate,' Trump Shows How He Uses Conspiracy Theories to Erode Trust." *The New York Times*, May 28. https://www.nytimes.com/2018/05/28/us/politics/trump-conspiracy-theories-spygate.html

67   Martin Pengelly, "'Sharpiegate': Trump Insists Dorian Was Forecast to 'Hit Or Graze' Alabama." *The Guardian*, September 5. https://www.theguardian.com/us-news/2019/sep/05/trump-hurricane-dorian-alabama-map-sharpiegate

68   Bryan Metzger and Grace Panetta, 2021. "Trump Promotes Lies about Ilhan Omar and Suggests She Apologize for 'Abandoning' Somalia, Which She Fled as a Child." *Business Insider*, November 30. https://www.businessinsider.com/trump-ilhan-omar-should-apologize-for-abandoning-her-former-country-2021-11)

69   Glenn Kessler, 2020. "Trump's Claim That He's Done More for Black Americans Than Any President Since Lincoln." *The Washington Post*, June 5. https://www.washingtonpost.com/politics/2020/06/05/trumps-claim-that-hes-done-more-blacks-than-any-president-since-lincoln/

70   Ibid.

71   Daniel Dale, 2021. "The 15 Most Notable Lies of Donald Trump's Presidency." *CNN*, January 16. https://www.cnn.com/2021/01/16/politics/fact-check-dale-top-15-donald-trump-lies/index.html

72   Stelter.

73   Christopher Paul and Miriam Matthews, 2023. *The Russian "Firehose of Falsehood" Propaganda Model: Why It Might Work and Options to Counter It*. Retrieved April 17, from https://www.rand.org/pubs/perspectives/PE198.html

74   Donald J. Trump (with Tony Schwartz), 1987. *The Art of the Deal*. New York: Ballentine.

75   Travis M. Andrews, 2020. "Commander in Tweets: The Dispatches that Define the Trump Presidency." *The Washington Post*, October 14. https://www.washingtonpost.com/graphics/2020/technology/trump-twitter-tweets-president/

76   Jane C. Timm, 2023. "Dominion and FOX News reach $787.5 Million Settlement in Defamation Lawsuit." *NBC News*, April 18. https://www.nbcnews.com/media/fox-news-settles-dominion-defamation-lawsuit-rcna80285

77   Jeremy W. Peters and Katie Robertson, 2023. "'The Whole Thing Seems Insane': New Documents on Fox and the Election," *The New York Times*, March 7. https://www.nytimes.com/2023/03/07/business/media/fox-dominion-2020-election.html

78   Jennifer Agiesta and Ariel Edwards, 2021. "CNN Poll: Most Americans Feel Democracy Is under Attack in the US." *CNN*, September 15. https://www.cnn.com/2021/09/15/politics/cnn-poll-most-americans-democracy-under-attack/index.html

79   Mark Murray, 2023. "Poll: 71% of GOP Voters Stand with Trump Amid Investigations." *NBC News*, July 31. https://www.nbcnews.com/meet-the-press/meetthepressblog/poll-71-gop-voters-stand-trump-investigations-rcna97305

4   Cheating

Nearly Everyone Cheats

Cheating refers to deceptive or deceitful actions intended to obtain a goal by unfairly and dishonestly gaining an advantage over others. When you think of cheating, and particularly among school-aged children and college students, the first thing likely to come to mind is cheating in school, or academic cheating. To one extent and form or another, nearly all students engage in academic cheating. So too have most parents. Students cheat on tests and exams by copying answers from others; obtaining questions or answers ahead of time; using a cheat sheet or unauthorized notes; and obtaining answers from a cell phone, smartwatch, or in other dishonest and often creative ways. Also common is cheating by copying the work of others, which includes copying someone else's homework and writing a paper that includes the work or material produced by someone else while presenting it as their own (i.e., plagiarism).

Students cheat by fabricating or falsifying information used in a paper or presentation. They cheat by having someone else complete their work for them or by accepting credit for work they did not produce themselves or contributed little to (e.g., a project or assignment completed largely by only one member of a workgroup or by a parent). They cheat by gaining an extension or exemption for required work by lying, such as claiming falsely that they were sick. I recently learned of a more modern and creative way to cheat by gaining an extension on work that is due. A student in one of my courses used a software program, available for free on the internet, to deliberately corrupt files of a paper that was not completed when due. As an excellent example of cheating *and* lying she falsely claimed that her computer had a virus that destroyed the files and thus requested an extension (the student was caught cheating and dismissed from the university). Another more recent form of academic cheating is use of artificial intelligence (AI) chatbots (e.g., ChatGPT), which has caused many universities to change how they teach. Many now require fewer written assignments and use programs designed to detect AI-generated text.[1]

DOI: 10.4324/9781003401278-4

Cheating is common in games and sports, both in and outside of school. Cheating in sports often entails an athlete or coach intentionally violating explicit or implicit rules of the sport to gain an unfair advantage over an opponent. Garnering much national attention in the media has been athletes in nearly every sport using steroids or other banned performance-enhancing substances. Infamous among those athletes are Lance Armstrong and Floyd Landis in cycling; Olympians Marion Jones and Ben Johnson in track; Barry Bonds, Mark McGuire, and Alex Rodriguez in baseball; Diego Maradona in soccer; Maria Sharapova in tennis; and Vijay Singh in golf. Hall of Fame horse trainer Bob Baffert was charged with cheating when steroids were found in a blood sample of his Kentucky Derby-winning horse Medina Spirit.[2] Other popular models of athletes cheating, but not with use of banned substances, are boxer Mike Tyson (who bite his opponent's ear off), NASCAR driver Clint Bowyer (used an illegal car), Olympian ice skater Tanya Harding (conspired to attack and maim an opponent), baseball player Sammy Sosa (used an illegal bat with cork inserted), and multiple coaches in college sports who were found guilty of illegal recruiting.

People cheat at places of work or business, and sometimes *as* a business. They cheat using many of the same methods of cheating that students use in school, including plagiarism, falsifying and fabricating information, and taking credit for the work of others. As often seen with cheating in business, cheating often entails lying; thus, cheating and lying can be one and the same. For example, prospective or current employees falsify information on their vitae, employees fail to work the full hours claimed, and employers cheat employees out of wages, benefits, and pensions. This also includes both employers and employees cheating customers by overcharging, misrepresenting merchandise, inflating prices, using bait and switch tactics, selling poor products, delivering poor services, and reneging on a contract. There are "businesses" that cheat and lie via telephone, email, and website scams designed to steal money from the elderly or anyone else who falls for their scams.

Customers also cheat businesses, as seen in customers not paying the bill or the full amount at a restaurant or store, sneaking into a theater or event without paying, or engaging in what is called "return fraud," "wardrobing," or "free renting." The latter is when a customer purchases, uses, and then returns clothes or other merchandise without ever intending to keep them. Although not generally viewed as illegal, this form of cheating constitutes fraud. Other forms of fraud include lying about one's property value or income to avoid taxes or to obtain a loan and making false claims to insurance companies or for unjustified government benefits (e.g., social welfare, social security, and Medicare benefits).

In addition to cheating in academics, sports, and business, another common form of cheating is self-cheating. Self-cheating is when people break the rules of a regimen that they set for themselves, such as not sticking to a diet, exercise plan, or a financial budget to which you had committed.

Finally, there is infidelity, wherein a person is disloyal or unfaithful in a romantic or sexual relationship. In the context of marriage, infidelity is commonly referred to as adultery. Infidelity also can occur outside the scope of marriage, such as in a close relationship, including during adolescence, wherein a couple has committed to dating only one another but become romantically or sexually involved with others. Although infidelity and adultery are widely viewed as a form of cheating, they differ from most other forms of cheating in that the behavior is not typically intended to obtain one's goal by unfairly and dishonestly gaining an advantage over others. Instead, the behavior is considered cheating because either spoken vows or unwritten rules are broken within a committed relationship.

Cheating Likely Includes You

Given the many different types of cheating noted above, it is safe to conclude that nearly everyone cheats, or has cheated. This very likely includes you. To see if this is correct, respond to each statement below with either "yes" or "no" while reflecting briefly about your answer.

	Yes	*No*	*Why, or why not?*
1. In school, I copied someone's homework.			
2. In school, I cheated on a test.			
3. In school, I knowingly plagiarized (used copied material without stating the source).			
4. In school, I allowed others to copy my homework or answers on a test.			
5. Either at school or home, I gave or accepted help on schoolwork when the teacher said students were not to (e.g., a parent completed much of my project or assignment, I helped a classmate with a paper or project).			
6. I cheated in a game with others.			
7. I cheated when playing a sport.			
8. I cheated on my vita or job application.			
9. I cheated at work (e.g., claimed hours I didn't actually work, left work early without permission while being paid)			
10. I cheated on a loan application (e.g., inflated net worth or failed to report all debts).			
11. I cheated a store or business (e.g., did not pay or underpaid the full amount, accepted more money than I was due, returned items I purchased and used but never intended to keep).			
12. I cheated on my taxes (e.g., claimed deductions I really didn't have; didn't claim income, such as tips; fudged the numbers).			
13. I cheated in a romantic relationship.			
14. I cheated in my diet, exercise plan, or financial budget.			

How did you do? If you are a parent, you have probably told your children not to cheat but your answers to the above quiz reveal that to one extent or another you have cheated yourself. Perhaps you also gave the same reasons for cheating that your children likely give. Keep your reasons in mind when reading the remainder of the chapter, and Chapter 10 on moral reasoning, to see if this is true.

We Know It's Wrong but Most of Us Cheat Anyway

If you admit to cheating, then you are not alone. Although survey results vary greatly due to differences in definitions of cheating and what types of cheating are included in surveys, it is not uncommon to find that most students cheat in high school and college. Cheating typically begins in elementary school and increases in middle school when grades and pressure to succeed academically become increasingly important. Academic cheating peaks in high school and continues at a high rate in college. A national survey of over 20,000 high school students in the United States found that 75% cheated in one form or another, with 63% admitting cheating on a test and 54% to plagiarism.[3] A survey of over 70,000 college students conducted over an 8-year period (2002–2010 found that 65% admitted to least one form of cheating while in college.[4]

In both high school and college, academic cheating tends to be more common among low-achieving than higher-achieving students.[5] However, as in college, cheating is rampant in high schools comprised largely of high-achieving, college-bound high school students. In a study of 4,316 high school students in middle- and upper-class communities, 93% reported cheating in one form or another.[6] The most common forms of cheating were in obtaining test questions or answers and working together when the instructor asked for individual work. A sizable number of the students admitted cheating in multiple ways: 40% reported that they had engaged in four to six of the 13 forms of cheating listed on the survey and 26% reported they had engaged in seven or more. In addition to obtaining test questions or answers and working together when not allowed, the 13 forms of cheating included various ways of copying, plagiarizing, and receiving help from others; unallowed use of electronic devices; helping someone cheat on a test; using cheat sheets; and getting an extension using a false excuse.

Academic Cheating: Students Are Not the Only Ones

Students are not the only ones who engage in academic cheating. So too do parents, teachers, and school administrators—adult role models who tell children to be honest but who show them how cheating gets things done. The role of parents in academic cheating received much national attention in 2019 when 33 parents of high school students applying to universities were charged with criminal conspiracy to influence the admission decisions.[7] Many of those universities were difficult to get into such as Yale and Stanford. Most of the parents pleaded guilty to paying the organizer of the scheme, William Rick Singer, to bribe coaches and school officials or to fraudulently increase their children's college entrance exam scores. Parents paid Singer over $25 million. Most of the parents were of considerable wealth; they included prominent businessmen and well-known actors and actresses. After getting rich in a business built largely on cheating and lying, Singer told the truth when he was caught, admitting cheating by facilitating the college admissions of students from over 750 families. Upon pleading guilty to racketeering conspiracy, money laundering conspiracy, conspiracy to defraud the United States, and obstruction of justice, he was sentenced to 3.5 years in federal prison.

One fraudulent scheme Singer used to assure admission to a chosen university was having students recruited by one of the university's coaches to play a collegian sport. In assisting college applicants in this scheme, Singer had applicants submit fake videos and photos (often created by their parents) of them participating in or practicing for sports for which they were recruited. Coaches of tennis, soccer, water polo, rowing, football, sailing, and volleyball were aware of the scheme, and found guilty of accepting bribes and assisting in falsifying application materials. Some of the students had never even played the sport for which they were recruited.

More common than assisting in fraudulent recruitment was Singer assisting college applicants in obtaining higher scores on the college entrance exam. He did so in various ways. Most common and lucrative was simply doctoring answers and scores on the exams, which were taken at his own facilities or facilities where Singer could pay others to partake in the cheating. Singer also paid others to pose for students while taking the exam. A graduate of Harvard who directed test preparation at a private boarding school was paid $10,000 for each test taken. Others involved in the scheme were paid to take pre-college, online classes for applicants with the understanding that the fraudulent grades in those classes would be submitted as part of the students' college applications.

A less common way Singer used to improve scores was assisting parents in having their children fraudulently diagnosed by a psychologist as having a learning disability or attention deficit-hyperactivity disorder (ADHD). With such a diagnosis, a student is typically granted extra time on the college admission exam and often is administered the exam in a room separate from most others (where cheating can more easily occur). In helping fake a learning disability, Singer told one father to tell his daughter: "when she gets tested, to be as, to be stupid, not to be as smart as she is. The goal is to be slow, to be not as bright, ..." When the father then asked if students at Singer's school received extra time, Singer responded: "'Everywhere.' .... Yeah, everywhere around the country. What happened is, all the wealthy families that figured out that if I get my kid tested and they get extended time, they can do better on the test. So most of these kids don't even have issues, but they're getting time."[8] Singer promised the father that his daughter would get "whatever score we need it to be." The parents paid Singer $75,000 for his services, which included arranging for someone to proctor the daughter's ACT exam and to correct incorrect answers after she completed it.

Singer was correct in noting that cheating by having their children falsely diagnosed with a disability is most common among wealthy parents (which I personally observed as a practicing school psychologist at a private school). In 2019, the *New York Times* conducted a thorough investigation and comprehensive analysis of federal data on students designated as having a disability, particularly a learning disability, ADHD, or an anxiety disorder, and thus qualifying for extra time on tests and other accommodations. The *New York Times* found that wealth was clearly associated with this type of cheating.[9]

Schools Cheat Too

Academic cheating is much less common among teachers and school administrators than among students and their parents, but teachers and school administrators cheat too. They cheat for the same major reason students and their parents cheat: It gets things done! Getting things done means winning (i.e., achieving higher scores), gaining rewards associated with winning (including school honors and salary bonuses), and avoiding negative consequences for performing poorly. Cases of cheating by educators have been reported nationwide, with the largest and most popular case occurring in the Atlanta Public Schools. In 2015, 11 educators in Atlanta were convicted on charges of racketeering. They were guilty of being part of a conspiracy in which they benefitted financially by fabricating students' test scores on statewide standardized tests. Sentences ranged from probation to 20 years in prison.[10]

Many students who cheat on tests report that they do so because of pressure to achieve in school.[11] The pressure is generally from parents or is self-imposed with the aim of performing better than others and to get into the most selective colleges. Interestingly, during the Atlanta trial, the school administrators and teachers reported that they cheated for a similar reason: They were under intense pressure to improve standardized state testing scores in their schools. Administrators and teachers who improved their scores received raises or bonuses, while those who failed to do so were punished with poor evaluations (and those who reported cheating were fired). Although a small percentage of the educators in Atlanta who fabricated scores were convicted, it was revealed that cheating occurred in most Atlanta schools.

Schools, and particularly coaches, also cheat in sports. This is most often seen in coaches encouraging athletes to disregard rules of the game (e.g., intentionally fouling opponents) and breaking the rules themselves, such as playing ineligible players. In 2019 the Cardinal Ritter College Prep High School in St. Louis, Missouri, then undefeated and nationally ranked in football, had to forfeit its conference title and all its games due to playing an ineligible player. That player had been ejected from the 2018 state championship game and thus was ineligible for the first game of the 2019 season. The coaches played him in that game while using a different name.[12]

Perhaps the most infamous case of coaches of youth teams cheating by playing ineligible players occurred not at school but in Little League Baseball during the 2001 Little League World Series.[13] Part of the Little League pledge is "I will play fair." One would assume that not only players but also coaches take that pledge and model good sportsmanship. The coach of the championship baseball team for 12-year-olds from the Bronx falsified the birth certificate of their star pitcher. After the World Series had ended it was discovered that the pitcher was two years older than all his opponents. This explained how he got things done—with a 70-mph fastball!

Why People Cheat in School, and Elsewhere

Both cheating and lying are forms of deceitfulness. Thus, it should be expected that they share many of the same influencing factors. This includes factors within individuals and their environments. As discussed in Chapter 2 on lying, antisocial behavior has a genetic basis, with genetic influences being greater for aggressive behaviors than nonaggressive rule-breaking behaviors such as lying and cheating. Shortly after birth and in early childhood, the role of genetics in those behaviors is seen in differences between children, and often within the same family, in dispositions reflecting temperament and such personality traits as irritability, attentiveness, activity, emotionality (e.g., expression of happiness, anger, fear), self-regulation, and sociability. As also discussed earlier, whereas genetics plays a greater role than the environment in aggressive behaviors, the opposite is true with nonaggressive rule-breaking behaviors. It is one's environment that is most influential in moderating the development of cognitive and emotional processes within individuals that underlie continuity and discontinuity in temperament and personality and that either inhibit or promote lying, cheating, and bullying. And it is environmental factors that greatly influence the impact of those processes on behavior in a given situation. For example, even self-centered students lacking in inhibitory control, emotion regulation, moral reasoning, and empathy are unlikely to cheat on a test when the teacher is standing right next to them. Conversely, students not lacking in any of those areas are more likely to cheat when others are doing the same, when there is great pressure to succeed, and when there is no risk of being caught.

As with prosocial lies, there are some situations in which cheating is prosocial, moral, or the right thing to do, such as cheating to help others and not oneself. Little, if any, harm is caused to others, or the benefits to others outweigh any harm caused. Examples include breaking in line to help someone in distress or helping complete the homework of a classmate who had a good reason for not having completed it.

Environmental Factors Related to Cheating

As with scammers, con artists, and used-car salesmen, children cheat for many of the same reasons they lie and bully, and primary among them is that cheating gets things done and thus it is reinforced. They also watch others exhibit the same behaviors, not only learning new and more effective ways to cheat, but also finding comfort in knowing they are not alone in their cheating.

Positive Reinforcement: Cheating Gets Things Done

Reinforcement typically lies in the cheating being effective in achieving one's goal such as passing a test, winning in a game or sport, or obtaining greater wealth or a prized possession. Another common source of reinforcement is social such as receiving attention or praise from others for "winning" or achieving a goal valued by others. As with all other behaviors, when cheating is reinforced, it is repeated. Cheating is especially likely to be repeated if the cheater is rarely caught and avoids significant negative consequences. When there is minimal or no fear of getting caught and being punished, then the anticipation of positive gain, or positive reinforcement, is likely to prevail in determining if one cheats. Thus, as with lying, cheating often entails a cost-benefit analysis.

One might guess that as with other antisocial behaviors, praising or rewarding students for *not* cheating helps deter cheating. Generally, this is true, as the effects of praising and rewarding honest behavior are both direct and indirect. Directly, when praise and rewards follow honest behavior, honesty is reinforced. As discussed in Chapter 13, when used wisely and strategically, praise also highlights why honesty and trustworthiness are important. Indirectly, use of praise and rewards by parents, teachers, or others promotes positive relationships and an overall positive climate, which in turn helps deter undesired behavior. The effectiveness and usefulness of rewards in changing behavior is often greatly exaggerated, however. That is, rewards are not as magical as many guidebooks on parenting and teaching often claim. This is especially true in adolescence when children are more autonomous and aware that rewards can be used to manipulate and control their behavior.

The relationship between the use of rewards and behavior is far more complex than many guidebooks suggest. For example, although rewards for honesty often help deter cheating, cheating is more, not less, prevalent in classrooms and schools where rewards and social comparisons are highly salient. In many of those settings, students come to believe that grades and doing better than others (or winning) are much more important than learning or mastering the material, and that cheating is an easy way to obtain better grades. Thus, cheating reaps a greater reward (i.e., a high grade) than the minor tangible rewards that schools often dispense for not cheating.

Although I know of no research examining if tangible rewards at home can have the same negative effects as in school, it seems likely that an overemphasis on tangible rewards (e.g., stickers, prizes, money) and social comparisons at home has the same effect as at school. A common reason that students give for cheating in school is pressure from their parents to get high grades, and one way that parents impose such pressure is by emphasizing tangible rewards (e.g., "If you get all A's we'll give you new iPhone") and with social comparisons (e.g., "Your brother got better grades"). This does not mean that parents and teachers should refrain from praising or rewarding children for good grades, but that they should do so wisely and strategically, following advice in Chapter 13.

Watching Others Cheat: Cheating Can Be Contagious

In addition to basic principles of reinforcement and punishment, and as is true with much of human behavior, modeling largely explains how children learn to cheat. Children (and adults) are more likely to cheat when others are doing the same, especially when those being observed are successful in their cheating, with their behavior positively reinforced and not punished. This is readily seen in homes where parents cheat by lying about their children's age to get a discount at a restaurant, theater, or amusement park, or by falsifying their children's college admission scores and records. Modeling also explains much of cheating in classrooms and schools, in sports, and in everyday violations of common rules and laws.

In demonstrating the powerful effects of modeling on both children's cheating and lying, researchers Chelsea Hayes and Leslie Carver presented preschoolers and school-age children with a task in which they were tempted to cheat by peeking at a hidden toy they were told not to look at. They were then asked if they had peeked. Prior to the task, half of the children were told a lie by an adult and half were not. School-age children who observed the adult lie were much more likely to cheat and lie about it than those who were not lied to. This was not found among preschoolers, likely because preschoolers are much more obedient to adult authority. These findings have important implications for parents, teachers, coaches, and others, and especially after early childhood: Children watch and learn to lie and cheat.

Cheating, and especially academic cheating, is more likely to occur in settings where cheating is the norm. A strong predictor of academic cheating is the degree of cheating in the classroom or school. Quite simply, students are much more likely to cheat if others are doing the same. It becomes contagious. Conversely, students are less inclined to cheat if such behavior goes against the established norm of honesty.[14] Note that a norm is not the same as a rule. A norm reflects the social acceptance and obedience to a rule. A rule becomes a norm once it is adopted by the group. Rules need not be written, but having rules in writing often makes behavioral expectations clearer. Academic cheating is less likely, and thus the norm of honesty is more prevalent, when rules against cheating are clear to students. Cheating also is less likely when students believe there is a good chance of getting caught (e.g., the teacher closely monitors students during a test), and when the consequences for being caught are not minor (e.g., more than a verbal reprimand).[15]

In establishing rules and norms against cheating, and thus deterring cheating, school honor codes have been shown to be helpful.[16] Honor codes require that students sign an honor pledge not to cheat and to report incidents of cheating that they observe. In many schools with honor codes, students also join faculty in the adjudication process for alleged cases of cheating, which includes enforcing rules against cheating.

Perceptions Often Matter More Than Reality

Academic cheating often hinges on student perceptions of their teachers and school. Rules, including those against cheating, are more likely to be followed, and thus norms against cheating established, in classrooms and schools where students view the relationships with their teachers and peers favorably;[17] the quality of the teaching to be good;[18] the teachers, and rules, as fair;[19] and when students do not feel alienated from school.[20] Whether or not the teacher is actually a poor instructor, is uncaring, or unfair, and if peer rejection is occurring, is much less important than students' *perceptions* of those conditions. Perceptions of reality, more so than reality per se, best predicts human behavior.[21] For example, a teacher may have clear and fair rules and is kind, caring, and fair—characteristics that typically predict less cheating—but those characteristics matter little if a student perceives the teacher as lacking in them.[22]

The importance of children's perceptions of the quality of relationships with others also applies to the home. As noted in Chapter 2 on lying, children, and especially adolescents, are more likely to disobey rules at home when they perceive them as unfair and when parents are overly harsh and lacking in responsiveness to their children's social and emotional needs.[23] With respect to cheating, much more research has been conducted on teacher and classroom characteristics than on parent and home characteristics. Considering that research shows that the most effective teachers and parents share the same characteristics in preventing antisocial behavior, in general, and in developing self-discipline,[24] it makes sense that this also applies to cheating. Those characteristics are found in the authoritative style of parenting, and teaching, consisting of a balance of responsiveness and demandingness. As discussed in much more depth in Chapter 13, authoritative parents understand that maintaining positive and supportive relationships, developing social and emotional competencies, close monitoring and supervision, and immediate and fair correction of misbehavior are critical to preventing cheating and other misbehavior.

Social Cognitive and Emotional Processes Related to Cheating

To one extent or another, the same cognitive and emotional processes related to lying, as discussed in Chapter 2, are related to cheating. This should come as no surprise since both lying and cheating are forms of deceitfulness. Whether one is deceiving others by lying or cheating, the underlying processes are basically the same. Primary among them are executive functioning, social perspective taking, moral reasoning and emotions, and mechanisms of moral disengagement, as described next.

Executive Functioning and Social Perspective Taking

As discussed in Chapter 2 on lying, executive functioning skills include impulse control, working memory, goal-oriented planning, adaptive and flexible thinking, and emotion regulation. With age, those skills become increasingly complex and sophisticated. The same holds true with social perspective taking. As with lying, more complex and sophisticated executive functioning and social perspective taking skills are a double-edged sword when it comes to cheating. They can either help deter cheating or make one a more successful cheater. Think of the classic used-car salesman who cheats customers and is calm, knowledgeable, reflective, persuasive, goal-oriented, adaptive, flexible, and aware of the customer's perspective.

Among executive functioning and social perspective skills, impulse control is the one most consistently found to be associated with cheating, but the association is not particularly strong. Being impulsive, or lacking impulse control, does not necessarily cause cheating but it does place individuals at greater risk. Lacking in impulsive control, individuals tend to make decisions quickly, while seeking immediate rewards, failing to resist temptation and delay gratification, and failing to think about the consequences of their behavior. Hence, they are more likely than others to cheat. This includes academic cheating,[25] competitive cheating (e.g., in sports and games, at work, and lying on resumes),[26] violating social contracts (e.g., sneaking into an event without a ticket; cutting in line; not paying at a restaurant),[27] and cheating in romantic and marital relationships.[28]

Moral Reasoning and Moral Emotions

As discussed later, individuals high in impulsivity and sensation-seeking are more prone than others to cheat. However, often cheating is neither impulsive nor does it generate what is referred to as the *cheater's high*. And there are many impulsive and sensation-seeking individuals who cheat no more than others. If not impulsivity and sensation seeking, what other factors best explain differences in cheating, both between individuals and within individuals? In other words, why do some people cheat more than others and nearly everyone cheats sometimes? What cognitive and emotional factors help explain why environmental and situational factors, such as norms and the saliency of getting caught, may or may not determine if one cheats?

As with lying (and bullying), cheating is a moral behavior influenced by one's moral reasoning and moral emotions, both across situations (i.e., what is referred to as trait behaviors) and within a given situation (i.e., what is referred to as state behaviors). The development of moral reasoning and moral emotions and their relation to moral behavior, including cheating, are discussed in much greater length in Chapter 10. In short, as children mature, their moral reasoning tends to become less self-centered; less driven by seeking rewards and avoiding punishment; and centered more on the needs of others and the impact on one's behavior on others, which includes relationships and how one is perceived by others. Children come to recognize and understand the importance of trust in relationships and communication; that most people do not trust or like liars and cheaters. They recognize that honesty and trust are cornerstones of valued social relationships and effective communication. They also come to understand that not all cheating is the same: cheating in a game with siblings or taking an item from a vending machine without paying because the machine malfunctioned is not the same as plagiarizing a paper, not paying at a restaurant, or cheating in a romantic relationship.

With maturity, children recognize that in some situations cheating and other antisocial behaviors can be prosocial and viewed as the "right" thing to do such as cheating to help someone in great need.[29] In judging if cheating is right or wrong, and to what degree, one's motivation or intentions now matter. They understand that not all cheating is the same and neither are all cheaters. It is when cheating is non-normative, frequent, illegal, and/or harms others that it is likely to lead to serious negative consequences, including social rejection.

As true with lying, by middle to late childhood, children have learned to evaluate the wrongness of cheating based on moral standards mentioned above. For most children, the development of more mature moral reasoning and the internalization and adoption of moral standards serve as strong deterrents against cheating, with violations of self-sanctions sparking feelings of guilt or shame.[30] Unfortunately, as was noted in the chapter on lying, not all children come to value the importance of honesty and trustworthiness. Indeed, there are many adolescents and adults who continue to reason that cheating can be very effective in getting things done and getting what one wants. From this immature, hedonistic, self-centered perspective, there is nothing wrong about cheating, if it is rewarded and not punished. One of the primary reasons students give for cheating in school is their failure to have studied for an exam or to have completed their work (which includes "too lazy to study").[31] Cheating takes much less time than studying. When seeking rewards and avoiding punishment predominate one's moral reasoning, no other self-sanctions deter antisocial behavior. As with pathological liars, self-centered moral reasoning and lack of moral emotions are found among chronic cheaters, many of whom meet the psychiatric criteria for conduct disorder and antisocial personality disorder.

Mechanisms of Moral Disengagement

Whereas hedonistic, self-centered moral reasoning and a lack of moral emotions explain the cheating of the most chronic, or pathological, liars and cheaters, it does not explain why nearly everyone cheats, including individuals quite capable of mature moral reasoning and moral emotions. Here again, the same cognitive and emotional processing that largely explains why most people lie also explains why they also cheat. For moral reasoning and moral emotions to guide behavior, the individual must view the behavior as a moral issue. In adolescence, when cheating tends to peak, this often is not the case. In defending cheating, students often admit that cheating is wrong but also argue that it is not a moral issue, or at least not a serious one.[32] Instead of viewing cheating as immoral, they view it as *amoral*, as an action that is not to be judged morally as right or wrong. When cheating is not viewed as harming others or otherwise inherently immoral, it does not trigger moral reasoning or moral emotions. For chronic cheaters and liars, those situations are far too common. As with lying, in those situations, various mechanisms of moral disengagement are used to neutralize cheating.

A recent comprehensive review of the research literature on academic cheating in college found that use of mechanisms of moral disengagement is a strong predictor of cheating: Students who find it easy to neutralize or justify their dishonest behavior are the ones most likely to cheat.[33] Mechanisms of moral disengagement commonly used in cheating are denying that one cheated (it helps to also believe your lie), denying that cheating harms anyone, blaming others, and excusing or justifying cheating, such as believing that it is fair to cheat if others are doing it too. The justification that everyone else is doing the same, and thus it really isn't cheating, is quite common among students who cheat academically[34] and among those who cheat in sports.[35] Such justification is especially common in what is viewed as less serious types of academic cheating (e.g., cheating by copying homework or getting help from others vs. cheating on an exam).[36] When more serious types of cheating become normative, however, they are viewed similarly to less serious types. In many schools cheating on exams is the norm. McCabe and colleagues found that only 35% of high school students responded that copying on a test/exam constituted serious cheating, and 7% responded that it was not cheating.[37]

The justification that everyone else is doing it, and thus it really isn't cheating, also is common in business and politics. A good example is Republican Congressman George Santos, who recently cheated his way to being elected by fabricating his education (he claimed degrees from two colleges that he never attended) and work experiences on his resume. When caught, he admitted lying on his resume while calling it "embellishing" and insisting that he "had done nothing unethical."[38] As reported by *The New York Times*, Santos is "in a class of his own," but he is not the only politician to have embellished his resume or misrepresented themselves in campaigns for election, noting that Trump, Biden, Hillary Clinton, and many members of Congress did the same.[39]

Sensation Seeking and the Cheater's High

Intriguingly, researchers show that some cheaters not only fail to experience guilt or shame about their cheating but feel good about it. This is most common among sensation seekers. Sensation seeking is generally viewed as a personality trait that characterizes individuals who desire to engage in activities that are novel, stimulating, and that rouse feelings of euphoria or an emotional high. Often, the activities are physical such as engaging in risky sports (e.g., sky diving, boxing), experimenting with drugs, and driving dangerously. Sensation seeking also entails a preference for risks that are less- or non-physical, including financial, legal, social, and sexual risks.[40] Those risks include cheating, with sensation seeking shown to be related to greater academic cheating,[41] cheating in competitive sports,[42] and cheating in relationships.[43] Sensation-seeking often coexists with impulsivity. That is, sensation seekers tend to be impulsive and impulsive individuals are more inclined than others to engage in risky behaviors that arouse their emotions.[44]

The euphoria or emotional high experienced by sensation seekers when cheating is called a *cheater's high*. The emotional affect is a form of self-reinforcement: the behavior is positively reinforced by the euphoric sensation that occurs during and after the behavior (and at times in anticipation of the behavior). One does not have to be a sensation seeker, to experience the cheater's high. The term was coined by a team of researchers led by Dr. Nicole Ruedy at the University of Washington.[45] Ruedy and colleagues examined the emotions that college students experience when cheating. They found that students who cheated most frequently were delighted, or felt "giddy," when they cheated (and were not caught). As with others who did not cheat in the contrived laboratory setting, cheaters reported beforehand that they would likely experience guilt upon cheating. However, unlike those who did not cheat or cheated less frequently, the frequent cheaters failed to experience any increase in feelings of guilt after cheating. Those cheaters felt like they had gotten away with something or had won, despite doing so unethically. They either failed to think of harm caused to others and how others viewed them, or perhaps thought about it but it did not bother them. Their cheating was positively reinforced, but internally and not externally. That is, they were delighted with themselves having won, regardless of any tangible or social reward.

Ruedy and colleagues attributed the cheater's high to three psychological benefits that often result from cheating and other unethical behaviors:

(1) the cheater reaps a personal benefit or reward such as a higher grade or financial gain; (2) the cheater benefits psychologically, experiencing a sense of control over the outcome and feeling a sense of accomplishment; and (3) the cheater takes pride in successfully challenging what is perceived as unfair or unduly burdensome rules designed to constrain his or her behavior.

As seen in the next chapter, cheating is highly predictable among sensation seekers, and those also characterized by self-centered moral reasoning, the lack of empathy, guilt, and shame, and who are prone to frequent use of mechanisms of moral disengagement.

Notes

1 Kalley Huang, 2023. "Alarmed by A.I. Chatbots, Universities Start Revamping How They Teach." *The New York Times*, January 16. https://www.nytimes.com/2023/01/16/technology/chatgpt-artificial-intelligence-universities.html?campaign_id=190&emc=edit_ufn_20230117&instance_id=82886&nl=from-thetimes&regi_id=114283553&segment_id=122722&te=1&user_id=41103b961eca74aad9b0b5c95fd2e359

2 Joe Drape, 2021. "On the Airwaves, Baffert Rails against Cheating Allegations." *The New York Times*, May 10. https://www.nytimes.com/2021/05/10/sports/horse-racing/baffert-medina-spirit-cheating-preakness.html

3 Donald L. McCabe, Kenneth D. Butterfield, and Linda K. Treviño, 2012. *Cheating in College: Why Student Do It and What Educators Can Do About It.* Baltimore: John Hopkins University Press.

4 Ibid.

5 Eric M. Anderman and Tamera B. Murdock, 2007. "The Psychology of Academic Cheating," in *Psychology of Academic Cheating,* edited by Eric M. Anderman and Tamera B. Murdock. San Diego, CA: Elsevier, 1–8.
   McCabe et al.

6 Mollie K. Galloway, 2012. "Cheating in Advantaged High Schools: Prevalence, Justifications, and Possibilities for Change." *Ethics & Behavior* 22, no. 5: 378–399. https:doi.org//10.1080/10508422.2012.679143

7 Melissa Korn, Jennifer Levitz, and Erin Ailworth, 2019. "Federal Prosecutors Charge Dozens in College Admissions Cheating Scheme." *The Wall Street Journal*, March 13. https://www.wsj.com/articles/federal-prosecutors-charge-dozens-in-broad-college-admissions-fraud-scheme-11552403149

8 Laura Smith (Special Agent FBI), 2019. "College Admissions Bribery Scheme Affidavit." *The Washington Post,* March 12. https://www.washingtonpost.com/college-admissions-bribery-scheme-affidavit/d216435e-e073-41f6-b6fa-33ed835d053d_note.html
   Dana Goldstein and Jugal K. Patel, 2019. "Need Extra Time on Tests? It Helps to Have Cash." *The New York Times*, July 30. https://www.nytimes.com/2019/07/30/us/extra-time-504-sat-act.html
   Anderman and Murdock.
   "Cheating in High School Sports," 2019. *eMissiouian.com*, Oct 24. https://www.emissourian.com/opinion/editorials/cheating-in-high-school-sports/article_3e869542-f59b-11e9-89ce-e71afa06fe10.html

9 Robert D. McFadden, 2001. "Little League Star Is 14, and Bronx Team Is Disqualified." *The New York Times*, September 1. https://www.nytimes.com/2001/09/01/sports/little-league-star-is-14-and-bronx-team-is-disqualified.html

10 Alan Blinder, 2015. "Atlanta Educators Convicted in School Cheating Scandal." *New York Times*, April 1. https://www.nytimes.com/2015/04/02/us/verdict-reached-in-atlanta-school-testing-trial.html

11 Alexandra S. Burt, 2009. "Are There Meaningful Etiological Differences within Antisocial Behavior? Results of a Meta-Analysis." *Clinical Psychology Review* 29, no. 2: 163–178. https://doi.org/10.1016/j.cpr.2008.12.004

    George G. Bear, 2020. *Improving School Climate: Practical Strategies to Reduce Behavior Problems and Promote Social-Emotional Learning.* New York: Taylor & Francis.

12 Anderman and Murdock.

    Galloway.

    Tamera B. Murdock, Natalie M. Hale, and Mary J. Weber, 2001. "Predictors of Cheating among Early Adolescents: Academic and Social Motivations." *Contemporary Educational Psychology*, 26, no. 1: 96–115. https://doi.org/10.1006/ceps.2000.1046

13 Ibid.

    Chelsea Hays and Leslie J. Carver, 2014. "Follow the Liar: The Effects of Adult Lies on Children's Honesty." *Developmental Science* 17, no. 6: 977–983. https://doi.org/10.1111/desc.12171

14 McCabe.

15 Galloway.

16 Dan Ariely, 2012. *The (Honest) Truth about Dishonesty: How We Lie to Everyone—Especially Ourselves.* New York: Harper Perennial.

17 Aaron Kupchek, James Highberger, and George G. Bear, 2022. "Helpfulness of School Climate: Skipping School, Cheating on Tests, and Elements of School Climate." *Psychology in the Schools* 59, no. 1. https://doi.org/10.1002/pits.22692

18 Tamera B. Murdock, Angela Miller, and Julie Kohlhardt, 2004. "Effects of Classroom Context Variables on High School Students' Judgments of the Acceptability and Likelihood of Cheating." *Journal of Education Psychology* 96, no. 4: 765–777. https://doi.org/10.1037/0022-0663.96.4.765

19 Richard Arum, 2003. *Judging School Discipline: The Crisis of Moral Authority.* Boston, MA: Harvard University Press.

20 Kristin Voelkl Finn and Michael R. Frone, 2004. "Academic Performance and Cheating: Moderating Role of School Identification and Self-Efficacy." *The Journal of Educational Research*, 97, no. 3: 115–122. http://dx.doi.org/10.3200/JOER.97.3.115-121

21 Albera Bandura, 1986. *Social Foundations of Thought and Action: A Social Cognitive Theory.* New York: Prentice-Hall.

22 Arum.

23 Diana Baumrind, 2013. "Authoritative Parenting Revisited: History and Current Status" in *Authoritative Parenting: Synthesizing Nurturance and Discipline for Optimal Child Development* edited by Robert E. Larzelere, Amanda Sheffield Morris, and Amanda W. Harrist. Washington, DC: American Psychological Association, 35–58.

24 Bear.

25 Melissa McTernan, Patrick Love, and David Rettinger, 2014. "The Influence of Personality on the Decision to Cheat." *Ethics & Behavior* 24, no. 1: 53–72. https://doi.org/10.1080/10508422.2013.819783

26 Ibid.

27 Ibid.

28 Ibid.

29 Maureen A. Manning and George G. Bear, 2011. "Moral Reasoning and Aggressive Behavior: Concurrent and Longitudinal Relations." *Journal of School Violence* 11, no. 3: 258–280. https://doi.org/10.1080/15388220.2011.579235
30 Bandura.
31 McCabe.
32 Kyle A. Burgason, Ophir Sefiha, and L. T. Briggs, 2019. "Cheating Is in the Eye of the Beholder: An Evolving Understanding of Academic Misconduct." *Innovative Higher Education* 44 no. 3: 203–218. https://doi-org.udel.idm.oclc.org/10.1007/s10755-019-9457-3
33 Samuel D. Lee, Nathan R. Kuncel, and Jacob Gau, 2020, "Personality, Attitude, and Demographic Correlates of Academic Dishonesty: A Meta-Analysis." *Psychological Bulletin*, 146, no. 11: 1042–1058. https://dx.doi.org/10.1037/bul0000300
34 Tamera B. Murdock, Anne S. Beauchamp, and Amber M. Hinton, 2008. "Predictors of Cheating and Cheating Attributions: Does Classroom Context Influence Cheating and Blame for Cheating." *European Journal of Psychology of Education* 23, no. 4: 477–492. https://doi.org/132.174.254.72
35 Alan Traclet, Philippe Romand, Orlan Moret and Maria Kavussanu, 2011. "Antisocial Behavior in Soccer: A Qualitative Study of Moral Disengagement." *International Journal of Sport and Exercise Psychology* 9, no. 2: 143–155. https://doi.org/10.1080/1612197X.2011.567105
36 McCabe.
37 McCabe.
38 Aaron Katersky, Luke Barr, and Soo Rin Kim, 2022. "Prosecutors Looking at George Santos amid Lies, Questions about His Wealth." *ABC News*, December 28. https://abcnews.go.com/Politics/prosecutors-george-santos-amid-lies-questions-wealth/story?id=95902176
   Neil Vigdor, 2022. "George Santos Is in a Class of His Own. But Other Politicians Have Embellished Their Resumes, Too." *The New York Times*, December 28. https://www.nytimes.com/2022/12/28/us/politics/george-santos-resume-lies-politicians.html
39 Vigdor.
40 Marvin Zuckerman, 1994. *Behavioral Expressions and Biosocial Bases of Sensation Seeking*. Boston, MA: Cambridge University Press.
41 David C. DeAndrea, Christopher Carpenter, Hillary Shulman, and Timothy R. Levine, 2009. "The Relationship between Cheating Behavior and Sensation-Seeking." *Personality and Individual Differences* 47, no. 8: 944–947. https://doi.org/10.1016/j.paid.2009.07.021
42 Marvin Zuckerman, 1983. "Sensation Seeking and Sports." *Personality and Individual Differences* 4 no. 3: 285–292. https://doi.org/10.1016/0191-8869(83)90150-2
43 Lewis Donohew, Rick Zimmerman, Pamela Cupp, Susan Colon, and Ritta Abell, 2000. "Sensation Seeking, Impulsive Decision-Making, and Risky Sex: Implication for Risk-Taking and Design of Interventions." *Personality and Individual Differences*, 28, no. 6: 1079–1091. https://doi.org/10.1016/S0191-8869(99)00158-0
44 Joseph Glicksoh, Revital Naor-Ziv, and Rotem Leshem, 2018. "Sensation Seeking and Risk-Taking" in *Developmental Pathways to Disruptive, Impulse-Control, and Conduct Disorders* edited by Michelle Martel. San Diego, CA: Academic Press, 183–208.
45 Nicole E. Ruedy, Celia Moore, Francesca Gino, and Maurice E. Schweitzer, 2013. "The Cheater's High: The Unexpected Affective Benefits of Unethical Behavior." *Journal of Personality and Social Psychology*, 105, no. 4: 531–548. https://doi.org/10.1037/a0034231

5 Trump

A Role Model for Cheating

Cheating Gets Things Done

There are plenty of adult role models for children to learn how cheating gets things done. As seen in the previous chapter, popular stories in the media have reported parents paying bribes for their children's fabricated college entrance scores, school administrators falsifying test scores of students, and coaches and athletes cheating in multiple ways. As with lying and bullying, cheating isn't new in our society. What is new is a president who has cheated in nearly all aspects of life, whether by avoiding taxes, scamming students enrolled in his "university," adultery, bribery, nepotism, cronyism, fudging his score in golf, or attempting to falsify the election count and inciting his supporters to overthrow the government.

How might Trump respond to the quiz about cheating presented in the previous chapter? Based on his history of lying and obsession with presenting a false and perfect self he would likely answer "no" to most, if not all, of the statements. But, as noted in Chapter 3, he once said he never lies; thus, if true, a response of "yes" to every item should be expected.

As seen in this chapter, no other president has provided such an exemplary role model of getting things done by cheating—promoting norms and a culture among many Americans (i.e., MAGA Republicans) in which cheating is viewed as acceptable, if not highly valued. In that culture, winning is everything and cheating makes winning easier, especially if you avoid getting caught and punished. Of course, power and wealth certainly help avoid punishment, as seen in Trump's protection of the presidency, threats of retribution, support from fellow MAGA Republicans, and a bottomless war chest to fund lawsuits and delay or thwart criminal investigations and trials.

Did Trump Cheat in School?

Little is known about Trump cheating in school. This can largely be attributed to schools that he attended having signed under threat of lawsuit that they would not release his school records.[1] I found no reports that

DOI: 10.4324/9781003401278-5

Trump cheated while in school or in scholastic sports. However, according to his niece, Dr. Mary Trump, her Uncle Donald cheated on his Scholastic College Exam by paying a friend to take it for him.[2] Given that Trump has a well-documented history of cheating as an adult, it is likely that he also cheated as a student. It also is likely that Trump cheated in school in light of possessing personality characteristics associated with cheating: hedonistic, self-centered values and moral reasoning; a lack of empathy, guilt, and shame; a fear of failure; impulsivity; sensation seeking; and a proclivity for using mechanisms of moral disengagement.

There are two good reasons, however, why Trump might have cheated less or no more than others in school. Firstly, it appears that he was a good, although not exceptional, student who did not need to cheat to obtain passing grades, especially at New York Military Academy (NYMA) where many of the students were sent for academic and behavioral remediation. They were not New York's finest. In college, there is no record of him being a stellar student, while majoring in real estate—something he already knew a lot about. Thanks to his father, Trump was already a millionaire and had a nice job lined up upon graduation working in his father's very successful real estate business. If he failed in college, he was still going to be a millionaire. Thus, there was little pressure to excel academically. Secondly, NYMA was not the type of school where academic cheating tends to be rampant. That is, students are less likely to cheat in schools where they perceive the rules to be strict, yet fair, and their relationships with teachers favorably,[3] and Trump perceived NYMA that way. As reported by his biographer, Michael D'Antonio, in the *Truth about Trump*, Trump loved the authoritarian atmosphere and admired his instructors and coaches.[4]

To be sure, cheating occurs in military schools with strict rules, and especially in those where students experience much pressure to succeed. That students cheat in military schools with strict rules was recently seen at the United States Military Academy at West Point. In 2020, 73 cadets (72 were freshmen) were accused of cheating on a calculus exam (taken online, not in person).[5] Cheating scandals also occurred at other service academies, including one in 2007 at the Air Force Academy that involved 18 cadets and one in 1994 at the United States Naval Academy that involved 125 midshipmen. Each of those military schools differs greatly from NYMA, however. Unlike NYMA where being wealthy and the need for remediation were greater predictors of admission than intellect and talent, cadets at America's military colleges are among the brightest and most talented students in higher education. Thus, they are under great pressure to succeed, not only to please their parents but themselves. Also unlike at NYMA, the competition to excel is keen and cadets have a realistic fear of losing their scholarships. Few cadets are millionaires who have jobs waiting for them regardless of their performance and with the promise of greater wealth regardless of their grades.

Whereas Trump might not have cheated more than others in grade school and college, his cheating afterward is another story. As seen below, as an adult and real estate developer in New York City, Trump became very skilled in cheating, not getting caught, and avoiding punishment when he was caught.

Cheating in Business

As a businessman, Trump viewed cheating as amoral, not immoral; it was justified, expected, and the norm among New York City real estate developers. Early on, he learned firsthand from his father how cheating got things done. His father, Fred Trump, was investigated by the U.S. Senate and the State of New York for profiteering. And as was noted in Chapter 3, his father was sued by the U.S. Justice Department's Civil Rights Division for violating the Fair Housing Act (i.e., he discriminated against Blacks). Additionally, Fred conducted various fraudulent schemes in unsuccessful attempts to save his son's Atlantic City casinos from bankruptcy. For example, he bought 3.5 million dollars of gambling chips in one of his son's casinos, with no intention of ever cashing them in.[6]

Biographers and others who have studied Trump's life history attribute his fondness and skills for cheating in business and elsewhere in life not only to his father but also to Roy Cohn. For more than 20 years Cohn was Trump's close friend and personal lawyer. As discussed in Chapter 12, Cohn, who was viewed by many as "evil," modeled how cheating, lying, and bullying can greatly enhance one's wealth, power, and fame. With two masters at cheating as mentors, Trump learned how to play the system. A 2018 story in *The New York Times* estimated that prior to that year Trump had received at least $885 million in tax breaks, grants, and other subsidies for his properties in New York City. Upon examining over 100,000 pages of bank statements, financial audits, invoices, court filings, and other documents, the *Times* found that much of Trump's fortune came from his parents and as the result of "dubious tax schemes during the 1990s, including instances of outright fraud." [7]

The report by the *Times* led to several lawsuits against the Trump empire. In 2022, the Trump Organization and the Trump Payroll Corporation were convicted by a jury on 17 counts of tax fraud and other crimes. The crimes included falsifying records, conspiracy, and not reporting large perks given to company executives on large gifts (e.g., luxury apartments, Mercedes-Benzes, private school tuition, real estate, large amounts of cash) for which no taxes were paid. Trump was not charged personally for the crimes, but as noted by the prosecutors Trump "knew exactly what was going on."[8]

Money laundering also was used to avoid paying taxes. Several of his casinos were fined for "willfully failing to report" transactions of over $10,000, which is a violation of the Bank Secrecy Act. In 2015, shortly before Trump announced his bid for the presidency, the Taj Mahal casino was fined $10 million for 106 violations dating back to 1993. The fine was the largest in American history for violation of the Bank Secrecy Act.[9]

Trump not only cheated local, state, and federal governments but he also was notorious for cheating companies and individuals by simply underpaying or refusing to pay for their work. This included illegal immigrants, such as the "Polish Brigade," which he hired, bypassing union workers, to perform the demolition work on the Trump Tower at four dollars an hour, which was about one-fifth the going rate.[10] There were many others whom he simply did not pay for their work. As noted in a report by the *USA TODAY NETWORK*:

"At least 60 lawsuits, along with hundreds of liens, judgments, and other government filings reviewed by the USA TODAY NETWORK, document people who have accused Trump and his businesses of failing to pay them for their work. Among them: a dishwasher in Florida. A glass company in New Jersey. A carpet company. A plumber. Painters. Forty-eight waiters. Dozens of bartenders and other hourly workers at his resorts and clubs, coast to coast. Real estate brokers who sold his properties. And, ironically, several law firms that once represented him in these suits and others."[11] Additional examples of Trump lying and cheating individuals were presented in Chapter 3, with Trump University being a classic case.

Cheating Charities

Many people, especially Trump supporters, might turn their backs to cheating in business, especially in New York real estate, thinking that it is the norm and acceptable. However, few people stoop so low as to cheat charities. Trump and his children, Ivanka, Donald Jr., and Eric made cheating charities a common practice. To be fair, they donated millions to various charities, but it was a very small fraction of their personal wealth and was usually for self-serving purposes (i.e., expecting favors in return or media attention). As revealed after Trump was finally forced by the courts to release his federal tax returns, during one year as president (2020) the billionaire Trump claimed no charitable contributions.[12] Trump had promised to donate all his annual salary as president to charities.[13]

Unlike most other wealthy people who establish charity foundations, the Trump family used the Trump Foundation they created as a means to an end: to cheat others out of their money and increase the family's wealth. Trump served as president of the Foundation. Its board members, who included Donald Jr., Eric, and Ivanka, never met for 19 straight years, with decisions being made by its president (Donald).[14]

In 2019 the New York Supreme Court found the Trumps guilty of fraud and waste that cheated contributors to the Trump Foundation for many years. Although the Trump Foundation contributed large sums of money to various charities, it repeatedly used the Foundation's money, including money donated by others, for Trump and his family's own personal benefit.[15] Among those benefits were:

- Spending $12,000 on a Tim Tebow autographed football helmet that Trump added to his personal collection of sports memorabilia.
- Spending $20,000 on two portraits of Trump, including one displayed at his Doral golf course in Miami.
- Using charity money to contribute to political campaigns, including Trump's own campaign for president.
- Using charity money to pay debts of his for-profit businesses and to settle lawsuits that had nothing to do with the charity.

As restitution and penalty for the Trump Foundation's cheating, the Trumps were forced to pay $2 million and to close the Trump Foundation charity. They were not allowed to operate a charity again in New York without close audits and an attorney supervising the charity. Eric, Donald Jr., and Ivanka also were required to take training on how to be more ethical board members.

The court case also revealed Trump's fondness for cronyism. Whereas Trump donated nothing from 2009 to 2015 to the Trump Foundation's charity, his billionaire friends Vince and Linda McMahon, founders of World Wrestling Entertainment, contributed a total of $5 million. The McMahons were later rewarded; when Trump became president, he appointed Linda McMahon as head of the U.S. Small Business Administration.

In his book *Plaintiff in Chief: A Portrait of Donald Trump in 3500 Lawsuits*,[16] James D. Ziren cites multiple cases, including those in the lawsuit above, where Trump used money from the Trump Foundation to settle lawsuits. Trump sued the town of Palm Beach for fining him over $120,000 ($250 a day) for violating zoning codes by flying a massive American flag atop an 80-foot flagpole on the front lawn of Mar-a-Lago. He lost the lawsuit, agreeing to replace the flag and donate $100,000 to Iraqi War veterans. He paid that amount not from personal funds, but from the Trump Foundation, which likely constituted charity fraud.

In another, and somewhat amusing, lawsuit against Trump that involved the Trump Foundation, Trump was sued for reneging on a promise to pay $1 million to anyone who made a hole-in-one during one of his golf tournaments.[17] Martin Greenberg made a hole-in-one. Trump refused to pay up and Greenberg sued him. Trump settled out of court, paying $158,000 out of charity funds of the Trump Foundation.

Cheating in Relationships

Although it is unclear how many women Trump had affairs with while married, it is clear that he cheated on his first two wives and likely cheated on the third.[18] He even bragged about his cheating, stating in a 1994 interview with *ABC*'s *Primetime Live*, while he was married to his first wife, Ivana, that "My life was so great in so many ways. The business was so great … a beautiful girlfriend, a beautiful wife, a beautiful everything. Life was just a bowl of cherries."[19] While married to Ivana, Trump took his mistress, and next wife,

Marla Maples, on a family ski trip to Aspen, CO, where Marla informed Ivana that she loved her husband. Shortly thereafter, a front-page story in the *New York Post* quoted Marla as saying, "Best sex I ever had." Trump gloated about the headline. While married to Ivana and dating Marla, Trump bragged about having "three other girlfriends" and stated that he would never marry Marla.[20] He married her two months after she had their baby, Tiffany. They divorced four years later.

Allegations of Trump cheating on his third wife, Melania, surfaced early in his presidency. As directed by Trump, his personal lawyer, Michael Cohen, paid porn star Stephanie Clifford ("Stormy Daniels") over $130,000 to stay silent about the alleged affair. Trump denied the affair, yet reimbursed Cohen with a check drawn from campaign funds. The payment was illegal; a violation of campaign-finance regulations. It was among the crimes for which Cohen served time in prison. It also was the primary basis of Trump being indicted by a New York grand jury on 34 felony accounts in March 2023. Most of the indictments related to Trump falsifying business records in a scheme to cover up his payment to the porn star before the 2016 election.[21]

Trump also denied allegations that he had an affair with Karen McDougal, the 1998 *Playboy's* Playmate of the Year. In his book, *Disloyal*, Cohen claimed that the Daniels and McDougal affairs both occurred.[22] There were 18 additional women who alleged sexual harassment by Trump from the 1980s to 2013.[23] One of them, E. Jean Carroll, sued him for rape and defamation, alleging that he raped her in 1996 (when Trump was married to Marla Maples) and defamed her with verbal insults (e.g., "mentally sick," "a nut job") after she wrote a book in 2019 about the incident. In May 2023, a civil jury in New York found Trump liable for sexually abusing and defaming Carroll, awarding her $5 million in damages.[24] Denying the charges, Trump appealed. After the verdict, he continued to attack Carroll on social media and in an interview on CNN, calling her a "wack job" and "not my type" and asserting that her claims were "fake," a "made-up story," "a rigged deal," "a complete con job," and "a Hoax and a lie." As a result of those and other allegedly defamatory comments that Trump made before, during, and after the trial, Carroll revised her defamation lawsuit, increasing the requested compensatory damages for defamation to over $10 million.[25]

Cheating Even in Golf

As with academics, little is known about Trump cheating in sports in childhood. However, as an adult, his cheating in golf is a different story. As revealed in Rick Reilly's *Commander in Cheat: How Golf Explains Trump*,[26] Trump cheats in nearly every aspect of golf. Reilly documents not only Trump's cheating in playing the sport, but also in building and managing his international empire of golf courses. As Reilly notes:

You might be thinking, 'What does golf have to do with being president? What does it matter that he cheats at it? What's that got to do with leading the country?' Everything.

If you'll cheat to win at golf, is it that much further to cheat to win an election? To turn a congressional vote? To stop an investigation? If you lie about every aspect of the game, is it that much further to lie about your taxes, your relationship with Russians, your groping women? If you're adamant that the poor don't deserve golf, is it that much further to think they don't deserve health care, clean air, safe schools?[27]

Reilly gives plenty, and often humorous, examples of the many ways Trump cheats in golf. They include him moving his ball from the rough to the fairway and his opponent's ball from the fairway to the rough; denying that his ball landed in the water, while dropping a ball on the fairway; claiming a "give me" on putts that most others would have to make; taking extra shots (i.e., "Mulligans"); lying about his score; and using a super-charged golf cart to make sure he arrives where his ball lands so he can move it to a better sport before others see where it actually landed. His caddies, who called him "Pele" for his practice of kicking his opponent's golf ball, often assisted him in cheating. Some were awarded handsomely for doing so. Trump appointed his former caddie, Dan Scavino, as White House Deputy Chief for Communications and Director of Social Media.

Cheating as President

As president, Trump was perhaps better known for his pathological lying than for his cheating. It was cheating, however, often combined with lying and bullying, that he will most likely be remembered. He will be remembered as the only president in American history whose cheating led to impeachments but also as perhaps the foremost example of a president whose cheating was seen in bribery, nepotism, conflicts of interest, cronyism, and abusing the presidency for unethical and illegal personal profit and partisan political politics.

Bribery

In business and government, bribery typically involves giving money or gifts to government/public officials in exchange for favors or preferential treatment, such as tax breaks, the awarding of government contracts, and not enforcing government regulations and laws (e.g., building codes). Such bribery is a form of cheating and a criminal act.

When Trump became president, he had a long-established history of bribing others to get things done. As noted by Trump's biographers, it was common in New York City and Atlantic City for real estate developers to give gifts to local and state politicians and other government officials, including tax assessors, in exchange for favors. Trump and his father were no exceptions. Bribery is less common as a president, however, with Trump being among the exceptions, and perhaps the only one who made it clear that bribery should be a standard and acceptable way for conducting business. In their book, *A Very Stable Genius: Donald J. Trump's Testing of America*, Philip Rucker and Carol Leonnig quote Trump as stating in a meeting with Secretary of State Rex Tillerson that it was "just so unfair that American companies aren't allowed to pay bribes to get business overseas" and that "I need you to get rid of that law."[28] "That law" was a major federal law enacted in 1977 to prohibit companies operating in the United States from bribing foreign officials in order to gain their business. Demonstrating the integrity that eventually got him fired, Tillerson refused to follow through.

Proving that giving gifts, money, or other favors in exchange for preferential treatment constitutes the illegal act of bribery requires proof that a "quid pro quo" relationship exists, as evidenced by the gift directly influencing, or intending to influence, the recipient's behavior. As discussed in Chapter 3 on Trump's lying, it was quid pro quo, an exchange of favors, that led to his first impeachment. The quid pro quo consisted of Trump withholding military aid to Ukraine unless that country investigated actions by former Vice President Joe Biden's son, Hunter Biden.

Nepotism and Conflicts of Interest

Nepotism refers to people favoring their relatives or friends. To be sure, nepotism is not uncommon in families, especially those that own businesses; it helps ensure that a family's hard work and wealth remains in the family and the business is protected by those believed to be most loyal. Trump was handed over his father's real estate empire and will do the same for Donald Jr., Eric, and Ivanka. One may well argue that such nepotism is well justified. Much more contentious, and less common, however, is blatant nepotism as a president of the United States, as seen below.

Often associated with President John Kennedy appointing his brother, Robert, as attorney general, in 1967 Congress passed the Federal Anti-Nepotism Statute. The law forbids a public official, including the president, from appointing or employing a relative to a "civilian position in the agency in which he is serving." The law further notes that "An individual appointed, employed, promoted, or advanced in violation of this section is not entitled to pay, and money may not be paid from the Treasury as pay to an individual so appointed, employed, promoted, or advanced." Throughout his presidency, Trump employed his daughter, Ivanka, and son-in-law, Jared, in the White House as advisors. Trump's Justice Department Office of Legal Counsel opined that the law was not being violated because the White House is not an agency and because neither Ivanka nor Jared received a salary.[29]

One might well argue that although they were not given salaries, Jared and Ivanka benefited financially in other ways that many would consider as conflicts of interest. For example, while in the White House, Jared continued to hold his family's real estate companies, which were valued at over $750 million. He met with financial executives in the White House who afterward loaned his companies approximately $500 million.[30] Jared also served as a negotiator of a Middle East peace plan while having close business ties with the Saudi Arabian government, including he and Ivanka being part owners of a company building a Trump property in that country.[31] Shortly after leaving the White House, Jared received a $2 billion investment from a fund headed by Saudi Crown Prince Mohammed bin Salman.[32]

Prior to Trump's election, and with substantial financial support from her father, Ivanka ran her own Trump business creating and marketing jewelry, clothing, and fashion accessories. Its primary store was in the Trump Tower. As reported by *The Wall Street Journal*, in approximately two-thirds of her Twitter, Facebook, and Instagram postings shortly before becoming White House adviser, and while she still owned her fashion business, Ivanka wore dresses, shoes, handbags, or jewelry that she sold in her business. The report noted: "Yet every time she steps out sporting Ivanka Trump merchandise, Ms. Trump—wittingly or not—is a walking billboard for her brand, and an example of the conflicts that arise when government employees have both public and private professional interests."[33] Ivanka was not the only one in the White House who hawked her merchandise. In a clear conflict of interest, and a likely ethical violation, during a television interview from the White House, Kellyanne Conway, a top Trump adviser, encouraged viewers to buy clothes from Ivanka's line of merchandise.[34]

Although they were not handed positions in the White House, Trump's two sons, Donald Jr. and Eric, are additional examples of nepotism at the expense of taxpayers and competing businesses. During Trump's presidency both served as executive vice presidents and trustees of the Trump Organization, consisting of approximately 500 businesses. Instead of placing his businesses in a blind trust or otherwise ridding himself of conflicts of interest, as done by previous presidents, Trump remained the sole proprietor or owner of the businesses.[35]

Multiple groups including Citizens for Responsibility and Ethics in Washington (CREW), the state of Maryland, Washington, D.C., and members of Congress filed lawsuits alleging that Trump violated the emoluments clause in the Constitution by he and his family accepting gifts and profiting from foreign governments doing business with the Trump Organization while serving as president.[36] CREW documented 3,737 alleged conflicts of interest during Trump's time in office. Among them were Trump visiting his own properties 547 times (including 328 visits to his golf courses, 145 visits to Mar-a-Lago, and 33 visits to the Trump International Hotel in Washington, DC). Government officials, both American and foreign, also were frequent visitors to his properties.

They included 346 officials of the executive branch, who visited close to 1,000 times; 143 members of Congress, with a total of 361 visits (mostly MAGA Republicans, with Lindsey Graham, Matt Gaetz, and Rand Paul visiting 20 or more times); and 150 government officials from 77 foreign governments. Special interest groups spent over $13 million at his properties, while various political groups that supported Trump spent $11.8 million. Trump's campaign committees and super PACs spent $7 million. Together, special interest groups, foreign governments, and political groups held over 250 events at Trump properties. Trump and his family profited not only from the millions in increased revenue created by those visits, but also in other ways, such as the Trump organization obtaining 69 foreign trademarks.

In the lawsuit filed by the District of Columbia against the 58th President Inauguration Committee, Trump International Hotel (in downtown DC), and the Trump Organization, it was revealed that the nonprofit inaugural committee illegally paid excessive rates to Trump's hotel, with much of money used to divert charitable contributions to Trumps' private holdings. An example was given of the committee paying $175,000 to Trump International Hotel to rent the main ballroom to host a private reception for Trump's children the night before his inauguration. On the same day, another organization had paid only $5,000. In 2022, the inauguration committee and the Trump Organization agreed to pay D.C. $750,000 to settle the suit.[37]

CREW documented that in addition to visiting and hosting visitors at his properties, Trump promoted his properties and businesses by referring to or mentioning them publicly 378 times while president. There were over 400 additional instances of other White House officials verbally promoting Trump properties.

Visits to Trump properties by the Trump family directly generated income for the family businesses, costing taxpayers millions of dollars.[38] The Secret Service paid nightly rates as high as $650 per room while staying at Mar-a-Lago and other Trump luxury hotels.[39] During one three-month period alone, the Secret Service paid $137,000 for use of golf carts at Trump's Florida and New Jersey clubs.[40] Instead of the Trump family paying the bill, taxpayers also paid for secret service protection for the president's children while they were on vacation. This included about $75,000 for Donald Jr. to hunt endangered long-horned sheep in Mongolia.[41]

Cronyism

Cronyism refers to appointing family or friends to positions of influence and authority irrespective of their qualifications. As with nepotism, cronyism helps ensure that those working for you are loyal. It also is a way to return favors. Without experience in government prior to being appointed advisers to the president, Jared and Ivanka, but especially Jared, are examples not only of nepotism but also cronyism. With no experience in either government or medicine, Jared was charged with leading the government's response to the coronavirus. His inexperience was largely to blame for the government's failure to slow the virus's spread.[42]

Countless friends, associates, and especially those who contributed large sums of money to Trump's election or otherwise supported him, also were rewarded with government positions, including ambassadorships and positions in his cabinet. Many of them resigned or were fired for ethical violations, illegal activities, or mismanagement and cheating taxpayers. Most were similar to Trump in their self-serving and egoistic character, but lacked the same political and financial power to avoid punishment when they were caught for ethical violations and cheating taxpayers. Prime examples were Edward Scott Pruitt, Administrator of the Environmental Protection Agency, who ordered a $43,000 soundproof phone booth for his office, and David Shulkin, Secretary of Veterans Affairs, who with his wife attended Wimbledon, toured Westminster Abbey, and took a river cruise on the Thames during a taxpayer-funded business trip to Europe.[43]

Hatch Act Violations

The 1939 Hatch Act is a federal law prohibiting federal employees, excluding the president and vice president, from using their official federally funded positions to promote or influence partisan politics. This includes the "official authority or influence for the purpose of interfering with or affecting the result of an election." The law applies to most federal employees only when they are on duty or in the workplace, but for some, such as those involved in national security, law enforcement, or elections, it applies when either on or off duty.

Instances of Hatch Act violations of the law are documented in a comprehensive October 2020 report by Senator Elizabeth Warren and her staff, entitled "*Lawlessness and Disorder: The Corrupt Trump Administration Has Made a Mockery of the Hatch Act.*"[44] The report documented that 14 officials in the Trump administration violated the Hatch Act 54 times. At least 22 more top Trump officials were under investigation at that time for nearly 100 additional violations. In campaigning for Trump's re-election, they conducted multiple television interviews and made numerous postings on social media. The report noted that the violations of the law by Kellyanne Conway, Senior Counselor to the President "were so egregious that the Office of Special Counsel recommended directly to President Trump that she be removed from her position—a recommendation that was ignored by the President."[45] When asked about their violations of the Hatch Amendment, Chief of Staff Mark Meadows dismissed the ethical and legal violation commenting "Nobody outside of the Beltway really cares." In mocking the Act, Conway added "Let me know when the jail sentence starts."[46]

Whether within or outside the beltway, many Trump Republicans really didn't care, and Trump helped make sure that was the case. Again, he cheated the system. In the White House, the Hatch Act and other laws are to be enforced by the Office of Special Counsel (OSC), which at the time was run by Trump-appointee Special Counsel Henry J. Kerner. Under his directorship, OSC simply ignored nearly all Hatch Act violations. To further ensure that Conway and other violators did not need to worry about "when the jail sentence starts," the Board (i.e., the Merit Systems Protection Board) that was to evaluate Hatch Act complaints never had a quorum during Trump's presidency. At times, it had no sitting members. In the absence of a quorum or board members, the OSC recommended that Trump, and not the practically non-existent Board, impose disciplinary actions against violators of the Hatch Act, including Conway. Trump did nothing to those who violated the Act, and at times clearly encouraged their cheating and unethical behavior.[47]

2020 Election

Getting caught and impeached the first time, as well as an onslaught of charges of nepotism, conflicts of interest, cronyism, and violations of the Hatch Act did not stop Trump from continuing to lie, cheat, and bully. In the last days of his presidency, he continued to rely on the same combination to get things done, which led to his second impeachment. Refusing to concede that he lost the election, he engaged in countless dishonest attempts to stay in power and overturn an honest and free election. As noted previously in Chapter 3, his firehose of lies claiming the election was rigged and that he won by "a landslide" led to his 2023 criminal indictment on four counts. The indictment also revealed a firehose of cheating.

The groundwork was first laid back in 2016 when Trump falsely claimed that "millions" voted illegally in the 2016 election and that if those votes had not been counted then he would have won not only the Electoral College count but also the popular vote (he lost the popular vote by nearly 3 million votes). The deceit continued in the 2018 and 2020 elections with Trump and many fellow Republicans repeatedly asserting that more mail-in votes were inherently fraudulent. Historically, most democrats cast mail-in votes than Republicans (ironically, Trump was among Republicans who had voted by mail).

Trump encouraged his supporters not to vote by mail. He believed that by not doing so the count would be skewed in his favor on Election Day since mail-in votes are often counted after in-person votes are counted, including several days following election day. As noted by reporter Ed Kilgore of the New York *Intelligencer* in an article entitled "Trump's Long Campaign to Steal the Presidency: A Timeline," "Trump's goal seemed clear: By asserting that voting by mail is tantamount to voter fraud, he was setting up a bogus justification for contesting election results in any state he lost."[48] Indeed, in the very morning of the day after the election and when it was becoming clear that Trump's lead was dwindling as mail-in votes were counted (as many had predicted and Trump had feared), Trump told his supporters that they were witnessing massive voter fraud to overturn his victory. Trump stated that "We want all voting to stop" and "as far as I'm concerned, we already have won it." Fortunately, he did not stop the voting, as his legal advisors counseled him out of it.

After knowing that he had lost both the Electoral College count and the popular vote, Trump shifted to other plans for cheating to stay in office. A legal team, called the "Elite Strike Force" and led by Rudy Giuliani, was quickly assembled to challenge the election in state and federal courts. They filed 62 lawsuits, with all but one being rejected (the one not rejected was in Pennsylvania, involving a small number of ballots with technical errors).[49] Trump supporters asked the Supreme Court to hear and overturn two of the cases that ruled against them, but the court rejected both requests.

Although members of the White House team that challenged the election changed often, Giuliani, Trump's attorney, was a constant member. The "Elite Strike Force" also included conspiracy theorist Sidney Powell, who Trump removed from his team after she revealed one of her conspiracy theories at a press conference—that Venezuelan communists hacked voting machines. This did not stop Powell from advising the team or filing lawsuits in support of the team (which led to actions to disbar her). Nor did her removal stop MAGA Republicans from posting her conspiracy theory on social media.[50] The team was advised, and roundly supported, by "MyPillow Guy" Mike Lindell, a multi-millionaire, evangelical Christian, reformed crack cocaine addict, staunch Trump ally, and major GOP donor. Lindell frequently appeared in the conservative media spreading lies and ungrounded conspiracy theories about the election being stolen.[51]

As revealed in Michael Bender's book, *Frankly We Did Win This Election: The Inside Story of How Trump Lost*, Jared Kushner and William Barr referred to the team as a "clown show."[52] Kushner, Barr, Trump, and others in the White House knew that claims in the "clown show" were bogus. Among the conspiracy theories they promoted were ones espoused by Powell—that a group consisting of communists, "globalists," George Soros, Hugo Chavez (who died in 2013), the Clinton Foundation, the CIA, and others infiltrated voting machines to rig the election. They frequently identified the machines made by Dominion Voting Systems and Smartmatic as being rigged. For example, Lindell claimed that Dominion "built them to cheat."

Dominion and Smartmatic sued Giuliani, Powell, Lindell, and others (including *One America News*, *Fox News*, and *Newsmax*) for defamation. The day that the trial was to begin in Dominion's lawsuit against Fox, the two companies settled out of court, with Fox agreeing to pay Dominion $787.5 million.[53] The judge had already ruled that Fox's claims about Dominion's machines being rigged were false. He also noted that Lindell frequently profited by lying about Dominion, often telling his audiences to buy *MyPillow* products (telling them that "President loves" *MyPillow* and offering promotional codes, including "FightforTrump"). Giuliani also profited. As noted by the judge, Giuliani "cashed in by hosting a podcast where he exploited election falsehoods to market gold coins, supplements, cigars and protection from 'cyberthieves.'"[54] Like Trump, Lindell and Giuliani knew that their lies and cheating would make them richer, as there were millions of Trump supporters willing to donate to their cause and buy products that they sold or endorsed. (At the time of this writing, only Dominion's lawsuit against Fox had been heard by a judge.)

As explained in the report of the House of Representatives Select Committee to Investigate January 6th Attack on the United States Capitol,[55] and further included in the special counsel's four-count indictment of Trump related to the 2020 election,[56] Trump had another plan for cheating Biden out of the presidency. It involved Republican legislators in seven states in which Biden had narrowly won to challenge their state's Electoral College votes. Those legislators were to refuse to certify their state's real electoral votes and appoint a separate slate of Trump electors to represent their state when the Electoral College was to meet on December 14 and electoral votes were to be counted. That attempt at cheating also failed, as the Trump electors were denied representation at the Electoral College meeting.

Another cheating scheme Trump considered was having the Department of Homeland Security, Justice Department, the Pentagon, or other agencies seize voting machines in states where he narrowly lost. This scheme, which was promoted by Sidney Powell and Trump advisor Michael Flynn, was shot down by Attorney General William Barr, as well as by Giuliani.[57,58]

Trump tried another scheme. He contacted Republican leaders in several states that he narrowly lost, asking them to somehow show that he had more votes than Biden. Georgia, where he lost by only 11,779 votes, was the state primarily on his radar. He first called Georgia Governor Brian Kemp asking him to overturn the election results by convening the state legislature and having the legislators appoint Trump electors. Kemp, who had already certified Biden as the winner, refused to do so. Trump then contacted other state officials for help, including Georgia Secretary of State Brad Raffensperger (like Kemp, a Republican) asking them to find him more votes. In the recorded phone call to Raffensperger Trump stated: "So look. All I want to do is this," the president said in a recorded conversation. "I just want to find 11,780 votes, which is one more than we have. Because we won the state." After the phone call failed to bully Raffensperger into pursuing Trump's false claims of election fraud, Trump tweeted that Raffensperger was "unwilling, or unable, to answer questions such as the 'ballots under table' scam, ballot destruction, out of state 'voters', dead voters, and more. He has no clue!" Worthy of a Profiles in Courage Award, and a good example of how to respond to a bully, Raffensperger refused to submit to the bullying and responded in his own tweet: "Respectfully, President Trump: What you're saying is not true."[59]

That phone call and additional actions (i.e., cheating, lying, and bullying) by Trump to reverse the election results in Georgia led to Georgia prosecutor,

Fani Willis, establishing a grand jury. In August 2023 the grand jury indicted Trump on 13 counts, including being part of a "criminal organization" that conspired to defraud the state, "unlawfully soliciting" a public officer to violate their oath (i.e., Raffensperger), conspiring to impersonate a public officer, and making false statements and writings. Trump and 18 other defendants and co-conspirators, who included Trump's attorney Rudy Giuliani and his Chief of Staff Mark Meadows, were charged on a total of 41 counts. As stated in the indictment: "Trump and the other Defendants charged in this Indictment refused to accept that Trump lost, and they knowingly and willfully joined a conspiracy to unlawfully change the outcome of the election in favor of Trump."[60] The nearly 100-page indictment listed 161 separate acts taken by the alleged criminal conspirators to overturn election results. Among those acts were the telephone call to Raffensperger, soliciting Vice President Pence to co-conspire, creating fake pro-Trump electors, and perhaps the most brazen act of all—breaching a voting machine, stealing data, and then covering up the transgression. At time of this writing, Powell is the only defendant noted above whose case had been heard in court. Several days before she was to be tried before a jury, she pleaded guilty to six counts of conspiracy to commit intentional interference with performance of election duties, which included breaching a voting machine.[61]

As reported by the Select Committee, Trump also pressured Acting Attorney General Jeffrey Rosen to lie about the election results. Rosen was serving as attorney general after William Barr had resigned, unwilling to participate in Trump's schemes. After Rosen also refused to go along with Trump's schemes, telling him that the Department of Justice would not and could not change the election outcome, Trump told him "Just say that the election was corrupt and leave the rest to me and the Republican Congressmen."[62] Rosen refused, but this did not stop Trump from trying to leave the rest to him and Republican Congressmen.

Short of a violent insurrection, Trump's last-ditch effort to reverse the election results and stay in power was his tried-and-true combination of lying, cheating, and bullying for getting things done. Supported by his loyal MAGA Republicans in Congress, the effort entailed a two-prong plan: (1) bully Vice President Pence into refusing to follow his Constitutional duty of declaring that Biden had the number of electoral votes to be president and (2) have members of Congress challenge the electoral count certifications in states that Trump narrowly lost and thus block confirmation of Biden's election.

Trump wanted Pence to "do the right thing" by either declaring outright that Trump had won or claiming that the election was disputed and thus Trump would continue in office until the Republican-controlled House of Representatives resolved the dispute or until state legislators replaced the existing electors with Trump electors. The mastermind behind this plan, which Federal District Court Judge David Carter later referred to in court hearings as "a coup in search of a legal theory," was John Eastman, an ultra-conservative attorney and adviser to Trump.[63] Pence refused to go along with the unconstitutional plan. In justifying his decision, Pence asserted there is "I had no right to overturn the election. The Presidency belongs to the American people, and the American people alone. And frankly, there is no idea more un-American than the notion that any one person could choose the American president."[64]

Knowing that Part 1 of the plan would fail, Part 2 was executed. In a joint session of Congress on January 6 to tally the Electoral College vote results, hard-core MAGA Republicans challenged the results. The challenge was led by Mo Brooks (Alabama), Ted Cruz (Texas), and Josh Hawley (Missouri). After the electoral votes from Alabama and Alaska were certified, they objected to the results from Arizona. At the same time of their challenge, however, an insurrection was occurring, forcing an emergency recess. When Congress returned, only six Senators voted to reject the Arizona electoral count (121 of the 302 members of the House voted the same).

Recognizing that his vice-president, whom Trump called a "wimp" and "pussy"[65] (and also "too honest"[66]) would not go along with the plan and that he would not have enough votes in Congress to block certification of electoral count, Trump proceeded with his final back-up plan: He incited a violent insurrection. Planned several weeks beforehand, with conservative radio hosts Steve Bannon, and Alex Jones, and others rallying to arms the Oathkeepers, Proud Boys, and other extremist groups to attend the January 6 "Stop the Steal" protest on the National Mall, Trump tweeted "Statistically impossible to have lost the 2020 Election … . Big protest in DC on January 6th. Be there, will be wild!"[67] After multiple speeches by Trump, Trump Jr., Bannon, Giuliani, MyPillow CEO Mike Lindell, and others, including several Republican members of Congress, claiming that Trump had won and that Pence and Congress were undermining democracy, Trump charged the crowd to descend on the Capitol. He was to lead the way, but the secret service prevented it out of fear for his safety. The rest is history. As the Capitol was attacked with insurrectionists yelling "Hang Pence," Trump watched on TV in the White House. He refused to intervene until after more than three hours of watching the insurrection play out. Upon recognizing that it had failed, he finally tweeted: "So, go home. We love you; you're very special."[68]

Notes

1 Grace Ashford, 2019. "Michael Cohen Says Trump Told Him to Threaten Schools Not to Release Grades." *The New York Times,* February 27. https://www. nytimes.com/2019/02/27/us/politics/trump-school-grades.html
2 Mary L. Trump, 2020. *Too Much and Never Enough: How My Family Created the World's Most Dangerous Man.* New York: Simon & Schuster.
3 Aaron Kupchik, James Highberger, and George G. Bear, 2022. "Identifying the Helpfulness of School Climate: Skipping School, Cheating on Tests, and Elements of School Climate." *Psychology in the Schools* 59 no. 8: 1538–1555. https://doi.org/10.1002/pits.22692

4 Michael D'Antonioo, 2016. *The Truth about Trump*. New York: Thomas Dunne Books, 40.

5 Ed Shanahan, 2020. "More Than 70 West Point Cadets Are Accused in Cheating Scandal." *The New York Times*, December 21. https://www.nytimes.com/2020/12/21/nyregion/west-point-cheating.html?auth=login-email&login=email

6 David Barstow, Susanne Craif, and Russ Buettner, 2018. "Trump Engaged in Suspect Tax Schemes as He Reaped Riches from His Father." *The New York Times*, October 2. https://www.nytimes.com/interactive/2018/10/02/us/politics/donald-trump-tax-schemes-fred-trump.html

7 Ibid.

8 Graham Kates, 2022. "Trump Organization Found Guilty on All Charges in Tax Fraud Trial in New York." *CBS News*, December 6. https://www.cbsnews.com/news/trump-organization-trial-verdict-tax-fraud-charges/

9 David Sirota and Lydia O'Neal, 2017. "Trump's Businesses Have a History of Money Laundering Charges." *International Business Times*, June 15. https://www.ibtimes.com/political-capital/trumps-businesses-have-history-money-laundering-charges-2552684

10 David C. Johnston, 2017. *The Making of Donald Trump*. Brooklyn, NY: Melville House.

11 Steve Reilly, 2018. "Hundreds Allege Donald Trump Doesn't Pay His Bills." *USA TODAY*, April 25. https://www.usatoday.com/story/news/politics/elections/2016/06/09/donald-trump-unpaid-bills-republican-president-laswuits/85297274/

12 David Goldman, Jeremy Herb, Jeanne Sahadi, and Maegan Vazquez, 2022. "Key Takeaways from Six Years on Donald Trump's Federal Tax Returns." *CNN*, December 30. https://www.cnn.com/2022/12/30/politics/donald-trump-tax-returns-released/index.html

13 David Taintor, 2021. "Mystery of $220,000 of Trump's Presidential Salary That He Promised to Donate but Disappeared." *The Independent*, July 30. https://www.independent.co.uk/news/world/americas/us-politics/trump-salary-donation-white-house-b1893787.html

14 David A. Fahrenhold and Joshua Partlow, 2019. "Trump Ordered to Pay $2 Million to Charities over Misuse of Foundation, Court Documents Say." *The Washington Post*, November 7. https://www.washingtonpost.com/politics/trump-ordered-to-pay-2-million-to-charities-over-misuse-of-foundation-court-documents-say/2019/11/07/b8f804e2-018e-11ea-9518-1e76abc088b6_story.html

15 Ibid.

16 David Goldman, Jeremy Herb, Jeanne Sahadi, and Maegan Vazquez, 2022. "Key Takeaways from Six Years of Donald Trump's Federal Tax Returns." December 30. https://www.cnn.com/2022/12/30/politics/donald-trump-tax-returns-released/index.html

17 Rick Reilly, 2019. *Commander in Cheat: How Golf Explains Trump*. New York: Hachette Books.

18 Kate Taylor, 2018. "Porn Star Stormy Daniels Is Taking a Victory Lap After Michael Cohen's Guilty Plea. Here's A Timeline of Trump's Many Marriages and Rumored Affairs." *Business Insider*, August 25. https://www.businessinsider.com/trump-melania-stormy-daniels-affairs-marriages-timeline-2018-3#melania-trump-is-not-the-presidents-first-wife-that-would-be-ivana-trump-who-married-donald-trump-then-a-young-real-estate-developer-in-1977-1

19 James D. Zirin, 2020. *Plaintiff in Chief: A Portrait of Donald Trump in 3,500 Lawsuits*. New York: All Points Book, 153.

20 Melina Delkic, 2018. "How Many Times Has Trump Cheated on His Wives? Here's What We Know." *Newsweek*, January 12. https://www.newsweek.com/how-many-times-trump-cheated-wives-780550

21 Jonah E. Bromwich, Ben Protess, William K. Rashbaum, and Michael Gold, 2023. "The Case against Donald Trump: What Comes Next?" *The New York Times*, April 5. https://www.nytimes.com/article/trump-indictment-criminal-charges.html

22 Michael Cohen, 2020. *Disloyal: A Memoir: The True Story of the Former Personal Attorney to President Donald J. Trump.* New York: Skyhorse Publishing.

23 Jessica Estepa, 2018. "Meet 19 Women Who Claim Affairs with Trump or Accuse Him of Unwanted Advances." *USA Today*, March 20. https://www.usatoday.com/story/news/politics/onpolitics/2018/03/20/meet-19-women-who-claim-affairs-trump-accuse-him-unwanted-advances/443685002/

24 Shayna Jacobs, Kim Bellware, and Mark Berman, 2023. "Jury in Civil Trial Finds Trump Sexually Abused, Defamed E. Jean Carroll." *The Washington Post*, May 9. https://www.washingtonpost.com/national-security/2023/05/09/e-jean-carroll-trump-jury/

25 Benjamin Weiser, 202. "Judge to Allow Trump's New Comments in Carroll Defamation Suit." *The New York Times*, June 13. https://www.nytimes.com/2023/06/13/us/politics/e-jean-carroll-trump-defamation-lawsuit.html

26 Reilly.

27 Reilly, 241.

28 Philip Rucker and Carol Leonnig, 2020. *A Very Stable Genius: Donald J. Trump's Testing of America.* New York: Penguin Press, 170.

29 Ciara Torres-Spelliscy, 2019. "Nepotism and the Impeachment Inquiry, Brennan Center for Justice." November 25. https://www.brennancenter.org/our-work/analysis-opinion/nepotism-and-impeachment-inquiry

30 Jesse Drucker, Kate Kelly, and Ben Protess, 2018. "Kushner's Family Business Received Loans after White House Meetings." *The New York Times*, February 28. https://www.nytimes.com/2018/02/28/business/jared-kushner-apollo-citigroup-loans.html

31 Jessica Kwong, 2019. "Jared Kushner Attending Saudi Conference Raises 'Red Flag' with Saudi Arabia in His Financial Disclosure: Ethics Experts." *Newsweek*, October 30. https://www.newsweek.com/jared-kushner-saudi-disclosure-ethics-1468809

32 David D. Kirkpatrick and Kate Kelly, 2022. "Before Giving Billions to Jared Kushner, Saudi Investment Fund Had Big Doubts." *The New York Times*, April 10. https://www.nytimes.com/2022/04/10/us/jared-kushner-saudi-investment-fund.html

33 Jean Eaglesham and Lisa Schwartz, 2017. "How Ivanka Trump Is a Walking Billboard for Her Namesake Fashion Business." *The Wall Street Journal*, December 27. https://www.wsj.com/articles/how-ivanka-trump-is-a-walking-billboard-for-her-namesake-fashion-business-1514389465

34 Richard Pérez-Peña and Rachel Abrams, 2017. "Kellyanne Conway Promotes Ivanka Trump Brand, Raising Ethics Concerns." *New York Times*, February 9. https://www.nytimes.com/2017/02/09/us/politics/kellyanne-conway-ivanka-trump-ethics.html

35 Andy Sullivan, Emily Stephenson, and Steve Holland, 2017. Trump Says Won't Divest His Business While President. *Reuters*, January 11. https://www.reuters.com/article/us-usa-trump-finance/trump-says-wont-divest-from-his-business-while-president-idUSKBN14V21I

36 Alex Altman, 2017. "Donald Trump's Suite of Power: How the President's D.C. Outpost Became a Dealmaker's Paradise for Diplomats, Lobbyists and Insiders." *Time*, June 8. https://time.com/donald-trumps-suite-of-power/

37 Eric Lipton, 2022. "Trump Settles Suit over Payments to Hotel for 2017 Inauguration." *The New York Times*, May 3. https://www.nytimes.com/2022/05/03/us/politics/trump-hotel-lawsuit-settlement.html

38 Liz Johnstone, 2017. "Tracking President Trump's Visits to Trump Properties." *NBC News*, December 29. https://www.nbcnews.com/politics/donald-trump/how-much-time-trump-spending-trump-properties-n753366

39 David A. Fahrenthold, Jonathan O'Connell, Carol D. Leonnig, and Josh Dawsey, 2020. "Secret Service Has Paid Rates as High as $650 a Night for Rooms at Trump's Properties." *The Washington Post,* February 7. https://www.washingtonpost.com/politics/secret-service-has-paid-rates-as-high-as-650-a-night-for-rooms-at-trumps-properties/

40 Gabriel Florit, Jonathan O'Connell, David A. Fahrenthold, and Teddy Amenabar, 2018. "Tracking Who Is Spending Money at President Trump's D.C. Hotel." *The Washington Post,* May 4. https://www.washingtonpost.com/graphics/2018/politics/trump-hotel-events/

41 Kate Bennett, 2020. "Trump Jr.'s Mongolian Sheep Hunting Trip Cost Taxpayers about $75,000, Documents Show." *CNN*, June 9. https://www.cnn.com/2020/06/09/politics/donald-trump-jr-mongolia-sheep-secret-service/index.html

42 Veronica Stracqualursi, 2020. Inexperience and Cronyism Slowed Kushner-led Efforts to Procure Medical Supplies. *CNN*, May 6. https://www.cnn.com/2020/05/06/politics/jared-kushner-white-house-volunteers-coronavirus/index.html

43 David Leonhardt and Ian Prasad Philbrick, 2018. Trump's Corruption: The Definitive List. *New York Times*, October 28. https://www.nytimes.com/2018/10/28/opinion/trump-administration-corruption-conflicts.html

44 Elizabeth Warren, 2020. *Lawlessness and Disorder: The Corrupt Trump Administration Has Made a Mockery of the Hatch Act.* Washington, DC: Office of Senator Elizabeth Warren. https://www.boston.com/wp-content/uploads/2020/10/Hatch-Act-Violations-by-Trump-Administration-Final.pdf

45 Ibid., 52.

46 Ibid., 52.

47 Ibid.

48 Ed Kilgore, 2022. "Trump's Long Campaign to Steal the Presidency: A Timeline." *New York Intelligencer*, July 14. https://nymag.com/intelligencer/article/trump-campaign-steal-presidency-timeline.html

49 Katelyn Polantz, 2021. "Judge Allows Defamation Lawsuits against Sidney Powell, Rudy Giuliani and MyPillow CEO to Go Forward." *CNN,* August 11. https://www.cnn.com/2021/08/11/politics/defamation-lawsuits-sidney-powell-rudy-giuliani-mike-lindell/index.html

50 Charles R. Davis, 2020. "Trump Campaign Purges Conspiracy-Theorist Sidney Powell from Legal Team." *Business Insider,* November 22. https://www.businessinsider.com/trump-campaign-purges-conspiracy-theorist-attorney-sidney-powell-2020-11

51 Casey Tolan, Curt Devine, and Drew Griffin, 2021. "MyPillow Magnate Mike Lindell's Latest Election Conspiracy Theory Is His Most Bizarre Yet." *CNN*, August 5. https://www.cnn.com/2021/08/05/politics/mike-lindell-mypillow-ceo-election-claims-invs/index.html

52 Michael Bender, 2021, *Frankly We Did Win This Election: The Inside Story of How Trump Lost.* New York: Twelve.

53 Jane C. Timm, 2023. "Dominion and Fox News Reach $787.5 Million Settlement in Defamation Lawsuit." *NBC News*, April 18. https://www.nbcnews.com/media/fox-news-settles-dominion-defamation-lawsuit-rcna80285

54 Ibid.

55 U.S. House of Representatives, Select Committee. to Investigate the January 6th Attack on the United Capitol, 2022. *Final Report of the Select Committee to*

Investigate the January 6th Attack on the United States Capitol. House Report 117-663, December 22. https://www.govinfo.gov/app/details/GPO-J6-REPORT/

56 United States District Court, District of Columbia, 2023. United States of America v. Donald J. Trump. Retrieved August 2, 2023 from https://www.justice.gov/storage/US_v_Trump_23_cr_257.pdf

57 Alan Feuer, Maggie Haberman, Michael S. Schmidt, and Luke Broadwater, 2022. "Trump Had Role in Weighing Proposals to Seize Voting Machines." *The New York Times*, January 31. https://www.nytimes.com/2022/01/31/us/politics/donald-trump-election-results-fraud-voting-machines.html

58 Michael Flynn was a client of Powell's law firm. Intriguingly, Powell met with Trump, requesting that Flynn be pardoned for lying to the FBI in Trump's first impeachment (which Flynn admitted, and was to serve time in prison). Shortly after Trump pardoned Flynn, Powell filed lawsuits challenging the election results.

59 Amy Gardner, 2021. "I Just Want to Find 11,780 Votes": In Extraordinary Hour-Long Call, Trump Pressures Georgia Secretary of State to Recalculate the Vote in His Favor." *The Washington Post*, January 3. https://www.washingtonpost.com/politics/trump-raffensperger-call-georgia-vote/2021/01/03/d45acb92-4dc4-11eb-bda4-615aaefd0555_story.html

60 Fulton County Superior Court, 2023. The State of Georgia v. Donald John [and 18 others], 14. Retrieved August 15, 2023 from https://www.washingtonpost.com/documents/1ccdf52e-1ba2-434c-93f8-2a7020293967.pdf?itid=lk_inline_manual_5

61 Kate Brumback, 2023. "Sidney Powell Pleads Guilty Over Efforts to Overturn Trump's Loss in Georgia and Agrees to Cooperate." *The Washington Post*, October 19. https://www.washingtonpost.com/politics/2023/10/19/sidney-powell-plea-deal-georgia-election-indictment/b9191478-6e88-11ee-b01a-f593caa04363_story.html

62 U.S. House of Representatives, Select Committee, 386.

63 Ibid., 102.

64 Ibid., 31–32.

65 Ibid., 458, 489.

66 United States District Court, 33.

67 Ibid., 499.

68 Ibid., 92.

6   Bullying

Bullying and School Shootings

Bullying is not new in schools or elsewhere in society, but during the past several decades it has captured increased attention among parents, educators, and the general public. School shootings, such as at Columbine High School in 1999 where 12 students and one teacher were killed, awakened the American public to issues of bullying and school safety. The primary suspected motive of the two high school shooters at Columbine was their revenge for having experienced vicious bullying from their classmates. They were called "faggots," laughed at, and physically harassed. Columbine students and their parents described the school as one where bullying was the norm. It soon became evident to many parents in the United States, and around the world, that Columbine was not alone in having a school climate in which bullying was common, and that their children could become victims too of bullying and school shootings.

Sadly, school shootings have continued, with a record number occurring in 2022; 51 school shootings, resulting in 100 people injured and 40 people killed (32 students or other children).[1] As seen later in this chapter, bullying continues to be a major factor in school shootings, with victims of bullying often seeking revenge. In addition to school shootings, bullying via electronic devices, or cyberbullying, has garnered much attention during the past decade, with cyberbullying triggering suicides among victims of vicious bullying. Indeed, "online safety," which focused largely on cyberbullying, was one of the three main "pillars" of First Lady Melania Trump's BE BEST campaign, with the "goal of encouraging children to BE BEST in their individual paths, while also teaching them the importance of social, emotional, and physical health." As was noted on Melania Trump's BeBest website, and with respect to cyberbullying, "Mrs. Trump believes that children should be both seen and heard, and it is our responsibility as adults to educate and reinforce to them that when they are using their voices—whether verbally or online—they must choose their words wisely and speak with respect and compassion."[2] The extent to which her husband, Donald Trump, has heeded her advice is the focus of the next chapter. This chapter focuses on

DOI: 10.4324/9781003401278-6

the different aspects and types of bullying, the harm bullying causes, warning signs of victimization and bullying, and risk factors associated with being either a victim or a bully.

Four Aspects of Bullying

The United States Department of Education defines bullying as "unwanted, aggressive behavior among school aged children that involves a real or perceived power imbalance. The behavior is repeated, or has the potential to be repeated, over time."[3] As found in most other definitions of bullying, this definition highlights three key aspects of bullying: (1) the behavior is aggressive and unwanted; (2) the behavior is repeated over time, and (3) an imbalance of power exists, which can be real or perceived as real by the victim. Let's look at each of these.

First, bullying is a *form of aggression,* and more specifically *aggression that is unwanted.* Bullying and aggression are not necessarily one and the same. The key difference is whether the person on the receiving end of an act of aggression invites the aggression or otherwise is okay with it. To constitute bullying, the aggression must be unwanted. Not all aggression is unwanted, with prime examples being aggression in many sports such as football, soccer, and especially boxing and wrestling. Aggression that is not bullying also is seen when two children get into a physical fight or exchange verbal insults when both are willing participants.

The second key aspect of bullying is *repetition.* Bullies repeat their unwanted acts of aggression, establishing histories of inflecting unwanted psychological or physical harm on others.

The third aspect of bullying is an *imbalance of power,* either real or perceived to be real by the victim. This aspect of bullying is not always as clear as the previous two. Physical size is likely to first come to mind when thinking of an imbalance of power: Bullies are generally bigger and stronger than their victims. To be sure, physical size often characterizes an imbalance of power, but there are other common sources. Primary among them are wealth, social power, position of authority, and power via access and control of information. Wealth can be used against the less wealthy to bully and punish, such as using one's wealth to sue others to get what one wants or out of spite. Likewise, a position of authority provides a powerful means of bullying others, such as forcing them to perform the least desired tasks and firing them for spiteful reasons. Social power is seen in snubbing or excluding classmates or coworkers and telling others to do the same. Social power becomes particularly influential during adolescence when the importance of peer approval peaks.

Finally, greater access and control of information as a source of an imbalance of power is commonly seen in cyberbullying. It occurs when the bully has greater access to various forms of media or greater skills in using media to harm others. A victim of verbal bullying is at a major disadvantage when the bully has many more followers on Facebook, Instagram, or *X*

(the social media platform previously called Twitter) or is skilled in manipulating video and uses those sources and skills to spew insults. This source of
imbalance of power is also seen when the bully literally controls the bully
pulpit such as insulting others while speaking at the podium. This is especially
true when the targets of bullying are not present, have no opportunity to
respond, or risk being verbally insulted by the speaker and ostracized by others
if they do respond.

Oddly, the Department of Education's definition lacks a fourth aspect of
bullying widely recognized by most researchers and experts on bullying:
intentionality. This is likely because intentions are difficult to determine,
especially given that many bullies lie about their intentions, often claiming
they did not mean to hurt the victim. Nevertheless, intentionality is commonly viewed as a core aspect of bullying and thus included in most definitions. Accordingly, for an action to constitute bullying it must be intentional,
with the intention being to inflict physical, psychological, or social harm. This
excludes actions that are accidental or impulsive. For example, a student
accidentally bumping into another in the hallway is not bullying, and neither
is impulsively blurting out in anger to someone "you're stupid," even if it
makes that person cry.

The criterion of intentionality is especially important when it comes to
teasing. Far too often children are accused of bullying others when they are
caught teasing. Teasing can be a form of bullying, but often teasing and
bullying are not one and the same. Teasing is not bullying when two classmates joke and tease about what each other is wearing, what grade they got,
how they played in a game, etc., *unless* the teasing hurts, is intended to hurt,
and is repeated over time (and especially when repeated after the victim tells
the bully to stop the teasing or shows that the teasing hurts).

In sum, to be considered bullying an aggressive act must be unwanted,
repeated over time, intentional, and occur in the context of an imbalance of
power. Unless all four criteria are met, the behavior should not be considered
bullying. By applying those criteria, many occurrences of fighting, social
rejection, and especially teasing are not bullying. Sure, they are hurtful and
still wrong (and thus should be corrected), but they should not result in the
culprit being labeled a bully.

Three Types of Bullying

Three types of bullying are widely recognized by most educators and researchers: physical, verbal, and social. Whereas behaviors constituting physical
and verbal bullying are rather obvious, those constituting social bullying are
often overlooked as forms of bullying. *Physical bullying* refers to such
behaviors as hitting, kicking, pushing, tripping, making rude hand gestures,
spitting, and stealing or breaking others' belongings. It also includes threats of
any of those behaviors, although some researchers include threats as a type of
verbal bullying. *Verbal bullying* consists of attacks by words such as teasing,

name-calling, saying hurtful or mean things, threatening, taunting, and making inappropriate sexual comments. *Social bullying*, also called relational or social/relational bullying, refers to behaviors that cause, or threaten to cause, damage to relationships with peers such as excluding others, spreading rumors about others, embarrassing others publicly, and telling others not to be friends with or to be mean toward someone.

Cyberbullying is often presented as another type of bullying. Cyberbullying refers to the use of digital devices such as computers, tablets, and cell phones to send mean or hurtful messages about others or to post them on social media (e.g., via X, Facebook, Instagram, Snapchat), in forums, and in gaming. Not all experts on bullying agree that cyberbullying is a distinct type of bullying. Instead, many view cyberbullying as the *means* (i.e., electronically) of engaging in verbal, physical, and social bullying. As such, they would view using social media to send hurtful messages as verbal bullying. Likewise, threatening others physically on social media would be viewed as physical bullying, and spreading rumors about others on social media would be considered social bullying. This is how cyberbullying is viewed in this book—as a means of bullying others and not as a distinct type of bullying.

About One in Five Children Are Bullied

Estimates of bullying vary greatly and depend largely on how bullying is defined and measured.[4] Nevertheless, national surveys indicate that about 20% of students ages 12 to 18 report having been bullied at least once during the school year.[5] Verbal bullying is most common, with 13% of students reporting being made fun of, called names, or insulted (10% of boys, 16% of girls). With respect to physical bullying, 5% report being pushed, shoved, tripped, or spit on (6% boys, 4% girls) and 4% report being threatened with harm (4% for boys and girls). For social bullying, 13% report being the subject of rumors (9% boys, 18% girls), and 5% report being excluded from activities on purpose (4% boys, 7% girls). As can be seen in those percentages, girls tend to experience greater verbal and social bullying than boys, whereas boys tend to experience greater physical bullying. Nevertheless, both sexes are victims of each type of bullying.

Where is bullying most likely to occur in school? Of the 20% of students who reported being bullied, 43% reporting that it occurred in the hallway or stairwell, 42% inside the classroom, 27% in the cafeteria, 22% outside on school grounds, 15% online or via text messaging, 12% in the bathroom or locker room, 8% on the school bus, and 2% somewhere else in the school building.

It Hurts, and More

At some point in childhood, nearly everyone is teased and called names, and some are truly bullied. For most victims, psychological harm is short-lived.

For others, however, the effects are much more damning and lasting. Children who are bullied are at increased risk of a host of negative outcomes, including headaches, stomach pain, sleeping problems, lower self-esteem, anxiety, depression, loneliness, and skipping school.[6] Whether operating alone or in combination, with the latter being more often the case, each of those negative outcomes places victims of bullying at additional risk of being rejected by peers and declining academic engagement.[7] In turn, those two negative outcomes place victims at greater risk for further bullying. This is especially the case when the victims lack social support from peers, teachers, and the home.[8] When the negative emotional, physical, and social effects of bullying spiral and exist over time, the risks increase for greater social and emotional problems, including delinquent behaviors (e.g., physical fighting, stealing, vandalism), substance use, self-injury, suicide, and bringing a weapon to school.[9]

Bullying harms not only victims and perpetrators, but also those who are involved indirectly and witness the bullying. In school, bystanders of bullying are at increased risks for many of the same emotional, social, and physical problems, as listed above, that are experienced by victims of bullying. This includes anxiety, depression, psychosomatic symptoms, hostility, paranoid ideation, substance use, and skipping school.[10]

The perpetrators of bullying (i.e., the bullies) also experience a host of negative outcomes, with many of them being the same as those experienced by their victims and witnesses. Bullies are at increased risk for anxiety and depression; psychosomatic symptoms; suicide ideation and attempts; delinquency, substance abuse, and criminality; less school bonding, or connectedness; and poorer academic engagement and achievement.[11] Perpetrators of bullying are particularly at risk for those negative outcomes if they are the victims of bullying themselves, which is often the case.

Finally, bullying creates a negative environment for learning and development, whether it is in the classroom, school, home, or workplace. This is especially true when bullying is pervasive and normative. For example, in classrooms and schools where it is normative, students and teachers alike report poor teacher-student, student-student, and home-school relationships; increased worries among students and staff about school safety; and less overall student engagement.[12]

Warning Signs of Bullying

What are the signs that a child is being bullied? The U.S. Department of Education's website www.stopbullying.gov gives the following warning signs (it also gives ways to help stop the bullying):[13]

- Unexplainable injuries;
- Lost or destroyed clothing, books, electronics, or jewelry;
- Frequent headaches or stomach aches, feeling sick or faking illness;

- Changes in eating habits, like suddenly skipping meals or binge eating. Kids may come home from school hungry because they did not eat lunch;
- Difficulty sleeping or frequent nightmares;
- Declining grades, loss of interest in schoolwork, or not wanting to go to school;
- Sudden loss of friends or avoidance of social situations;
- Feelings of helplessness or decreased self-esteem;
- Self-destructive behaviors such as running away from home, harming themselves, or talking about suicide.

Parents should be concerned if their child exhibits one or more of the above signs of bullying. When observed, parents should discuss with their child what is causing the behavior and what might be done to address it. Depending on the situation and severity of the behavior, this may entail seeking support from teachers and staff at school, counseling, or talking to the parents of the bully. (The latter is recommended in cases in which the bullying is *not* occurring in school. If it is occurring in school, it's best to let the school handle it, while keeping parents informed.)

Signs That A Child Might Be a Bully

In addition to giving warning signs that a child is being bullied, and drawing from research on the topic, the Stopbullying.gov website gives the following signs that a child is bullying others.

- Gets into physical or verbal fights;
- Has friends who bully others;
- Is increasingly aggressive;
- Is sent to the principal's office or to detention frequently;
- Has unexplained extra money or new belongings;
- Blames others, or otherwise doesn't accept responsibility for his or her actions;
- Is competitive and worries about his or her reputation or popularity.

A parent should be concerned if their child exhibits behavioral signs above, especially if they are seen often and are resistant to attempts to stop them. That is, of particular concern is when bullying behaviors continue despite age-appropriate disciplinary practices commonly found to be effective as discussed in Chapter 13 (e.g., practices found in authoritative parenting).

A Child Is More Likely to Be Bullied If ...

As with lying and cheating, whether a child is a victim or perpetrator of bullying is a product of a combination and interaction of multiple individual and environmental factors. Certain characteristics of individual children, as described below, increase the odds of a child being a victim or perpetrator. Individual differences largely explain why children in the same classroom or home have entirely different experiences with respect to bullying: why some are victims, some are bullies, and others are witnesses or bystanders who may or may not intervene. Individual and environmental characteristics shown to increase or decrease the risk of bullying follow.

Individual Child Characteristics

Of the Victim

Children are at increased risk of being bullied if they are perceived by their peers as different, or deviant. For example, children experience greater bullying if they have physical features perceived as different from peers (e.g., being overweight or underweight, being smaller or younger in their class, dressing differently than peers);[14] if their sexual orientation is lesbian, gay, bisexual, transgender, or questioning;[15] and if they have a disability.[16] Personality and behavior also play a major role in bullying victimization: Bullies tend to pick on those who are lacking in social skills. Victims tend to be submissive, socially anxious, and lacking in assertiveness; annoying and provoking to their peers; or those who fail to regulate their emotions effectively when teased, excluded, or threatened.[17] The failure to regulate emotions is seen in the victim either withdrawing and crying or exploding in anger—responses that reinforce the bullying by conveying to the bully that their behavior is effective in controlling others, or otherwise getting what the bully wants.

None of the individual characteristics above dictates that a child will necessarily be a victim of bullying. However, each characteristic increases the risk of being bullied, and the risk increases with each increase in the number of factors. For example, children with disabilities are at risk of being bullied, especially those who lack social skills and disrupt the learning of others. Those characteristics are commonly found among children with certain disabilities more so than other disabilities such as children with emotional disabilities (e.g., conduct disorder, oppositional defiant disorder, anxiety disorder, depression), autism spectrum disorder, and attention deficit hyperactivity disorder (ADHD).[18]

As one might expect, just as there are certain individual characteristics that increase the risks of being bullied there also are individual characteristics that help *protect* children from bullying. Many are simply the opposite of the risk factors. Indeed, the strongest protection against bullying and its negative effects are children's social and emotional competencies. Children are less likely to be bullied if they have good social skills. Particularly instrumental in preventing bullying and lessening any negative impact when bullying occurs is the ability to avoid and negotiate situations of potential conflict and disagreement with peers and the ability to control one's emotions.[19] When bullied, victims experience fewer and less lasting negative effects if they possess and apply effective social problem-solving and coping strategies such as seeking support from close friends, peers, teachers, and parents.[20] The negative impact of bullying also is less among those who view themselves positively, as seen in high self-esteem and self-confidence.[21]

Of the Bully

Less is known about individual characteristics of bullies than about victims, particularly what contributes to or explains a bully's proclivity for hurting others. It is known, however, that bullies tend to differ from others in behavior other than their bullying per se and in how they think and feel about their behavior. Bullying others is not the only behavior problem found among many bullies. Bullies tend to have other conduct problems—conduct problems that frequently lead to peer rejection. Common among them are forms of aggression other than bullying, acts of dishonesty (e.g., lying and cheating), and disobedience of rules and laws that they perceive as restricting them from doing what they want. Not all bullies, however, have behavior problems that typically lead to peer rejection. This might explain why many bullies are not rejected by their peers and remain popular despite their bullying.[22] Popularity of bullies is especially found in middle school and high school. Readers might recall bullies during their adolescence who were perhaps the most athletic, the most attractive, the wealthiest, and the most charming—those who possessed highly valued characteristics that made others overlook their bullying, especially their bullying of victims that they disliked or were not their friends.

As noted in previous chapters, many of the same social cognitive and emotional processes that underlie lying and cheating (and narcissism) underlie bullying and other antisocial behaviors, including executive functioning and social perspective-taking skills. And as also noted previously, and discussed more thoroughly in Chapter 10, bullies, liars, cheaters, and narcissists have in common self-centered, hedonistic moral reasoning; the lack of empathy, guilt, and shame; and the frequent use of various mechanisms of moral disengagement. Whereas those characteristics foster bullying, their opposites serve as protective factors against bullying perpetration.[23]

Role of Genetics in Bullying

Being either a bully or a victim of bullying has a genetic basis.[24] In a national study of 1,116 families with ten-year twins, Dr. Harriet Ball and colleagues found that genetic factors explained 61% of the variation in bullying and 73% of the variation in victimization (the remainder was explained by non-shared environmental factors such as different parenting and friends). The finding that bullying has a genetic basis is consistent with research reported earlier in Chapter 2 showing that genetics account for 65% of the variance in aggressive antisocial behavior. Finding that both bullying and bullying victimization have a genetic basis makes sense in light of research linking genetics to multiple individual characteristics noted above, ranging from physical features (e.g., size, shape, disability) to personality characteristics(e.g., impulsivity, lack of emotion regulation, proneness to anxiety), shown to be associated with bullying and its impact on victims.

Clearly, some individual characteristics are more genetically determined, and thus less malleable than others. As such, parents of children with physical and intellectual disabilities are greatly limited in changing characteristics within their children that make them more susceptible to bullying. Not only are those parents greatly limited in changing physical features, but many also are more limited in developing social and emotional skills that will help their children avoid bullying and respond and cope effectively when bullying occurs. Likewise, with respect to bullying, the odds of a child being a bully are greater when genetically wired to be physically large, impulsive, aggressive, and lacking in empathy. Having a child with those traits increases the odds, especially if the parents are overly harsh or overly permissive and indulgent, as discussed next. In sum, with respect to developing individual characteristics associated with bullying, genetics can make it more or less likely that a child will become a victim or perpetrator. However, as emphasized below, the greater determinant of being either a victim or perpetrator of bullying is a child's environment, which includes factors at school and home (especially parenting).

Characteristics of the Child's Environment

Regardless of children's genetic makeup and individual characteristics, the environment is greatly influential in determining the extent to which children not only learn many characteristics that either promote or deter bullying victimization and perpetration, but also the extent to which those characteristics are expressed. Primary among those environmental factors are the home, and especially parenting, and the school.

Of the Home and Parenting

Bullying is a learned behavior, often taught at home by parents, siblings, and others. As with aggression and violence, basic principles of social learning largely explain how parents teach bullying to their children. Quite simply, children watch others engage in verbal, physical, social, and cyberbullying and do the same. They are especially likely to copy the behavior of those they look up to and admire, such as parents, siblings, popular peers, star athletes, and media celebrities. Upon observing that bullying works, they try it themselves. If it works for them too (i.e., the behavior is reinforced and not punished), they are on their way to becoming a bully. The reinforcer might be tangible, such as the money or item taken from a victim, or it might be a self-fulfilling sense of power, dominance, and control over others.

Bullies tend to have parents who are bullies themselves and who fail to develop social and emotional competencies in their children that help deter bullying. Parents of bullies tend to be aggressive, overly harsh and controlling, rejecting, and derisive (i.e., demeaning and belittling), and lacking in warmth, understanding, and support.[25] As such, with high demandingness and low responsiveness, they best fit the authoritarian style of parenting. In homes with authoritarian parenting, bullies observe and learn the skills of effective bullying. Perhaps of equal importance is what they *fail* to learn. They fail to learn the forms of moral reasoning, moral emotions, problem-solving, and social skills (e.g., conflict resolution, anger management, coping skills) commonly found among non-bullies.

Not all parents of bullies are authoritarian; some are permissive or disengaged.[26] Instead of being overly punitive, harsh, and lacking in warmth and responsiveness, permissive parents tend to be low in demandingness and are non-punitive. Believing their children can do no harm, they set few restrictions and are overly protective. They are always there to comfort and protect them—either from other bullies or from the consequences of their engaging in bullying (e.g., when caught bullying, the parents join their bullying child in blaming the victim or otherwise in justifying the behavior). As with permissive parents, disengaged parents set few restrictions and fail to correct misbehavior, but in contrast to permissive parents they also fail to provide for their children's psychological needs, including the need for warmth and support. Interestingly, both the permissive and disengaged parenting styles are associated with greater bullying *and* victimization. This makes sense when one stops and thinks about the likely consequences of being raised by parents who fail to correct misbehavior, including bullying, and who coddle or otherwise fail to teach their children social and emotional competencies that help protect them from bullying and to cope with bullying when it occurs.

Not all children of authoritarian, permissive, and disengaged parents become bullies or victims. The majority do not. Those styles of parenting simply place children at greater risk of being bullies, victims, or both. Fortunately, children are resilient, and the effects of even poor parenting can be offset by various protective individual child and environmental factors. For example, children of authoritarian, permissive, or disengaged parents may learn from others the social and emotional competencies that help prevent them from being bullies or victims; spend most of their time in environments in which bullying rarely if ever occurs (and is stifled immediately when it does); or choose not to act like their parents and others who model or otherwise foster bullying and victimization.

Children are less likely to be perpetrators or victims of bullying in homes characterized by the authoritative style of parenting.[27] Authoritative parents set high behavioral expectations, closely monitor their children's behavior, and are quick to reinforce prosocial behavior and correct antisocial behavior. They provide the guidance and support needed for their children to develop the broad range of social and emotional competencies that promote prosocial behavior, inhibit antisocial behavior, and are associated with positive mental health. In providing their children with needed comfort and support when they are the targets of bullying, they help prevent internalizing problems such as depression.[28]

Of the School

As with the home, the school environment is greatly influential in bullying. Teachers replace parents and classmates replace siblings as either models and promoters of bullying or as deterrents to bullying and sources of support to victims when bullying occurs. Research shows that bullying is much less likely to occur in schools characterized by a positive school climate. Key aspects of a positive school climate are supportive and respectful relationships between teachers and students and between students—positive relationships that establish norms that prevent bullying and that support victims when bullying occurs. When students view their teachers and classmates favorably, and understand that others support them, they are less likely to engage in bullying; they respond and cope more effectively when bullied; and they intervene against bullying when they witness it.[29] Research also shows that less bullying occurs in classrooms and schools in which teachers and staff are characterized by the authoritative (not authoritarian) approach to classroom management and school discipline.[30] Teachers, administrators, and staff work hard to prevent bullying by developing positive relationships with students and among students and by developing their social and emotional competences. They make it clear that bullying is unacceptable, and are attuned to peer interactions that foster it. They monitor and supervise students accordingly, especially in locations where bullying most often occurs, such as the playground and cafeteria, and respond immediately and effectively to all forms of bullying.

In schools that are most effective in preventing bullying, students are taught the signs of bullying and to either wisely try to stop it or to report it.[31] Teaching and encouraging students to report peers they suspect might be planning to harm others is widely recognized as the most effective way of preventing school shootings.[32] Students who know or suspect that a classmate plans to shoot someone, and who report it, prevent more shootings than do school resource officers, metal detectors, surveillance cameras, the fear of suspension/expulsion, and many bully prevention programs. Unfortunately, many children, especially after early elementary school, do not inform their teachers when they are bullied. Victims also are reluctant to inform their parents. They feel too embarrassed or ashamed, fear retaliation and further bullying, or think that nothing will or can be done to stop the bullying.[33] Thus, too often bullying is discovered only after friends or classmates of the victim notice and report it, typically to a teacher, school nurse, or school administrator. In most school shootings, and with many suicides, at least one classmate knew about the active violence ahead of time but failed to inform an adult.[34] Students are much more likely to report bullying and potential threats of violence in schools where they are strongly encouraged to do so and where students believe adults will support them and take action to stop or prevent harmful behavior.[35]

Should You Worry If a Child Is a Victim or a Bully?

If you know of a child who is a victim or perpetrator of bullying, the negative outcomes above are not meant to scare you. Although being bullied increases the risk of negative outcomes, those outcomes are not found among most victims and perpetrators of bullying, especially the most serious negative outcomes of suicide and school shootings (although the news coverage of bullying, suicide, and school shootings might make you believe otherwise). The vast majority of victims and bullies do not attempt suicide, bring a gun to school, shoot others, abuse substances, or engage in delinquent behaviors. Thus, whether a child is a victim or perpetrator of bullying, generally there is little need to worry about those serious outcomes.

However, one should be concerned when multiple risk factors associated with being bullied or being a bully exist, especially when a child shows multiple signs, or symptoms, listed earlier of victimization and bullying. This includes being concerned about the potential of suicide or a shooting when multiple risk factors are present. Risk factors shared by both of those tragic outcomes are depression, social withdrawal, family history of mental health problems (especially a family history of depression in cases of suicide and of violent behavior in school shootings), stress factors at home (e.g., experiencing emotional or physical abuse), peer rejection, declining grades, exposure to suicidal or violent behavior, poor problem-solving and coping skills, the availability of means to commit either suicide or a school shooting (e.g., access to guns at home), and the lack of social support networks. In general, as the number of risk factors increases so too does the likelihood of suicide and a school shooting.

In addition to risk factors listed above, other factors are more specific to either suicide or school shootings. More specific to suicide are having a previous history of self-harm, suicidal threats, and suicidal attempts; the death of an important family member; substance abuse (particularly alcohol in male adolescents); perfectionism; and being an adolescent with a sexual orientation of lesbian, gay, bisexual, or transgender. Those are critical risk factors for suicide, irrespective of bullying. Indeed, bullying is seldom the primary cause of suicides. However, when bullying co-exists with additional risk factors, the likelihood of depression and suicidal attempts is much greater.

Although school shootings are rarer than suicides, bullying plays a predominant role in many school shootings. An extensive study of school shooters conducted by the United States Secret Service found that being a victim of bullying was one of the most common characteristics shared by school shooters.[36] Among the school shooters studied, 80% had been bullied by their classmates, with more than half of them being victims of persistent bullying. Additional characteristics of school shooters were a school history of disciplinary problems, an interest in violent topics (including weapons), intense or escalating anger, expressed grievance toward the target, and previously threatening or intending to attack the target of the shooting or others. Social stressors at school, such as rejection by peers, rejection in romantic relationships, and especially for bullying, also were found to be risk factors.

Interestingly, the Secret Service study found that many school shooters had a narcissistic personality. They had inflated self-esteem and a sense of superiority and were lacking in empathy and remorse. They also were prone to lying, manipulation, and a disregard for rules. By noting that many school shooters are narcissists is not meant to imply that narcissistic children become school shooters. The odds of that happening are very slim. Although most school shooters are narcissists, most narcissists are not bullies and extremely few are school shooters. As seen in Chapter 9, rather than shooting someone, narcissists are much more likely to brag about being able to do so if they want, and to get away with it, such as shooting someone in the middle of Fifth Avenue without harming their reputation.

Notes

1 Evie Blad, Laura Baker, Hyon-Young Kim, and Holly Peele, 2023. "School Shootings in 2022: 4 Key Takeaways." *Education Week*, January 27. https://www.edweek.org/leadership/school-shootings-in-2022-4-key-takeaways/2022/12

2 "Be Best: First Lady Melania Trump's Initiative." Retrieved May 21, 2023 from https://trumpwhitehouse.archives.gov/bebest/

3 Stopbullying.gov (n.d.). "What Is Bullying?" Retrieved March 28, 2023 from https://www.stopbullying.gov/bullying/what-is-bullying

4 George G. Bear, Lindsey Mantz, Joseph Glutting, Chunyan Yang, and Deborah Boyer, 2015. "Differences in Bullying Victimization Between Students with and without Disabilities." *School Psychology Review* 44 no. 1: 98–116. https://doi.org/10.17105/SPR44-1.98-116

5 National Center for Education Statistics, 2022. "Bullying at School and Electronic Bullying. *Condition of Education*. U.S. Department of Education, Institute of Education Sciences." Retrieved April 30, 2023, from https://nces.ed.gov/programs/coe/indicator/a10

6 Gianluca Gini, 2008. "Associations between Bullying Behavior, Psychosomatic Complaints, Emotional and Behavioral Problems." *Journal of Pediatrics and Child Health* 44 no. 3: 492–497. https://doi.org/10.1111/j.1440-1754.2007.01155.x

7 Sandra Y. Rueger and Lyndsay N. Jenkins, 2014. "Effects of Peer Victimization on Psychological and Academic Adjustment in Early Adolescence." *School Psychology Quarterly* 29 no. 1: 77–88. https://doi:10.1037/spq0000036

8 Albert Reijntjes, Jan H. Kamphuis, Peter Prinzie & Michael J. Telch, 2010. "Peer Victimization and Internalizing Problems in Children: A Meta-Analysis of Longitudinal Studies." *Child Abuse & Neglect* 34 no. 4: 244–252. https://doi.org/10.1016/j.chiabu.2009.07.009

9 Leanne Lester, Donna Cross, and Therese Shaw, 2012. Problem Behaviors, Traditional Bullying, and Cyberbullying Among Adolescents: Longitudinal Analyses. *Emotional and Behavioral Difficulties* 17 no. 3–4: 435–447. https://doi.org/10.1080/13632752.2012.704313

   Jessica A. Heerde and Sheryl A. Hemphill, 2018. "Are Bullying Perpetration and Victimization Associated with Adolescent Deliberate Self-Harm? A Meta-Analysis." *Archives of Suicide Research* 23 no. 3: 353–381. https://doi.org/10.1080/13811118.2018.1472690

10 Ian Rivers, Paul V. Poteat, Nathalie Noret, and Nigel Ashurst, 2009. "Observing Bullying at School: The Mental Health Implications of Witness Status." *School Psychology Quarterly* 24 no. 4: 211–223. https://psycnet.apa.org/doi/10.1037/a0018164

11 Bear, G. G. (2020). *Improving School Climate: Practical Strategies to Reduce Behavior Problems and Promote Social-Emotional Learning.* New York: Taylor & Francis.

12 Ibid.

13 Signs a Child is Bullying. Retrieved March 29, 2023 from https://www.stopbullying.gov/bullying/warning-signs

14 Moja Kljakovic and Caroline Hunt, 2016. "A Meta-Analysis of Predictors of Bullying and Victimisation in Adolescence." *Journal of Adolescence* 49: 134–145. https://doi: 10.1016/j.adolescence.2016.03.002

   Xi Ma, 2002. "Bullying in Middle School: Individual and School Characteristics of Victims and Offenders." *School Effectiveness and School Improvement* 13 no. 1: 63–89. https://doi.org/10.1076/sesi.13.1.63.3438

15 Michelle Birkett, Dorothy L. Espelage, and Brian Koenig, 2009. "LGB and Questioning Students in Schools: The Moderating Effects of Homophobic Bullying and School Climate on Negative Outcomes." *Journal of Youth and Adolescence* 38 no. 7: 989–1000. https://doi.org/10.1007/s10964-008-9389-1

16 Bear, 2020.

17 Filippos Analitis, Mariska Klein Velderman, Ulrike Ravens-Sieberer, Symone Detmar, Michael Erhart, Mike Herdman, Silvina Berra, Jordi Alonso, and Luis Rajmil; European Kidscreen Group, 2009. "Being Bullied: Associated Factors in Children and Adolescents 8 to 18 Years Old in 11 European Countries." *Pediatrics* 123 no. 2: 569–77. https://doi.org/10.1542/peds.2008-0323

   Silja Saarento, Antti Karna, and Ernest V. E. Hodges, 2013. "Student-, Classroom-, and School-Level Risk Factors for Victimization." *Journal of School Psychology* 51 no. 3: 421–434. https://doi.org/10.1016/j.jsp.2013.02.002

18 Bear et al., 2015.

19 Jun Sung Hong, Dorothy L. Espelage, Andrew Grogan-Kaylor, and Paula Allen-Meares, 2012. "Identifying Potential Mediators and Moderators of the Association between Child Maltreatment and Bullying Perpetration and Victimization in School." *Educational Psychology Review* 24 no. 2: 167–186. https://doi.org/10.1007/s10648-011-9185-4

20 Becky Kochenderfer-Ladd and Karey Skinner, 2002. "Children's Coping Strategies: Moderators of the Effects of Peer Victimization?" *Developmental Psychology* 38 no. 2: 267–278. https://doi.org/10.1037/0012-1649.38.2.267

21 Mitch van Geel, Anouk Goemans, Wendy Zwaanswijk, and Kini Gianluca, 2018. "Does Peer Victimization Predict Low Self-Esteem, or Does Low Self-Esteem

Predict Peer Victimization? Meta-Analyses on Longitudinal Studies." *Developmental Review* 49: 31–40. https://doi.org:10.1016/j.dr.2018.07.001

22 Amanda L. Duffy, Sarah Penn, Drew Nesdale, and Melanie J. Zimmer-Gembeck, 2017. "Popularity: Does It Magnify Associations between Popularity Prioritization and the Bullying and Defending Behavior of Early Adolescent Boys and Girls?" *Social Development* 26, no. 2: 263–277. https://onlinelibrary.wiley.com/doi/abs/10.1111/sode.12206

23 Izabela Zych, Maria M. Ttofi, Vicente J. Llorent, David P. Farrington, Denis Ribeaud, and Manuel P. Eisner, 2018. "Longitudinal Study on Stability and Transitions among Bullying Roles." *Child Development* 91 no. 2: 527–545. https://doi.org/10.1111/cdev.13195

24 Harriet A. Ball, Louise Arseneault, Alan Taylor, Barbara Maughan, Avshalom Caspi, and Terrie E. Moffitt, 2008. "Genetic and Environmental Influences on Victims, Bullies and Bully-Victims in Childhood. "*Journal of Child Psychology and Psychiatry* 49 no. 1:104–112. https://doi.org/10.1111/j.1469-7610.2 007.01821.x

25 Kyriakos Charalampous, Constantina Demetriou, Loukia Tricha, Myria Ioannou, Stelios Georgiou, Militsa Nikiforou, and Panayiotis Stavrinides, 2018. "The Effect of Parental Style on Bullying and Cyber Bullying Behaviors and the Mediating Role of Peer Attachment Relationships: A Longitudinal Study." *Journal of Adolescence*, 64 no. 1: 109–123. https://doi.org/10.1016/j.adolescence. 2018.02.003

26 Jessica R. Norton and Adrienne M. Duke, 2021. "The Influence of Parenting on Bullying Prevention: Parenting as a Moderator of Adolescents' Bullying Behaviors." *Journal of Child and Family Studies* 30: 2913–2924. https://doi.org/10.1007/s10826-021-02014-1

27 Anna C. Baldry and David P. Farrington, 2000. "Bullies and Delinquents: Personal Characteristics and Parental Styles." *Journal of Community & Applied Social Psychology* 10 no. 1: 17–31. https://doi.org/10.1002/(SICI)1099-1298(200001/02)10:1<17::AID-CASP526>3.0.CO;2-M

28 Hillary K. Morin, Catherine P. Bradshaw, and Juliette K. Berg, 2015. "Examining the Link between Peer Victimization and Adjustment Problems in Adolescents: The Role of Connectedness and Parent Engagement." *Psychology of Violence* 5, no. 4: 422–432. https://doi.org/10.1037/a0039798

29 Bear, 2020.

30 Ibid.

31 Claire F. Garandeau, Elisa Poskiparta, and Christina Salmivalli, 2014. "Tackling Acute Cases of School Bullying in the Kiva Anti-Bullying Program: A Comparison of Two Approaches." *Journal of Abnormal Child Psychology* 42 no. 6: 981–991. https://doi.org/10.1007/s10802-014-9861-1

32 Eric Madfis, 2014. *The Risk of School Rampage: Assessing and Preventing Threats of School Violence.* New York: Palgrave Pilot.

33 Khaerannisa I. Cortes and Becky Kochenderfer-Ladd, 2014. "To Tell or Not to Tell: What Influences Children's Decisions to Report Bullying to Their Teachers?" *School Psychology Quarterly* 29 no. 3: 336–348. https://doi.org/10.1037/spq0000078

34 Randy Borum, Dewey G. Cornell, William Modzeleski, and Shane R. Jimerson, 2010. "What Can Be Done about School Shootings? A Review of the Evidence." *Educational Researcher* 39 no. 1: 27–37. https://doi.org/10.3102/0013189× X09357620

Daniel J. Flannery, James A. Fox, Lacey Wallace, Edward Mulvey, and William Modzeleski, 2020. "Guns, School Schooters, and School Safety: What We Know

7 Trump
A Role Model for Bullying

The Classic Bully

No other president, and very few other public figures, has provided a better role model of a classic bully than Trump. It is not only verbal bullying for which he is well known, especially via social media and campaign rallies, but also his physical and social bullying. Indeed, Trump clearly meets each of the four recognized criteria presented in the previous chapter for being a full-fledged bully. His bullying behaviors are aggressive and unwanted, intentional, repeated over time, and occur in the context of an imbalance of power. As seen below, Trump meets each of those four criteria and does so across all three forms of bullying—verbal, social, and physical. Trump has all the characteristics of a classic schoolyard bully: He denies responsibility and blames others, is aggressive and easily frustrated, has difficulty following rules, thinks badly of others, views violence in a positive way, has friends who bully others, and has unexplained extra money or new belongings. There are few other exemplary role models of bullying for our youth and America's present and future leaders.

Trump the Verbal Bully

Documented examples of Trump's bullying as a child are scarce, but it is very likely that his verbal, social, and physical bullying began at an early age. As described by one of his childhood neighbors: "He was a loud-mouthed bully" who often would "shout and curse very loudly" when riding his bike around the neighborhood.[1] From ages 13 to 18, he lived at New York Military Academy where bullying was the norm.[2]

As an adult and long before becoming president, Trump was notorious for verbally insulting, mocking, ridiculing, and harassing those who challenged, offended, or disagreed with him. His verbal bullying escalated when he assumed the presidency; he harnessed greater power and authority and occupied the world's biggest bully pulpit. His victims included most news reporters and agencies, members of his own cabinet, the FBI, the nation's military leaders, leaders of other countries, RINO Republicans

DOI: 10.4324/9781003401278-7

and Directions for Change." *School Psychology Review* 50 no. 2–3: 237–253. https://doi.org/10.1080/2372966X.2020.1846458
   Birkett et al.
35 United States Secret Service, 2019. *Protecting American Schools: A U.S. Secret Service Analysis of Targeted School Violence.* U.S. Department of Homeland Security, United States Secret Service.
36 Bryan Vossekuil, Robert A. Fein, Marisa Reddy, Randy Borum, and William Modzeleski, 2004. *The Final Report and Findings of the Safe School Initiative: Implications for the Prevention of School Attacks in the United States.* Washington, DC: U.S. Secret Service and U.S. Department of Education.

(i.e., Republicans In Name Only who failed to support him), his own lawyers, election officials, the chief justice and other members of the Supreme Court, the chairman of the Federal Reserve Board, judges and special counsels investigating him, nearly all Democrats, and practically anyone else who challenged or questioned him. Examples of his verbal insults and bullying follow.

Fake Media and Rude Reporters

As noted in Chapter 3 on his lying, Trump is notorious for accusing the media of lying whenever they say anything negative about him or report facts that he does not want to hear. Such attacks on the media are not only excellent examples of his lying, but also are often choice examples of verbal bullying. During his presidency, hardly a week went by without him referring to any news that questioned or criticized him as "fake," "garbage," "terrible," and "lamestream." In one tweet he made it clear which news agencies he hated the most, and that the public should share his hatred toward them, tweeting: "The FAKE NEWS media (failing @nytimes, @NBCNews, @ABC, @CBS, @CNN) is not my enemy, it is the enemy of the American People!"[3] Trump continued to use that language after being told that Hitler and Stalin referred to the media as the enemy of the people before censoring the press, imprisoning and killing news reporters, and establishing their own propaganda machines.[4]

The most frequent targets of Trump's verbal bullying and insults were individual news reporters, as seen in the following examples:

- A "bimbo," "liar," "dopey," "only average in looks," "third-rate reporter," "sick," "over-rated," and "crazy." That's what Trump called Megyn Kelly, *Fox News* host and the moderator of Trump's first presidential debate with Hilary Clinton. The verbal insults were in retaliation for a question Kelly asked Trump during the debate: "You've called women you don't like 'fat pigs,' 'dogs,' 'slobs,' and 'disgusting animals.' Does that sound to you like the temperament of a man we should elect as president?" In a nationally televised interview, Trump raised eyebrows even among some of his supporters when he accused Kelly of deliberately trying to trip him up during the debate, making the sexist remark: "You could see there was blood coming out of her eyes, blood coming out of her wherever."[5]
- "You're a third-rate reporter. What you just said is a disgrace. You will never make it," Trump lashed out at *ABC*'s reporter Jonathan Karl at a White House news conference in which the reporter questioned Trump about his mishandling of the coronavirus.[6]
- "Your record is so bad you ought to be ashamed of yourself" and "You probably have the worst record in the history of broadcasting," Trump told *CNN*'s reporter Bob Acosta at a White House news conference. At another news conference, Trump shouted to Acosta, "*CNN* should be ashamed of

itself having you working for them. You are a rude, terrible person. You shouldn't be working for *CNN* .... You're a very rude person. The way you treat Sarah Huckabee [Trump's press secretary] is horrible. And the way you treat other people are horrible. You shouldn't treat people that way" [i.e., the way Trump treats people, as he then modeled].[7]

In an unprecedented move, and in addition to verbally insulting news correspondents who questioned him, Trump revoked many of their White House presses, including Acosta's (CNN successfully sued to have it reinstated).[8] Trump had done the same during the 2016 presidential campaign, revoking the passes of all reporters of *The Washington Post* from his events.[9]

The Choice Insult: Calling Others a "Dog"

As was stated by Megyn Kelly above, Trump had a proclivity for calling women who crossed him "fat pigs," "dogs," "slobs," and "disgusting animals." Whether they were women or men, Trump had a particular fondness for calling reporters and other critics a dog. The reporters mentioned previously were just a few of Trump's victims of his verbal insults and bullying. As listed in a report in *New York* magazine, the dogs included *NBC*'s "not nice!" David Gregory; "irrelevant" *Fox*'s Glenn Beck; *NBC*'s "sleepy eyes" and "moron" Chuck Todd; "the most boring political pundit on television" *ABC*'s George Will; *ABC*'s "jerk" and "spectacular prick" Bill Maher; *National Review*'s "lightweight" Brent Bozell; and "a dog who wrongfully comments on me," freelancer Laura Goldman.[10]

Trump's dogs included not only reporters but individuals whom Trump hired and fired in the White House, as well as pretty much anyone who crossed him. He tweeted that Steve Bannon, former White House advisor and a person whom many credited for Trump being elected as president, "cried when he got fired and begged for his job. Now Sloppy Steve has been dumped like a dog by almost everyone. Too bad!"[11] In another tweet he called Omarosa Manigault, his former White House advisor (and former contestant on *The Apprentice*), "that dog" and a "crazed, crying lowlife."[12] Firing and then insulting one of the very few Black people and women in his administration was viewed by many as both racist and sexist.

Perhaps the most vicious, harmful, and infamous case of Trump's verbal bullying of someone he called a dog was the juvenile feud between Trump and Rosie O'Donnell that began before he was president and continued into his presidency. It started when O'Donnell called Trump a "snake-oil salesman" and mentioned his bankruptcies and failed marriages on national TV (on *The View*, which she co-hosted). In retribution, Trump called her a "fat slob" and "a real loser," and promised to sue her, once stating "I look forward to taking lots of money from my nice, fat little Rosie" (it was an empty threat, as he never sued).[13]

In addition to dog, among the litany of verbal insults, Trump wielded toward O'Donnell in interviews, tweets, and speeches were "true loser," "a total loser," "a peg," "crude, rude, obnoxious, and dumb," "a total train-wreck," and a "degenerate" (after she revealed she was a lesbian). He viciously attacked her physical appearance even while she was experiencing serious depression, telling *Entertainment Tonight* "If I looked like Rosie, I'd struggle with depression too." In one speech he told a crowd of supporters that he knew the "cure" for her depression: "If she stopped looking in the mirror, I think she'd stop being so depressed."[14] Few children and adolescents are crueler.[15]

Interestingly, Trump never had a pet dog, being the first president in over a century without one in the White House. As supported by research on children having a pet dog,[16] perhaps if Trump had a dog he might have greater empathy, caring, and acceptance of responsibility. A dog would have given him the unconditional love that he often lacked as a child. And perhaps he would not be a germophobe.

Worse Than Dogs? All Democrats and Some Republicans

Trump had much harsher words for others who challenged his authority and power. Democrats leading his impeachment were "savages." He called Californian congressman, Adam Schiff, Chair of the House Committee on Intelligence who led Trump's impeachment trial in the House of Representatives, "little Adam Schitt," "Shifty Schiff," "dumb as a rock," "a deranged human being," "a sick person," corrupt, a liar, and a traitor.[17] Trump implied that two other Democrats leading his impeachment, House Speaker Nancy Pelosi and Sen. Chuck Schumer, were terrorists. He did so in a clearly doctored video that he retweeted showing the fake images of the two dressed in Middle Eastern attire standing in front of an Iranian flag with a caption of the photo reading "the corrupted Dems trying their best to come to the Ayatollah's rescue" (Twitter removed the tweet).[18]

Included with the "savages," "traitors," and "terrorists" that Trump believed did not belong in America were Democratic members of Congress who were women of color. In what many viewed as both a racist and sexist comment lodged toward four liberal freshmen members of the House of Representatives, Trump tweeted: "Why don't they go back and help fix the totally broken and crime infested places from which they came." All four members were women, Democrats, and American citizens elected to Congress by their constituents. Only one was born outside of the United States.[19]

Although far more Democrats than Republicans experienced his verbal bullying, Trump did not spare the very few Republicans who had the courage to challenge or criticize him. After Senate Minority Leader Mitch McConnell refused to support Trump's false assertions that he won the 2020 election, Trump called McConnell a "stone-cold loser," a "dumb son of a bitch," and "gutless and clueless," while also mocking his wife, Elaine Chao who served as his Secretary of Transportation (and who resigned immediately after Trump incited the Capitol insurrection).[20] For voting in favor of his impeachment and challenging his Big Lie (i.e., that he won re-election), he called Congresswoman Liz Cheney "a warmongering fool" who would "maybe embarrass her family by running for president."[21]

A Fucking Dumb Cabinet, and Not Much Kinder Words about the Supreme Court, FBI, and Other Government Agencies

Trump was verbally brutal toward members of his own cabinet. As documented by Daniel Drezer in *The Toddler in Chief: What Donald Trump Teaches Us about the Modern Presidency*, Trump's frequent verbal bullying and insulting of staff often occurred in the context of a temper tantrum thrown by a screaming "bratty toddler."[22] His first Attorney General, Jeff Sessions was "fucking worthless," a "fucking idiot," a "fucking jerk off," a "fucking moron," and "fuck head."[23] He ranted that he should get credit for nominating "the first mentally retarded Attorney General" in history.[24]

His Secretary of Defense, James Mattis, was "the worlds most overrated general" and "just a PR guy." Mattis resigned, while later noting: "when I was basically directed to do something that I thought went beyond stupid to felony stupid, strategically jeopardizing our place in the world and everything else, that's when I quit."[25] After his Secretary of Defense Rex Tillerson resigned, Trump tweeted that Tillerson "didn't have the mental capacity needed. He was dumb as a rock and I couldn't get rid of him fast enough. He was lazy as hell."[26] After four years of being perhaps the most loyal member of the president's cabinet, Vice President Pence also witnessed the one-way street of loyalty. For refusing to support Trump's efforts to overturn the 2020 election, Trump accused him of lacking the "courage to do what should have been done to protect our Country and our Constitution" and called him a "wimp" and "pussy."[27]

No branch of government or governmental agency was spared Trump's abusive verbal bullying. For not supporting Trump's fraudulent claims of massive voter fraud, Trump used his bully pulpit to tweet that Supreme Court judges (including three he had appointed) were "totally incompetent and weak" and that "The 'Justice' Department and the FBI have done nothing about the 2020 Presidential Election Voter Fraud, the biggest SCAM in our nation's history, despite overwhelming evidence. They should be ashamed."[28] In retribution for Attorney General William Barr asserting that the election was not rigged, Trump called him "slow," "lethargic," "lazy," and "a coward."[29]

Military Generals? "A Bunch of Fucking Pussies"

Regarding his military generals and the Pentagon, Trump had this to say: "my fucking generals are a bunch of pussies. They care more about their alliances than they do about trade deals."[30] He once yelled to his chief of staff, General John Kelly, "You fucking generals, why can't you be like the German generals?" (Kelly reminded him that Hitler's generals tried to kill him three times).[31] In their presence, he told the generals "I wouldn't go to war with you people ... . You're all losers. You don't know how to win anymore." ... "You're a bunch of dopes and babies." As noted by authors Carol Leonnig and Philip Rucker in *A Very Stable Genius*, "for a president known for verbiage he euphemistically called 'locker room talk,' this was the gravest insult he could have delivered to these people, in this sacred space. [i.e., the Tank room)."[32] The insult led Secretary of State, Rex Tillerson, to defend the generals at the meeting and calling Trump "a fucking moron."[33] Shortly thereafter Trump fired him.

It is ironic that insulting our nation's military leaders came from a draft dodger of the Vietnam war. Avoiding serving his country, Trump was diagnosed with bone spurs by a doctor, reportedly as a favor to his landlord, Fred Trump.[34] The draft dodging Trump once compared his avoiding sexually transmitted diseases as his "personal Vietnam," while noting that "vaginas are landmines" and that "I feel like a very great and very brave soldier."[35]

Leaders of Other Democratic Countries, Especially Women, Also Are Stupid and Nasty

Trump verbally bullied leaders of other countries, especially women. In phone calls, he told British Prime Minister Theresa May that she was a "fool" and "spineless" and German Chancellor Angela Merkel that she was "stupid."[36] After Denmark's Prime Minister, Mette Frederiksen, gave a cold shoulder to Trump's idea that the US should buy Greenland (which belongs to Denmark), and called the idea "absurd," Trump canceled his planned visit to Denmark and tweeted that Frederidsen was "nasty."[37] Although less frequently, Trump insulted male leaders. He tweeted that the Canadian Prime Minister, Justin Trudeau, was "very dishonest & weak."[38] Trump refrained, however, from bullying authoritarian leaders such as Russia's Putin, Turkey's Erdogan, and the Philippines' Rodrigo Duterte—leaders that he tended to praise.

Intimidating Witnesses

In addition to calling them names, Trump repeatedly threatened and discredited multiple potential and actual witnesses in his impeachment trials. This was perceived by many as witness intimidation and tampering; thus, supporting the obstruction of justice charges against him. For example, Trump publicly threatened the whistleblower who filed the original formal complaint about his behavior with Ukraine. Trump called anyone who gave information to the whistleblower "close to a spy" who should be tried for treason.[39] While testifying before Congress, Marie Yovanovitch, the former US ambassador to Ukraine, was verbally attacked in tweets by Trump.

Trump's "perfect" phone call to Ukrainian President Volodymyr Zelensky, which led to Trump's first impeachment, is a classic case of a bully preying upon a much weaker victim. With his country having already been invaded by Russia, and with Russia spending millions on influencing elections in Ukraine, Zelensky was desperate for positive relations with the United States and in much need for weapons. As noted in *The Atlantic*: "This weakness and dependency are exactly the things that the bully hopes to exploit."[40]

Not learning from his first impeachment, Trump's second impeachment entailed verbal bullying and what many consider bribery and extortion. In an hour-long phone call, Trump tried to bully Brad Raffensperger, the Georgia secretary of state and a Republican, in which he asked him to "find" 11,780 votes, Trump first flattered and begged him, but when that did not work he threatened him with potential criminal liability.[41]

Intimidating witnesses continued well after his presidency. After being indicted on the four counts related to his lying and cheating in the 2020 election, which was his third indictment in 2023, Trump posted on his Truth Social platform "IF YOU GO AFTER ME, I'M COMING AFTER YOU!" Several days later, the federal judge trying the case issued a protective order, warning Trump about intimidating witnesses and making false statements about the evidence presented in court.[42]

Okay to Mock Children and Revered Republican War Heroes

There is no greater imbalance in power than a president targeting a child and dead people, but this was not below Trump, especially if those he targeted had somehow offended or challenged him. Trump used Twitter to mock a child, 16-year-old Greta Thunberg, who was recognized by *Time* magazine as *Person of the Year*. Thunberg's offense, and the reason she won the *Time* magazine's honor, was working to improve global climate (Trump believed that climate change was a "hoax"). Trump's 80 million Twitter followers read that in the eyes of the president of the United States, Thunberg's honor was "So ridiculous," and that "Greta must work on her Anger Management problem, then go to a good old-fashioned movie with a friend! Chill Greta, Chill!"[43]

Perhaps worse than an adult verbally bullying a child is mocking someone who is dead and literally cannot defend themselves, including war heroes who returned from a war and chose to serve their country as national leaders. Trump strongly disliked Senator John McCain, a leader of the Republican party and presidential candidate in 2008. As a Navy pilot in the Vietnam war, McCain's plane was shot down during his 23rd bombing mission. He was captured, held prisoner, and tortured for five and a half years. McCain died of a brain tumor in 2018. Among the reasons Trump gave for disliking McCain (and many were political) was that Trump likes "people who weren't captured."[44] As is a tradition, after the death of a national leader American flags fly at half mask at all government buildings. The exception, however, was at the Trump White House where Trump ordered the flag not to be lowered after McCain died of brain cancer (he later succumbed to political pressure and had it lowered that afternoon). Adding to his disrespect of McCain, after his death Trump called McCain a "fucking loser." Trump also called former President George H.W. Bush a "loser" because he piloted a Navy plane that was shot down (in World War II; Bush was not captured).[45]

Trump the Social Bully

As defined in the previous chapter, social bullying is intended to damage the victim's relationships with peers. Because this can be done verbally, such as by publicly insulting and embarrassing someone, many of the examples above of Trump's verbal bullying constitute both verbal *and* social bullying. Trump's calling reporters and critics names that reflect incompetence is meant not only to insult them but to make others think less of them and thus to harm their social standing.

Another common way in which Trump has engaged in social bullying is by excluding others. Over the years, nearly everyone in his social network has been wealthy or in a position of power, and White (Mike Tyson, a classic physical and verbal bully, being an exception). If not wealthy or powerful, you were excluded. Trump's social bullying is more directly seen in Trump repeatedly telling his supporters to treat opponents, and particularly Democrats, poorly. However, targets of his social bullying also have included Republicans who challenged or criticized him. To Trump, those "RINO" Republicans do not deserve to belong to the Trump Republican Party.

Primary among those who Trump targeted for exclusion from the Republican party were the ten Republican members of Congress who joined Democrats to impeach him the second time and the two senators who voted to convict him (Mitt Romney of Utah and Lisa Murkowski of Alaska). In retribution for their votes, he told his conservative supporters to "Get rid of them all" and pledged to do whatever it took to defeat the twelve. The top target on his list for revenge was Congresswoman Liz Cheney of Wyoming, the third-ranking Republican in the House of Representatives, who had tweeted "There is no question that the president formed the mob, the President incited the mob, the President addressed the mob. He lit the flame."[46] Trump helped lead the Republicans in Congress to remove Cheney from her position of leadership in Congress and endorsed another Republican to run against Cheney for her reelection (Cheney lost by a landslide).

Trump also announced that he would actively campaign against the "disloyal and very bad senator" Murkowski (she won re-election to the senate, however).[47] After hearing Romney justify his vote by saying "As a Senate juror, I swore an oath before God to exercise impartial justice." Trump accused the "pompous ass" and "failed presidential candidate" of using his religion as a "crutch."[48]

In the book *The Cult of Trump*, author Steven Hassan presents a convincing case that Trump's behavior, and especially his verbal and social bullying, matches that of cult leaders.[49] To keep everyone in the fold, cult leaders reward those who support them, while shunning or banishing and publicly insulting those who disagree with them. Other common tactics of cult leaders are holding rousing rallies among supporters and creating false enemies. In Trump's rallies, the major false enemies have been Democrats, Mexicans, Muslims, and the media.

Trump the Physical Bully

Trump told his biographer Michael D'Antonio "I loved to fight. I always loved to fight ... all types of fights, any kind of fight, I loved it."[50] Although Trump has bragged about fighting, and his biographers have noted that his bullying began in early childhood, that he was a terror at home, and often was in detention in elementary school,[51] I found very few actual examples of Trump being in a physical fight or otherwise causing bodily harm as a child or adult. As seen below, Trump was much more likely to harm others physically and emotionally by threatening to take their possessions, especially money, by means of lawsuits.

Physical Bullying via Bodily Harm and Threats Thereof

Exceptions of Trump not inflecting bodily harm are his pummeling a kid in his neighborhood when he was young and attempting to throw a smaller cadet out of the window at New York Military Academy, who was much smaller. The other cadet physically struck first, however, hitting Trump with a broomstick after Trump ripped the sheets off the fellow cadet's bed because he didn't make it properly.[52]

In his book *The Art of the Deal*, Trump boasted that in second grade he gave a Black eye to a music teacher because "I didn't think he knew anything about music and I almost got expelled. I'm not proud of that, but it's clear evidence that even early on I had a tendency to stand up and make my opinions known in a very forceful way."[53] However, given that Trump is prone to lying, reporters Michael Kranish and Marc Fisher of *The Washington Post* investigated the validity of this claim when writing their book *Trump Revealed: An American Journey of Ambition, Ego, Money, and Power*.[54] They found no one at the school he attended, including his classmates and teachers, had ever heard of him striking a teacher.

Whereas few examples exist of Trump harming anyone physically, there are plenty of examples of him threatening to do so, encouraging others to engage in physical aggression, and reinforcing others for physical aggression and bullying. In response to his many posts glorifying violence, Trump was suspended from Twitter.

At multiple campaign rallies, with the crowds cheering him on (and with children often watching), Trump called for violent treatment toward those who protested against him, calling them "thugs," "sick," and encouraging his supporters to "Get him out of here!" and "knock the crap out of him" while offering to pay the resulting legal fees if they did. Regarding one protester, Trump stated "I'd like to punch him in the face ... You know what they used to do to a guy like that in a place like this? They'd be carried out on a stretcher, folks."[55] Not specific to protesters, he also advised police officers "don't be too nice" when placing suspects in squad cars. Perhaps his most infamous call for violence was inciting the January 6 insurrection that led to the deaths of five people.[56]

Other examples of Trump espousing or condoning physical bullying, hate, racism, and violence follow:

- At a Republican primary debate, Trump said if he were elected president he would "bring back a hell of a lot worse than waterboarding."[57]
- Two days after a protester was punched in the face by Trump supporters at a campaign rally, Trump commented that such violence was "very, very appropriate" and the kind of action "we need a little bit more of."[58]
- As reported by the *The New York Times*, to help keep migrants from crossing the Mexican border Trump entertained the options of shooting migrants in the legs; filling trenches with water, snakes, and alligators; and installing an electrified wall with spikes that could "pierce human flesh."[59]
- In his book, "*A Sacred Oath*," Secretary of Defense Mark Esper wrote that Trump asked him at least twice if the military could "shoot missiles into Mexico to destroy the drug labs" while adding "no one would know it was us."[60]
- After George Floyd was killed by a policeman in Minneapolis, Trump threatened to shoot the protesters who were looting stores in Minneapolis, calling them "thugs" and tweeting "when the looting starts, the shooting starts" (Twitter flagged this tweet for "glorifying violence"). According to Esper, Trump wanted to deploy 10,000 troops in Washington, D.C. in response to the protestors and asked him "Can't you just shoot them? Just shoot them in the legs or something."[61]
- At a 2016 campaign rally in Iowa, Trump, in describing the loyalty of his supporters, notoriously said, "I could stand in the middle of Fifth Avenue and shoot somebody and I wouldn't lose voters."[62] (A claim that might not be a lie.)

Physical Harm via Lawsuits

Whereas few examples can be found of Trump personally inflicting bodily harm on others, plenty of examples can be found of him inflicting another form of physical harm often found among schoolyard bullies—taking another person's money or threatening to do so. Prior to becoming president, Trump filed over 3,500 lawsuits, averaging three per day (the count is now well over 4,000). As noted by attorney and author James D. Zirin in *Plaintiff in Chief:*

A Portrait of Donald Trump in 3,5000 Lawsuits, many of Trump's lawsuits were about bullying others:

> Trump saw litigation as being only about winning. He sued at the drop of a hat. He sued for sport; he sued to achieve a sense of control; and he sued to make a point. He sued as a means of destroying or silencing those who crossed him. He became a 'plaintiff in chief.' … He sued to make headlines, for the entertainment value, and to reinforce his power over others.[63]

As noted by Zirin, Trump sued his first ex-wife, Ivana, for $25 million for revealing his finances. Claiming defamation of character, he sued one of his biographers, Timothy L. O'Brien, author of *TrumpNation: The Art of Being the Donald*, and the book's publisher for 5 billion dollars. The book correctly revealed that Trump's wealth was far less than Trump claimed and that he was not a billionaire. Trump lost the lawsuit. In an interview with *The Washington Post*, Trump bragged that losing the case didn't bother him, stating: "I spent a couple of bucks on legal fees, and they spent a whole lot more. I did it to make [O'Brien's] life miserable, which I am happy about."[64]

In perhaps his most frivolous and spiteful lawsuit, Trump even sued Bill Maher, a comedian, for joking on *The Tonight Show* that he would pay Trump $5 million if he would prove his father was not an orangutan. Trump eventually dropped the case: Comedians can't be sued for their jokes.[65]

As president and since then, Trump continued to sue or threaten to sue authors and others who wrote or spoke negatively about him. Authors of books who were threatened or sued by Trump or his administration include his niece, Dr. Mary Trump, author of *Too Much and Never Enough: How My Family Created the World's Most Dangerous Man*; Omarosa Manigault, White House aide and author of *Unhinged: An Insider's Account of the Trump White House*; Michael Wolff, author of *Fire and Fury: Inside the Trump White House*; John Bolton, national security adviser to Trump and author of *The Room Where It Happened*; and Bob Woodward, author of multiple books about Trump, including the audiobook *The Trump Tapes: Bob Woodward's Twenty Interviews with President Donald Trump* (for which he was sued). Of the lawsuits filed, Trump won none of them (the suit against Woodward is pending).

Claiming unfair coverage, defamation, libel, or slander, he sued *The New York Times* and *The Washington Post* in 2020. In 2022 he sued *CNN* for $475 million. In that recent lawsuit Trump *cited* *CNN*'s "lies" about election and unfair criticism over his policies, while claiming that *CNN* caused him to suffer "embarrassment, pain, humiliation and mental anguish."[66] Again, he won none of the lawsuits (the lawsuit against *CNN* is pending).

Several of his lawsuits and threats backfired. Trump sued Hillary Clinton and some of her advisers, FBI Director James Comey and other FBE officials, Congressman Adam Schiff, and nearly 50 others, alleging that they spread disinformation about his campaign during the 2016 election (including that Russia interfered in support of Trump). A federal judge in Florida ruled in favor of the defendants, ordering Trump to pay nearly $1 million in sanctions to cover their attorneys' fees and costs. The judge noted "This case should never have been brought. Its inadequacy as a legal claim was evident from the start. No reasonable lawyer would have filed it." In his order, he wrote "Intended for a political purpose, none of the counts of the amended complaint stated a cognizable legal claim" and that Trump has a "pattern of misusing the courts to serve political purposes."[67]

Trump's Imbalance of Power and Intentionality

Trump's history of verbal, physical, and social aggression is well documented, with his aggression clearly meeting the first two criteria for being a bully—it is unwanted and repeated over time. As discussed in the previous chapter, two additional criteria must be met for someone to be recognized as a full-fledged bully: The unwanted aggression occurs within the context of an imbalance of power, and is intentional, as seen below.

Imbalance of Power

In most cases of bullying, an imbalance of power refers to greater physical size or strength, with the bully being larger or stronger than the victim. However, greater power also can reside in greater wealth, authority, social status, and access and control of information. As a billionaire businessman and president, Trump possessed each of those sources of power. Despite being physically larger than most women and many men, Trump has little history of using his size and strength to bully others, except with verbal threats. This is because Trump understood that harming others physically would likely lead to serious negative consequences such as being sued, arrested, or losing the fight. Trump also understood that he could use his wealth and authority to cause even greater anguish and harm to others by suing or firing them, destroying their reputations, or publicly belittling them.

As is the case when a schoolyard bully is bigger and stronger, it is difficult, if not impossible, for victims to successfully defend themselves against bullies who use their greater wealth, position of authority, and control of information to harm them. As seen in examples of Trump's bullying presented earlier in this chapter, he verbally insulted, shunned, fired, or otherwise punished those who criticized, challenged, or questioned him. Another example of his abuse of power, as well as the imbalance in power, Trump blocked people who criticized or mocked him from following his Twitter account. This presidential act was overturned by the courts, which ruled that Trump had violated the First Amendment rights of U.S. citizens.[68]

That Trump was aware of his power to bully others was made clear in an interview with Bob Woodward for his book *Rage*. As asserted by Trump:

"I have a opposition like nobody has. And that's OK. I've had that my whole life. I've always had it. And this has been—my whole life has been like this. In the meantime, right now, I'm looking at the White House. Okay? I'm staring right at the walls of the White House." As noted by Woodward, "It seemed to be his way of reminding me that he was the president."[69]

Intentionality

As a businessman, and prior to becoming president, Trump expressed in multiple speeches that when insulting and bullying others his intention is to inflict psychological harm. The purpose of harming others is to punish those who cross him but also to warn others that they should not think about offending or crossing him because they too will experience the same punishment.

As noted in a 2016 article by David Corn in *Mother Jones*, when asked in 2011 about the keys to his success, at the top of Trump's list was "Get even with people. If they screw you, screw them back 10 times as hard. I really believe it."[70] Trump expanded on this in a speech in 2012, stating:

> One of the things you should do in terms of success: If somebody hits you, you've got to hit'em back five times harder than they ever thought possible. You've got to get even. Get even. And the reason, the reason you do, is so important ... The reason you do, you have to do it, because if they do that to you, you have to leave a telltale sign that they just can't take advantage of you. It's not so much for the person, which does make you feel good, to be honest with you, I've done it many times. But other people watch and you know they say, 'Well, let's leave Trump alone.'[71]

In a 2017 interview with CBS veteran journalist Lesley Stahl of *60 Minutes* Trump further revealed the intentions behind his bullying, and more specifically for constantly attacking the press. When Stahl asked the president why he repeatedly called news outlets and the press corps "fake news" and "enemy of the people," Trump responded: "I do it to discredit you all and demean you all so when you write negative stories about me, no one will believe you."[72]

In sum, Trump's bullying is intended to demonstrate his power and make the lives of others miserable. As seen in two of Bob Woodward's books about Trump, *Fear* and *Rage*,[73] his bullying is intended to strike fear and rage in others. It makes him feel good.

Additional Bullying Characteristics That Trump Models

By now it should be evident that Trump is a true bully, having met the four criteria for bullying and doing so for all three types of bullying. But what makes him a truly exemplary role model of bullying is that he also possesses all other characteristics of bullies, as discussed in the previous chapter. Applied to Trump, those characteristics are as follows:

Denies Responsibility and Blames Others

Trump falsely blamed millions of immigrants who voted illegally for him not winning the popular vote in 2016, China for the coronavirus, Obama for the lack of medical supplies for treating the virus, Democrats for preventing him from focusing on the coronavirus during his impeachment, rigged voting machines for him losing the 2020 election, and Antifa for the storming of the Capitol. He blamed either the "fake" media or "hateful" Democrats for the same things and just about all other of his mistakes and failures. Plenty of additional examples of Trump denying responsibility and blaming others are presented in Chapter 10 on his use of mechanisms of moral disengagement.

Is Aggressive and Easily Frustrated

That Trump is aggressive and easily frustrated when he doesn't get what he wants is well documented by all his biographers and in nearly all books written by reporters, members of his staff, and others who worked with him. Included are numerous documented reports of him throwing child-like temper tantrums in which he cursed, yelled at others, pouted, and fired off a rapid stream of insults and false accusations via social media, the telephone, or in person. He also has been known to kick and throw objects and to walk out of meetings, including with members of Congress. Daniel W. Drezer gives plenty of examples of Trump's tantrums in his book *The Toddler in Chief: What Donald Trump Teaches Us about the Modern Presidency*.[74] Maggie Haberman does the same in *Confidence Man*.[75]

Has Difficulty Following Rules

In elementary school, Trump was in detention so often for not following rules that his peers began referring to detentions as the "DTs" (Donald Trumps).[76] As noted previously, because of his poor behavior his father sent him to the New York Military Academy (NYMA), which was noted at the time as a popular place where parents sent children with disciplinary problems or ADHD. He responded well to the school's authoritarian and regimental style of discipline, as there is no history of Trump having disciplinary problems at the military academy or in college. Defiance of rules resurfaced, however, after he joined his father's real estate business. He learned from his father that rules were to be broken and laws circumvented, wherever possible, if it increased your wealth or otherwise got things done. Ample examples of Trump not following rules were presented in Chapter 5 on his cheating.

Thinks Badly of Others

For sure, Trump has not thought kindly about those he has bullied including those listed throughout this chapter. As revealed in one of his interviews for Bob Woodward's 2020 book *Rage*, Trump perceived the media and Democrats as hating him. In turn, he believed this justified his hatred toward them. Likewise, he is well known for his hate speeches, in which he spews and incites hatred not only toward the media and Democrats but also toward Mexicans, (including famous athletes who protested racial inequality), previous presidents (e.g., Obama, Clinton, G.W. Bush), and others.

Views Violence in a Positive Way

To be fair, Trump has swung from denouncing violence to encouraging and provoking it. When president, denouncements (and denials) typically came after the violence he provoked had already occurred. A classic example was Trump inciting his supporters to storm the Capitol, telling them earlier that day at a rally near the Capitol that the election had been stolen from him and that "We fight like hell, and if you don't fight like hell, you're not going to have a country anymore." After listening, the crowd stormed the Capitol, resulting in five deaths.[77]

Another example of Trump both encouraging and denouncing physical violence was the Unite the Right Rally, held by right-wing militants in Charlottesville, VA. Most of the militants were Trump supporters who espoused White supremacist and neo-Nazi beliefs. Several waved Confederate flags. The militants were met with counter-protesters, and the two groups fought. One of the militants drove a car into a group of counter-protesters, killing one and injuring 19 others. Many attributed this tragic event to Trump's constant attacking of Muslims, Mexicans, and others, which stoked the anger of many White supremacists and neo-Nazis. As described by Bob Woodward in his book *Fear: Trump in the White House*, Trump first refused to respond to the protests and the violent death. Under pressure from White House advisers, he relented and agreed to read a speech written largely by one of his aides, Rob Porter, that condemned the violence. However, he departed from the prepared speech, commenting that the hatred, bigotry, and violence were "On many sides. On many sides."[78] That comment was roundly criticized as being racist and supportive of right-wing extremists. Critics included most prominent Republicans.

As noted earlier, as an adult Trump has seldom acted in a physically violent manner, excluding his throwing tantrums, and I found no validated incidents of him hitting anyone or being in a fistfight. Not hitting others, however, does not mean that Trump fails to view physical violence in a positive way. This was seen earlier in the chapter in examples of Trump either threatening or endorsing physical violence.

In Atlantic City, he was a big promoter, supporter, and fan of boxing and professional wrestling. At his casinos, he hosted many matches, including the heavyweight championship match between Mike Tyson and Michael Spinks. Trump even participated in some of the wrestling shows he hosted, as when he served as manager of a wrestler in the "Battle of the Billionaires" at WrestleMania 23. Trump was inducted into the WWE (World Wrestling Entertainment) Hall of Fame and into the New Jersey Boxing Hall of Fame. That Trump views violence in a positive way is also seen in tweets and campaign speeches quoted previously in which he engaged in verbal bullying while encouraging physical bullying and violence.

Has Friends Who Bully Others

A *New York Times* article on Trump's friendships reported that although Trump always had many acquaintances, he had few close friends before becoming president and even fewer by the end of his presidency.[79] Trump commented at one of his 2020 campaign rallies "I lost all my friends." Trump's number of friends peaked during his presidency, as he befriended many conservative members of Congress and talk show hosts who supported and defended him and shared in his bullying. Perhaps a good indication of who his closest friends were when he was president is who he invited most often to play golf and stay at his Margo Largo palace. Primary among them were former mayor and presidential advisor Rudy Guiliani; Republican members of Congress Lindsey Graham, Rand Paul, and Matt Gaetz; Sean Hannity and Bret Baier of Fox News, and popular radio talk show host Rush Limbaugh (whom Trump awarded the Medal of Freedom).[80] Many of those friends would qualify as meeting all of the criteria for being a bully. Other friends of Trump who are classic bullies (as well as narcissists, liars, and cheaters) are Roy Cohn and Roger Stone, who are profiled in Chapter 12.

Has Unexplained Extra Money or New Belongings

This characteristic of bullies is the one that applies the least to Trump. Having unexplained extra money or new belongings is associated much more with physical bullying than verbal and social-relational bullying. It is also much more common among bullies who are not lacking money or cannot afford what they want, which has never been Trump. One might well argue, however, that despite never needing extra money or new belongings, Trump has nevertheless demonstrated this characteristic in many instances of his cheating, which were described in Chapter 5. He did so by having his properties greatly under-appraised, not paying a fair share of taxes, and by suing others to gain their money or belongings. His possession of sport memorabilia and self-paintings illegally paid for by the Trump Foundation charity also might be considered as examples of having unexplained new belongings. Additionally, unexplained new belongings would include documents, some of which were classified as top secret, that he removed from the White House and took with him to Mar-a-Lago.

Although the characteristic of having unexplained extra money or new belongings fits Trump less so than the other characteristics above, it still fits. Furthermore, one needs not possess all the characteristics of bullies to be recognized as a full-fledged bully. All that is necessary is to demonstrate behavior that is aggressive and unwanted, intentional, repeated over time, and occurs within the context of an imbalance of power. Trump meets each of those criteria, and does so verbally, physically, and socially. As with lying and cheating, for bullying there is no better role model.

In sum, Trump meets all criteria for being a full-fledged, classic bully: His verbal, physical, and social bullying is aggressive and unwanted, intentional, repeated over time, and occurs in the context of an imbalance of power. As with other bullies, he denies responsibility and blames others, is aggressive and easily frustrated, has difficulty following rules, thinks badly of others, views violence in a positive way, has friends who bully others, and has unexplained extra money or new belongings. There are few better role models.

Notes

1 Paul Schwartzman and Michael E. Miller, 2016. "Confident. Incorrigible. Bully: Little Donny Was a Lot Like Candidate Donald Trump." *The Washington Post*, June 22. https://www.washingtonpost.com/lifestyle/style/young-donald-trump-military-school/2016/06/22/f0b3b164-317c-11e6-8758-d58e76e11b12_story.html
2 Michael D'Antonio, 2016. The Truth about Trump. New York: Thomas Dunne Books, 277.
3 Donald J. Trump (@realDonaldTrump), 2017. "The FAKE NEWS media (failing @nytimes, @NBC News, @ABC, @CBS, @CNN) is Not My Enemy, It Is the Enemy of the American People!" *Twitter*, February 17, 2017. https://twitter.com/realDonaldTrump/status/832708293516632065
4 Jonathan Karl, 2020. *Front Row at the Trump Show*. New York: Dutton.
5 Tara Golshan, 2016. "For 9 Months Donald Trump Bullied Megyn Kelly. Tonight Fox Will Air Their One-On-One Interview." *Vox*, May 17. https://www.vox.com/2016/1/27/10842640/donald-trump-megyn-kelly-tweets
6 Aaron Rupar, 2020. "'You're a Third-Rate Reporter': Trump Lashes Out in Response to Questions About Damning IG Report," *Vox*, April. 6. https://www.vox.com/2020/4/6/21211345/trump-coronavirus-briefing-hhs-ig-report-jon-karl-kristin-fisher
7 Lindsey Bever, 2018. "You're a Very Rude Person." "That's Enough." "Sit Down." Trump's News Conference Turns Hostile." *The Washington Post*, November 7. https://www.washingtonpost.com/politics/2018/11/07/youre-very-rude-person-thats-enough-sit-down-trumps-news-conference-turns-hostile/
8 Mathew Ingram, 2019. "White House Revokes Press Passes for Dozens of Journalists." *Columbia Journalism Review*, May 9. https://www.cjr.org/the_media_today/white-house-press-passes.php
9 Sarah Begley, 2016. "Donald Trump Revokes Washington Press Credentials," *Time*, June 13. https://time.com/4367449/donald-trump-washington-post-press-credentials/

10 Madeleine Aggeler, 2018. "For Some Unknown Reason, Trump Thinks Dogs Are Constantly Getting Fired." *The Cut,* August 15. https://www.thecut.com/2018/08/everyone-donald-trump-has-called-a-dog.html

11 Ibid.

12 Ibid.

13 D'Antonio. 2016.

14 Madeleine Sheehan Perkins, 2017. "A Complete Timeline of Trump's Years-Long Feud with Rosie O'Donnell." *Business Insider,* May 12. https://www.businessinsider.com/trump-rosie-odonnell-history-2017-5

Andrew Kaczynski, 2016. "Donald Trump Viciously Mocked Rosie O'Donnell's Depression During Their Public Feud." *Buzzfeed News,* March 28. https://www.buzzfeednews.com/article/andrewkaczynski/donald-trump-viciously-mocked-rosie-odonnells-depression-dur

15 **Warning**: If you are a parent and your child says similar things to a depressed peer who later commits suicide, not only are you likely to be sued, but based on recent court rulings your child's school also is likely to be sued if they knew about the bullying and did nothing to stop it.

16 Nancy R. Gee, Aubrey H. Fine, and Peggy McCardle (eds.), 2017. *How Animals Help Students Learn: Research and Practice for Educators and Mental-Health Professionals.* New York: Routledge.

17 John Wagner, 2019. "Trump Lashes Out Again at Whistleblower, Questions Whether Schiff Should Be Arrested for 'Treason'." *The Washington Post,* September 30. https://www.washingtonpost.com/politics/trump-lashes-out-again-at-whistleblower-questions-whether-schiff-should-be-arrested-for-treason/2019/09/30/932840ba-e370-11e9-a6e8-8759c5c7f608_story.html

18 Anushay Hossain, 2020. "Trump's Outrageous Retweet of Hate." *CNN,* January 14. https://www.cnn.com/2020/01/14/opinions/trump-hateful-retweet-schumer-pelosi-hossain/index.html

19 Laurie Kellman, 2019. "A Look at the 'Squad' That Trump Targeted in Racist Tweets." *AP News,* July 15. https://apnews.com/article/f80a96ce799348609 36ebdc2127c28fc

20 Josh Dawsey, 2021. "Trump Slashes at McConnell as He Reiterates Election Falsehoods at Republican Event." *The Washington Post,* April 11. https://www.washingtonpost.com/politics/trump-mcconnell-election/2021/04/11/297a8 2da-9879-11eb-962b-78c1d8228819_story.html

Andrew Solender, 2021. "Trump Blames Pence, McConnell for Election Loss as He Blasts Liz Cheney." *Forbes,* May 5. https://www.forbes.com/sites/andrewsolender/2021/05/05/trump-blames-pence-mcconnell-for-election-loss-as-he-blasts-liz-cheney/?sh=3b3d55aa3088

21 Thomas Colson, 2021. "Trump Says Liz Cheney Is a 'Warmongering Fool' Who Would 'Embarrass Her Family by Running for President'." *Business Insider,* April 28. https://www.businessinsider.com/donald-trump-says-liz-cheney-warmongering-fool-presidential-hopes-wyoming-2021-4

22 Daniel W. Drezner, 2020. *The Toddler in Chief: What Donald Trump Teaches Us about the Modern Presidency.* Chicago: The University of Chicago Press.

23 Philip Rucker and Carol Leonnig, 2020. A *Very Stable Genius: Donald J. Trump's Testing of America.* New York, Penguin Press, 139.

24 Maggie Haberman, 2022. *Confidence Man: The Making of Donald Trump and the Breaking of America.* New York: Penguin Press, 334.

25 Bob Woodward, 2020. *Rage.* New York: Simon & Schuster, 143.

26 Matthew Choi, 2018. "Trump Calls Tillerson 'Dumb as a Rock' and 'Lazy as Hell.'" *Politico,* December 07. https://www.politico.com/story/2018/12/07/trump-tillerson-dumb-lazy-1051485

27 Rosalind S. Helderman and Josh Dawsey, 2020. "Mounting Evidence Suggests Trump Knew of Danger to Pence When He Attacked Him as Lacking 'Courage' Amid Capitol Siege." *The Washington Post*, February 11. https://www. washingtonpost.com/politics/trump-tweet-pence-capitol/2021/02/11/cc7d9 f7e-6c7f-11eb-9f80-3d7646ce1bc0_story.html

28 James Crowley, 2020. "Trump Attacks FBI, DOJ, Supreme Court and GOP Senators in Twitter Tirade." *Newsweek*, December 26. https://www.newsweek. com/trump-attacks-doj-fbi-supreme-court-gop-senators-mitch-mcconnell-twitter-1557376

29 Chris Cillizza, 2022. "The 20 Most Outlandish Lines from Donald Trump's Letter to Lester Holt." *CNN*, March 7. https://www.cnn.com/2022/03/07/politics/ trump-lester-holt-letter-bill-barr/index.html

30 Woodward, *Rage*, 37.

31 Peter Baker and Susan Glasser, 2022. *The Divider: Trump in the White House, 2017–2021*. New York: Doubleday.

32 Rucker and Leonnig, 135–136.

33 Ibid., 138.

34 Aaron Blake, 2019. "Trump's Flippant Talk about the Vietnam War." *The Washington Post*, June 5. https://www.washingtonpost.com/politics/2019/06/ 05/trumps-flippant-talk-about-vietnam-war/

35 Ibid.

36 J. Edward Moreno, 2020. "Trump Insulted UK's May, Called Germany's Merkel 'Stupid' in Calls: Report." *The Hill*, June 30. https://thehill.com/homenews/ administration/505182-trump-insulted-uks-may-called-germanys-merkel-stupid-in-calls-report

37 Allie Malloy, 2019. "Trump Refers to Another Woman As 'Nasty'—This Time the Danish PM." *CNN*, August 21. https://www.cnn.com/2019/08/21/politics/ trump-nasty-woman-denmark-mette-frederiksen/index.html

38 Rucker and Leonnig, 260.

39 Maggie Haberman and Katie Rogers, 2019. "Trump Attacks Whistle-Blower's Sources and Alludes to Punishment for Spies." *The New York Times*, September 26. https://www.nytimes.com/2019/09/26/us/politics/trump-whistle-blower-spy. html

40 Franklin Foer, 2019. "Trump's Classic Bully Move." *The Atlantic*, September 25. https://www.theatlantic.com/ideas/archive/2019/09/donald-trump-bullied-ukrainian-president-zelensky/598798/

41 Amy Gardner, 2021. "'I Just Want to Find 11,780 Votes': In Extraordinary Hour-Long Call, Trump Pressures Georgia Secretary of State to Recalculate the Vote in His Favor." *The Washington Post*, January 3. https://www.washingtonpost.com/ politics/trump-raffensperger-call-georgia-vote/2021/01/03/d45acb92-4dc4-11eb-bda4-615aaefd0555_story.html

42 Ryan J. Reilly and Daniel Barnes, 2023. "Judge Warns Trump about Intimidating Witnesses and Disclosing Secrets in 2020 Election Case." *NBC News*, August 11. https://www.nbcnews.com/politics/donald-trump/trump-lawyers-face-jack-smiths-prosecutors-discovery-rules-rcna99070

43 Allan Smith, 2019. "Trump Mocks Greta Thunberg after She Wins Time Person of the Year." *NBC News*, December 12. https://www.nbcnews.com/politics/ donald-trump/trump-mocks-greta-thunberg-after-she-wins-time-person-year-n1100531

44 Aaron Blake, 2020. "Trump's Callous Alleged Comments About Military Veterans vs. What He's Said Very Publicly." *The Washington Post*, September 4. https://www.washingtonpost.com/politics/2020/09/04/trumps-callous-alleged-comments-about-veterans-vs-whats-hes-said-very-publicly/

45 Ibid.
46 David Morgan, 2021. "'Banana Republic Crap:' Some Republicans Turn on Trump over Capital Violence." *Reuters*, January 6. https://www.reuters.com/article/us-usa-election-republicans/banana-republic-crap-some-republicans-turn-on-trump-over-capitol-violence-idUSKBN29B33W
47 Jim Acosta and Aaron Pellish, 2021. "Trump Says He'll Campaign against Murkowski in Alaska Next Year." *CNN*, March 6. https://www.cnn.com/2021/03/06/politics/murkowski-trump-endorsement-alaska-senate-race-2022/index.html
48 Brakkton Booker, 2020. "Trump Blasts Romney Over Impeachment Vote." *NPR*, February 6. https://www.npr.org/2020/02/06/803445433/trump-blasts-romney-over-impeachment-vote
49 Steven Hassan, 2019. *The Cult of Trump*, New York: Free Press.
50 D'Antonio, 10.
51 Michael Dranish and Marc Fisher, 2016. *Trump Revealed: An American Journey of Ambition, Ego, Money, and Power*. New York: Scribner.
52 Ibid.
53 Donald J. Trump (with Tony Schwartz), *Trump: The Art of the Deal*. New York: Ballentine, 73.
54 Dranish and Fisher.
55 Michael E. Miller, 2016. "Donald Trump on a Protester: 'I'd Like To Punch Him in the Face.'" *The Washington Post*, February 23. https://www.washingtonpost.com/news/morning-mix/wp/2016/02/23/donald-trump-on-protester-id-like-to-punch-him-in-the-face/
56 U.S. House of Representatives, Select Committee to Investigate the January 6th Attack on the United Capitol, 2022. *Final Report of the Select Committee to Investigate the January 6th Attack on the United States Capitol*. House Report 117–663, December 22. https://www.govinfo.gov/app/details/GPO-J6-REPORT/
57 Fabiola Cineas, 2021. "Donald Trump Is the Accelerant." *Vox*, January 9. https://www.vox.com/21506029/trump-violence-tweets-racist-hate-speech
58 Ibid.
59 Michael D. Shear and Julie Hirschfeld Davis, 2019. "Shoot Migrants' Legs, Build Alligator Moat: Behind Trump's Ideas for Border." *The New York Times*, October 1. https://www.nytimes.com/2019/10/01/us/politics/trump-border-wars.html
60 Mark T. Esper, 2022. *A Sacred Oath: Memoirs of a Secretary of Defense During Extraordinary Times*. New York, William Morrow, 312–313.
61 Esper, 1.
62 Jeremy Diamond, 2016. "Trump: I Could 'Shoot Somebody And I Wouldn't Lose Voters.'" *CNN*, January 24. https://www.cnn.com/2016/01/23/politics/donald-trump-shoot-somebody-support/index.html
63 James D. Zirin, 2019. *Plaintiff in Chief: A Portrait of Donald Trump in 3,5000 Lawsuits*. New York: All Points Books, xi.
64 Paul Farhi, 2016. "What Really Gets under Trump's Skin? A Reporter Questioning His Net Worth." *The Washington Post*, March 8. https://www.washingtonpost.com/lifestyle/style/that-time-trump-sued-over-the-size-of-hiswallet/2016/03/08/785dee3e-e4c2-11e5-b0fd-073d5930a7b7_story.html
65 Ibid.
66 Michael M. Grynbaum, 2022. "Trump Sues *CNN* for Defamation, Seeking $475 Million," *The New York Times*, October 3. https://www.nytimes.com/2022/10/03/business/media/trump-cnn-lawsuit.html

67 Thao Nguyen, 2023. "Trump and His Lawyers Sanctioned Nearly $1 M in 'Frivolous' Lawsuit against Hillary Clinton." *USA Today*, January 20. https://www.usatoday.com/story/news/politics/2023/01/19/donald-trump-lawsuit-sanctions-hillary-clinton-2016-campaign/11086773002/

68 Charlie Savage, 2019. "Trump Can't Block Critics from His Twitter Account, Appeals Court Rules." *The New York Times,* July 9. https://www.nytimes.com/2019/07/09/us/politics/trump-twitter-first-amendment.html

69 Woodward, *Rage*, 383.

70 David Corn, 2016. "Donald Trump Is Completely Obsessed with Revenge." *Mother Jones*, October 19. https://www.motherjones.com/politics/2016/10/donald-trump-obsessed-with-revenge/

71 David Corn, 2016. "The Debate Tonight Could Be All about Payback." *Mother Jones*, October 19. https://www.motherjones.com/politics/2016/10/donald-trump-obsessed-with-revenge/

72 Dan Mangan, 2018. "President Trump Told Lesley Stahl He Bashes Press 'To Demean You and Discredit You So … No One Will Believe' Negative Stories about Him." *CNBC*, May 22. https://www.cnbc.com/2018/05/22/trump-told-lesley-stahl-he-bashes-press-to-discredit-negative-stories.html

73 Woodward, *Fear*.
    Woodward, Rage.

74 Rick Reilly, 2019. *Commander in Cheat: How Golf Explains Trump*. New York: Hachette Books.

75 Maggie Haberman, 2022. *Confidence Man: The Making of Donald Trump and the Breaking of America*. New York: Penguin.

76 Kranish and Fisher, 34.

77 U.S. House of Representatives, Select Committee, 2022.

78 Woodward, Fear, 239.

79 Alan Feurer, 2016. "For Donald Trump, Friends in Few Places." *The New York Times*, March 11. https://www.nytimes.com/2016/03/13/nyregion/for-donald-trump-friends-in-few-places.html

80 Ellen Cranley, 2019. "23 Celebrities, Professional Athletes, and Politicians Trump Has Golfed with as President." *Business Insider*, March 24. https://www.businessinsider.com/trump-golf-partners-while-president-2019-3

8 Narcissism

What Is Narcissism?

Wearing a red cape and pretending to be Superman, at age three our son Brian leaped off an overturned and unstable laundry basket to fly across the family room. The basket flipped and he landed with his face hitting the fireplace hearth, requiring three stitches over his eye. Always persistent and persevering, several months later he repeated the stunt (no, he was not a slow learner), resulting in three more stitches in nearly the same place and creating a small equal sign above one eye for the rest of his life. Pretending that they too had supernatural powers and believing they were the greatest, our other son and four grandchildren exhibited similar behaviors when they were toddlers and preschoolers (fortunately, with no scars).

Among young children, pretending that you possess superpowers and believing that you are the greatest is normal. Indeed, such self-confidence and creativity are quite healthy. For most children, pretending and believing that you are the greatest quickly dissipates shortly after entering elementary school. Exceptions are narcissists—those who continue throughout adolescence and into adulthood to believe they are the greatest.

The term narcissism evolved from the Greek myth about a handsome young hunter named Narcissus. Narcissus rejected romantic advances by beautiful nymphs and fell in love with himself. Upon admiring his reflection in a pool of water, for hours every day he stared at his reflection until he withered away and died. A lovely flower grew at the place where he adored himself and it became known as the Narcissus (also called a daffodil).

Narcissism refers to excessive self-admiration and feelings of self-importance, superiority, and entitlement.[1] Persons high in narcissism are preoccupied about themselves and how others view them, perceiving themselves to be superior to others in physical attractiveness, intelligence, leadership, creativity, wealth, achievement (e.g., sports, academics, business), or areas of self-importance. Their perceptions of superiority and entitlement are inflated or exaggerated—inconsistent with objective evidence. Narcissists fantasize and project that they are the most successful, powerful, or greatest, but very few really are.

DOI: 10.4324/9781003401278-8

Narcissists are braggarts, arrogant, and conceited. To validate their sense of superiority, they crave and seek constant self-enhancing rewards, attention, praise, and admiration from others. Unlike non-narcissists with healthy self-esteem, narcissists love themselves *and* are obsessed about conveying to others their importance, superiority, and entitlement. Validation of their perceived superiority is often gained most readily by being in positions of power, leadership, or celebrity—positions they crave and seek.

Narcissists tend to be assertive extroverts who project dominance, boldness, and fearlessness. Few are lacking in social skills, and most are quite charming. Many are showmen, or desire to be such. They use their social skills and showmanship for their self-enhancement, which includes manipulating and exploiting others. Narcissists love the limelight, but only when they, not others, bask in it. Others in the limelight (i.e., *their* entitled limelight) are viewed as threats to their superiority—threats to be eradicated. Narcissists respond to threats and those who disagree with them by ridiculing, criticizing, belittling, or otherwise conveying that they are inferior. When in positions of sufficient authority, wealth, or physical power, their bullying includes firing, suing, or assaulting those they dislike.

Narcissists are viciously competitive, obsessed about winning, and unwilling to accept defeat. To them, there is only one winner, and all others are losers. They are enamored and obsessed about their own achievements and possessions and feel that others should share in their personal admiration. They believe they are entitled to special treatment, which includes others admiring and obeying them and demonstrating their unwavering loyalty.

Self-centered, selfish, and hedonistic, narcissists are lacking in empathy: They are insensitive or dismissive of the perspectives, needs, and feelings of others, as well as the impact of their behavior on others. Exceptions, however, are when demonstrating empathy to further their own narcissistic needs and desires or to alleviate their own personal distress. In such exceptions, empathy may be expressed in words or actions, but it is rarely truly felt, such as when narcissists thoughtlessly go through the motions of conveying sorrow and understanding (after being cued or told to do so, and perhaps reading what others had written for them).

The lack of empathy makes it easy for narcissists to take advantage of others and to treat others poorly. If this means taking credit from others, so be it. Gaining rewards and "winning" always outweighs any costs to others. Self-enhancement by claiming more credit than one deserves, exploiting others, and devaluing the achievements and contributions of others is a hallmark of the narcissist. Exploitation of others includes lying, cheating, stealing, and aggression—immoral behaviors found to be more common among narcissists than others.[2] Their greater aggression exists in all forms, which include verbal, social-relational, and physical bullying, as well as violent behavior.[3]

In their comprehensive review of over 400 studies of narcissism and aggression, researchers Sophie Kjærvik and Anne Herlache concluded that "narcissism is an important risk factor for aggression and violence."[4]

This is because narcissists are thin-skinned. They are quick to react with anger, aggression, and even rage at the slightest provocation or threat, whether real or imagined. This includes when criticized or corrected or when they believe others are treating them unfairly. Believing that others are treating them unfairly may occur simply when they fail to receive the attention, praise, admiration, and loyalty that they think they are entitled.

Interestingly, studies show that narcissists are quite insightful about their selfish, arrogant, and self-enhancing behavior and its negative impact on others; they simply don't care. It doesn't bother them if they hurt others or even if others think they are jerks as long they are the center of attention. Relationships are self-serving; they exist for self-enhancement or personal pleasure. Indeed, narcissists view narcissism as a favorable personality trait, although not necessarily a socially desirable one, and they intend to be more narcissistic.[5]

Narcissism and Self-Esteem Are Not the Same

Both self-esteem and narcissism refer to thinking favorably about oneself, but they differ in an important way. Self-esteem refers to an individual's overall evaluation of oneself, or global feelings of self-worth, general happiness, and self-acceptance.[6] In contrast, narcissism refers to feeling *superior* to others. The difference between thinking "I like myself" and "I'm the greatest" matters when it comes to behavior and mental health, as discussed later in this chapter. The difference also matters with respect to raising children. That is, nearly all parents want their children to have high self-esteem, but few want them to be narcissistic.

What accounts for high or low self-esteem? According to Dr. Susan Harter's research-based theory of self-concept, there are two major pathways to self-esteem.[7] The first pathway consists of an individual's perceptions of competence or adequacy in specific domains of life. For children in elementary and middle school, the most common domains are academic competence, social acceptance, behavioral competence, athletic competence, and physical appearance. The number of domains increases with age: job competence, close friendships, and romantic appeal become important during adolescence. Children and adolescents who perceive themselves as competent or adequate in those or other domains are likely to have high self-esteem. This is particularly true if the domains are ones the individual highly values. Competence, or the lack thereof, in domains not highly valued is much less important, as it has little negative impact on overall self-esteem. For example, it is easy for one to discount not being a star athlete or physically attractive when those two domains are not viewed as important.

The second major pathway to self-esteem consists of perceptions of social support from significant others. For most children, significant others are their parents, teachers, classmates, and close friends. For some children, however, significant others also include coaches, grandparents, additional relatives, and other members of the community. As with perceptions of competence in various domains, positive perceptions of social support, especially from those sources the individual values most highly, are associated with positive self-esteem. Among the various sources of social support and across all grade levels, parental support is the strongest predictor of self-esteem. During adolescence, however, often social support from peers is equally influential as that from parents.

In many ways, the pathways to narcissism are the same as for self-esteem. That is, perceptions of competence and social support are critically important. With respect to the first pathway, which is via self-perceptions of competence, narcissists are preoccupied about being *better* than others in one or more domains. Being competent or good enough is not sufficient; narcissists need to be the greatest (and want others to know it). The most common domains of superiority are physical appearance, achievement (academic or financial), athletics, social acceptance (including popularity), and romantic relations (e.g., for a narcissist, think trophy date or spouse). The behavioral domain, also often called the moral domain, is *not* among the domains most narcissists value highly. This is because the honest viewing of oneself as morally competent and living up to that self-view would likely interfere with the narcissist's self-perceived superiority. Thus, to protect overall self-esteem, many narcissists discount or dismiss the importance of the moral domain, allowing them to conclude "I'm great in all areas of life that are important!" They also dismiss or discount the importance of any other domain in which they do not claim to be superior.

With respect to the second pathway to self-esteem and narcissism, which is via perceived social support, narcissists are concerned mostly about being admired and praised by others, particularly those who feed their narcissism and serve their hedonistic needs. Parents, peers, and close friends are the primary sources of teaching and reinforcing narcissism in childhood and adolescence, as well as often throughout life. However, when it comes to sources of admiration, narcissists are not very selective, welcoming praise and rewards from almost anyone, believing "If they love me, they must have high standards and be beautiful people."

Parents want their children to have high self-esteem—to like themselves and to feel worthwhile. Few, however, want them to believe they are superior to all others. Even if their children *are* better than others, such as in physical attractiveness, sports, math, or music, few parents want their children bragging about it. Most people are not particularly fond of those who are conceited, braggards, and who care less about others. Fortunately, most children with high self-esteem are *not* narcissists. Unfortunately, too many parents overly reward and indulge their children, conveying a sense of entitlement, while thinking they are enhancing their children's self-esteem when they are enhancing both self-esteem *and* narcissism.

Contrary to the popular belief that narcissists are insecure and think poorly about themselves, high self-esteem is common among narcissists. This makes sense given that self-esteem and narcissism have similar roots or pathways.[8] It is a myth that deep down inside narcissists have feelings of insecurity, inadequacy, and inferiority. Some do, but most do not.

High self-esteem and high narcissism are a dangerous combination, especially its impact on others. Narcissists with high self-esteem believe "I love myself, am superior to all others, and care less about others who are inferior (i.e., nearly everyone else)." Whereas individuals with high self-esteem smile when they look in the mirror, those high in narcissism pound their chests, post daily photos or videos bragging about their achievements, and otherwise routinely and proudly communicate to others that they are superior, entitled, and in love with themselves. They are quick to attack anyone who challenges their superiority and entitlement.

As noted earlier, narcissists are competitive and aggressive. This is particularly true among narcissists with high self-esteem compared to those with modest self-esteem.[9] High self-esteem and high narcissism often translates into greater lying, cheating, and bullying, and even criminal acts, especially if those acts lead to greater fame and thus ego enhancement. As one might suspect, this combination magnifies negative relations with others.

When Is Narcissistic Behavior Normal?

Until about the age of about seven, children have positively biased perceptions of themselves. They believe they are competent, if not the greatest, at almost everything. Thus, they often think and act like narcissists.[10] Unlike narcissists, however, they do not view others as inferior. Sure, they often believe they are superior, but they also believe that everyone else can join them in pretending to be Superman, Wonder Woman, or otherwise possess superpowers. At this age, cognitive distortions and fantasies are normal, not pathological.

Self-perceptions of competence and overall self-esteem tend to decline as children move into middle childhood (grades 2 through 6) and again when they move into early adolescence (grades 7 through 9).[11] A rebound in self-esteem tends to occur in high school when adolescents discover more specific areas in which they can excel and experience personal satisfaction and success (e.g., sports, music, close relationships). Greater social support from close friends also helps enhance self-esteem during adolescence.

With increasing cognitive maturity, young children come to evaluate themselves more critically and realistically.[12] In early elementary school they begin to understand that they are better in some areas than others; that there is a real self and a make-believe self; that when compared to others, they are not as great as they thought; and that the evaluations by important others, whose perspectives they now understand, may not be positive but are realistic. They learn that others often differ in their evaluations—one teacher gives them an A, while another makes it clear that similar work is less deserving.

Such cognitive developments help children come to understand that they do not always get, or deserve, a sticker or grade of A for acceptable schoolwork, or a trophy for simply participating in a sport. With age, children's self-evaluations become increasingly consistent with external indicators, including valid evaluations by teachers and others based on objective criteria such as performance, progress made, and comparisons with others. Reality sets in. If external evaluations are favorable in areas a child values most highly, then self-esteem is likely to remain very high. Social support also matters greatly; it buffers the negative effects of external evaluations on self-esteem. A comforting parent, teacher, or friend is invaluable in helping a child cope with disappointment or failure and in fostering positive self-esteem.

Narcissistic children and adolescents who grow up to be narcissistic adults follow a different developmental course. Their self-perceptions of superiority and high self-esteem rarely waiver.[13] Unlike others, they never outgrow the unrealistically positive and inflated views of themselves held in early childhood. They learn from their parents, peers, and others, and they come to believe, that they are special, entitled, and superior to others despite evidence to the contrary—evidence that they disregard.

When Is Narcissistic Behavior Abnormal?

As true with lying, cheating, and bullying, narcissism falls along a continuum.[14] The distribution for narcissism tends to be a bell-shaped curve like one for intelligence, height, weight, aggression, generosity, and most human behaviors.[15] On one end of the continuum are individuals who rarely, if ever, exhibit the characteristics of a narcissist. Regardless of their actual wealth, intellect, athleticism, and achievements, they do not perceive themselves as superior and others as inferior. They are modest, humble, and caring.

Falling in the middle of the continuum are most of us: Individuals who exhibit narcissistic behaviors every now and then. Here I am not referring to behaviors commonly found among narcissists and non-narcissists alike that are related to positive mental health and life satisfaction such as high self-esteem, self-confidence, socially appropriate assertiveness, extraversion, and competitiveness. Instead, I am referring to the defining and maladaptive traits of narcissism such as a sense of superiority or grandiosity, the constant craving for admiration, and the lack of empathy (often seen in exploitation of others). To one degree or another, most children and adults display these narcissistic behaviors, but few do so to the point to which they harm relationships with others and others view them as a "narcissist."

At the other end of the continuum, or bell-shaped curve, are those individuals who frequently and continually display maladaptive narcissistic traits. Those are the individuals we commonly refer to as "narcissists," and whom psychologists recognize as having either a *narcissistic personality or a narcissistic personality disorder.* They are the individuals to whom I am referring when I use the term narcissist. However, recognize that most narcissists have not been diagnosed nor seen by a psychologist, as seeking help would greatly diminish their feelings of superiority and invincibility.

Although narcissistic personality and a narcissist personality disorder fall near the end of the continuum, the latter falls at the extreme end, reflecting a true psychiatric, or mental, disorder, mental illness, or pathology that interferes with personal functioning. Both narcissistic personality and a narcissist personality disorder share the same narcissistic traits; *the difference is a matter of degree, not kind.* It is estimated that 6.2% of all individuals (7.7% men, 4.8% women) warrant the diagnosis of a narcissistic personality disorder.[16] Many more, however, are considered to have a non-pathological narcissistic personality.

Narcissistic Personality Disorder

Narcissistic personality disorder is a clinical diagnosis made by a psychologist or other licensed mental health professional. The diagnosis must meet the criteria set forth in the American Psychiatric Association's *Diagnostic and Statistical Manual of Mental Disorders, Fifth Edition, Text Revision (DSM-V-TR)*. Accordingly, "the essential feature of narcissistic personality disorder is a pervasive pattern of grandiosity, need for admiration, and lack of empathy" as seen in five or more of the following nine symptoms, or traits:[17]

1 A grandiose sense of self-importance (e.g., exaggerates achievements and talents, expects to be recognized as superior without commensurate achievements).
2 Preoccupation with fantasies of unlimited success, power, brilliance, beauty, or ideal love.
3 Belief that he or she is "special" and unique and can only be understood by, or should associate with, other special or high-status people (or institutions).
4 Requires excessive admiration.
5 A sense of entitlement (i.e., unreasonable expectations of especially favorable treatment or automatic compliance with his or her expectations).
6 Interpersonal exploitation (i.e., takes advantage of others to achieve his or her own ends).
7 Lack of empathy: unwilling to recognize or identify with the feelings and needs of others.
8 Being often envious of others or believing that others are envious of him or her.
9 Showing arrogant, haughty behaviors or attitudes.

To warrant diagnosis, the above traits must be severe, lasting (not temporary), and exhibited across a variety of social contexts. Severity is seen in the traits causing significant impairment in relationships with others or serious personal distress. As noted in the DSM–5–TR: "Many highly successful individuals display personality traits that might be considered narcissistic. Only when these traits are inflexible, maladaptive, and persisting, and cause significant functional impairment or subjective distress, do they constitute narcissistic personality disorder."[18]

Although it is recognized that a narcissistic personality typically develops in childhood and adolescence, the diagnosis of narcissistic personality disorder should not be made until early adulthood. This is because it is not uncommon for children, and especially adolescents, to exhibit narcissistic behaviors; however, those behaviors are more transient, less pervasive, more normative, and less likely to interfere with personal functioning during that point in development.

As noted earlier, believing that one is superior to others, and even has superpowers, is common in early childhood. Likewise, narcissistic behaviors are common during adolescence.

Narcissistic behavior, such as frequent postings on Instagram, TikTok, and Facebook highlighting one's physical attractiveness, talents, or achievements does not necessarily make an adolescent, or you, a narcissist. However, frequent, and continual postings, especially when combined with other narcissistic behaviors (e.g., bragging, arrogance, lack of empathy, sense of superiority, exploitation of others), may well reflect the development of narcissistic personality or even a narcissistic personality disorder.

The Upside to Narcissism

There are certain positive aspects of narcissism. In addition to being associated with high self-esteem, narcissism is associated with popularity and leadership, including leadership positions in the military and large corporations.[19] This is because narcissists tend to be extroverts who exhibit assertiveness, charisma, social charms, motivation, and self-confidence. Many narcissists possess additional qualities that appeal to others such as physical attractiveness, humor, and wearing the latest fashions. Thus, they make favorable first impressions, and quickly emerge as leaders, especially when other leaders are absent, and the leadership takes place among those who have not known the narcissist for any length of time. First impressions are not very lasting, however, as the leadership effectiveness of narcissists deteriorates over time. This is particularly true among individuals with high, as opposed to moderate, levels of narcissism.[20]

The declining leadership effectiveness of narcissists over time can be attributed largely to their selfishness, self-centered motivation, intolerance of criticism and disagreement, and lack of empathy and caring about others. Because they are more concerned about their own success than that of others, they are not team players. Their relationships with others tend to be superficial, exploitative, and self-serving—serving to reinforce their feelings of superiority or to further enhance their ego and own ambitions.

Not only do narcissists fail to recognize the contributions of others (often falsely claiming credit themselves), but they also devalue others. They do so to make themselves look greater. Additional reasons why narcissists fail as leaders over time is that others figure out that narcissists are not as great as they claim or were first perceived. Moreover, arrogance, conceit, exaggerations, and bragging become wearing. All these factors come to alienate co-workers, who come to recognize that they pay the price for the narcissist's own self-enhancement.

Research on narcissism and leadership among children has yielded similar findings to that among adults: Children high in narcissism tend to be highly visible, popular (but not necessarily more "likable") and emerge as leaders. In a longitudinal study of children ages 7–14, Dr. Eddie Brummelman and colleagues found that children high in narcissism often emerged as leaders in their classrooms.[21] As expected, these narcissistic children viewed their leadership qualities more favorably than their peers. However, they were not as great of leaders as they thought they were. When given a group task to perform, they failed to display leadership behaviors any greater than other leaders who were lower in narcissism, nor were they viewed any more favorably (or negatively) than other leaders by their classmates. Another study followed children as they transitioned from primary into secondary school and found that whereas popularity was maintained among narcissists with modest self-esteem, it faded among those with high self-esteem.[22]

And the Downside

Whereas high self-esteem and leadership are positive outcomes associated with narcissism, there are negative outcomes. Primary among them is that narcissists are at increased risk for mental health problems, including depression, anxiety, mood disorders, aggression, obsessive-compulsiveness, phobias, substance abuse, and personality disorders in addition to narcissistic personality disorder.[23] It might seem paradoxical that someone with high self-esteem is at high risk for depression and high anxiety since those two mental health disorders, and especially depression, are commonly linked with *low* self-esteem. The combination of depression or anxiety with high self-esteem occurs when narcissists discover that they are not as great as they think, when they no longer receive the attention and admiration they crave, and when interpersonal relationships fail. In those situations, and when blaming others and denying responsibility are ineffective in avoiding responsibility, self-esteem takes a major hit.

Other negative outcomes are indirectly associated with narcissism and the result of problem behaviors being triggered by certain maladaptive aspects of narcissism. This is true with delinquent behavior. Research shows that narcissistic behavior adds to the prediction of delinquent behavior.[24] Believing they are entitled, loving the limelight, and being determined to exploit others for their own self-enhancement, narcissistic adolescents and adults, and more so males than females, are prone to engage in delinquent or criminal acts such as lying, cheating, stealing, drug abuse, vandalism, weapon possession, and assault.[25] In turn, those behaviors greatly increase the odds of social rejection and incarceration. As noted above with respect to the downside to possessing certain leadership qualities, over time narcissism also takes its toll on others who are the victims of the narcissist's aggression, bullying, lying, and cheating. This includes victims of failed romantic relationships and infidelity, which is all too common among narcissists.[26]

Are You, or Your Child, a Narcissist?

You might be wondering if you, your children, and others are narcissists. I designed the test below to help you make that determination. The test consists of 13 items characterizing a narcissist and 13 contrasting items characterizing someone with high self-esteem. The 13 statements were not designed for diagnosis, as there are plenty of valid measures of narcissism and self-esteem available to mental health specialists for that purpose. I have not administered the items to others, except our grandchildren and some of their friends (I was relieved to find that all were high in self-esteem and low in narcissism).

For each of the 13 items below, please read the sentence in both columns and CIRCLE the one sentence, either a or b, that better describes you. If neither sentence describes you well, circle "Neither."

1 a. I like myself. | b. I am greater than most others. | c. Neither
2 a. I get angry when others don't pay attention to me and don't praise or reward me. | b. There are times when I like to be recognized or rewarded for doing well. | c. Neither
3 a. Sometimes I make mistakes. | b. I never, or rarely, make mistakes. | c. Neither
4 a. I wish I were even greater than I am. | b. I am happy. | c. Neither
5 a. I work well with others. | b. I am a natural leader, and others should listen to me. | c. Neither
6 a. Others wish they were me. | b. I'm pleased with myself. | c. Neither
7 a. I care about others. | b. I care only about those who like me. | c. Neither
8 a. Others should help me more than they do. | b. I like to help others. | c. Neither
9 a. I'm a good person. | b. I am very special. | c. Neither
10 a. I am much better looking than most others. | b. I am pleased with how I look. | c. Neither
11 a. I do some things very well. | b. I'm better than others. | c. Neither
12 a. I love to show off to others. | b. I try to do my best, especially when others are watching me. | c. Neither
13 a. When I grow up, I want to be happy and successful. | b. When I grow up, I want to be famous. | c. Neither
14 a. I deserve to be treated better. | b. Most of the time I'm treated fairly. | c. Neither

---

Scoring your responses. For the odd items (1, 3, 5, 7, 9, 11, and 13), assign a score of 1 for each circled response of *b*. For the even numbers (2, 4, 6, 8, 10, 12, 14), score 1 for each circled response of *a*. Do not score responses of *c*. Enter your two total scores below:

Number of responses of *b* for odd numbered items: _____
Number of responses of *a* for even numbered items: _____
Total Score for Narcissism (adding the two entries above): _____

The higher the score, the greater the narcissism. Although I have not developed norms for this brief scale, my guess is most children and adults (i.e., non-narcissists) would receive a score of 3 or lower, although many adolescents would score slightly higher. Scores above 7 (responding in a narcissistic manner to over half the items) suggest narcissism.

Whereas a high score reflects narcissism, a low score reflects a very healthy self-concept. Items 1a, 4b, 6b, and 9a look more specifically at self-esteem; thus, circling those items would reflect high self-esteem (and without high narcissism).

Becoming a Narcissist (or Not)

As with other aspects of personality and mental health, ranging from happiness to personality disorders, narcissism is the product of a combination of nature and nurture.[27] Some people are born with temperamental and personality traits that drive narcissism such as greater impulsivity, frustration, demandingness, sensation seeking, and the lack of empathy. Others are born without those temperamental and personality traits but with traits that hinder narcissistic behavior such as empathy and agreeableness. The expression of temperamental and personality traits that either foster or hinder narcissistic behaviors is greatly influenced by environmental factors, including an array of sociocultural and contextual factors.

The influence of sociocultural factors is clearly seen in marked cultural differences in the prevalence of narcissism. For example, both narcissism and self-esteem are higher in Western countries, and particularly in the United States, than in Asian countries.[28] Interestingly, despite lower self-esteem among Asian students, ample research shows that they outperform nearly all other cultural groups in academic achievement. My colleagues and I have also found that Chinese and Japanese students not only outperform others academically but also exhibit fewer behavior problems in school and view their teachers and schools more favorably.[29] Such findings support the view of many experts that the importance of self-esteem in human behavior is often greatly exaggerated. As concluded in a comprehensive review of the research literature, "self-esteem per se is not the social panacea that many people once hoped it was."[30]

Differences in narcissism and behavior between individuals in Asian and Western countries can largely be attributed to the contrasting styles in how parents and teachers manage children's behavior. In brief, Asian parents and teachers place tend to be authoritative in their style of discipline, placing great emphasis on the development of self-discipline, especially the development of moral reasoning and moral emotions that underlie the assumption of responsibility and in turn, moral behavior.[31] This contrasts with American parents and teachers who place greater emphasis on the external control of children's behavior while relying highly on the use of rewards and punishment. Such emphasis on the frequent and controlling use of external praise and rewards, and especially the latter, is likely to promote narcissism, as seen in an overindulgent style of parenting.

Overindulgent and Permissive Parenting > Narcissism

If you have been told over and over that you are great, special, and superior to others, and have been treated as such, you are likely a narcissist. If you have children, they are likely to become narcissists too, for both genetic and environmental reasons. Children of narcissists are likely to inherit their parents' narcissistic-promoting temperament and personality traits,[32] and learn how to best express them.

Research on parenting shows that overindulgent, permissive, and authoritarian parenting styles are associated with narcissism.[33] Parents of narcissists excessively admire and overly valuate their children (and likely themselves), while communicating to their children that they are infallible and more attractive, talented, and smarter than others. Yes, this leads to high self-esteem, but it also leads to high narcissism. Like most other parents, those of narcissists praise and reward their children, but they do so excessively, not reasonably. They lavish their children with whatever their children so desire or whatever they think the greatest children—their children—are entitled, especially whatever might impress their neighbors and their children's peers. Their children internalize their parents' view that they are the greatest and entitled. When budding narcissists do not get what they want, they respond with indignation and tantrums, if not rage. In turn, their parents acquiesce to please their little princesses or princes and end their protesting. This stops the tantrum in the short term, but for the long-term tantrums are reinforced.

Not wanting to harm their children's self-esteem and sense of superiority, many parents of narcissistic children walk on eggshells, refraining from criticism and especially punishment. They also are quick to protect or defend their children from criticism by others and anything else their children find aversive. Thus, they blame teachers for their children's poor grades, coaches for their children performing poorly in a game (or for not starting in a game), and "mean" peers for not inviting their children to a party. Their children are not taught to learn from their mistakes, but instead, they learn that mistakes are not their fault. Avoiding criticism and punishment might enhance self-esteem in the short term, but it often leads to failure in the long term, as children fail to learn from their mistakes, accept responsibility, cope with failure, and persevere when faced with hardship. Eventually, narcissistic children experience a rude awakening when they discover that not everyone pampers or feeds their egos, such as when a teacher, coach, friend, classmate, or employer makes it clear that they are not as great as they think. When the response of tantrums or rage is no longer developmentally appropriate, or fails to change how they are treated, the outcome of believing that one has not lived up to the expectations of others, especially parents, and one's own expectations of being great is poor self-esteem.

Poor self-esteem is often associated with depression and anxiety. Although certainly not the only cause of suicide recently becoming the leading cause of death among American adolescents, surpassing accidents, overindulgent parenting is likely among contributing factors; not every adolescent can be what their parents have told them and treated them—the greatest.

Narcissistic children are spoiled, and what spoiled and narcissistic children have in common is overindulgent parents. However, it is important to note that *whereas nearly all narcissistic children are spoiled, most spoiled children are not narcissists.* Spoiling children is not the same as teaching them to be narcissists. Neither is good, but the latter is a lot worse. Spoiled children do not necessarily believe that they are entitled (which includes entitled to being spoiled) and that they are superior to others. Perhaps more importantly, unlike narcissists, spoiled children are not necessarily lacking in empathy. You can be spoiled and still care about others. Caring about others, especially the many others believed to be inferior, is very difficult for narcissists.

Overindulgent Parenting + Authoritarian Parenting > Narcissism

Whereas most parents of narcissistic children are overly indulgent and permissive, others are authoritarian.[34] Some are both: They lavish their children with praise and rewards while also being overly controlling and demanding perfection. Control, either psychological or physical, is a major characteristic of authoritarian parenting.[35] Authoritarian parents have high behavioral expectations, expecting their children to be the best, and they will do whatever it takes to ensure it. This often means controlling their children's lives, either psychologically (e.g., love withdrawal, shaming) or physically. They supervise and monitor their children constantly and closely. With tethered cell phones, narcissistic children and their parents are in constant communication. Constant supervision and external control are detrimental to children's social and emotional development. It stifles self-discipline, resilience, and grit, while fostering narcissism. When their children do not live up to their expectations, parental criticism is often overly harsh and shaming; communicating that if you aren't number one then you are inferior and a loser. Among many authoritarian parents, criticism is accompanied by overly harsh punishment, including corporal punishment. Their children come to treat, and manipulate, others the same when they do not live up to their expectations.

Birds of a Feather

Next to parenting, the environmental factor influencing narcissism and self-esteem the greatest is relations with peers and close friends. This is especially true in adolescence and adulthood. Narcissists are attracted to and admire one another. Because most people do not care much for others who are braggards, bullies, self-centered, and noncaring, it should come as no surprise that narcissists have few friends, especially close ones, and the friends they do have tend to be fellow narcissists.[36]

Narcissists feed on one another's egos; they share in demonstrating to others how great they are. Relationships are mutually self-enhancing. This applies not only to peer relationships but also to intimate relationships.[37] Romantic partners are seen as trophies or great conquests. Star athletes, billionaires, models, and other celebrities are attracted to one another. The relationships are reciprocal and mutually self-enhancing ("I'm great and so are you"), but also expendable. When their partner no longer feeds the narcissist's ego and desires, another partner is sought who is equally or more beautiful, wealthy, powerful, socially prominent, loyal, and admiring of the narcissist. Ending a romantic relationship with a narcissist can be very ugly, as narcissists must prove that they are not at fault for their failed relationships and that they are always the winners in absolving any relationship. Lacking empathy and viewing harm to others as either amoral or morally defensible, narcissists can readily move on to other self-enhancing conquests.

Narcissistic Thoughts and Emotions

As with lying, cheating, and bullying, basic principles of social learning, particularly positive reinforcement, modeling, and punishment (i.e., in the case of narcissism, it is often the *absence* of punishment or negative consequences following misbehavior), largely explain how children learn each of the symptoms or traits of narcissism. Learned primarily at home but also from the media and peers, those symptoms and traits are applied and reinforced at home, school, in sports, and in media they control themselves, such as TikTok and Instagram. The same principles of social learning that largely explain narcissistic behaviors also explain how children develop thoughts and emotions that underlie and support those narcissistic behaviors. Primary among them are the three cognitive and emotional characteristics, or character traits, of individuals mentioned in previous chapters and discussed more thoroughly in Chapter 10. As applied to narcissism, those three traits are:

1 *Amorality and Immature Moral Reasoning.* As with liars, cheaters, and bullies, narcissists view their self-promoting and self-centered behavior as either amoral (i.e., not a moral issue) or morally justified. Moral justifications for narcissistic behaviors are grounded in the same immature and hedonistic moral reasoning commonly found among young children and

juvenile delinquents when justifying their bullying, cheating, lying, and other antisocial behaviors—that nothing is wrong with maximizing rewards, manipulating, and dominating others, and believing others are inferior. Entitlement is granted by birthright or position of power or wealth. By being king, president, or rich, any behavior is justified that makes the narcissist feel superior, especially if the behavior results in being in the limelight (and with cheering fans).

2 *Lack of empathy, guilt, and shame.* Narcissists focus on themselves, not on others, which is easy to do when lacking the moral emotions of empathy, guilt, and shame. As noted previously, lack of empathy is a common characteristic of narcissism. Likewise, related to the lack of empathy, narcissists tend to experience less guilt and shame than others.[38] Research also shows that as in the "cheaters high," narcissists often take pleasure in the harm and suffering they cause others in their social relations.[39]

3 *Moral disengagement.* Immature self-centered moral reasoning and the lack of moral emotions are common among narcissists and often explain their immoral behavior. However, many narcissists are quite capable of engaging in mature moral reasoning, such as thinking about the needs of others, and in experiencing empathy, guilt, and shame. The problem is that they fail to do so unless it serves their own self-interests. Narcissists use various mechanisms of moral disengagement, such as denial and blaming, to convince themselves, and often others, that moral reasoning and moral emotions are not applicable in given situations—situations that benefit them. This absolves themselves of any sense of responsibility for harm done to others. Narcissists are more prone than others to use mechanisms of moral disengagement, especially when engaged in aggression and other antisocial behaviors, including in contact sports (e.g., soccer, rugby, football, hockey)[40] and when cheating on their spouses.[41]

In *The Narcissism Epidemic: Living in the Age of Entitlement,* authors Dr. Jean Twenge and Dr. W. Keith Campbell convincingly argue that narcissism has become epidemic. They chronicle the development in America of "the corrosive narcissism that threatens to infect us all" and warn readers that "narcissism causes almost all the things that Americans hoped high self-esteem would prevent, including aggression, materialism, lack of caring for others, and shallow values. In trying to build a society that celebrates high self-esteem, self-expression, and 'loving yourself,' Americans have inadvertently created more narcissists and a culture that brings out the narcissistic behavior in all of us."[42] The book was published in 2009, before America elected a president who for decades has been the epitome of a role model of narcissism, as seen in the following chapter. Children have watched and learned how lying, cheating, and bullying get things done and that they should feel good about it.

Notes

1 Sander Thomaes and Eddie Brummelman, 2016. "Narcissism" in *Developmental Psychopathology: Maladaptation and Psychopathology, Vol. 3*, edited by Dante Cicchetti. New York: John Wiley and Sons, 679–725. https://doi.org/10.1002/9781119125556.devpsy316

   Emily Grijalva and Luyao Zhang, 2016. "Narcissism and Self-Insight: A Review and Meta-Analysis of Narcissists' Self-Enhancement Tendencies." *Personality and Social Psychology Bulletin* 42 no. 1: 3–24. http://dx.doi.org/10.1177/0146167215611636

2 Ziatan Krizan and Anne D. Herlache, 2021. "The Link between Narcissism and Aggression: A Meta-Analytic Review." *Psychological Bulletin* 147 no. 5: 477–503. https://doi.org/10.1037/bul0000323

   Charles A. O'Reilly III and Bernadette Doerr, 2020. "Conceit and Deceit: Lying, Cheating, and Stealing among Grandiose Narcissists." *Personality and Individual Differences* 154: 1–10. https://doi.org/10.1016/j.paid.2019.109627

3 Krizan and Herlache.

4 Ibid., 477.

5 Erika N. Carlson, 2013. "Honestly Arrogant or Simply Misunderstood? Narcissists' Awareness of Their Narcissism." *Self and Identity* 12 no. 3: 259–277. https://doi.org/10.1080/15298868.2012.659427

6 Maureen A. Manning, George G. Bear, and Kathleen M. Minke, 2006. "Self-Concept and Self-Esteem" in *Children's Needs III: Development, Prevention, and Intervention*, edited by George G. Bear and Kathleen M. Minke. Bethesda, MD: National Association of School Psychologists, 341–356.

7 Susan Harter, 2012. *The Construction of the Self, Second Edition: Developmental and Sociocultural Foundations, 2nd Edition*. New York: Guilford.

8 Jean M. Twenge and W. Keith Campbell, 2009. *The Narcissism Epidemic: Living in the Age of Entitlement*. New York: Free Press.

9 Ibid.

10 Harter.

   Eddie Brummelman, Sander Thomaes, Stefanie A. Nelemans, Bram Orobio de Castro, Geertjan Overbeek, and Brad Bushman, 2015. "Origins of Narcissism in Children." *PNAS Proceedings of the National Academy of Sciences of the United States of America* 112 no. 12: 3659–3662. https://doi.org/10.1073/pnas.1420870112

11 Harter.

   Manning and Bear.

12 Harter.

13 Thomaes and Brummelman.

14 Ziatan Krizan and Anne D. Herlache, 2018. "The Narcissism Spectrum Model: A Synthetic View of Narcissistic Personality." *Personality and Social Psychology Review* 22 no. 1: 3–31. https://doi.org/10.1177/1088868316685018

15 Thomaes and Brummelman.

16 Frederick S. Stinson, Deborah A. Dawson, Rise B. Goldstein, Patricia Chou, Boji Hunag, Sharon M. Smith, W. June Ruan, Attila J. Pulay, Tulshi D. Saha, Roger P. Pickering, and Bridget Grant, 2008. "Prevalence, Correlates, Disability, and Comorbidity of DSM-IV Narcissistic Personality Disorder: Results from the Wave 2 National Epidemiologic Survey on Alcohol and Related Conditions." *Journal of Clinical Psychiatry* 69 no. 7: 1033–1045. https://doi.org/10.4088/jcp.v69n0701

17 American Psychiatric Association, 2022. *Diagnostic and Statistical Manual of Mental Disorders, Fifth Edition, Text Revision*. Washington, DC: American Psychiatric Association, 760.

18 Ibid., 764.

19 Carlson.
Emily Grijalva, Peter D. Harms, Daniel A. Newman, and Blaine H. Gaddis, 2015. "Narcissism and Leadership: A Meta-Analytic Review of Linear and Nonlinear Relationships." *Personnel Psychology* 68 no. 1:1–47. https://doi.org/10.1111/peps.12072

20 Grijalva and Zhang.

21 Eddie Brummelman, Barbara Nevicka. and Joseph M. O'Brien, 2021. "Narcissism and Leadership in Children." *Psychological Science* 32 no. 3: 354–363. https://doi.org/10.1177/0956797620965536

22 Astrid M. G. Poorthuis, Meike Slagt, Marcel A. G. van Aken, Jaap J. A. Denissen, and Sander Thomaes, 2012. "Narcissism and Popularity among Peers: A Cross-Transition Longitudinal Study." *Self and Identity* 20 no. 2: 282–296. https://doi.org/10.1080/15298868.2019.1609575

23 Stinson et al.
Albert Reijntjes, Marjolijn Vermande, Sander Thomaes, Frits Goossens, Tjeert Olthof, Liesbeth Aleva, and Matty Van der Meulen, 2016. "Narcissism, Bullying, and Social Dominance in Youth: A Longitudinal Analysis." *Journal of Abnormal Child Psychology* 44 no. 1: 63–74. https://doi.org/10.1007/s10802-015-9974-1

24 Christopher T. Barry, Paul J. Frick, Kristy K. Adler, and Sarah J. Grafeman, 2007. "The Predictive Utility of Narcissism among Children and Adolescents: Evidence for a Distinction between Adaptive and Maladaptive Narcissism." *Journal of Child and Family Studies* 16 no. 4: 508–521. https://link.springer.com/article/10.1007/s10826-006-9102-5

25 O'Reilly III and Doerr.

26 Laura Widman and James K. McNulty, 2011. "Narcissism and Sexuality." In *The Handbook of Narcissism and Narcissistic Personality Disorder: Theoretical Approaches, Empirical Findings, and Treatments,* edited by W. Keith Campbell and Joshua D. Miller. New York: John Wiley and Sons, 351–359.

27 Joel Paris, 2014. "Modernity and Narcissistic Personality Disorder." *Personality Disorders: Theory, Research, and Treatment* 5 no. 2: 220–226. https://doi.org/10.1037/a0028580

28 Joshua D. Foster, W. Keith Campbell, and Jean M. Twenge, 2003. "Individual Differences in Narcissism: Inflated Self-Views across the Lifespan and around the World." *Journal of Research in Personality* 37 no. 6: 469–486. https://doi.org/10.1016/S0092-6566(03)00026-6

29 George G. Bear, Dandan D. Chen, Lindsey Mantz, Chunyan Yang, Xishan Huang, and Kunior Shiomi, K., 2016. "Differences in Classroom Removals and Use of Praise and Rewards in American, Chinese, and Japanese Schools." *Teaching and Teacher Education,* 53: 41–50. https://doi.org/10.1016/j.tate.2015.10.003
George G. Bear, Chunyan Yang, Joseph Glutting, Xishan Huang, Xianyou He, Wei Zhang, and Dandan Chen, 2015. "Teacher–Student Relationships, Student-Student Relationships, and Conduct Problems in China and the U.S." *Journal of International School and Educational Psychology,* 2 no. 4: 247–260. https://doi.org/10.1080/21683603.2014.883342

30 Roy F. Baumeister, Jennifer D. Campbell, Joachim I. Krueger, and Kathleen D. Vohs, 2003. "Does High Self-Esteem Cause Better Performance, Interpersonal Success, Happiness, or Healthier Lifestyles?" *Psychological Science in the Public Interest* 4 no. 1: 1–44, 26. https://doi.org/10.1111/1529-1006.01431

31 George G. Bear, Maureen A. Manning, and Kunio Shiomi, 2006. "Children's Reasoning about Aggression: Differences between Japan and the United States and Implications for School Discipline." *School Psychology Review* 35 no. 1: 62–77. https://doi.org/10.1080/02796015.2006.12088002

32 Philip A. Vernon, K. V. Petrides, Denis Bratko, and Julie Aiken Schermer, "A Behavioral Genetic Study of Trait Emotional Intelligence." *Emotion* 8, no. 5, 2008: 635–642. https://doi.org/10.1037/a0013439
33 Brummelman et al.
    Robert S. Horton, 2011. "Parenting as a Cause of Narcissism: Empirical Support for Psychodynamic and Social Learning Theories." In *The Handbook of Narcissism and Narcissistic Personality Disorder: Theoretical Approaches, Empirical Findings, and Treatments,* edited by W. Keith Campbell and Joshua D. Miller. New York: John Wiley and Sons, 181–190.
34 Ibid.
35 Astrid et al.
36 Ulrike Maab, Lena Lämmle, Doreen Bensch, and Matthias Ziegler, 2016. "Narcissists of a Feather Flock Together: Narcissism and the Similarity of Friends." Personality and Social Psychology Bulletin 42 no. 3: 366–384. https://dx.doi.org/10.1177/0146167216629114
37 Widman and McNulty.
38 Pauline Georgees Poless, Linda Torstveit, Ricardo Gregorio Lugo, Marita Andreassen, and Stefan Sütterlin, 2018. "Guilt and Proneness to Shame: Unethical Behaviour in Vulnerable and Grandiose Narcissism." *European Journal of Psychology* 14 no. 1: 28–43. https://doi.org/10.5964/ejop.v14i1.1355
39 Seda Erzi, 2020. "Dark Triad and Schadenfreude: Mediating Role of Moral Disengagement and Relational Aggression." *Personality and Individual Differences* 157 no. 15: 109827. https://doi.org:10.1016/j.paid.2020.109827
40 Benjamin D. Jones, Tim Woodman, Matthew Barlow, and Ross Roberts, 2017. "The Darker Side of Personality: Narcissism Predicts Moral Disengagement and Antisocial Behavior in Sport." *The Sport Psychologist* 31: 109–116. https://doi.org/10.1123/tsp.2016-0007
41 Widman and McNulty.
42 Tweege and Campbell, 9.

9   Trump
A Role Model for Narcissism

On a Scale of 1–10, He's a 10

Just as Trump is a pathological liar, cheater, and bully, so too is he a narcissist. On a scale of 1 to 10, he certainly rates 10. Nearly all mental health experts would agree that he is a classic narcissist. For example, in *The Dangerous Case of Donald Trump*, 37 widely known psychiatrists and mental health experts present their opinions about Trump's mental health.[1] With respect to narcissism, there was overwhelming consensus that Trump is a narcissist. For ethical reasons, however, they refrained from giving Trump a formal psychiatric diagnosis, including the diagnosis of a narcissistic personality disorder. Following the ethical code that guides psychiatrists, they are not to diagnose anyone without first conducting an examination and are not to share the results with others unless granted permission from the patient to do so.[2]

In the *New York Times* Bestseller, *Too Much and Never Enough: How My Family Created the World's Most Dangerous Man*, Dr. Mary L. Trump, a clinical psychologist and Trump's niece, asserts that her uncle clearly meets all criteria set forth in the DSM for the diagnosis of narcissistic personality disorder. Many other psychologists and psychiatrists concur, referring to Trump as a "textbook narcissistic personality disorder"[3] and "incapable of attending to any issue beyond his own personal need for adulation"[4] and noting that "Remarkably, virtually all definitions apply to Donald Trump."[5]

In addition to narcissistic personality disorder, some mental health professionals assert that Trump meets criteria in the DSM for *antisocial personality disorder*—a more serious diagnosis commonly made for individuals considered as psychopaths or sociopaths (neither of which are formal psychiatric diagnoses).

Although there is consensus that Trump is a model narcissist, not all mental health experts agree with Dr. Mary Trump and others that Trump's narcissism meets all DSM criteria for the psychiatric diagnosis of narcissistic personality disorder, and fewer agree that he meets the criteria for antisocial personality disorder. In this chapter we look at Trump's narcissism and

DOI: 10.4324/9781003401278-9

whether it is severe enough to warrant the psychiatric diagnosis of narcissistic personality disorder. Additionally, we look at whether Trump meets the criteria for antisocial personality disorder. Finally, we ask if it is more fitting to describe Trump not as "crazy" as in having a psychiatric disorder but instead as "crazy as a fox."

To What Extent Does Trump Exhibit the Nine Symptoms or Traits of Narcissistic Personality Disorder?

As stated in the most recent (2022) edition of the DSM, which is the *Diagnostic and Statistical Manual of Mental Disorders, Fifth Edition, Text Revised* (DSM–V–TR), "The essential feature of narcissistic personality disorder is a pervasive pattern of grandiosity, need for admiration, and lack of empathy beginning in early adulthood and present in a variety of contexts."[6] Nine symptoms, or traits, of the disorder are presented. To be diagnosed with narcissistic personality disorder, an individual must exhibit five or more of them. Let's look at each of the nine symptoms and traits and the extent to which Trump's behavior matches each one.

A Grandiose Sense of Self-Importance (e.g., Exaggerates Achievements and Talents, Expects to Be Recognized as Superior without Commensurate Achievements)

According to Trump, no one knows as much, has achieved as much, and is as great as he is. As he stated in his acceptance speech as presidential candidate at 2016 Republican National Convention, he believes "I alone can fix it!"[7] The following are quotes of Trump bragging and proclaiming his superiority about almost everything, as reported by Aaron Blake in *The Washington Post*[8] and by Haley Britzky in *Axios.*[9]

The Economy, Trade, and Jobs
"Nobody knows more about trade than me."
"Nobody knows jobs like I do!"
"I think I know about it [the economy] better than [the Federal Reserve]."

Banking, Debt, and Taxes
"Nobody knows banking better than I do."
"Nobody knows more about debt. I'm like the king. I love debt."
"I think nobody knows more about taxes than I do, maybe in the history of the world. Nobody knows more about taxes."

Construction and Infrastructure
"[N]obody knows more about construction than I do."
"Nobody in the history of this country has ever known so much about infrastructure as Donald Trump." [Note that Trump has often referred to himself in the third person, which is another telltale sign of a narcissist).

Technology
"Technology—nobody knows more about technology than me."

Courts and Lawsuits
"I know more about courts than any human being on Earth."
"[W]ho knows more about lawsuits than I do? I'm the king."

Immigration
"Because nobody knows the system better than me. I know the H1B. I know the H2B. Nobody knows it better than me."

U.S. Government and Politicians
"Nobody knows the [government] system better than I do." (This statement was made after only four months of experience in government, and as president).
"Nobody knows politicians better than Donald Trump."

Others on Television
"I know more about people who get ratings than anyone."

Military and Even Drones
"There's nobody bigger or better at the military than I am."
"I know more about ISIS [the Islamic State militant group] than the generals do. Believe me."
"I know more about offense and defense than they will ever understand, believe me. Believe me. Than they [military generals] will ever understand."
"I know more about drones than anybody."

Coronavirus
"I like this stuff. I really get it .... People are really surprised I understand this stuff .... Every one of these doctors said, 'How do you know so much about this?' Maybe I have a natural ability." (Boasting to reporters while visiting the Centers for Disease Control.)

Trump claimed not only to be "really smart" but so smart he should "qualify as not smart, but genius ... and a very stable genius at that!" to be "so great looking and smart, a true Stable Genius," and to be "the super genius of all time."[10] If Trump were a true genius, he would not have hired someone to take the college entrance exam for him, as claimed by his niece. Likewise, his performance in high school and college would not have been judged by his teachers as mediocre. If he is a genius, or even "really smart," one also would think that his name would appear on the list of honor students in the colleges he attended. It doesn't.

That Trump is no genius is attested to by very reliable sources, including several Cabinet secretaries and multiple others in the government who worked closely with him. Indeed, many of them often mocked Trump's knowledge deficits and his frequent refusal to read or listen to important briefing reports. As reported in Carol Leonnig and Philp Rucker's book *A Very Stable Genius: Donald J. Trump's Testing of America*, Trump's former Secretary of State, Rex Tillerson, described Trump as "a man who is pretty undisciplined, doesn't like to read, doesn't read briefing reports, doesn't like to get into the details of a lot of things, but rather just kind of said, 'Look, this is what I believe and you can try to convince me otherwise, but most of the time you're not going to do that.'"[11]

Others have been less kind when commenting about Trump's intelligence, or lack thereof, viewing his IQ not at the genius level but closer to intellectually challenged, especially when it comes to decision-making. Several in the White House called him an "idiot," including Treasury Secretary Steven Mnuchin, chief of staff Reince Priebus, economic advisor Gary Cohn (who also said that Trump was "dumb as shit" and "an idiot surrounded by clowns"), and advisor Sam Nunberg. John Down, Trump's White House lawyer, also was among those who called him an idiot, insisting that Trump not testify in person before Congress during his first impeachment trial because he would certainly lie, and thus be stupid enough to cause himself more harm than good. National security advisor H.R. McMaster called him "an idiot with the intelligence of a kindergartener" and a "dope." Secretary of Defense James Mattis was a bit more generous, saying that Trump acted like and had the understanding of a "fifth-or sixth-grader."[12]

Consistent with boasting of being the smartest living genius, Trump claims to have achieved more than any other president in history. After his first two years in office, he boasted "Nobody has ever done so much in the first two years of a presidency as this administration. Nobody. Nobody." On another occasion, Trump conceded that Abraham Lincoln was a greater president, placing himself as #2 among all presidents.[13] However, in a 2022 interview in which he claimed to have been elected president twice, he also asserted that he was more popular and well-liked than both Lincoln and Washington, stating "I think it would be hard if George Washington came back from the dead and he chose Abraham Lincoln as his vice president, I think it would have been very hard for them to beat me."[14]

Preoccupation with Fantasies of Unlimited Success, Power, Brilliance, Beauty, or Ideal Love

Trump's preoccupation with fantasies of unlimited success and brilliance is seen in most of the quotes presented above. With respect to beauty, Trump also proclaimed to be "great looking," while stating at one campaign rally that he is so attractive that he had been told that he looked like Elvis Presley (ironically, while also stating at the same rally that he is not conceited).[15] Reflecting his preoccupation with fantasies of success and beauty, and fusing the two, Trump once stated that "Part of the beauty of me is that I am very rich."[16] One of his most infamous quotes speaks to his preoccupation with both power and what he sees as ideal love: "And when you're a star, they let you do it. You can do anything ... Grab'em by the pussy. You can do anything."[17] On another occasion, Trump similarly stated "It doesn't really matter what [the media] write as long as you've got a young and beautiful piece of ass."[18] And, upon admiring a woman entering his Mar-a-Lago golden resort Trump commented "there is nothing in the world like first-rate pussy."[19]

While in office, Trump often viewed himself more as a king than the president of the U.S. (and his family as the royal family). Among the examples of Trump perceiving himself to have the power of be a king was his responses to reporters during one of his infamous televised White House conferences on the coronavirus. During that conference Trump commented that he would not allow any governor of a state to shut down the state's economy regardless of the number of coronavirus-related deaths, stating: "The President of the United States has the authority to do what the President has the authority to do, which is very powerful. The President of the United States calls the shots."[20] When a reporter noted that the 10th Amendment of the Constitution does not give him that power, Trump responded: "when somebody is the President of the United States, the authority is total, and that's the way it's got to be." The reporter replied: "It's total? Your authority is total?" Trump answered: "It's total. It's total." To which the reporter asked: "But who told you the President has the total authority?" The president ended the conversation with: "Enough. Please." Constitutional experts strongly disagreed with Trump that he had such power.[21] Several days later he retracted, via tweet, his insistence on having "total authority."

Like a young child, Trump enjoys playing pretend, or acting out a fantasy. Many children pretend to be a doctor or scientist who wins the Nobel Peace Prize, a military hero worthy of receiving a Purple Heart or a Medal of Honor, or a superhero with magical powers who defeats evil. Trump never won the Nobel Peace Prize, but he tried to arrange to be granted one. Envious of Obama receiving that honor in the first year of his presidency, Trump reportedly lobbied Japanese Prime Minister Shinzo Abe and other Asian heads of state to nominate him.[22]

Although he never served in the military (having been granted draft deferments for bone spurs on his heel), Trump also suggested that he should award himself the Presidential Medal of Honor. Fortunately, his aides persuaded him against it.[23]

Immediately after being elected, Trump began expressing some of his fantasies: He falsely claimed that he had the largest inauguration crowd in history. His fantasies continued to the bitter end of his presidency, and to this day, with him repeatedly claiming that he won re-election and "BY A LOT." Many additional examples of child-like fantasizing were seen throughout his presidency. This included fantasizing about having his own military parade on the National Mall. That idea originated when he was watching the Bastille

Day celebrations in France with French President Emmanuel Macron. Trump asked his top military brass to arrange for a similar parade.[24] Drawing from his days as a television producer, Trump fantasized about choreographing war planes flying over the Capitol, tanks and missile carriers plowing down the streets of Washington, D.C., and fireworks bursting "TRUMP" in the background while he gave a nationally televised address about the greatness of America (while claiming all the credit).[25]

Trump also fantasized about joining George Washington, Thomas Jefferson, Abraham Lincoln, and Theodore Roosevelt at the Mount Rushmore National Memorial in South Dakota, proposing the idea to the state's governor. Later, he denied having proposed this, but nevertheless tweeted that it was a "good idea" based on his accomplishments being "perhaps more than any other Presidency."[26] This was tweeted on August 12, 2020, when the daily average death count for the coronavirus was spiking for the summer and was over 1,000.[27]

It is not uncommon for young children to enjoy pretending being tough, head-bashing wrestlers who power over all opponents on a stage while thousands of spectators cheer. As an adult, Trump appeared numerous times on stage with "professional" wrestlers. His staged campaign rallies had a similar "beat the bad guys and win at any cost" atmosphere. Among his staged wrestling events was WrestleMania's Battle of the Billionaires. Trump picked the wrestler, Bobby Lashley, to represent him in a match against Umaga who represented the billionaire owner of World Wrestling Entertainment (WWE), Vince McMahon. For winning his bet in the match, Trump shaved McMahon's head on stage and on national television. Trump was later inducted into the WWE Hall of Fame. (He also received millions of dollars in campaign contributions from McMahon, and his wife, Linda. After his election, Trump appointed Linda McMahon as Administrator of the Small Business Administration.)[28]

Perhaps the best example of Trump's fantasizing about unlimited power as president was his plan to pretend to be Superman.[29] After being released from the hospital for the coronavirus, he seriously considered a publicity stunt in which he would wear a Superman tee-shirt under his dress shirt, coat, and tie. Upon arriving at the White House in the presidential helicopter, he would then climb up to the balcony and dramatically peel aside his mask. Trump performed those first three steps of his fantasy. Fortunately, others wisely talked him out of what he had planned next. Next, he would open his sports coat and rip open his button-down dress shirt to reveal the Superman logo as a sign of strength that he defeated the evil enemy. The enemy was the virus, which Americans no longer needed to fear because Superman had survived the battle!

Trump's narcissistic fantasies of being Superman continued in 2023 after losing reelection, with him producing and hawking digital trading cards, at $99 each, with images of him as Superman-like superheroes, a Top Gun fighter pilot, an astronaut, a hunter in camo gear holding a shotgun, a sheriff, and a boxer.[30]

Requiring Excessive Admiration

In an article entitled, "The Psychopath in Chief," Tony Schwartz, ghostwriter for Trump's book *The Art of the Deal*, concluded that after he had spent considerable time with Trump it was quite clear that Trump was lacking in empathy, obsessed about always winning at any cost, and "driven by an insatiable narcissistic hunger to be loved, accepted, admired, and praised."[31] Critics and supporters alike agree that Trump has always required constant and excessive admiration, and willing to say or do almost anything to receive it. Examples abound. A few of my favorites follow.

At his second wedding, to Marla Maples, guests at each of the tables were presented with a life-size photo of Trump's head on a stick. Seeking excessive admiration, but also fantasizing about being someone powerful, Trump also arranged to be introduced to the wedding guests in a fashion of a championship boxing match. As described by D'Antonio in *The Truth about Trump*, guests watched Trump enter the ballroom to "the rousing theme music from the movie *Rocky*, as the announcer bellowed, 'let's hear it for the king!'—and Trump burst through a large paper screen. He emerged wearing big red boxing gloves and a red robe draped over a tuxedo. Then, as if this weren't sufficiently awkward, Trump casino executive Nick Ribis offered the crowd a paean to his boss in the style of Muhammad Ali: 'He was tough and resilient and he had no fear. He made the comeback of the year. Against all odds, his opponents buckled with a thump. The winner was, Donald J Trump.'"[32]

Trump has always expected applause and admiration, especially upon entering any stage. When Democrats did not applaud him during his first State of the Union address, he accused them of "bad energy," being "un-American," and treason (which is punishable by death).[33]

Requiring excessive admiration is perhaps best seen in Trump's obsession that his name be emblazoned in golden letters on his buildings and products; in Trump's love of performing at campaign rallies before his adoring supporters; and in his thousands of self-congratulatory tweets and announcements of his greatness. His self-admiration and other characteristics of narcissism are on display in over a dozen self-promoting books he wrote (nearly all of which are believed to be written largely, if not entirely, by ghostwriters). When a reporter once asked Trump to name his favorite books, Trump named two of his own books, *The Art of the Deal* and *How to Get Rich*.[34] (In another interview, however, he did concede that the Bible was better, while also noting that his favorite verse or story in the Bible is "an eye for an eye.")[35] One of his favorite movies is *The Greatest Showman*,[36] which is about fellow entertainer and narcissist P.T. Barnum's rise to fame with his circus.

When the government issued stimulus checks to millions of Americans to help offset the negative effects of the coronavirus on the economy, Trump insisted that his name appear on each check, which slowed the delivery of the checks. This act of vanity was the first for an American president, as no other had his name on a check sent from the Internal Revenue Service.[37]

Throughout his presidency Trump's excessive hunger for admiration was largely fed by his cabinet members, staff, and family members, and in campaign rallies. In his infamous first full cabinet meeting, each member of his cabinet took turns lavishing him with praise and what looked like kneeling before their king. His chief of staff, Reince Priebus, proclaimed "On behalf of the entire senior staff around you, Mr. President, we thank you for the opportunity and the blessing that you've given us to serve your agenda and the American people."[38]

When the coronavirus restricted his campaign rallies, Trump substituted them with daily coronavirus briefings, which often lasted over 90 minutes and during which time he monopolized the stage. As commented by the Editorial Board of the conservative *Wall Street Journal*, Trump's "wasted briefings" were "a showcase for him," "all about the President," and "more about the many feuds of Donald J. Trump" than about the virus. The board further noted that during Trump's self-produced showcase, "His first-rate health experts have become supporting actors, and sometimes barely that, ushered on stage to answer a technical question or two."[39]

A Sense of Entitlement (i.e., Unreasonable Expectations of Especially Favorable Treatment or Automatic Compliance with His or Her Expectations)

Trump always had a sense of entitlement, with his billionaire father telling him he was be become a "king" and "killer."[40] Although entitled to become king (or president), Trump viewed the White House as beneath his standards. As reported by Rick Reilly in *Commander in Cheat*, upon being elected president Trump once told golfers at his Bedminster resort in New Jersey that "I can't believe I got to live in the White House. What a fucking dump."[41] He thought similarly about the government's Camp David in the nearby mountains of Maryland, where previous presidents vacationed and played golf. Trump viewed Camp David as too rustic and not worth staying more than 30 minutes.[42] Whenever he could, including most weekends, he thus escaped to either his glitzy 110,000 square foot Mar-a-Lago or to his secluded castle-like Bedminster golf resort.

It was at Mar-a-Lago that Trump, after losing reelection, illegally stored government documents, many of which were classified and top-secrets. He believed that they belonged to him, as seen in Trump telling advisers "They're mine."[43] As noted by Maggie Haberman of *The New York Times*, "For four years, former President Donald J. Trump treated the federal government and the political apparatus operating in his name as an extension of his private real estate company."[44] Having covered Trump for several decades, Haberman described Trump as a "pack rat" who finds it exciting to collect and show others objects that reflect how important or great he is, fusing sports memorabilia, such as a pair of Shaquille O'Neal's basketball shoes with top secret records.

Trump also believed he was entitled to, and thus demanded, complete loyalty from those who worked with him, which meant automatic and unwavering compliance with his expectations. As both the head of his businesses and as president of the United States, demanding especially favorable treatment was reflected in the expected general understanding among everyone who worked for him that they were not to question him. Very rarely did anyone do so.[45] When someone did question him, failed to comply immediately to his demands, did not praise him, or stole the limelight, they were deemed disloyal and were likely to be a victim of his rage, to be fired, or to be forced to resign. Trump even appointed a White House staff member whose job was to seek out those in his government who were disloyal to him, including the Department of Justice and Federal Bureau of Investigation—two federal agencies with long histories of impartiality.[46]

Interpersonal Exploitation (i.e., Takes Advantage of Others to Achieve His or Her Own Ends)

Like many other narcissists, Trump has never lacked social skills. He turns on the charm when it so serves him, which includes when exploiting others. As noted by Bob Woodward, Trump lives in a paradox, "capable of being friendly and appealing. He can also be savage and his treatment of people is often almost unbelievable."[47]

In a commentary appearing in *The Atlantic*, entitled "Unfit for Office," attorney George T. Conway, III presents a strong case for Trump meeting each of the criteria for narcissistic personality disorder.[48] In addressing whether Trump meets the interpersonal exploitation criterion, Conway writes: "*Interpersonally exploitative?* Just watch the *Access Hollywood* tape, or ask any of the hundreds of contractors Trump the businessman allegedly stiffed, or speak with any of the two dozen who have accused Trump of sexual misconduct, sexual assault, or rape. (Trump has denied all their claims.)"

Trump exploited hundreds of those who worked in his election campaigns and served under him in the White House, firing them as soon as they no longer met his narcissistic needs.

As noted by CNN reporter Chris Cillizza in his article "Donald Trump Gets Sick of Everyone, Except for Donald Trump": "If you are close to him (unless you are a member of his immediate family) you are on the clock. It's only a matter of time before he tires of you—and turns on you. Consider these names (and this is far from a complete list): Michael Cohen, Omarosa Manigault Newman, Rex Tillerson, James Mattis, Jeff Sessions, Steve Bannon, John Kelly, Paul Ryan, Cliff Sims, Donald McGahn, Chris Christie and Scaramucci. All were once close to Trump. All were once publicly praised by Trump. And all are now on the outs with him, the result—in virtually every circumstance—of Trump finding fault with them, whether in how they were performing the job he had tasked them with or in how they defended him (or didn't) at all costs."[49] To that list, by the end of his presidency one would add

Secretary of Defense, Mark Esper; Attorney General William Barr; and Chair of the Joint Chiefs of Staff, General Mark Milley; Vice President Michael Pence; and others.

Lack of Empathy: Unwilling to Recognize or Identify with the Feelings and Needs of Others

Plenty of examples of Trump's lack of empathy are presented in Chapter 10 on the moral emotions of empathy, guilt, and shame. If it were not for Trump's failure to experience and display empathy, he might still be president. That is, multiple advisors warned him that the coronavirus pandemic was likely to cost him re-election, and largely because of his unwillingness, or incapability, to recognize and identify with the feelings and needs of those individuals and families who contracted the virus or experienced economic hardship related to the pandemic.[50]

In an analysis of 35 coronavirus briefings in which Trump spoke for 13 hours (about 60% of the time), *The Washington Post* found that Trump spent 45 minutes lavishing praise on himself and his administration, two hours attacking others, and only 4 and 1/2 minutes expressing condolences for victims of the coronavirus. He devoted much more time to promoting unproven and dangerous treatments and presenting false or misleading information than he did to expressing empathy. On three occasions he presented self-congratulatory, other-blaming, and misinformative videos produced by White House aides (at taxpayer expense).[51]

Reflecting both his vanity and lack of empathy, Trump refused to wear a mask during the pandemic, stating at one time or another:

> "I just don't want to wear one."
> "Somehow sitting in the Oval Office behind that beautiful Resolute desk ... I don't see it for myself,"
> "Wearing a mask is a sign of weakness,"
> "You look weak if you wear a mask."

Trump often ridiculed those who wore masks, insisting that others in the White House not be photographed wearing a mask while near him.

Being Often Envious of Others or Believing That Others Are Envious of Him or Her

With his great wealth and power, Trump has envied very few others. President Obama is one of them, and perhaps the one he has envied the most. As commented by *The Washington Post* columnist Eugene Robinson, "Trump seems terrified that history will look more kindly on Obama's presidency than on his own. If that's the case—on this one point—he couldn't be more right."[52] President Obama was not born into wealth, graduated at the top of his class at Harvard, is more intelligent and articulate than Trump, won the

Nobel Peace Prize, and won reelection. Historians rank Obama among the top ten presidents, and Trump among the bottom five.[53]

Trump also envied the late senator, war hero, and presidential candidate John McCain.[54] Because a hardcore narcissist cannot handle anyone being superior, Obama and McCain were constant targets of Trump's wrath. For years, Trump refused to recognize the legitimacy of Obama's presidency, falsely claiming that he was not born in America. Upon McCain's death, Trump refused to lower the flag to half-mast over the White House, and later he directed the Pentagon to keep the destroyer USS John S. McCain out of sight when he visited a naval base.[55]

Trump also often expressed envy toward authoritarian leaders who yielded more power than him, especially Russia's Vladimir Putin, China's Xi Jinping, Turkey's Recep Tayyip Erdoğan, Egypt's Abdel Fattah el-Sisi, Philippine's Rodrigo Duterte, and North Korea's Kim Jong-Un. He envied their power and how brutal they could be toward the media and others who challenged or criticized them. Whereas he envied dictators, he frequently ridiculed leaders of America's traditional allies—a common strategy of narcissists used to elevate themselves above others, and in this case, to the level of dictators he envied.

Trump bragged about others envying him, asserting that they envied him because he was rich and "because I fuck super-models."[56] As president, and in his mind, he likely moved up to being the most envied person in the world, if not in history, as seen in his tweeting after his 2019 Independence Day celebration "Our Country is the envy of the World. Thank you, Mr. President!"[57]

Belief That He or She Is "Special" and Unique and Can Only Be Understood By, or Should Associate with, Other Special or High-Status People (or Institutions)

As discussed previously in Chapter 1, Trump's enablers, but especially his evangelical base, have viewed him as God-like, supporting his self-proclamations of uniqueness that "I alone can fix it," and particularly his delusion "I'm the chosen one." Trump claimed to be the chosen one after quoting a conspiracy theorist who described him as being like the King of Israel and said that Jews "love him like the second coming of God."[58] Trump said he was joking. Joking or not, how many other presidents have claimed to be the second coming of God?

Despite his craving for attention, Trump is known to have very few close friends, preferring to spend time away from work with family.[59] The friends he has had and most others he associated with were like him: rich or famous and fellow narcissists, such as his close friends and personal attorneys Roy Cohn and Rudy Giuliani. As discussed in Chapter 12, perhaps no other friend influenced Trump more than Cohn, and no other was a greater narcissist, liar, cheat, and bully.

Showing Arrogant, Haughty Behaviors or Attitudes

Haughty behaviors and attitudes are those that convey one's superiority and disdain or contempt for others. Persons who are haughty are arrogant, conceited, cocky, patronizing, demanding, full of pride, and often rude, obnoxious, and abusive. As such, this criterion is largely redundant with several criteria above; thus, many of the examples above of Trump's narcissism also fit here. Additional examples of Trump's rudeness are given in Chapter 7 on his verbal bullying, such as Trump rudely calling reporters, co-workers, and anyone who questioned or criticized him every name in the book (often preceded by the modifier "fucking" as in "fucking loser").

Another excellent example of Trump's arrogant superiority and disdain of others was his response to a reporter who simply questioned if he would ever concede the election that he had lost, to which Trump responded: "*Don't talk to me that way, I'm the president of the United State don't ever talk to the president that way.*"[60] Perhaps the most fitting example, however, of his haughtiness, arrogance, and sense of superiority is his infamous quote: "I could stand in the middle of Fifth Avenue and shoot somebody and I wouldn't lose any voters."

Trump believes his behavior is so perfect that he once stated in an interview that he does not need to ask God for forgiveness, noting (in language that resembles that of a kindergartener) "I like to be good. I don't like to have to ask for forgiveness. And I am good. I don't do a lot of things that are bad. I try to do nothing that is bad."[61] In perceiving himself to be God-like he is not to bow to anyone, including God; however, he expects others to bow to *him*.

Does Trump Meet Additional Criteria for Diagnosis of a Narcissistic Personality Disorder?

As seen above, a very strong case can be made that Trump meets each of the nine criteria with respect to exhibiting symptoms or traits associated with narcissistic personality disorder. However, to warrant the DSM–V–TR diagnosis, it is required that the symptoms are lasting (not temporary), exhibited across a variety of social contexts, and are severe. As seen in the examples above, as well as in Trump's developmental history reviewed in Chapter 12, it is evident that for over 60 years Trump has exhibited the nine symptoms at home, school, in his businesses, as a presidential candidate, and as president. He continues to do so.

With respect to severity, the symptoms must cause a significant impairment in relationships with others (e.g., friends, relatives, co-workers, and romantic partners) or cause serious personal distress. Trump has very few friends, and likely fewer now than before being president. A litany of co-workers, including the many he fired and countless others who resigned, have despised working with him. He has had countless romantic partners, including three wives. Even his relatives dislike him. Clearly, his narcissism has impaired relationships with others. However, one can counterargue that despite his narcissism, over 70 million Americans voted for him, with most of them continuing to like him. Thus, it is debatable if Trump meets the criterion that his narcissism causes significant impairment in relationships with others.

With respect to symptoms or traits causing personal distress, the case for Trump meeting this criterion is weaker than the case of impairing relationships with others. (Note, however, that to be diagnosed with a narcissistic personality disorder, the symptoms or traits must impair relationships *or* cause personal distress. Only one, not both, is required.) Symptoms of personal distress are clearly seen in his tantrums, rages, and expressed hatred toward others. But, if one were to interview Trump and inquire about his emotional state, I suspect that it is very likely he would convey that although he is obsessed about losing an election that he still thinks was stolen from him (and continues to seek revenge), he nevertheless sees himself as he truly desires: as a very rich, powerful, and famous person with a beautiful young wife. Thus, he would claim to be a very happy man and superior to all others. But then again, he is a pathological liar.

Based on the wealth of examples of narcissistic behaviors documented above, it is evident that Trump meets all nine of the behavior criteria for a narcissistic personality disorder. It is truly difficult to find another person whose behavior more closely matches the nine criteria. However, as discussed later, it is debatable if his narcissism meets an additional criterion for the diagnosis of narcissistic personality disorders, which is that the disorder is "usually associated with significant distress or disability in social, occupational, or other important activities."[62]

A Narcissist, Pathological Liar, Cheat, and Bully, but Is He Crazy?

Although Trump might not be diagnosed with narcissistic personality disorder, he nevertheless is a classic narcissist, as well as pathological liar, cheat, and bully. As noted earlier, some experts argue that in addition to narcissistic personality disorder, he meets most, if not all, diagnostic criteria for *antisocial personality disorder*. Antisocial personality disorder is on a spectrum, with the most severe form seen in sociopaths and psychopaths. Trump's niece, Dr. Mary Trump, is among those who argue that Trump meets all diagnostic criteria in DSM for antisocial personality disorder. Others who also know Trump well concur and among them are attorney George Conway and Trump's ghostwriter Tony Schwartz. As noted earlier, both have argued that Trump meets all DSM criteria for narcissistic personality disorder. They feel the same about antisocial personality disorder. Conway makes the case that Trump is a psychopath in an article titled "Unfit for Office,"[63] and Schwartz does the same in another article "The Psychopath in Chief."[64] Are Dr. Trump, Conway, Schwartz, and others correct in claiming that Trump's antisocial behaviors are serious enough to warrant the diagnosis of antisocial personality disorder?

As noted in the previous chapter, deceitfulness is among the seven defining behavioral criteria or symptoms of antisocial personality disorder. The other six symptoms are a failure to conform to social norms with respect to lawful behavior, lack of remorse, impulsivity, irritability and aggressiveness, reckless disregard for safety of self or others, and consistent irresponsibility. What they have in common is that they represent a pervasive pattern of disregard for and violation of the rights of others. DSM–V–TR requires that three or more of the seven behaviors are present for a clinical diagnosis. Below, drawing from extensive documentation of Trump's behavior, the extent to which Trump meets each of the seven behavioral criteria is examined.

"Deceitfulness, as Indicated by Repeated Lying, Use of Aliases, or Conning Others for Personal Profit or Pleasure"

Trump's lying certainly meets the deceitfulness criterion. As detailed in earlier chapters, he averaged 21 lies per day as president, often repeating the same ones over and over, and he often conned others for profit or pleasure (e.g., Trump University). When seeking media attention from reporters and editors, he also masqueraded over the phone as the fictitious John Miller or John Barron, while bragging about himself.[65] Thus, there is a slam-dunk case for Trump's deceitfulness.

"Lack of Remorse, as Indicated by Being Indifferent to or Rationalizing Having Hurt, Mistreated, or Stolen from Another"

As described in DSM–V–TR, individuals meeting this behavioral criterion: "may be indifferent to, or provide a superficial rationalization for, having hurt, mistreated, or stolen from someone (e.g., for example, 'life's unfair,' 'losers deserve to lose'). These individuals may blame the victims for being foolish, helpless, or deserving of their fate (e.g., 'He had it coming anyway'); they may minimize the harmful consequences of their actions; or they may simply indicate complete indifference. They generally fail to compensate or make amends for their behavior. They believe that everyone is out to 'help number one' and that one should stop at nothing to avoid being pushed around."[66]

As so described, this behavioral criterion encompasses both a lack of moral emotions and a proneness to the use of various mechanisms of moral disengagement. Both of which are discussed in Chapter 10, with examples of Trump's lack of empathy, guilt, and shame and use of mechanisms of moral disengagement presented in Chapter 11.

Among features commonly associated with antisocial personality disorder, and more specifically a lack of remorse, DSM–V–TR notes that in addition to being callous and lacking in empathy, individuals "may have an inflated and arrogant self-appraisal (e.g., feel that ordinary work is beneath them or lack a realistic concern about their current problems or their future) and may be excessively opinionated, self-assured, or cocky. Some antisocial individuals may display a glib, superficial charm and be quite voluble and verbally facile."[67] As noted in DSM–V–TR, those features also characterize narcissistic personality disorder, and a person may have both disorders. That combination is common in traditional conceptions of psychopathy and sociopathy. It is Trump's combination of narcissistic and antisocial features that Maggie Haberman, reporter for *The New York Times*, highlights and thoroughly describes in her book appropriately entitled *Confidence Man: The Making of Donald Trump and the Breaking of America*.[68]

In sum, as with deceitfulness, there is a very strong case for Trump meeting this behavioral criterion.

"Failure to Conform to Social Norms with Respect to Lawful Behaviors, as Indicated by Repeatedly Performing Acts That Are Grounds for Arrest"

As noted in DSM–V–TR, failure to conform to social norms is another behavior common among sociopaths and psychopaths. Among clear examples of Trump failing to conform to social norms with respect to lawful behaviors include the sheer number of lawsuits against him, including for sexual harassment; his two impeachments; his refusal to accept election results and inciting an insurrection; and his stealing government documents. Trump also is the first president to be indicted for a criminal offense. However, being arrested, or indicted, is not required to meet this criterion. As described and explained in *Untouchables: How Powerful People Get Away with It*, written by former New York prosecutor Elie Honig, there are many individuals, including psychopaths and sociopaths, who repeatedly break the law but are sufficiently skilled and manipulative, as well as wealthy and powerful, to avoid arrest and conviction.[69]

So far, Trump has scored three out of seven behavioral criteria for antisocial personality disorder, which is the required minimum for the diagnosis. As seen below, meeting each of the other four behavioral criteria is less straightforward.

"Impulsivity or Failure to Plan Ahead"

In describing this criterion, DSM–V–TR notes that "Decisions are made on the spur of the moment, without forethought and without consideration for the consequences to self or others; this may lead to sudden changes of jobs, residences, or relationships." To be sure, at times Trump's behavior, which includes much of his lying, is impulsive. Books about Trump are replete with examples of his impulsivity or failure to plan ahead. For example, General John Kelly, who served as Trump's Chief of Staff, often struggled to curtail Trump's impulsive decision-making. At times Kelly warned Trump that his lies and verbal threats could potentially lead to the deaths of thousands, such as when Trump impulsively threatened North Korea with "fire and fury."[70]

But while one might find plenty of examples of Trump's impulsivity or failure to plan ahead, one can counterargue that there as many, if not more, instances in which future planning contributed to his becoming a billionaire, president of the United States, and idolized by tens of millions of Americans. As he stated in 2000, "It's very possible that I could be the first presidential candidate to run and make money on it."[71] That planning succeeded. For example, as noted by Maggie Haberman in *Confidence Man*, Trump made over $20 million alone just in the sale of MAGA baseball caps, and during only three weeks of the 2020 reelection campaign he took in over $200 million (raised mostly under the pretense of fighting voting fraud).[72]

Planning ahead also was seen in him casting doubt on the 2022 election results long before the results were in, while strategically calculating that his lies would be welcomed by other Republican leaders and by voters, and result in positive political and financial consequences for himself.

"Irritability and Aggressiveness, as Indicated by Repeated Physical Fights or Assaults"

As true with him being impulsive, at times Trump is irritable and aggressive. As with his impulsivity, plenty of examples of Trump's irritability and aggressiveness are given in a number of books (e.g., to name a few, see *Confidence Man, The Divider, Rage, The Toddler in Chief*, and *Tower of Lies*[73]). Examples also are presented in Chapter 7 on his verbal bullying. But while Trump's irritability and aggressiveness are often displayed in verbal assaults, threats, sulking, whining, and physical childlike tantrums, including throwing things, he is not known to engage in physical fights or otherwise harming others physically, at least not directly. In describing behavior fitting this criterion, DSM–V–TR notes that the behavior is often seen in "spouse beating or child beating." Trump might have many flaws, but physical abuse of his wives and children is not among them. Thus, although Trump is irritable and verbally aggressive, the case that his behavior meets this criterion is not as strong as the cases for the criteria presented previously.

"Reckless Disregard for Safety of Self or Others"

One might well argue that there is no lack of examples of Trump's behavior being reckless and disregarding the safety of self or others. Examples of him exhibiting such behavior were on full display during the coronavirus pandemic when he refused to wear a mask and falsely assured the public that the virus would magically disappear. Inciting an insurrection at the Capitol also fits the bill, as does multiple additional times when he showed reckless disregard for the safety of others by verbally attacking them and arousing his supporters, such when calling his vice president a "wimp" and "pussy" for not illegally blocking the certification of President Biden's election and tweeting when the insurrection was underway that "Mike Pence didn't have the courage to do what should have been done," sparking shouts from the rioters "Hang Mike Pence!" In an interview after the insurrection, Trump defended the rioters wanting to hang Pence, saying it "was common sense" given the election fraud.[74]

Despite Trump's actions clearly jeopardizing the safety of others, it is doubtful that they are the types of actions that authors of the DSM–V–TR had in mind for meeting this criterion. As noted in DSM-V-TR, in meeting this criterion most individuals exhibit reckless and drunken driving, substance abuse, child neglect, or risky sexual behavior. Trump has no history of the first three of those behaviors. So, as with impulsivity, irritability, and aggressiveness, Trump may have displayed reckless disregard for the safety of self and others but not likely of the type that DSM–V–TR had in mind for the diagnosis of antisocial personality disorder.

"Consistent Irresponsibility, as Indicated by Repeated Failure to Sustain Consistent Work Behavior or Honor Financial Obligations"

Examples given in DSM–V–TR of behaviors meeting this criterion are long periods of unemployment despite jobs being available, repeated and unexplained absences from work, defaulting on debts, and failing to support dependents. Yes, Trump has a reputation for cheating, or not paying, contractors, banks (e.g., in Casino bankruptcies), and even his attorneys. However, there is no disputing that he has been a very hard worker, while experiencing great success in both business and politics. Among the seven behavioral criteria, this is the one that Trump most clearly fails to meet.

Antisocial Personality Disorder, or Not?

In sum, a strong argument can be made that Trump meets three of the seven behavioral criteria for diagnosis of antisocial personality disorder, which is the minimum number needed. Much weaker arguments can be made for Trump meeting the other four criteria, and especially the seventh one (i.e., consistent irresponsibility). In addition to the behavioral criteria, however, two other criteria must be met. First, as stated in DSM–V–TR, an individual is at least 18, and there "must be evidence of conduct disorder with onset before age 15 years."[75] Although his niece, Dr. Mary Trump, argues that her uncle had a history of bullying and disobeying his parents and was sent off to a military or reform school for his behavior, there is insufficient evidence that his behavior was severe enough to warrant the diagnosis of a conduct disorder. As a school psychologist who made such diagnoses on many occasions, I sincerely doubt if a convincing case could have been made when he was a child or adolescent for that diagnosis.

The second criterion, which was mentioned earlier with respect to narcissistic personality disorder and applies to antisocial personality disorder and most other mental disorders, is that the disorder is "usually associated with significant distress or disability in social, occupational, or other important activities."[76] Note that DSM–V–TR qualifies this criterion by prefacing the word "associated" with "usually." This allows for exceptions to this criterion. Clearcut exceptions would be a person with an alcohol or drug addiction and with no indication of significant distress or disability.

For example, substance use might occur daily, but the individual remains employed, maintains relationships with others, and shows no signs of depression. Thus, in cases of substance abuse exceptions are made to the significant distress or disability criteria.

As cogently argued by Dr. Allen Frances in an article titled "I Helped Write the Manual for Diagnosing Mental Illness: Donald Trump Doesn't Meet the Criteria," it is for the above reason that Trump does not have a mental disorder.[77] Although Dr. Frances was referring to narcissistic personality disorder when making this argument, what he says also applies to antisocial personality disorder. Dr. Frances is a foremost authority on the topic, having chaired the task force responsible for revising the fourth edition of the DSM and having written the criteria for narcissistic personality disorder. He states that "Trump certainly causes severe distress and impairment in others, but his narcissism doesn't seem to affect him that way." Thus, according to Dr. Frances, in the absence of showing significant personal distress or disability, Trump does not have narcissistic personality disorder, or antisocial personality disorder. Dr. Frances notes that Trump is like many other successful people who are extremely narcissistic but who are not being mentally ill, including "many politicians and most celebrities." He concludes that although not mentally ill, Trump is crazy—"crazy as a fox."

Crazy as a Fox

"Crazy as a fox" fits Trump well. Yes, he is a pathological liar and otherwise deceitful. He is also a classic narcissist. Those characteristics might make him "unfit for office" as stated by his Chief of Staff, General John Kelly, and agreed upon by multiple others who served under him in the White House. But this does not mean he is mentally ill. Rather than a hindrance and source of personal stress or a disability, his deceitfulness and bullying got things done—helping him achieve his cherished and self-serving goals of greater wealth, fame, and power. And after all, he did become president of the United States. If one were to assess his self-esteem and happiness, I would guess that he would respond that he is very happy, having become the "killer" and "king" that his father desired and helped create (but if he's not happy, he would likely lie that he is).

With *The Washington Post* having awarded him tens of thousands "Pinocchio's" for his lies, one might say that Trump best characterizes Pinocchio in Carlo Collodi's classic book and Disney's film *Pinocchio*. This is not only because of his pathological lying, but also because Pinocchio lacked a conscience (i.e., without Jiminy Cricket present). But a more fitting character in that story is the cunning fox, Honest John, who was socially skilled, happy, charming, persuasive, and a liar and cheat. Before becoming an adult, Pinocchio developed his own conscience. No longer needing Jiminy Cricket to guide him, he stopped lying and learned to be truthful, unselfish, and brave (i.e., "a real boy"). In contrast, Honest John never changed, and used his deceitfulness and social skills to manipulate Pinocchio (without Jiminy Cricket around) and to lead many other gullible and delinquent boys astray, leading them to Pleasure Island where they all became jackasses. Like Trump, Honest John got things done, and he was happy and proud of it.

Notes

1 Bandy Lee (ed.), 2019. *The Dangerous Case of Donald Trump*. New York: Thomas Dunne Books.
2 As a researcher, author, professor, and not a psychiatrist, I am not bound by this ethical code. Moreover, not all mental health experts agree that they must refrain from diagnosing Trump without an examination, arguing that sufficient documents exist to make some diagnoses, such as a narcissistic personality disorder, and that another ethical code supersedes the one pertaining to making a diagnosis—the ethical code to warn others of a client's immediate danger to others.
3 Henry Alford, 2015, "Is Donald Trump Actually a Narcissist? Therapists Weigh In!" *Vanity Fair*, November 11. https://www.vanityfair.com/news/2015/11/donald-trump-narcissism-therapists
4 James Crump, 2020, "Trump Has Narcissistic Personality Disorder, Says Leading Psychoanalyst." *Independent*, August 11. https://www.independent.co.uk/news/world/americas/us-politics/donald-trump-narcissistic-personality-disorder-mary-trump-john-zinner-bandy-x-lee-a9665856.html
5 Justin A. Frank, 2018. *TRUMP on the Couch: Inside the Mind of the President*, New York: Avery, 117.
6 American Psychiatric Association, 2022. *Diagnostic and Statistical Manual of Mental Disorders, Fifth Edition, Text Revision*, Washington, DC: American Psychiatric Association, 61.
7 Carol Leonnig and Philip Rucker, 2021. *I Alone Can Fix It: Donald J. Trump's Catastrophic Final Year*. New York: Penguin.
8 Aaron Blake, 2016. "19 Things Donald Trump Knows Better Than Anyone Else, According to Donald Trump." *The Washington Post*, October 4. https://wapo.st/2dFLY1T?tid=ss_mail&utm_term=.97c48aaea84f
9 Haley Britzky, 2019. "Everything Trump Says He Knows More about Than Anybody." *Axios*, January 5. https://www.axios.com/2019/01/05/everything-trump-says-he-knows-more-about-than-anybody
10 George T. Conway, III, 2019. "Unfit for Office." *The Atlantic*, October 3. https://www.theatlantic.com/ideas/archive/2019/10/george-conway-trump-unfit-office/599128/
   William Cummings, 2019. "Trump Says He's 'So Great Looking and Smart, a True Stable Genius' In Tweet Bashing 2020 Dems." *USA TODAY*, July 11. https://www.usatoday.com/story/news/politics/elections/2019/07/11/trump-again-calls-himself-stable-genius/1703154001/
11 Philip Rucker and Carol Leonnig, 2020. *A Very Stable Genius: Donald J. Trump's Testing of America*. New York: Penguin, 328.
12 Rebecca Morin, 2018. "'Idiot,' 'Dope,' 'Moron': How Trump's Aides Have Insulted the Boss." *Politico*, September 4. https://www.politico.com/story/2018/09/04/trumps-insults-idiot-woodward-806455
13 Chris Cillizza, 2017. "Donald Trump Ranked Himself 2nd in a List of Most 'Presidential' Presidents." *CNN*, July 26. https://www.cnn.com/2017/07/26/politics/donald-trump-abe-lincoln/index.html
14 Leonnig and Rucker, 508.

15 Jason Le Miere, 2018. "Donald Trump Claims People Said He Looked Like Elvis Presley: 'You'll Say I'm Very Conceited … I'm Not.'" *Newsweek*, November 26. https://www.newsweek.com/donald-trump-elvis-presley-lookalike-1232301

16 Neil King Jr., 2011. "Trump on 2012: 'Part of Beauty of Me Is I'm Very Rich.'" *The Wall Street Journal*, March 17. https://www.wsj.com/articles/BL-WB-29144

17 Danielle Paquette, 2016. "Why the Most Outrageous Part of Donald Trump's 'Hot Mic' Comments Isn't the Vulgar Language." *The Washington Post*, October 7. https://www.washingtonpost.com/news/wonk/wp/2016/10/07/the-real-issue-with-donald-trump-saying-a-man-can-do-anything-to-a-woman/

18 Alan Rappeport, 2016. "Donald Trump's Trail of Comments about Women." *The New York Times*, March 25. https://www.nytimes.com/2016/03/26/us/politics/donald-trump-women.html

19 Jill Filipovic, 2017. "Our President Has Always Degraded Women—and We've Always Let Him." *Time*, December 5. https://time.com/5047771/donald-trump-comments-billy-bush/

20 Jeremy W. Peters, Elaina Plott, and Maggie Haberman, 2020. "260,000 Words, Full of Self-Praise, from Trump on the Virus." *The New York Times*, April 26. https://www.nytimes.com/interactive/2020/04/26/us/politics/trump-coronavirus-briefings-analyzed.html

21 Meagan Flynn and Allyson Chiu, 2020. "Trump Says His 'Authority Is Total.' Constitutional Experts Have 'No Idea' Where He Got That." *The Washington Post*, April 14. https://www.washingtonpost.com/nation/2020/04/14/trump-power-constitution-coronavirus/

22 Reis Thebault, 2019. "Trump Can't Stop Talking about the Nobel Peace Prize. It Might Have Something to Do with Obama." *The Washington Post*, September 24. https://www.washingtonpost.com/politics/2019/09/24/trump-cant-stop-talking-about-nobel-peace-prize-it-might-have-something-do-with-obama/

23 Quint Forgey, 2019. "Trump Says He Wanted to Give Himself Medal of Honor." *Politico*, August 21. https://www.politico.com/story/2019/08/21/donald-trump-give-himself-medal-of-honor-1470950

24 Stephen Collinson, 2019. "Trump's July 4 Extravaganza Sets a Political Trap." *CNN*, July 3. https://www.cnn.com/2019/07/03/politics/donald-trump-july-4-military-politics-parade/index.html

25 Chris Cillizza, 2018. "The Trump Military Parade Was Always a Really Bad Idea." *CNN*, August 17. *CNN*. https://www.cnn.com/2018/08/17/politics/parade-trump/index.html

26 Cummings.

27 Robin Foster and E.J. Mundell, 2020. "U.S. Coronavirus Death Tally Hits New High for Summer." *U.S. News & World Report*, August 13. https://www.usnews.com/news/health-news/articles/2020-08-13/us-coronavirus-death-tally-hits-new-high-for-summer

28 Matt Flegenheimer, 2018. "Linda McMahon Gets a Ringside Seat for TrumpMania." *The New York Times*, February 24. https://www.nytimes.com/2018/02/24/us/politics/linda-mcmahon-gets-a-ringside-seat-for-trumpmania.html

29 Annie Karni and Maggie Haberman, 2020. "Trump Makes First Public Appearance Since Leaving Walter Reed." *The New York Times*, October 12. https://www.nytimes.com/2020/10/10/us/politics/trump-white-house-coronavirus.html

30 Michael C. Bender and Maggie Haberman, 2022. "Trump Sells a New Image as the Hero of $99 Trading Cards." *The New York Times*, December 15. https://www.nytimes.com/2022/12/15/us/politics/trump-nft-trading-cards-superhero.html

31 Tony Schwartz, 2020. "The Psychopath in Chief." *Gen*, May 28. https://gen.medium.com/the-psychopath-in-chief-aa10ab2165d9

32 Michael D'Antonio, 2016. *The Truth about Trump*. New York: Thomas Dunne Books, 223–224.

33 Ryan Teague Beckwith, 2018. "President Trump Said Democrats Who Didn't Clap at the State of the Union Were 'Treasonous'." *Time*, February 6. https://time.com/5134150/donald-trump-state-union-democrats-treasonous/

34 D'Antonio, 253.

35 Brandon Gates, 2020. "WATCH: All the Times Trump Used the Bible—His "Favorite" Book—as a Prop." *Courier*, June 5. https://couriernewsroom.com/2020/06/05/watch-all-the-times-trump-used-the-bible-his-favorite-book-as-a-prop/

36 Maggie Haberman, 2022. *Confidence Man: The Making of Donald Trump and the Breaking of America*. New York: Penguin.

37 Jim Acosta and Caroline Kelly, 2020. "Trump's Name Will Be Added to Stimulus Checks." *CNN*, April 15. https://www.cnn.com/2020/04/14/politics/trump-name-checks-coronavirus/index.html

38 Allan Smith, 2017. "Why Trump's Sycophantic Cabinet Meetings Seem So Oddly Familiar." *Business Insider*, December 22. https://www.businessinsider.com/trump-praise-filled-cabinet-meetings-sound-like-the-apprentice-2017-12

39 Editorial Board, 2020. "Trump's Wasted Meetings." *The Wall Street Journal*, April 8. https://www.wsj.com/articles/trumps-wasted-briefings-11586389028

40 Michael Kranish and Marc Fisher, 2016. *Trump Revealed: The Definitive Biography of the 45th President*. New York: Scribner, 37.

41 Rick Reilly, 2019. *Commander in Cheat: How Golf Explains Trump*. New York: Hachette Books, 132.

42 Emily Jane Fox, 2017. "How Mar-a-Lago Became the New Camp David." *Vanity Fair*, February 21. https://www.vanityfair.com/news/2017/02/mar-a-lago-camp-david

43 Maggie Haberman, 2022. "Another Trump Mystery: Why Did He Resist Returning the Government's Documents?" *The New York Times*, August 26. https://www.nytimes.com/2022/08/18/us/politics/trump-fbi-classified-documents.html

44 Maggie Haberman, 2022. "Another Trump Mystery: Why Did He Resist Returning the Government's Documents?" *The New York Times*, August 26. https://www.nytimes.com/2022/08/18/us/politics/trump-fbi-classified-documents.html

45 Yasmeen Abutaleb and Damian Paletta, 2021. *Nightmare Scenario: Inside the Trump Administration's Response to the Pandemic That Changed History*. New York: Harper.

46 Philip Rucker and Carol Leonnig, 2020. *A Very Stable Genius*. New York: Penguin Press, 95.

47 Woodward, 390.

48 Conway, III.

49 Chris Cillizza, 2019. "Donald Trump Gets Sick of Everyone, except for Donald Trump." *CNN*, August 13. https://www.cnn.com/2019/08/13/politics/donald-trump-anthony-scaramucci/index.html

50 Yasmeen and Damian, 2021.

51 Phillip Bump and Ashley Parker, 2020. "13 Hours of Trump: The President Fills Briefings with Attacks and Boasts, but Little Empathy." *The Washington Post*, April 26. https://www.washingtonpost.com/politics/13-hours-of-trump-the-president-fills-briefings-with-attacks-and-boasts-but-little-empathy/2020/04/25/7eec5ab0-8590-11ea-a3eb-e9fc93160703_story.html

Yasmeen Abutaleb and Damian Paletta, 2021. *Nightmare Scenario: Inside the Trump Administration's Response to the Pandemic That Changed History.* New York: Harper.

52 Eugene Robinson, 2019. "Opinion: Trump's Obama Envy Is Getting Even Worse" *The Washington Post*, August 26. https://www.washingtonpost.com/opinions/trumps-obama-envy-is-getting-even-worse/2019/08/26/5dadc7d0-c83a-11e9-be05-f76ac4ec618c_story.html

53 Gillian Brockell, 2021. "Historians Just Ranked the Presidents. Trump Wasn't Last," *The Washington Post*, June 30. https://www.washingtonpost.com/history/2021/06/30/presidential-rankings-2021-cspan-historians/

54 Conway, III.

55 Max Burman and Courtney Kube, "Navy Acknowledges Request Was Made to Hide USS John S. Mccain during Trump Visit." *NBC News*, June 1, 2019. https://www.nbcnews.com/politics/donald-trump/navy-acknowledges-request-was-made-hide-uss-john-s-mccain-n1012731

56 Rick Reilly, 2019. *Commander in Cheat: How Golf Explains Trump.* New York: Hachette Books, 249.

57 Donald J. Trump @realDonaldTrump. "Our Country Is the Envy of the World. Thank You, Mr. President!" Twitter, July 6, 2019. https://twitter.com/realDonaldTrump/status/1147478123593785344

58 Chris Cillizza, 2019. "Yes, Donald Trump Really Believes He Is 'The Chosen One,'" *CNN*, August 24. https://www.cnn.com/2019/08/21/politics/donald-trump-chosen-one/index.html

59 Harry Jaffe, "Who Are Donald Trump's Closest Friends?" *Town & Country*, April 18, 2017. https://www.townandcountrymag.com/society/politics/a9521926/donald-trump-friends/

60 Sarah Polus, 2020. "'Don't Talk to Me That Way': Trump Lashes out at Reporter over Election Question." *The Hill*, November 27. https://thehill.com/homenews/news/527734-dont-talk-to-me-that-way-trump-lashes-out-at-reporter-over-election-question

61 Maxwell Tani, 2016. "Trump on God: 'I Don't Like to Have to Ask for Forgiveness'." *Insider*, January 17. https://www.businessinsider.com/trump-on-god-i-dont-like-to-have-to-ask-for-forgiveness-2016-1

62 DSM–V–TR, 14.

63 Conway III.

64 Schwartz.

65 Marc Fisher and Will Hobson, "Donald Trump Masqueraded as Publicist to Brag about Himself," May 13, 2026, *The Washington Post*, https://www.washingtonpost.com/politics/donald-trump-alter-ego-barron/2016/05/12/02ac99ec-16fe-11e6-aa55-670cabef46e0_story.html

66 DSM–V–TR, 749.

67 DSM–V–TR, 749.

68 Haberman, 2022.

69 Elie Honig, 2023. *Untouchable: How Powerful People Get Away with It.* New York: Harper.

70 Jonathan Karl, 2020. *Front Row at the Trump Show.* New York: Dutton.

71 Jerry Useem, 2000. "What Does Donald Trump Really Want?" *Fortune*, April 3. https://fortune.com/2000/04/03/what-does-donald-trump-really-want/

72 Maggie Haberman, 2022. *Confidence Man: The Making of Donald Trump and the Breaking of America.* New York: Penguin, 467.

73 Haberman.

Peter Baker and Susan Glasser, 2022. *The Divider: Trump in the White House, 2017–2021*, 2022, New York: Doubleday.

Barbara A. Res, 2020. *Tower of Lies: What My 18 Years of Working with Donald Trump Reveals about Him.* Los Angeles: Graymalkin Media.

Daniel W. Drezner, 2020. *The Toddler in Chief: What Donald Trump Teaches Us about the Modern Presidency.* Chicago: University of Chicago Press.

Bob Woodward, 2020. *Rage.* New York: Simon & Schuster.

74 U.S. House of Representatives, Select Committee to Investigate the January 6th Attack on the United Capitol, 2022. *Final Report of the Select Committee to Investigate the January 6th Attack on the United States Capitol.* House Report 117-663, December 22. https://www.govinfo.gov/app/details/GPO-J6-REPORT/

75 DSM–V–TR, 749.

76 DSM–V–TR, 14.

77 Allen Frances, 2017. "I Helped Write the Manual for Diagnosing Mental Illness. Donald Trump Doesn't Meet the Criteria." Statnews, September 6. https://www.statnews.com/2017/09/06/donald-trump-mental-illness-diagnosis/

10 Moral Reasoning, Moral Emotions, and Mechanisms of Moral Disengagement

Why People Don't Act Like Weathervanes

Undoubtedly, a major determinant of lying, cheating, bullying, and narcissism is observing others display those behaviors. This is especially true when the behaviors are modeled by individuals whom the observer highly respects or admires and when the behaviors observed lead to positive outcomes. Common positive outcomes for lying, cheating, and bullying are tangible rewards (e.g., gaining a valued object, increased wealth), social reinforcement (e.g., praise, recognition, fame), the personal satisfaction or thrill of "winning" (e.g., the "cheater's high"), and feelings of control, power, and superiority over others. In the absence of such positive outcomes, and especially when negative outcomes occur, observed behaviors are much less likely to be attempted or to continue.[1]

Although observing and experiencing outcomes, either positive or negative, are powerful determinants of human behavior, they fail to explain why most of us are not pathological liars, seldom cheat, and refrain from physically bullying and verbally berating those who stand in the way of getting things done. That is, despite watching others benefit from dishonest and antisocial behaviors, most people don't exhibit the same behaviors. Observational learning also fails to explain why many chronic liars, cheaters, and bullies come from homes where those behaviors are rarely observed, and where honesty, trustworthiness, and integrity are taught. As asserted by Dr. Albert Bandura, professor of psychology at Stanford University: "If actions were performed only on behalf of anticipated external rewards and punishments, people would behave like weathervanes, constantly shifting direction to conform to whatever influence happened to impinge upon them at the moment. In actuality, people display considerable self-direction in the face of competing influences."[2] In his social-cognitive theory of morality, Bandura asserts that moral behavior is determined by a variety of social-cognitive and emotional factors that mediate the influence of the environment. This chapter focuses on those key factors, and particularly moral reasoning; the moral emotions of empathy, guilt, and shame; and Bandura's mechanisms of moral disengagement.

DOI: 10.4324/9781003401278-10

Moral Knowledge Is Not the Same as Moral Reasoning and Moral Emotions

Nearly all children, and adults, can tell you what behaviors are "good" and "bad." Unfortunately, too often such knowledge, or moral content, has very little to do with their actual behavior; knowing right from wrong does not translate into moral behavior. This was well demonstrated nearly a century ago in classic research studies of deceit conducted by psychologists Dr. Hugh Hartshorne and Dr. Mark May of Columbia University.[3] Hartshorne and May presented over 10,000 students with multiple measures of cheating, lying, and stealing, including self-reports of dishonesty and contrived opportunities for the students to cheat in schoolwork, games, and athletic contests. Greatly challenging the popular method of character education at that time (and still popular in many schools today) was the finding that the direct teaching, or lecturing, of right and wrong and punishing children for not doing as told had little relation to dishonest behavior. As expected, Hartshorne and May found that students who were repeatedly taught in school, home, Sunday school, and the Scouts that cheating, lying, and stealing were wrong clearly knew that those behaviors were wrong, as they scored high on measures of moral knowledge. However, they found that those students were just as likely to lie, cheat, and steal as students who received much less drill and practice in moral knowledge (e.g., those who did not attend Sunday school or belong to the Scouts).

Hartshorne and May's findings on the relation of moral knowledge to moral behavior, which have been replicated many times since, do not mean that moral knowledge is unimportant. The odds are very high that students will lie, cheat, and bully if they are truly unaware that those behaviors are wrong. That is, *not knowing* that a behavior is wrong is a good predictor of engaging in that behavior; however, *knowing* it is wrong *is not* necessarily a good deterrent. For example, students who are unaware that plagiarism constitutes cheating are more likely to cheat on written assignments than those who are well aware. However, there are plenty of students who know that plagiarism is wrong but nevertheless plagiarize. The same applies to most crimes, including speeding, shoplifting, and using illegal drugs—the culprits know the behavior is wrong, but that doesn't stop them.

Consistent with Hartshorne and May's findings, nearly all psychology and moral philosophers recognize that when it comes to determining moral behavior, more important than moral knowledge per se are one's moral values and standards. Most people would agree that lying, cheating, and bullying are wrong, but some feel much more strongly about those behaviors than others. Individuals who feel more strongly about a given behavior being wrong are less likely to engage in that behavior.[4] As such, and as explained below, *why* a person thinks and feels that a behavior is right or wrong matters greatly, as it determines one's moral values and standards, and ultimately behavior. Those psychological processes—moral reasoning, moral emotions, and mechanisms of moral disengagement—underlie moral values, standards, and behavior.

Moral Reasoning

Moral reasoning refers to the cognitive processes of determining right from wrong and deciding what one *ought* to do. Moral reasoning guides both prosocial and antisocial behavior—behavior that helps or harms others, as well as oneself. In early childhood, moral reasoning tends to be self-centered and hedonistic, characterized by seeking and maximizing rewards and avoiding punishment. With age, moral reasoning becomes less self-serving and more oriented toward the impact of one's behavior on others, issues of fairness, the welfare of others, the inherent importance of rules (i.e., beyond the fear of punishment), and principles of justice. This is not to say that young children are incapable of empathy and unaware of or insensitive to the effects of their behavior on others, as those qualities are found in early childhood, and as early as age two.[5] However, as discussed below, self-centered moral reasoning is the developmental norm up to about early elementary school; it is between the ages of four to seven that the understanding of the outcomes of behavior, and intentions, perspectives, emotions, and needs of others grow exponentially with respect to making moral judgments and guiding moral behavior.[6]

Development of Moral Reasoning: Kohlberg's Stages

Since the 1970s, the most popular theory of moral reasoning has been that of Dr. Lawrence Kohlberg, who was a professor of psychology and human development at Harvard University. At the core of Kohlberg's cognitive-developmental theory of moral development is the idea that children are not passive learners who simply internalize what they are taught and observe.[7] Instead, they play an active role in understanding and determining what they internalize. This includes constructing, evaluating, and determining what is right and wrong. Kohlberg posited that moral reasoning occurs developmentally within the framework of increasingly complex stages of moral reasoning. Think of a stage as a structure, framework, or mindset that guides moral decision-making and behavior. Kohlberg argued that although individuals progress through stages in a given order, they progress at different rates and the endpoint is not the same for everyone. Whereas some advance to more mature stages of moral reasoning, others become fixated at lower stages.

Kohlberg described six stages embedded within three broader *levels* of moral reasoning: the preconventional, conventional, and postconventional levels. Preconventional moral reasoning encompasses Stages 1 and 2 and is predominant among children of preschool and early elementary age. Conventional moral reasoning includes Stages 3 and 4, with Stage 3 typically emerging in the upper grades of elementary school and Stage 4 in adolescence. Those two levels and four stages are described below. Because postconventional moral reasoning, which consists of Stages 5 and 6, is not found among school-age children and is seldom found among adults, those stages are not discussed much here. In brief, at the postconventional level individuals value principles of justice and human rights above laws, and often challenge laws and actions they view as violating human rights and other moral principles. At Stage 5 (which Kohlberg labeled *Social Contract or Utility and Individual Rights*), individuals understand and value that abiding by rules and laws is best for the general welfare and protection of the rights of everyone. However, they also believe it is morally right to challenge, and disobey, laws that violate such individual rights as life and liberty.

Stage 6 moral reasoning (labeled *Universal Ethical Principles*) is grounded in more abstract and universal ethical principles of justice, and particularly equality of human rights and respect for human dignity. Kohlberg gave Thomas Jefferson, Mahatma Gandhi, and Martin Luther King as examples of Stage 6 moral reasoning. Because Stage 6 moral reasoning is rarely found, most researchers question if it truly belongs in a developmental theory.

Stages 1 and 2: Immature Self-Centered, Hedonistic Moral Reasoning

Moral reasoning at the first two stages is considered preconventional or "immature" because there is a general lack of awareness or concern about social conventions and the impact of one's behavior on others. As with all stages, different types of moral reasoning exist within Stages 1 and 2; however, to one extent or another the orientation within those two stages is self-centered, or hedonistic. At Stage 1, which Kohlberg first labeled *Punishment and Obedience Orientation* in 1958 and later called *Heteronomous Morality* in 1976, "good" behavior is behavior that is rewarded and "bad" behavior is that which is punished. People in positions of authority (e.g., parents, teachers, clergy, authoritarian leaders) dictate what is morally right and wrong. At Stage 1, individuals obey to gain rewards and out of fear of punishment, believing that one way or another they *will* be punished for doing what they are told not to do. Punishment, whether immediate or in the future, is believed to be inevitable (e.g., going to hell for one's sins). It also is understood that those in positions of authority or otherwise more powerful are entitled to control others and get what they want—"might makes right."

Moral reasoning at Kohlberg's Stage 2 (which Kohlberg first labeled as *Naïve Instrumental Hedonism* and later changed to *Individualism, Instrumental Purpose, and Exchange*) is like that at Stage 1, with a self-centered focus on gaining rewards and avoiding punishment. However, it differs from Stage 1 in several important ways, reflecting its greater complexity and sophistication. First, children reasoning at Stage 2 realize that authority and punishment are *not* omnipresent: You *might* or *might not* get caught—parents, teachers, and other authorities aren't always watching. If you don't get caught, you won't be punished. Thus, if the risk of getting caught is slim, then there is little or no reason *not* to do whatever you so desire.

Second, at Stage 2 the child gains an understanding and appreciation of the concept of pragmatic reciprocity, as seen in the perspective of "If you're nice to me, I'll be nice to you." Good behavior is all about exchanges that benefit oneself and others, but mostly oneself. Retribution is justified: If others treat you badly, it's only fair to do the same to them. Choice of behavior is situational, pragmatic, and based on self-interest. The overall guiding philosophy is quid pro quo: "Scratch My Back and I'll Scratch Yours."

The third way that Stage 2 differs from Stage 1 is that empathy and the consideration of the needs of others, or "needs-oriented reasoning," is of greater importance. This might seem inconsistent with the pragmatic "instrumental exchange" and "just don't get caught" aspects of Stage 2 moral reasoning described above. However, Kohlberg argued that all three of those aspects of Stage 2 moral reasoning are similar in their increasing cognitive maturity; they reflect greater consideration and basic understanding of the perspective of others, which is lacking in Stage 1.

Stages 3 and 4: Focus on the Needs of Others, Interpersonal Relations, and Social Order

Stages 3 and 4 constitute Kohlberg's conventional level of moral reasoning, characterized by greater understanding and appreciation of the needs of others and of society's values, norms, expectations, and laws. The intentions and motives of others weigh much more heavily in moral judgments than at the preconventional level. It is understood that two people might commit the same moral transgression, but for entirely different reasons. Although intentions and motives certainly come into play at the preconventional level in early childhood, with age they come to matter much more.

Moral reasoning at Stage 3, which Kohlberg first labeled as *Good-boy Morality of Maintaining God Relations, Approval by Others* and later relabeled *Mutual Interpersonal Expectations, Relationships, and Interpersonal Conformity*, recognizes a major shortcoming of preconventional moral reasoning: Others are likely to disagree with you when you look out only for your own self-interests, especially when trying to solve interpersonal conflicts. To get along with others, and do what is right, one needs to consider the perspectives, intentions, motivations, and needs of others, which include individuals and groups. Shared values and norms are now viewed as important in helping guide moral decision-making. It is understood that rules should be followed because they are important for the welfare of others. It also is understood that rule-following behavior is good for one's reputation and moral identity and in maintaining positive interpersonal relations with others. One now understands and appreciates the Golden Rule of treating others as you want to be treated.

As with conventional level moral reasoning at Stage 3, at Stage 4 (first called the *Authority-Maintaining Morality* and later *Social System and Conscience*) it is understood that one has a moral duty or obligation to adhere to social norms and laws. One now thinks beyond rule-following and normative behavior being best for one's own self-interest. It also is best for society overall; if everyone operated based on their own self-interests and group loyalties then laws would not be upheld, and social disorder or chaos would likely result.

Moral Reasoning and Moral Behavior

In general, more mature moral reasoning is associated with less aggressive and antisocial behavior and greater prosocial behavior. Although the association is not particularly strong (with correlations generally in the low 30s), it becomes stronger, and is more consistently found, when one looks at specific types of moral reasoning both within and across Kohlberg's stages rather than at stages per se. For example, moral reasoning found at Stage 2 is commonly voiced by the most aggressive and disruptive students,[8] juvenile delinquents,[9] and bullies.[10] More specifically, the type of moral reasoning related to antisocial behavior centers on gaining or maximizing rewards, avoiding punishment, experiencing power or control over others, dispensing retribution, and lacking empathy, guilt, and shame. In contrast, a focus on the needs and rights of others, which characterizes Stages 3 and 4, is common among children and adults who refrain from antisocial behavior and who more frequently exhibit prosocial behavior—behavior that benefits rather than harms others such as helping, comforting, and sharing.[11]

The relation between self-centered moral reasoning and antisocial behavior has been found in multiple research studies, including several that my colleagues and I conducted.[12] In one of our studies, moral reasoning predicted not only the current behavior of students but also their behavior two years later.[13] In our research, we probed students' moral reasoning, asking them such questions as "Why should you not steal?" and "Why should you not bully others?" We also had teachers and classmates rate students as to extent to which they exhibited behavior problems such as stealing, hitting, teasing, saying mean things to others, excluding others from games, and being overly aggressive and disruptive in class. As predicted, we found that self-centered moral reasoning that characterizes Kohlberg's Stage 2 was the best predictor of behavior problems. Among students with greater behavior problems, the most common moral reason given for not exhibiting behavior problems was "you might get into trouble." In contrast, students with no or few behavior problems gave reasons reflecting concern about the emotional needs and welfare of others and their own self-concept or moral identity. Their responses were grounded in empathy, empathy-based guilt, integrity, respect of others, and their own reputations. As one might predict considering their less aggressive and more prosocial behavior, those students also were more socially accepted by their peers. Intriguingly, we also found it was not just their moral behavior that led to greater social acceptance but also their moral reasoning.[14] This finding provides insight into why many popular peers in adolescence are not lacking in assertiveness and aggression—their aggression, which is infrequent, is viewed by their peers as being good for moral reasons (e.g., defending victims of bullying, or themselves).

Why Moral Reasoning and Moral Behavior Are Not Always Related

Just as simply knowing what is right or wrong does not predict moral behavior, neither does mature moral reasoning necessarily lead to greater moral behavior. As discussed below, there are two primary reasons why moral reasoning is not a strong predictor of moral behavior. The first is specific to Kohlberg's approach to moral reasoning, whereas the second concerns not only Kohlberg's approach but any approach that focuses exclusively on the cognitive aspects of moral behavior.

Limitations to a Stage Approach to Moral Reasoning in Predicting Moral Behavior

Several limitations of Kohlberg's theory explain why the relationship between his stages of moral reasoning and moral behavior is not strong. First, both moral and immoral behavior can be justified at any one of the stages. That is, within each stage one type or another of moral reasoning can be used to justify whether one decides to lie, cheat, steal, bully, and exhibit other immoral behaviors. For example, on the one hand, Stage 1 moral reasoning guided by "It's wrong to steal because you will be punished" (or will go to hell) is associated with rule-abiding behavior, as we found in one of our studies.[15] On the other hand, in using Stage 1 moral reasoning a person might argue "He told me to steal" or "I stole because I wanted it." Likewise, Stage 2 moral reasoning can be used to justify cheating ("I will get a higher grade, and my parents will be happy") and not cheating ("I might get caught"). The same is true with moral reasoning at other stages. For example, at Stage 3 a student might argue against cheating, saying: "I would feel awful, as I would be violating the trust of others" or argue for cheating "In sharing my answers I help friends that I care about."

A second major limitation of Kohlberg's stage theory is that rarely does a child, or adult, reason at only one stage. Most people voice moral reasons across multiple stages. For example, it is uncommon for school-age children to voice a combination of Stages 1, 2, and 3 moral reasoning. A greater range of moral reasoning is found among adults, as the actions of even those adults capable of the most principled moral reasoning may be determined by self-serving personal considerations and contingencies of the moment.[16] Because arguments can be made either for and against a given behavior at each of Kohlberg's stages and few individuals reason at only one stage, it is understandable that the correlation between more reasoning and moral behavior is not particularly strong.

Considering the two major limitations above (as well as theoretical and philosophical limitations not discussed here), most modern-day theories of moral reasoning and behavior forego stage explanations and focus instead on specific types of moral reasoning. This includes specific types of moral reasoning that Kohlberg identified when researching his stages of moral reasoning, such as moral reasoning focused on seeking rewards, avoiding punishment, a focus on the needs and welfare of others, and being viewed favorably by self and others.

Types of moral reasoning include what social-cognitive researchers refer to as *cognitive scripts*. Cognitive scripts are latent knowledge structures stored in memory grounded in personal knowledge, past experiences, beliefs, values, and attitudes.[17] They guide social and moral behavior, particularly in situations like ones experienced previously. Stored in memory, cognitive scripts dictate how people respond in those situations. Because the same cognitive scripts have been used repeatedly and effectively in the past, there is no need to stop and reflect or reason about what to do again in similar situations; thinking about what to do is easy and automatic, as there is no need to reflect or engage in moral decision-making. Cognitive scripts are like scripts in a film or video that tell individuals what to expect or do in a given situation.[18] They underlie many habitual, as well as impulsive, behaviors. Among aggressive individuals, cognitive scripts support their aggression,[19] with the scripts being similar to, or supported by, the types of moral reasoning found in Kohlberg's Stage 2, such as "If someone hits you, hit them back." There also are cognitive scripts consistent with Kohlberg's preconventional level that support prosocial behavior, ranging from good manners and common acts of civility (e.g., saying please and thank you) to acts of honesty (e.g., "don't lie, cheat, or steal").

Countering Kohlberg and other cognitive-developmental theorists, social-cognitive researchers who focus on different types of moral reasoning and cognitive scripts do not claim that moral reasoning develops in a fixed order, with reasoning at higher stages being more mature or morally superior to reasoning at lower stages. They also make no attempt to lump various types of moral reasoning together into a given stage.

Additional Limitations to a Focus on Moral Reasoning

Although specific types of moral reasoning are more predictive of behavior than Kohlberg's more general stages, they too often fail to predict actual behavior. This is another major limitation of Kohlberg's theory, but also other cognitive-oriented theories of moral development and behavior. Moral reasoning is only one of multiple environmental and individual factors interacting in an ongoing dynamic and reciprocal fashion that determine whether a person lies, cheats, or bullies. Those factors not only influence moral reasoning and behavior in real-time and in a given situation but also future moral reasoning and behavior. That is, individuals learn from past behavior, which shapes their future moral reasoning and behavior. Without accounting for factors beyond moral reasoning—factors within both the environment and the individual—it is difficult to fully understand, much less predict moral behavior.

Environmental factors range from laws, customs, and norms to specific situational and circumstantial factors such as peer pressure, the salience of rewards and punishment, and the relationship one has with others in situational context. Interacting with environmental factors in determining behavior are multiple aspects of personality, such as temperament, impulsivity, and sensation seeking, and social cognitive and emotional processes in addition to moral reasoning that underlie moral decision-making and moral behavior. For example, many of the same social-cognitive information processes required for effective social problem-solving apply to moral decision-making.[20] They include moral awareness (e.g., awareness that a moral problem exists); cognitive and emotional understanding of the perspectives of others; self-management of emotions and impulses; generating and evaluating alternative solutions; and self-efficacy—believing that one has the ability to perform the behavior chosen, and is capable of doing so. A limitation in any one of those processes can negatively impact moral behavior, either directly or via the influence on moral reasoning and decision-making.

Perhaps more importantly, social-cognitive processes, including moral reasoning, cannot influence behavior unless they are engaged. As discussed later in this chapter, individuals use multiple mechanisms of moral disengagement to avoid other-oriented moral reasoning and absolve themselves of responsibility for their behavior. Moral reasoning also is not engaged when an individual views the behavior as not concerning issues of morality, as being amoral or not falling in the moral domain.

According to *social domain theory*, the moral domain is not the only domain that entails values and moral reasoning. Social domain theorists argue that children's values and moral reasoning fall into three general domains: *moral*, *social-conventional* (also called societal), and *personal* (also called psychological).[21] The moral domain entails behavior concerning issues of fairness, justice, rights, equality, and the welfare of others. The social conventional domain entails behavior governed by rules, laws, norms, conventions, and practices established by a particular social system or authority (including parents, teachers, the government, and one's religion). The personal domain concerns behavior of personal choice, pertaining to one's health, preferences, comfort, goals, autonomy, and identity. Examples are rules and expectations about dress, homework, curfews, choice of music, use of tobacco and alcohol, and romantic relations. Individuals vary in the extent to which they view issues as falling in the moral, social-conventional, and personal domains. Although they tend to view a behavior as more or less in one domain, it is not uncommon for some behaviors to be viewed as multifaceted, concerning two or three domains, such as judgments about friendships and social and romantic relations.

Whereas behaviors in the moral domain elicit moral reasoning, those in the social-conventional and personal domains tend to elicit reasoning more specific to those two domains—reasoning not always conceptualized in Kohlberg's and other theories of moral reasoning, and thus not expected to relate to moral behavior. In general, children and adolescents agree that parents, teachers, and others have the right to regulate behaviors they agree fall in the moral domain, and that they should regulate their moral behavior themselves. However, they often object to adults and others attempting to govern behaviors they believe are not moral, but are either social-conventional or personal, and especially the latter. Supporting the importance of differentiating the moral, social-conventional, and personal domains in predicting moral behavior, research shows that adolescents' moral reasoning is a stronger determinant of behaviors in the moral domain than in the social-conventional and personal domains.[22]

Moral Emotions That Engage Moral Behavior: Empathy, Guilt, and Shame

During the past several decades researchers have increasingly recognized that it is not only how individuals think but also how they feel—their emotions—that largely determine moral behavior.[23] Three moral emotions have received the greatest attention: empathy, guilt, and shame. They provide the spark often needed for persons to act in a manner consistent with their moral reasoning, beliefs, and values, motivating them to inhibit antisocial behavior and to act prosocially. It is the absence of moral emotions, also often referred to as the presence of callous and unemotional traits, that characterizes many of the most aggressive and antisocial individuals, particularly criminals.[24]

Empathy

Empathy is generally viewed as the ability to experience the feelings of others *and* care about how they feel (i.e., to experience sympathy). Empathy requires an awareness and recognition of the perspectives of others, or *social perspective taking*. To share the feelings of others, one must be aware of their feelings. Knowing how others feel, or what they are thinking, however, does not ensure empathy or caring. Whereas social perspective taking is necessary for empathy, it is not sufficient. One might be quite skilled in recognizing and assuming the perspective of others, especially how they think, but use the skill for their own self-interests, such as when lying, cheating, bullying, and manipulating others to achieve their self-centered goals.

Empathy goes beyond social perspective taking, adding an emotional component—the ability to share, or experience vicariously, how others feel. Although many emotion theorists add that empathy also includes caring or compassion, not all agree. Some argue that although an individual might take the perspective of others *and* experience feelings about the situation, the feelings are not necessarily those of *empathic concern*, which entails compassion and sympathy. It is for this reason that empathic concern is often differentiated from *personal distress*, with the latter referring to a focus not on the suffering or feelings of others but instead on one's own unpleasant feelings of discomfort. With personal distress, one thinks and feels "I need to help myself," which may or may not lead to helping others.[25]

In general, individuals high in empathy exhibit greater prosocial behavior and experience greater peer acceptance and academic success, but this is particularly true with empathic concern and not personal distress.[26] In contrast, those lacking in empathy tend to be unaware of and insensitive to the feelings of others. In failing to experience the same emotions as others, they are less likely to exhibit caring, concern, compassion, and to help others, and they are more likely to act in antisocial and harmful ways.[27] For example, bullies don't think about the impact of their behavior on others and the harm it causes, or they simply don't care.

Note that empathic concern and personal distress are not necessarily exclusive of one another, as they can be experienced simultaneously. This is often seen when someone comforts others to alleviate their suffering but also to alleviate his or her own worrying and anxiety.[28]

Guilt

Guilt is experienced when one fails to act in a manner consistent with his or her own moral standards. Recognized as the "quiescent moral emotion," guilt lies at the core of a sense of responsibility for one's actions, especially actions that harm others.[29] Guilt reflects the internalization of society's values and serves as a self-sanction. As with empathy, individuals who are prone to experiencing guilt are more likely to help others and act in a just and fair manner, whereas those lacking in guilt are more likely to exhibit aggressive and antisocial behavior.[30]

Guilt correlates positively and highly with empathy, and it is empathy that often triggers feelings of guilt, which is called *empathy-based guilt*. Empathy-based guilt occurs when someone experiences the negative emotions of others *and* feels responsible for causing those emotions, or for not doing anything about it. In addition to motivating prosocial behavior and inhibiting antisocial behavior, empathy-based guilt serves to help repair relationships and maintain one's moral self-identity. That is, it motivates reparation after acting in a manner that harms or otherwise adversely affects others. By apologizing, confessing, or making restitution, one can undo, repair, or amend their behavior and thus avoid or relieve feelings of guilt and feel better about themselves.

Although empathy is the most common source of guilt, it is not the only one. There are times when people feel responsible and badly, or a sense of guilt, over their actions without considering the perspectives or feelings of others. As such, guilt can be experienced without hurting or harming others. Concern about violating one's moral standards and the fear of experiencing personal distress are other common sources of the anticipation and experience of guilt. For example, a person with high moral standards might anticipate guilt when thinking about lying, cheating, or bullying, irrespective of the impact of those behaviors on others.

Shame

Both guilt and shame are "self-conscious" emotions experienced when violating self-imposed moral standards. They often co-occur and are not easy to differentiate; thus, the terms are often used interchangeably. Most emotion theorists, however, view guilt and shame as distinct emotions that differ in fundamental ways.[31] The primary difference is the focus or object of the negative feelings. With guilt, negative feelings center on a specific behavior that one has done or is thinking about doing (e.g., "I feel awful about hurting her feelings"). With shame, the negative feelings center on the self and thus are much more global, or pervasive (e.g., "I feel like I'm an awful person because what I did," or "If I did that, I couldn't live with myself.").

As with empathy and guilt, shame can influence behavior before or after it occurs. That is, the anticipation of experiencing shame often prevents immoral behavior, but the experience of shame also impacts future behavior by causing one to think twice before acting similarly in the future. Thus, lessons learned from experiencing shame can motivate people to reflect upon and change their behavior.

Although the fear of experiencing shame, and what is often perceived as personal failure, typically deters immoral behavior, it also can foster it. For example, shame is often experienced when one greatly disappoints others, with the disappointment of parents being a common source of shame.[32] Students can avoid such shame by cheating or lying to their parents. Of course, many adults also cheat and lie to avoid shame associated with disappointing others. As was seen in Chapter 9 on narcissism, for individuals with a narcissistic "win at all costs" and "never fail" personality, the fear of failure and disappointing oneself and others and the coinciding anticipation of shame often fosters rather than deters antisocial behavior.[33]

With respect to moral behavior, proneness to shame is largely positive and adaptive but there also is a dark, destructive side of shame, especially when one fails to regulate the emotion. Because it is much more difficult to change oneself than one's behavior, the impact of shame on psychological well-being can be much more damning than that of guilt. When repeated often, attributions of responsibility and uncontrollability for failing to meet internalized standards and the expectations and standards of others can lead to intense and pervasive negative feelings of shame becoming associated with low self-esteem, sadness, hopelessness, social withdrawal, depression, and at worse suicidal ideation.[34] Adolescents are particularly prone to the negative effects of shame, as they believe that peers, parents, and others are constantly evaluating them. Suicide is the second or third (depending on age) leading cause of death among adolescents and young adults,[35] with shame often being a contributing factor.

When unregulated, shame also can trigger anger and aggression directed not only toward oneself but also toward others. This is especially true when one blames others for their negative feelings of shame.[36] As was seen in Chapters 6 and 7 on bullying, blaming others is common among perpetrators of bullying. It also is common among hard-core criminals who engage in more harmful and violent behavior. Whereas many of them are lacking shame, others attempt to avoid it by blaming and attacking what they perceive to be the source of their shame.[37]

Whether shame is directed toward the self or others, researchers and therapists have always recognized its dark, destructive side.[38] Thus, the practice of parents, teachers, and others "shaming" children for their behavior is strongly discouraged. This does not mean that children should not be taught to feel responsible for their behavior, but that the focus of discipline should not be the badness of the self but the impact of the behavior on others and how to repair any harm caused.

Mechanisms of Moral Disengagement

Operating as self-sanctions, mature moral reasoning and moral emotions decrease the likelihood of someone lying, cheating, bullying, and being a narcissist. Unfortunately, moral reasoning and moral emotions often fail to explain moral behavior. Many individuals are quite capable of voicing mature moral reasoning and experiencing empathy, guilt, and shame, but nevertheless act immorally. Examples include individuals of all walks of life, with not only hardcore criminals but also clergy, lawyers, and government leaders often being in the news. As with moral reasoning, moral emotions have their limitations with respect to accurately predicting moral behavior and foremost among them is that they matter little if they are not activated or engaged.[39] Disengaging moral reasoning and moral emotions explains a moral paradox: how people who are fully capable of experiencing mature moral reasoning and moral emotions harm others and do not feel badly about their behavior or themselves. Indeed, mechanisms of moral disengagement explain how some people are even proud of the harm that they or others cause. In using mechanisms of moral disengagement, narcissists can feel great about their wealth, fame, and power without experiencing any guilt, shame, or personal distress over the harm they caused others.

Mechanisms of moral disengagement also largely explain how people can act hypocritically without experiencing cognitive dissonance. Their use of mechanisms of moral disengagement allows them to teach and preach high moral standards, and impose them on others, while violating those standards themselves. A good example is parents who teach children to follow the Ten Commandments, and expect other Americans to do the same, while defending and excusing their sins and the sins of others whom they admire. They do so by blaming others, denying or minimizing any harmful impact of their behavior, or otherwise justifying harmful behavior.

Bandura identified eight mechanisms of moral disengagement used to deactivate, or disengage, moral reasoning, moral emotions, and other self-regulatory processes, and, in turn, to excuse or justify harmful behavior.[40] Several decades of research have shown that children, adolescents, and adults prone to using mechanisms of moral disengagement are more likely than others to act in dishonest and antisocial ways.[41] This includes lying,[42] cheating,[43] and bullying.[44]

Bandura grouped his eight mechanisms of moral disengagement into four categories based on their common focus, or "locus." In the *Victim Locus* are the *attribution of blame* and *dehumanization*, with both mechanisms centering on the victim and more specifically on blaming the victim. The *Agency Locus* also entails blaming, but the two mechanisms in that category, *displacement of responsibility* and *diffusion of responsibility*, focus not on blaming the victim but displacing the blame onto others or sharing the blame. The *Behavioral Locus* includes three mechanisms: *advantageous comparison*; *moral, social, or economic justification*; and *euphemistic labelling*. Each of the three focuses on persuading the self and others that the harmful behavior is good, if not commendable. This is done by arguing that (1) the behavior is not as bad as alternative behaviors and outcomes (i.e., making advantageous comparisons); (2) the behavior, although harmful, serves worthy ends (i.e., engaging in moral, social, or economic justification); or (3) by using language that sanitizes or distorts the behavior or its outcomes. Finally, the *Effects Locus* consists of the mechanism of moral disengagement Bandura labeled *disregard, distortion, and denial of harmful effect*, which entails neutralizing harmful behavior by disregarding, distorting, and denying the harm done.

Mechanisms of moral disengagement are generally used in the context of harming others, or failing to help others, and for the purpose of avoiding responsibility for the harm done. They are more likely to follow rather than proceed harmful behavior. Children begin to use mechanisms of moral disengagement, especially blaming and denying, at an early age. By late adolescence, most are quite skilled in their use, with boys using them more frequently than girls.[45] When the mechanisms are found to be effective, and thus often practiced, self-sanctions are disengaged, leading to more frequent harm. For example, over time the occasional liar becomes a pathological liar, and the mildly aggressive child becomes a full-fledged bully.

Mechanisms of moral disengagement overlap with moral reasoning. Indeed, the two can be one and the same. This is especially true when the mechanisms of blaming and moral justification are used to defend one's harmful actions such as bullying. For example, bullies often blame others for their bullying ("He started it") or otherwise justify their bullying ("He's a real loser and deserves it."), while avoiding or refusing to think about the harm caused and why the behavior is wrong (e.g., "I don't care how he feels. I did nothing wrong"). The bully also might reason that the bullying was "fair" and the "right thing to do" because the victim started it and deserved the harm, or because bullying the victim is best for others (e.g., "We would get more things done if he shut up"). Whereas Bandura would view these as examples of moral disengagement, Kohlberg would argue that they reflect immature, self-centered moral reasoning such as "Might makes right" and "Deals: You scratch my back, I'll scratch yours."

Moral reasoning and mechanisms of moral disengagement differ in an important way. Moral reasoning entails making moral judgments about behavior being morally right or wrong and *why* (e.g., "bullying is wrong because it harms others"). In contrast, when using mechanisms of moral disengagement, moral judgments do not need to be made.

Use of mechanisms of moral disengagement is common among those who frequently lie, cheat, and bully, and among narcissists, but they aren't the only ones who use them. To one degree or another all of us use them to avoid negative emotions and responsibility for our actions and to protect our sense of self. Their occasional use is normal, as very few children and adults never deny what they did, never blame others, or otherwise never rationalize their wrongdoing. At times the use of mechanisms of moral disengagement can even be good for one's mental health, serving to protect one's self-esteem.

What follows are brief descriptions of Bandura's eight mechanisms of moral disengagement and examples of how children, and many adults, use them to absolve themselves of responsibility for lying, cheating, bullying, and other harmful behaviors. For heuristic purposes, Bandura's eight mechanisms are collapsed into three categories instead of Bandura's four loci. As such, the four mechanisms of moral disengagement that entail blaming are combined into one category instead of the two categories used by Bandura. More user-friendly labels also are used to describe the three categories and eight mechanisms (note: the language used by Bandura to describe each mechanism, and its corresponding loci, appear in parentheses).

When reviewing the mechanisms, keep in mind that they often are not used alone but in combination and simultaneously with others, such as when one denies responsibility, blames others, and dismisses the seriousness of what they did.

Blame Others (the Victim Locus and Agency Locus)

It's Someone Else's Fault (Attribution of Blame)[46]

If you are a parent of children over the age of two, you have heard them excuse their misbehavior by blaming others. In most homes the person blamed is a sibling: "She started it." "He did it first." "She did it too!" "Don't blame me! Blame him!" If the behavior happened in school, you likely heard "I wasn't the only one in class who did it" (e.g., cheated, didn't turn in homework, skipped class, etc.), "The teacher really doesn't care," "She doesn't do anything about it," or "She didn't do anything about it before" (e.g., cheating, violating rules). Among school-age children, bullies often blame their victims,[47] whereas cheaters tend to blame their teachers, the test ("it's too hard and unfair"), and their peers ("they cheat too").[48] Of course, blaming others is not found only among children. As will be seen in the next chapter, adults also are quite skilled in blaming others.

They're Evil, Animals, or Otherwise Nonhuman (Dehumanization)

With this mechanism, blame is attributed to others but more specifically to those whom the individual views as lacking in positive human qualities commonly associated with respect for an individual, such as intelligence and morality. At its very worst, this type of blaming consists of viewing someone as evil or nonhuman and thus deserving not only blame, but verbal abuse, violence, and even death. Examples in history include most wars, including religious wars (e.g., the Crusades) and wars for the sake of "ethnic cleansing," the execution of "witches" during the Salem witch trials, the massacre of American Indians, lynchings of Blacks, the holocaust, the My Lai massacre in Vietnam, and Russia's invasion of Ukraine to remove the "Nazis."

They Made Me Do It (Displacement of Responsibility)

Rather than blaming the victim, blame is attributed to a person, or persons, of higher authority who dictated the behavior (e.g., "He made me do it." and "I did what I was told to do."). Any harm caused is excused or neutralized because you had no choice and followed orders. A classic example is a soldier carrying out an order to kill others. Among children, displacing responsibility is often seen in claiming that a sibling or peer made them do it.

Others Did It Too (Diffusion of Responsibility)

Sharing in the blame, or diffusion of responsibility, is seen in common claims such as "Others did it too" and "I wasn't the only one." Cheaters often employ this popular mechanism of moral disengagement, including athletes in excusing their use of steroids and other illegal performance enhancers. A good example is Lance Armstrong, who won the Tour de France for seven consecutive years. Stripped of his title for using illegal performance-enhancing drugs, he shared blame in noting "The culture was what it was."[49]

Argue That Bad Behavior Is Good Behavior (the Behavioral Locus)

It Could Have Been Worse (Advantageous Comparison)

With this mechanism, responsibility is deflected or minimized by using comparisons to one's advantage. This takes one of two forms: (1) comparing the behavior to that of others or to an alternative (and worse) behavior that could have been chosen, and (2) comparing the *outcome* of the behavior to other (and worse) outcomes. An example of its first form is when children assert "I know I cheated, but not as much as others in my class" or

"I only shoved him a little. I should have shoved harder!" Examples of the second form of this mechanism are "I know I shoved him, but he isn't bleeding. It's only a scratch!" and "Okay, I was sent to the office for cheating, but at least I wasn't suspended."

It Was for a Good Reason (Moral, Social, or Economic Justification)

The strategy here is to convince others, and often oneself, that the harmful behavior is justified because it serves worthy ends. For example, lying, cheating, and bullying are justified because they "get things done." Moral, and religious, justifications are commonly used to absolve individuals and groups of responsibility for the most reprehensible behaviors. For example, slave owners justified owning, and often abusing, other humans not only on economic grounds but also on moral and religious grounds (i.e., that slaves were better off, and the Bible supported slavery). Likewise, it was argued that killing thousands of witches (whom at times in history could be anyone who questioned authority) was justified in the Bible.

More recently, and combined with dehumanization, this mechanism of moral disengagement was heard by White supremacists who justified mass shootings on moral and religious grounds.[50] Dylann Roof murdered nine African Americans during a Bible study at a church in Charleston in 2015 "to start a race war."[51] While in prison he wrote that "There's plenty of evidence to indicate that Christianity can be a warrior's religion."[52] Similarly, Robert Bowers, who murdered 11 people at a Pittsburgh synagogue, used religion to justify his actions. Bowers posted on the web that "Jews are the children of Satan (John 8:44)" and "The Lord Jesus Christ [has] come in the flesh."[53] Both Roof and Bowers pleaded not guilty. In showing no remorse, they were able to absolve himself of guilt and responsibility by citing scripture to justify the murdering of their innocent victims.

Let's Call It Something Else That Sounds Better (Euphemistic Labeling)

Another way to minimize, distort, or dismiss the significance or negative impact of behavior is by using labeling or language that sanitizes the behavior or attempts to convince others (and oneself) that the behavior was nonintentional or not really that bad. In euphemistic labeling, pleasant or neutral words are used when referring to what most people would view as unpleasant, threatening, anxiety-provoking, or blameworthy. Common examples are saying that someone "passed away" instead of died, referring to genocide as "ethnic cleansing," and calling unintentional deaths in war "collateral damage." Common examples of euphemistic labeling used by children after verbal or physically bullying a sibling or a peer are "I was only joking," "I was just kidding," and "We were just playing around."

Insist That No Harm Occurred (the Effects Locus)

It Didn't Harm Anyone! (Disregard, Distortion, and Denial of Harmful Effects)

Often, the easiest way for someone to avoid responsibility for their behavior is to simply lie about it. This isn't easy to do, however, when the liar is caught in the lie. For most people (i.e., those with moral standards and capable of mature moral reasoning and moral emotions), it is difficult to avoid feelings of guilt when they know that they have harmed someone, lied about it, and that others are aware of the harm (and lie) and view such negatively. One way around this conundrum is not to lie about what was done, but to minimize, distort, dismiss, or deny the significance of any harm caused. Yes, it's still lying, but not lying about what one did but about the harm caused. This is seen when a child hits a sibling and claims "It didn't hurt him!"

As seen in the next chapter, individuals who frequently use mechanisms of moral disengagement are often the same ones with immature, self-centered moral reasoning and who are lacking in empathy, guilt, and shame. The combination of self-centered moral reasoning, the lack of moral emotions, and a proclivity in the use of mechanisms of moral disengagement is a good predictor of lying, cheating, bullying, and narcissism. Any one of the above mechanisms of moral disengagement can be used to absolve oneself for the responsibility of harm caused to others, but mechanisms of moral disengagement are often used in combination, such as when a person blames others, dismisses the seriousness of any harm caused, and justifies his or her behavior. A good example is someone stating "I didn't start the riot. It didn't cause much harm—it was like tourists visiting the capitol. Besides, it was the right thing to do to save democracy from the big lie."

Notes

1 I use the terms positive and negative outcomes instead of positive reinforcement and punishment here because positive outcomes, such as tangible rewards or social praise, do not always reinforce behavior, nor do punitive outcomes or consequences necessarily decrease a behavior. Technically, a positive outcome is a positive reinforcer only if it increases the behavior. Likewise, a negative outcome constitutes punishment only if it decreases a behavior.

2 Albert Bandura, 2001. "Social Cognitive Theory: An Agentic Perspective." *Annual Review of Psychology* 52: 1–26, 7. https://doi.org/10.1146/annurev. psych.52.1.1

3 Hugh Hartshorne and Mark A. May 1928. *Studies in the Nature of Character: Vol. I: Studies in Deceit.* New York: Macmillan.
    Hugh Hartshorne and Mark A. May 1929. *Studies in the Nature of Character: Vol. II: Studies in Service and Self-Control.* New York: Macmillan.

4 Talia Carl and Kay Bussey, 2022. Cross-Sectional and Longitudinal Relationships between Children's Moral Standards and Their Antisocial Lie Telling. *Journal of Applied Developmental Psychology* 80: 1–10. https://doi.org/10.1016/j.appdev. 2022.101411

5 Melanie Killen and Judith G. Smetana, 2015. "Origins and Development of Morality" in *Handbook of Child Psychology and Developmental Science*, 7th edition, edited by Michael E. Lamb and Richard M. Lerner. New York: John Wiley & Sons, 701–749.
6 Ibid.
7 Lawrence Kohlberg, 1981. *Essays on Moral Development, Vol. II: The Psychology of Moral Development*. San Francisco, CA: Harper & Row.
8 Maureen A. Manning and George G. Bear, 2011. "Moral Reasoning and Aggressive Behavior: Concurrent and Longitudinal Relations." *Journal of School Violence* 10 no. 3: 258–280. https://doi.org:10.1080/15388220.2011.579235
9 Geert Jan Stams, Daniel Brugman, Maja Dekovic, Lenny van Rosmalen, Peter van der Laan, and John C. Gibbs, 2006. "The Moral Judgment of Juvenile Delinquents: A Meta-Analysis." *Journal of Abnormal Child Psychology* 34 no. 5: 697–713. https://doi.org:10.1007/s10802-006-9056-5
10 Michael von Grundherr, Anja Geisler, Manuel Stoiber, and Mechthild Schafer, 2017. School Bullying and Moral Reasoning Competence. *Social Development* 26 no. 2: 278–294. https://doi.org:10.1111/sode.12199
11 Nancy Eisenberg, Tracy L. Spinrad, and Ariel Knafo-Noam, 2015. "Prosocial Development" in *Handbook of Child Psychology and Developmental Science, Seventh Edition, Vol. 3. Socioemotional Processes,* edited by Michael E. Lamb and Richard M. Lerner. Hoboken, NJ: John Wiley & Sons. https://doi.org/10.1002/9781118963418.childpsy315
12 Manning and Bear.
   Gail Rys and George G. Bear, 1994. Moral Reasoning, Classroom Behavior, and Sociometric Status Among Elementary School Children. *Developmental Psychology* 30 no. 5: 633–638. https://doi.org/10.1037/0012-1649.30.5.633
13 Manning and Bear.
14 Rys and Bear.
15 Herbert C. Richards, George G. Bear, Anne L. Stewart, and Antony D. Norman, 1992. "Moral Reasoning and Conduct: Evidence of a Curvilinear Relationship." *Merrill-Palmer Quarterly* 38 no. 2:176–190. https://psycnet.apa.org/record/1992-29285-00
16 Noam M. Nisan, 1991. "The Moral Balance Model: Theory and Research Extending Our Understanding" in *Handbook of Moral Behavior and Development, Vol. 3: Application,* edited by William M. Kurtines and Jacob L. Gewirtz. Hillsdale, New Jersey: Erlbaum, 213–249.
17 Virginia S. Burks, Robert D. Laird, Kenneth A. Dodge, Gregory S. Pettit, and John E. Bates, 1999. "Knowledge Structures, Social Information Processing, and Children's Aggressive Behavior." *Social Development* 8 no. 2: 220–236. https://doi.org/10.1111/1467-9507.00092
18 L. Rowell Huesmann, 1988. "An Information Processing Model for the Development of Aggression." *Aggressive Behavior* 14 no. 1: 13–24. https://doi.org/10.1002/1098-2337(1988)14:1<13::AID-AB2480140104>3.0.CO;2-J
19 Arnaldo Zelli, Kenneth Dodge, John E. Lochman and Robert D. Laird, 1999. "The Distinction Between Beliefs Legitimizing Aggression and Deviant Processing of Social Cues: Testing Measurement Validity and the Hypothesis That Biased Processing Mediates the Effects of Beliefs on Aggression." *Journal of Personality and Social Psychology* 77 no. 1, 150–166. https://doi.org/10.1037/0022-3514.77.1.150
20 William F. Arsenio, 2014. "Moral Attributions and Aggression" in *Handbook of Moral* Development, 2nd edition, edited by Melanie. Killen and Judith G. Smetana. New York: Psychology Press, 235–255.

21 Judith Smetana, 2013. "Moral development: The Social Domain Theory View" in *The Oxford Handbook of Developmental Psychology: Body and Mind*, edited by Philip D. Zelazo. Oxford, England: Oxford University Press, 832–864. https://doi.org/10.1093/oxfordhb/9780199958450.001.0001
22 Nancy G. Guerra, Larry Nucci, and L. Rowell Huesmann, 1994. "Moral Cognition and Childhood Aggression" in *Aggressive Behavior: Current Perspectives*, edited by L. Rowell Huesmann. New York: Plenum, 13–33.
23 Martin L., 2000. *Empathy and Moral Development: Implications for Caring and Justice*. Cambridge, England: Cambridge University Press.
   June P. Tangney and Ronda L. Dearing. 2002. *Shame and Guilt*. New York: Guilford.
   June P. Tangney, Jeff Stuewig, and Debra J. Mashek, 2011. "Moral Emotions and Moral Behavior." *Annual Review of Psychology* 58: 345–372. https://doi.org/10.1146/annurev.psych.56.091103.070145
24 Paul J. Frick and Stuart F. White, 2008. "Research Review: The Importance of Callous-Unemotional Traits for Developmental Models of Aggressive and Antisocial Behavior." *Journal of Child Psychology and Psychiatry, and Allied Disciplines* 49 no. 4: 359–75. https://doi.org/10.1111/j.1469-7610.2007.01862.x
25 Nancy Eisenberg, Tracy L. Spinrad, and Ariel Knafo-Noam, 2015. "Prosocial Development" in *Handbook of Child Psychology and Developmental Science*, 7th edition, edited by Michael E. Lamb and Richard M. Lerner. New York: John Wiley & Sons, 610–656.
26 Ibid.
27 Ibid.
28 It is other-oriented empathic concern, not personal distress, that most people have in mind when they think of empathy and sympathy. Thus, unless noted otherwise, when the term empathy is used throughout this book, it refers to other-oriented empathic concern.
29 Tangney, Stuewig, and Debra J. Mashek.
30 Tina Malti and Tobias Krettenauer, 2013. "The Relation of Moral Emotion Attributions to Prosocial and Antisocial Behavior: A Meta-Analysis." *Child Development* 84 no. 2: 397–412. https://doi.org/10.1111/j.1467-8624.2012.01851.x
31 Carol E. Izard, 1991. *The Psychology of Emotions*. New York: Plenum.
   Tangney and Dearing 2002.
32 Holly A. McGregor and Andrew J. Elliot, 2005. "The Shame of Failure: Examining the Link Between Fear of Failure and Shame." *Personality and Social Psychology Bulletin* 31 no. 2: 218–231. https://doi-org.udel.idm.oclc.org/10.1177/0146167204271420
33 Ibid.
34 Tangney, Stuewig, and Debra J. Mashek.
35 Centers for Disease Control and Prevention, 2022. *Web-based Injury Statistics Query and Reporting System (WISQARS)*. Atlanta, GA: National Centers for Injury Prevention and Control, Centers for Disease Control and Prevention. Retrieved from https://www.cdc.gov/injury/wisqars/index.html
36 Tangney and Dearing.
37 Ibid.
   June P. Tangney, Jeffrey Stuewig, and Andres G. Martinez, 2014. "Two Faces of Shame: Understanding Shame and Guilt in the Prediction of Jail Inmates' Recidivism." *Psychological Science* 25 no. 3: 799–805. https://doi.org/10.1177/0956797613508790
38 Tangney and Dearing.

39 Albert Bandura, 2016. *Moral Disengagement: How People Do Harm and Live with Themselves.* New York: Worth Publishers.
    Hoffman.
40 Bandura.
41 Ibid.
    Gianluca Gini, Tiziana Pozzoli, and Shelley Hymel, 2014. "Moral Disengagement Among Children and Youth: A Meta-Analytic Review of Links to Aggressive Behavior." *Aggressive Behavior*, 40 no. 1: 56–68. https://doi-org.udel.idm.oclc.org/10.1002/ab.21502
42 Ida Foster, Joshua Wyman, and Victoria Talwar, 2020. "Moral Disengagement: A New Lens with Which to Examine Children's Justifications for Lying." *Journal of Moral Education* 49 no. 2: 209–225. https://doi.org/10.1080/03057240.2019.1656057
43 Tamera B. Murdock and Jason M. Stephens, 2007. "Is Cheating Wrong? Students' Reasoning about Academic Dishonesty in *Psychology of Academic Cheating*, edited by Eric M. Anderman and Tamera B. Murdock. New York: Elsevier Academic Press, 229–251. https://doi.org/10.1016/B978-012372541-7/50014-0
44 Zhaojun Teng, George G. Bear, Chunyan Yang, Qian Nie, and Cheng Guo, C. 2020. "Moral Disengagement and Bullying Perpetration: A Longitudinal Study of the Moderating Effect of School Climate." *School Psychology* 35 no. 1: 99–109 https://doi: /10.1037/spq0000348
45 Bandura.
46 Note that Bandura tends to limit this mechanism to attributing blame to the victim (the "The Victim Locus") but I include both the victim and others to whom blame is attributed.
47 Rober Thornberg and Tomas Jungert, 2014. "School Bullying and the Mechanisms of Moral Disengagement." *Aggressive Behavior* 40 no. 2: 99–108. https://doi.org/10.1002/ab.21509
48 Tamera B. Murdock, Anne S. Beauchamp, and Amber M. Hinton, 2008. "Predictors of Cheating and Cheating Attributions: Does Classroom Context Influence Cheating and Blame for Cheating." *European Journal of Psychology of Education* 234: 477–492. https://doi.org/132.174.254.72
49 Liz Clarke, 2013. "Lance Armstrong Interview Analysis: He confessed, but … " *The Washington Post*, January 18. https://www.washingtonpost.com/sports/othersports/lance-armstrong-interview-analysis-he-confessed-but-/2013/01/18/8b029dea-61b3-11e2-9940-6fc488f3fecd_story.html
50 Robert P. Jones, 2020. *White Too Long: The Legacy of White Supremacy in American Christianity.* New York: Simon & Schuster.
51 Ibid., 137.
52 Ibid., 140.
53 Stoyan Zaimov, 2018. "Robert Bowers, Shooter Who Killed 11 at Synagogue, Quoted the Bible, Talked about Jesus Christ, The Christian Post." *The Christian Post*, October 29. https://www.christianpost.com/news/robert-bowers-shooter-killed-11-synagogue-quoted-bible-talked-jesus-christ.html

11 How Trump Lies, Cheats, and Bullies While Still Loving Himself

A Model of More Than Behavior

Trump sees himself as "a great moral leader,"[1] and many Republicans agree with his self-assessment. If lying, cheating, bullying, and narcissism make a great moral leader, then Trump and his supporters are correct in their assessment. Others, however, including those who have served in his administration, view Trump differently. His Secretary of State, General James Mattis, described Trump as "dangerous," "unfit," and having "no moral compass,"[2] while his Chief of Staff, John Kelly, asserted that "He's a very flawed human being."[3] Likewise, before becoming a staunch ally of Trump, U.S. Senator Ted Cruz stated "The man is utterly amoral .... Morality does not exist for him."[4] They, and many others, have attested to his pathological lying, widespread cheating, vicious bullying, and grandiose narcissism, as was described in previous chapters. Unquestionably, Trump is an exemplary role model of those behaviors. As will be seen in this chapter, he also is an exemplary role model for immature, self-centered moral reasoning, a lack of moral emotions, and the masterful use of mechanisms of moral disengagement—individual characteristics that explain much of his behavior.

Trump's Moral Reasoning: "I Love Getting Even"

Trump's self-serving moral reasoning and behavior exemplifies Kohlberg's Stage 2 perspective of "Individualism, Instrumental Purpose, and Exchange," as described in the previous chapter, and a cognitive script that reads "Maximize Rewards, Avoid Punishment, Gain and Return Favors, and Seek Retribution." For Trump, obtaining greater wealth, power, and fame is a product of pragmatic reciprocity, instrumental exchange, or what is often referred to as a "scratch my back and I'll scratch yours" mentality. Trump is nice to those who are nice to him, and bullies and punishes those who aren't, while viewing the latter as disloyal, unfair, and the "enemy"—thus deserving his retribution.

   Examples abound. In exchanging favors with conservative media, as president, Trump typically called on reporters at news conference who praised and

DOI: 10.4324/9781003401278-11

reported favorably about him. As was seen in Chapter 7 on his bullying, Trump publicly berated reporters who questioned or criticized him. As an obsessed viewer of *Fox News*, while watching the network's MAGA-endorsing shows he frequently returned the hosts' and network's favorable coverage by ensuring that *Fox News* was the first, if not only, network to obtain interviews with him and his staff. In exchanging favors, Trump was in frequent contact via text messages, live-tweeting, and late-night telephone calls with his favorite *Fox News* hosts Sean Hannity, Lou Dobbs, Laura Ingraham, Jeanine Pirro, and Tucker Carlson. According to Stephanie Grisham, one of Trump's press secretaries, at times Trump dialed Hannity and Dobbs into Oval Office staff meetings.[5] As revealed in text messages and other documents disclosed in Dominion Voting Systems $1.6 billion defamation lawsuit against FOX (in which Dominion obtained a settlement of $787.5 million), it was common for *Fox News* hosts to knowingly lie for the sake of higher ratings, with the biggest lie being that Trump won the election. The exchanges with *Fox News* hosts were reciprocal and mutually beneficial, as both gained greater fame (i.e., ratings), wealth, and power. Additionally, in exchange for their favors, Trump awarded multiple Fox executives, reporters, and contributors to Fox with cabinet and staff positions, ambassadorships, and positions in federal agencies.[6]

Although clearly among his favorites, those associated with *Fox News* were not the only ones rewarded for their support and loyalty. As was seen in the chapter on Trump's cheating and cronyism, members of his cabinet and staff consisted almost exclusively of individuals who supported his presidential campaigns or were close friends of others who helped finance them. Many lacked qualifications for their positions, with several being forced to resign or fired for ethical violations. To be sure, some were much more qualified than others, but their appointments were almost always guided by Trump's moral reasoning of instrumental exchange, in which praise, adulation, and loyalty were more important than qualifications. Exceptions consisted mainly of generals and others who had served in the military and demonstrated integrity, such as Chief of Staff, General John Kelly; Chairman of the Joint Chiefs of Staff, General Mark Milley; Secretaries of Defense, General James Mattis and Dr. Mark Esper.

Trump's moral reasoning of instrumental exchange also is seen in how he dealt with leaders of other countries: belittling and bullying those who questioned, challenged, or criticized him, while praising and rewarding those who lavished him with praise. Whereas the former included powerful NATO allies such as Germany, France, Canada, and the United Kingdom, the latter included many authoritarian or fascist leaders. In reference to praise and flattering "love" letters from North Korean dictator Kim Jong Un, Trump commented "He wrote me beautiful letters, and they're great letters. We fell in love."[7]

Trump was the only American president to meet with the authoritarian leader, doing so at North Korea and South Korea's demilitarized zone.

As with other authoritarian leaders whom Trump admired, Kim Un learned quickly that Trump craves praise and returns the favor. Russian President Vladimir Putin was another authoritarian leader who knew Trump well. In defense of Trump's perplexing behavior toward Putin, which at times appeared to be a sense of awe and admiration, Trump once stated "If he says great things about me, I'm going to say great things about him."[8,9]

In an interview with Bob Woodward for his book *Rage*, Trump noted "the tougher and meaner they are the better I get along with them" while adding (in reference to Recep Erdogan of Turkey and Kim Un of North Korea) "I get along with these bad guys but not the good guys."[10] This is likely because it is the "bad guys" and not the "good guys" who praise him. It also can be attributed to Trump desiring to be more like them—dictators with absolute power.

Perhaps the best example of Trump's moral reasoning of instrumental exchange is him giving a "Get Out of Jail Free" card to his loyal friends caught lying and cheating and who were sent to prison. Nearly all were his allies and wealthy White Republican males who contributed or raised money for his campaigns or were friends thereof. Among the 74 that Trump granted pardons during his last days in office were Paul Manafort, Trump's former campaign manager, who had been sentenced to seven and a half years in prison for fraud; Roger Stone, Trump's adviser and longtime friend, who had been sentenced to more than three years in prison for seven felonies including lying under oath to a congressional committee and bullying a witness to those lies; Stephen Bannon, Trump's former chief strategist and adviser who was charged with fraud; and Charles Kushner, Jared Kushner's father who was in prison for 16 counts of tax evasion and for lying and retaliating against a federal witness (the witness was his brother-in-law, whom Charles Kushner was accused of videotaping having sex with a prostitute and then sending the tape to his wife, which was Charles' sister).[11] In addition to the above pardons, during the last days of his presidency, and in exchange for their (violent) support, Trump even considered pardons for all participants in the January 6 insurrection.[12] On multiple occasions after leaving the White House he promised full pardons and "with an apology to many" if elected in 2024.[13]

Trump's supporters and enablers entered a Faustian bargain, or pact, trading their moral values for whatever benefits Trump might reward them. For a few, it was a pardon, but for most it was a wall to keep Mexicans out, a ban to keep Muslims out, a tax cut, government deregulation, protecting their right to own assault weapons, and the appointment of conservative judges to the Supreme Court to make sure that Roe vs Wade was overturned and their religious freedoms were not infringed upon. In instrumental exchange the flipside of returning favors is retribution, and for Trump this means revenge—getting back at those who fail to return his favors, who disagree with or criticize him, who are disloyal, or who simply fail to do whatever he says. As asserted in his book *Trump: Think Big and Kick Ass*, "'Get even!' That is not your typical advice, get even, but it is real-life advice. If you do not get even, you are just a schmuck! I really mean it too."[14]

Trump is often vicious when putting those words into practice. An excellent example of this, and of retribution, is a letter he wrote to journalist Shannon Donnelly, writing: "Let's make a deal; if you promise not to get 'personal' with me, I will promise not to show you as the crude, fat and obnoxious slob which everyone knows you are. Sincerely, Donald J. Trump."[15] Many others received similar threats of retribution. Most of the examples in Chapter 7 of Trump's verbal, physical, and social bullying were grounded in his Stage 2 moral reasoning of instrumental exchange and retribution, and in the cognitive script "Always fight back and get even." As also noted in that chapter, during the 2016 presidential campaign Trump threatened to sue 26 people for speaking negatively about him, which including the media and GOP opponents and their supporters. As noted by the author and attorney James D. Zirin in *Plaintiff in Chief: A Portrait of Donald Trump in 3,5000 Lawsuits*, many of those and others of Trump's lawsuits were "to achieve a sense of control," "to reinforce his power over others" "to make a point," "for destroying or silencing those who crossed him," about "winning," "for sport," "for the entertainment value," "to make headlines," and "to reinforce his power over others."[16]

There is no dearth of examples of Trump's retribution as president, and among them are:

- Attempting to block the merger of AT&T and Time Warner. Warner Books was the publisher that Trump had sued for defamation and lost. The merger also was strongly opposed by Trump's supporter and owner of Fox, Robert Murdoch.[17]
- Firing James Comey, Director of the FBI, while the FBI was in the midst of investigating Russia's interference in the 2016 election. Many saw this not only as retribution, but also political interference.
- Firing, or forcing to resign, General James Mattis, Secretary of Defense, after he disagreed with Trump over the withdrawal of U.S. troops from Syria and Afghanistan and Trump's belittling of NATO and American allies.[18]
- Firing Christopher Krebs, director of the Cybersecurity and Infrastructure Security Agency, after his agency and other security experts told the truth about interference in the 2020 election that Trump lost—that there was absolutely no evidence to support Trump's claims.
- Revoking former CIA director John Brennan's security clearance after he criticized Trump on national television.
- Threatening to fire (before he resigned) Mark Esper, Secretary of Defense after Esper publicly disagreed with Trump wanting to use the 1807 Insurrection Act to deploy active-duty military personnel during the 2020 protests in Washington DC and other cities.
- After ten Republican members of Congress and two senators voted to impeach him (i.e., the second impeachment) he charged his supporters to

"get rid of them all" and worked hard to do so with a barrage of personal attacks and giving campaign rallies and financial support to their opponents in their GOP primaries.[19]

Trump's obsession with retribution did not end with his presidency. In losing the 2020 election, and believing the Big Lie that he had won, revenge and retribution only exacerbated. And, he has promised that more is to come. This was frighteningly seen in a speech he gave at the Conservative Political Action Conference on March 4, 2023, in which he told the MAGA crowd the following as to why he deserved their vote for president in 2024:

"In 2016, I declared: I am your voice. Today, I add: I am your warrior. I am your justice. And for those who have been wronged and betrayed: *I am your retribution*," [italics added]. "With you at my side, we will demolish the deep state. We will expel the war mongers ... We will drive out the globalists. We will cast out the communists. We will throw off the political class that hates our country ... We will beat the Democrats. We will rout the fake news media. We will expose and appropriately deal with the RINOs [Republicans in name only]. We will evict Joe Biden from the White House. And we will liberate America from these villains and scoundrels once and for all."[20]

Sparks of Mature Moral Reasoning?

To be fair, at times Trump shows sparks of mature moral reasoning, which is generally seen in speeches written by others and delivered via teleprompter. For example, Trump has often voiced that his actions benefit others (as commonly found at Stage 3), such as tax breaks, the border wall, and more law and order, but those actions are almost always self-beneficial, with him basking in the credit. It is difficult to find examples of Trump justifying those and other actions with other-oriented moral reasoning. Extremely rare is moral reasoning grounded in a sense of responsibility, moral identity, an appreciation of just laws that serve society, or moral principles of respect, dignity, equity, and justice (i.e., beyond an authoritarian law-and-order perspective).

Trump's Moral Emotions, or Lack Thereof

Most people appreciate that the moral emotions of empathy, guilt, and shame serve the adaptive and positive function of inhibiting antisocial behavior and promoting prosocial behavior. But, for individuals with self-centered moral reasoning and the aim of maximizing rewards and avoiding punishment, moral emotions can be more of a hindrance than of value— they interfere with getting things done and feeling good about it. Hedonistic aims can be achieved more easily if not bothered by feelings of empathy, guilt, and shame. Moreover, in the absence of moral emotions, one can experience a sense of pleasure or happiness regardless of any harm caused to others. This is seen in the cheater's high, the satisfaction and relief that pathological liars experience in avoiding punishment, the sense of power and control that bullies feel, and in the pleasure that cold and callous criminals feel in getting things done.

Although Trump is not void of moral emotions, as some of his critics have claimed, he is seriously lacking, as seen below.

Empathy: "It's Just Not My Thing"

In an article in *The Atlantic*, George Conway, a prominent attorney (and also at the time the husband of Kellyanne Conway, Trump's campaign manager and personal advisor), presents a strong case that Trump shares a trait commonly found among psychopaths or sociopaths—the absence of empathy. Conway agrees with "The notorious lawyer and fixer Roy Cohn, who once counseled Trump, said that 'Donald pisses ice water,'" while asserting that "Trump's utter lack of normal human empathy abound."[21] Some of the examples given by Conway of Trump's utter lack of empathy follow:

- Trump displayed no empathy (and bragged about it) when witnessing a guest at his Mar-a-Largo palace falling on the floor, hitting his head, and bleeding profusely. In telling this story to others, Trump commented "I thought he died." Trump's primary concern, however, was not the man's welfare or his screaming and crying wife, but about the blood on his "beautiful" expensive marble floor. He made no attempt to help the man or comfort his wife. Trump turned away, and after the man was taken away in a stretcher, ordered "Get that blood cleaned up! It's disgusting!" In confessing his lack of empathy, the following day Trump told others "I forgot to call [the man] to say is he okay … It's just not my thing." (This is a classic example of someone experiencing personal distress and not emphatic concern.)
- Hours after the New York Twin Towers collapsed on 9/11, in a call-in interview to a New York television station Trump bragged that one of his buildings was now the tallest building in New York City (which was not true as another building was taller).
- When giving eulogies, including at his father's funeral, Trump spoke much more about his own successes and how great he was than about the deceased (as with the 9/11 example above, Trump's narcissism overrode any feelings of empathy).
- Trump reportedly told the widow of a serviceman killed in action that he knew what he was getting into when he enlisted.

Here are some additional examples one might add of Trump demonstrating "It's just not my thing" with respect to empathy:

- As reported by John Kelly, a retired four-star Marine General who served as homeland security secretary and later his chief of staff, Trump showed little or no empathy toward soldiers who lost their lives serving our country, referring to members of the military as "suckers" or "losers" (recall that Trump avoided the draft during Viet Nam by claiming bone spurs; thus, avoiding being a sucker or loser). While standing with Kelly at the grave of Kelly's son who was killed in Afghanistan, Trump allegedly commented "I don't get it. What was in it for him?" On another occasion, after Trump's scheduled visit was canceled to a cemetery in France where American soldiers in World War I were buried, Trump dismissed the importance of the visit saying "Why should I go to that cemetery? "It's filled with losers."[22]
- When asked in an interview about over 1,000 Americans dying every day from the coronavirus, Trump responded "They are dying. That's true. ... It is what it is."[23]
- When firing members of his administration and others in the government or informing them of their replacements, Trump often did so publicly, via Twitter, instead of privately. It was by tweet that Reince Priebus, Trump's first chief of staff, learned from Trump that he was being replaced by John Kelly as the new chief of staff. Kelly was appalled to learn of this. Priebus was not surprised, commenting that Trump's cold and callous way of handling his departure (and the firing and resignations of many others) made perfect sense when you understood "The president has zero psychological ability to recognize empathy or pity in any way."[24]
- Often when Trump verbally expressed empathy, it was because he was told, cued, or reminded to do so by his chiefs of staff and their aides or whoever wrote his speech. When meeting with survivors of the Parkland, Florida school shooting in February 2018, an aide handed him a note card reminding him that he should say such things as "I hear you."[25] Having to remind them to show and express some empathy and compassion would have been unheard of among presidents Obama, G.W. Bush, Clinton, Reagan, G. Bush, Carter, and likely all others.

Trump's lack of empathy is perhaps best understood from the lens of his instrumental exchange perspective which shapes how he views others—as objects to be manipulated for his own self-interest. As commented by Trump, "For the most part, you can't respect people because most people aren't worthy of respect."[26] If not worthy of respect, they do not deserve sympathy.

Guilt and Shame: "Deny, Deny, Deny ... Never Admit"

Without empathy, one fails to experience the most common form of guilt, which is empathy-based guilt. As discussed in the previous chapter, empathy-based guilt underlies the assumption of responsibility and feelings of remorse over harming others. It often motivates one to repair any harm done, including harm to interpersonal relationships. Trump's lack of empathy largely explains why he also is lacking in guilt, as well as the more pervasive negative feeling of shame.

Multiple individuals who know Trump well or have studied him closely, including psychologists, have commented about his lack of guilt and shame. Some go so far as to say that he is incapable of those emotions. As discussed in Chapter 9, some also present a case for Trump having antisocial personality disorder, which is the formal diagnosis made of individuals commonly referred to as psychopaths and sociopaths. After observing Trump as president and having spent hundreds of hours with Trump as the ghostwriter of *The Art of the Deal,* Tony Schwartz concluded that Trump possessed a trait found among psychopaths: "the utter absence of conscience—the capacity to lie, cheat, steal, and inflict pain to achieve their ends without a scintilla of guilt or shame." Schwartz further stated that "What Trump's words and behavior make clear is that he feels no more guilt about hurting others than a lion does about killing a giraffe … His primary goal is to win at any cost and the end always justifies the means. Ultimately, he doesn't care what anyone else thinks or feels."[27]

Many others agree with Schwartz. General Colin Powell, Secretary of State under President George W. Bush, stated that "Trump has no sense of shame."[28]

Undoubtedly, Trump lacks empathy, guilt, and shame, but saying that he has no conscience and is *incapable* of experiencing moral emotions is an overstatement. Just as Trump is capable of moral reasoning beyond Stage 2 (but rarely displays such), so too is he capable of experiencing moral emotions. Examples of Trump demonstrating empathy can be found in several authoritative books. In Bob Woodward's *Fear: Trump in the White House.* Woodward noted that "a staffer who sat in on several calls that Trump made to Goldstar families was struck with how much time and emotional energy Trump devoted to them. He had a copy of material from the deceased service member's personnel file."[29] In another example of Trump demonstrating empathy (which might have been more personal distress than empathic concern), Woodward notes that Trump was visibly emotionally distraught over video of Syrian children being killed in a sarin gas attack on Syrian rebels by Syrian dictator Bashar al-Assad, responding "Let's fucking kill him! Let's go in. Let's kill the fucking lot of them" (which he did).[30] Although a few examples of Trump demonstrating empathic concern can be found, examples of guilt and shame are extremely rare (I found none).

Unquestionably, Trump is seriously lacking empathy, as we have seen earlier in multiple examples of the psychological harm he causes others, and his admitting with respect to empathy "It's just not my thing." His lack of empathy accounts for his lack of empathy-based guilt and shame. There is another major factor, however, that greatly explains not only his lack of guilt and shame but also his lack of empathy. In the words of Gary Cohn, Trump's Director of the National Economic Council, and chief economic advisor:

"He's 71. He's not going to admit he's wrong, ever." Never admitting he's wrong also explains why Trump often fails to experience guilt and shame even in the rare situations in which he just might feel empathetic or emotionally moved by someone's suffering. By believing he's never wrong, any empathy that might emerge is fleeting and the connection linking empathy to guilt or shame, as found in most humans, is quickly short-circuited.

Indeed, it is extremely rare to find instances where Trump admits he is wrong and accepts responsibility. However, instances of him denying responsibility abound. As seen later in this chapter, with respect to Trump using blaming as a mechanism of moral disengagement, he denies responsibility and blames others for just about every mistake he makes or whatever he does that is wrong. He denied any responsibility for the million deaths related to the coronavirus, for his actions leading to his two impeachments, for him and many fellow Republicans losing the 2020 election, for the storming of the Capitol and attempted coup, and for illegally storing classified documents at Mar-a-Lago. Most denials are supported by his lies.

As reported by Woodward in *Fear*, Trump once advised a friend who admitted to treating women badly that: "You've got to deny, deny, deny and push back on these women," he said. "If you admit to anything and any culpability, then you're dead. That was a big mistake you made. You didn't come out guns blazing and just challenge them. You showed weakness. You've got to be strong. You've got to be aggressive. You've got to push back hard. You've got to deny anything they said about you. Never admit."[31]

By never admitting wrongdoing one not only avoids guilt and shame, but also avoids, or minimizes, empathic concern, as any initial emotions of concern are quickly diminished by absolving oneself of responsibility. For Trump, admitting you're wrong is a sign of weakness. By never being wrong, and believing it, he escapes negative feelings of guilt and shame. This includes believing his own lies: A lie is not viewed as a lie when the liar believes the lie. Trump's father taught him to never admit wrongdoing or guilt; It is shameful to do so. This was reinforced at the church that his family attended, Marble Collegiate Church in Manhattan. The pastor was Norman Vincent Peale, author of the bestselling book *The Power of Positive Thinking: A Practical Guide to Mastering the Problems of Everyday Living*, which sold over 5 million copies. Peale taught his followers to "be free of a sense of guilt." He also preached that "every normal person wants power over circumstances, power over fear, power over weakness, power over themselves."[32] Trump got the message: At the core of positive thinking was power and being "free of a sense of guilt."

As discussed in the next chapter, it was as an adult, and under the tutelage of Roy Cohn, his unscrupulous lawyer and close friend, that Trump further developed and perfected the art of power without guilt and learned that the key was the strategic and frequent use of mechanisms of moral disengagement. As seen later in this chapter, he became a master of their use, absolving himself of any sense of responsibility and thus avoiding guilt and shame.

Trump mastered the use of mechanisms of moral disengagement, and discovered another strategy for avoiding negative emotions—simply avoid situations that induce them. For example, by not going to the cemetery in France Trump avoided a situation that just might have triggered empathic concern, or more likely, personal distress. Likewise, after attending a ceremony at Dover Air Force Base in Delaware in honor of the arrival of the body of a Navy SEAL killed in a combat mission ordered by Trump, he never attended another one. If viewing the body was not enough to trigger moral emotions, the soldier's father refused to meet with Trump saying, "my conscience won't let me talk to him."[33]

Trump is notorious for avoiding situations that are likely to induce personal distress, particularly embarrassment. Though proud of verbally attacking and bullying others, he is thin-skinned when it comes to receiving any form of criticism. A good example was his refusal to attend the annual dinner of the White House Correspondents and the annual Kennedy Center Honors event out of fear that the hosts and celebrities would criticize him (as Obama had humorously done at the Correspondents dinner in 2016).

Master of Mechanisms of Moral Disengagement

Although Trump's self-centered moral reasoning, lack of moral emotions, and mechanisms of moral disengagement largely account for his lying, cheating, and bullying (and to a lesser extent his narcissism), it is the latter that most fully explains those behaviors. Indeed, when reading and writing about mechanisms of moral disengagement I often thought that Trump could have written "the book" on their use. Mechanisms of moral disengagement are directly seen, or reflected, in almost every instance of his lying, cheating, and bullying—allowing him to disengage moral emotions and other-oriented moral reasoning and in doing so absolve himself of any sense of responsibility for harm caused to others. Mechanisms of moral disengagement also support his narcissism, for it is difficult for even narcissists to continue to truly believe they are greater than others when they are aware that they are morally flawed. Successful use of mechanisms of moral disengagement stifles such awareness.

As seen below, Trump has mastered use of each of Bandura's mechanisms of moral disengagement that were described in the previous chapter.

It's Someone Else's Fault (Attribution of Blame)[34]

As noted by his biographer Michael D'Antonio, Trump has a long history of blaming others:

> "This idea that you grab credit for everything and push responsibility off on others is something long-standing with him." ... When he [Trump] went

through his big bankruptcies in the early 1990s, he basically blamed his lenders and said they were responsible because they made the loans. He was not responsible because he failed to pay them back.[35]

There are plenty of other examples of Trump blaming others, such as:

- He blamed Democrats for just about everything he found to be wrong in the United States, including crime, poverty, riots, and the "tremendous anger" in the country caused by the second impeachment. He also blamed them for a government shutdown, despite declaring to Democratic leaders "I will be the one to shut it down. I'm not going to blame you for it."[36]
- He blamed the media, as much if not more than Democrats, for everything that reflected poorly upon him. He blamed the "fake news" when news coverage of the White House was unfavorable, including the reporting of deaths and loss of jobs caused by the coronavirus. He blamed the "liberal" media for the anger and hatred in the country that led to the mail bombs sent to CNN and democrats, and for multiple other instances of White Supremacists (and Trump supporters) threatening and killing others, including at Charlottesville, Pittsburgh, and the U.S. Capitol.[37]
- He blamed Attorney General Jeff Sessions (whom Trump appointed), the "Deep State," "the witch hunt," and Democrats for the Mueller investigation and his first impeachment.
- In addition to blaming Democrats, he blamed Federal Reserve Chairman Jerome Powell, whom Trump nominated for the job, when the stock market fell (but Trump took all the credit when the market rose).[38]
- During his 2016 campaign for president, Trump blamed, and fired, his pollsters when their polls were unflattering and showed he was not winning.[39]
- He blamed losing the popular vote in the 2016 election by about 3 million votes on voter fraud (and particularly voting by illegal immigrants). He continued to do so despite the fact that multiple independent experts and the Presidential Advisory Commission on Election Integrity, which was appointed by Trump and chaired by Vice President Mike Pence, found no evidence to support this lie.[40]
- After losing the 2020 election, he blamed phony paper ballots, rigged voting machines, inaccurate polls, and "voter suppression." He also blamed almost everyone else (except himself), including many Republican leaders at both the state and national levels, his own Attorney General William Barr, and court judges for not more aggressively challenging the election results. He blamed Vice President Michael Pence and Senate Majority Leader Mitch McConnell for failing to overturn the election results. Of course, he also blamed the "fake news" media—for supporting Joe Biden and failing to investigate his allegations of systematic voter fraud.[41]
- Trump blamed Antifa for the violence at the U.S. Capitol building.[42]

- For the multiple federal and state investigations, including for criminal offenses, tax evasion, interference in election results, instigating the January 6, 2020 attack on the U.S. Capitol, and storing classified documents illegally at Mar-a-Lago, he blamed the FBI, judges, Biden, and Democrats for a "weaponized" justice system, while also calling on Republicans to "defund" the Department of Justice and FBI.[43]

Perhaps the best example of Trump blaming others was his handling of the coronavirus, claiming "I don't take responsibility for this."[44] As viewed by Trump, the million deaths caused by the coronavirus (over half during his presidency) were not his fault. In his eyes he was not responsible for the government's lack of preparation for a pandemic, including the lack of respirators, protective medical gear, and testing for the virus. For this, he blamed governors. Trump also blamed the Obama/Biden administration, despite at that time Trump having been in power for three years during which he cut funding of federal programs that maintained those supplies. He also blamed Obama and Biden for the lack of COVID-19 test kits even though the virus did not exist while they were in office. Likewise, he blamed state governors for not testing large numbers of citizens even though the federal government had not provided the states with anywhere near the number of kits to deliver on his false claim made at news conferences that "If somebody wants to be tested right now, they'll be able to be tested."[45]

He blamed Democrats in Congress for deliberately exaggerating the negative effects of the virus, claiming that they had created a "hoax" to harm the economy and his chances for reelection. He blamed Democratic governors for increases of the virus in their states (while also accepting credit in any state where rates decreased and while praising Republican governors for ignoring increasing death rates and "opening back up"). He blamed China for creating the virus and not preventing its spread to the United States. Being racially insensitive, he labeled the virus the "Chinese virus," and the "Kung Fu virus." Before suspending flights to Europe, he blamed the European Union for "seeding" pockets of the "foreign virus" in the United States and failing to stop it in Europe. He blamed the World Health Organization for mismanaging the global response to the virus and punished them by suspending funding from the United States.[46]

For his own failure to wear a mask as president, Trump blamed Dr. Anthony Fauci, Director of the U.S. National Institute of Allergy and Infectious Diseases and member of the Trump's Coronavirus Task Force, arguing that Dr. Fauci had stated that masks were not recommended (which was a gross distortion of Dr. Fauci's recommendations).[47] By not wearing masks, berating others who wore them or endorsed doing so, tweeting about their insignificance, and railing against the wearing of masks at campaign rallies, he supported those who viewed having to wear a mask as an authoritarian affront to their individual rights (i.e., to reason at Stage 2 and act in a self-centered, hedonistic, and harmful manner).

Trump blamed the Democrats in Congress for spreading the virus, claiming that by impeaching him they distracted him from handling the virus effectively. With no evidence supporting the charge, he blamed the "deep state" and the U.S. Food and Drug Administration (including the head of the agency, whom he appointed) for prolonging the spread of the virus by intentionally delaying vaccine trials. The concern he voiced about prolonging the spread of the virus, however, was not the death of people but that it would cause him to lose reelection.[48]

According to Bob Woodward, Fauci warned Trump about lying to the public about the virus, noting that he would be criticized about his misleading information, Trump responded, "Who gives a shit? They criticize me no matter what I do anyway."[49]

Finally, upon contracting the virus himself, he suggested it was not from the campaign rallies, fundraising events, and meetings with White House Staff where he and others failed to wear masks and practice social distancing. Instead, he suggested that blame was attributed to Gold Star family members he invited to the White House—those whose relatives had died in military conflicts.[50]

Blaming others was commonly used in defense of Trump supporters storming the Capitol. One national poll found that over half of all Republicans believed that the riot was "mostly an antifa-inspired attack" as claimed by Trump and repeated by his supporters.[51] Many Republicans, including members of Congress (e.g., Mo Brooks, Matt Gaetz, Marjorie Greene, Paul Gosar), joined Trump in denying that many of the rioters were Republicans, while makir⸱ ⸱⸱ oaseless claim on Fox, Newsmax, and other conservative media networks that the rioters were Antifa or that the riot was orchestrated by Antifa or Black Lives Matter.[52] Another poll found that over half of Republican voters blamed Joe Biden, not Trump, for the insurrection.[53] By blaming Antifa and Biden, Trump and many of his supporters were able to absolve themselves of responsibility, avoiding the cognitive dissonance and negative emotions that most other people would experience when espousing law and order but acting in unlawful and violent ways.

They're Evil, Animals, or Otherwise Nonhuman (Dehumanization)

Trump has a long history of referring to humans as animals, particularly those he assumes to be criminals. He called a group of African American adolescents whom he accused (falsely) of rape in New York Central Park as animals and a "wolf pack"—noting that they were among many other wolf packs that roamed New York City at that time. He also called terrorists of the World Trade Center animals and members of the Islamic State "a vicious group of animals." Trump recommended the death penalty for all such animals. Reflecting both racism and dehumanization, in a tweet Trump referred to former aide Omarosa Manigault-Newman as a "dog" and members of Mexican gangs as "animals" who "aren't people" and "infest" our country.[54]

Trump repeatedly referred to Democrats as "very evil and sick people" and to both Democrats and the media as "enemy of the people."[55] Multiple Trump-supporting Republicans in Congress followed suit, as exemplified in Congresswoman Marjorie Greene calling democrats "Nazis" and equating the wearing of masks with the holocaust.[56]

Viewing others as animals, or otherwise lacking in human qualities, allows one to disengage the moral emotions of empathy, guilt, and shame and thus inflict pain without feeling poorly about one's behavior or self. Too often language such as "animals" and "terrorists" generalizes beyond individuals who have committed hideous crimes to cultural, racial, and ethnic groups to which they belong: Mexican immigrants are members of Mexican drug cartels, Muslims are members of the Islamic State and thus terrorists, Black American males are wolves, and Asians are creators of the deadly "Chinese" or "Kung Fu" virus. When repeated over and over a new normal of discrimination and hatred emerges.

Trump supporters, and especially alt-righters and White nationalists, are especially prone to dehumanizing others. When asked to rate the human qualities of certain groups on a scale of 1 to 100, alt-righters rated Muslims the lowest (55.4). Also viewed as lacking in human qualities were African Americans (64.7), Mexicans (67.7), and Jews (73). Whites received a rating of 91.8.[57]

It is not only people of color that Trump and his enablers view as lacking human qualities. When it comes to those who disagree with him, Trump is color blind. During protests in Minneapolis over the brutal killing of George Floyd by a police officer, Trump referred to the protesters as "thugs," tweeting that "When the looting starts, the shooting starts," while retweeting a video in which a supporter says, "The only good Democrat is a dead Democrat."[58] Alt-righters agree to his views of Democrats, rating them 60.4 on the scale of 1 to 100—higher than feminists (57) and journalists (58.6).[7]

With the apple not falling far from the tree, both of Trump's sons, Donald Trump, Jr. and Eric Trump, have dehumanized Democrats, viewing them as evil. Donald Jr. went so far as stating that Democrats are so evil and sick that they had hoped that the coronavirus "kills millions of people so that they could end Donald Trump's streak of winning."[59] Eric went even further with his dehumanization of Democrats, commenting during a television interview with Sean Hannity on Fox that Democrats are "not even people" and adding "It's so, so sad, I mean morality is just gone, morals have flown out the window. We deserve so much better than this as a country. You know, it's so sad."[60] (Hannity didn't disagree.) Yes, morality is just gone, and children in this country deserve much better role models than those who dehumanize over half of Americans.

Others Did It Too (Diffusion of Responsibility)

Interestingly, I found no example of Trump using shared blaming. I suspect, however, that examples are out there. You would think that he might share some of the blame for the deaths caused by the coronavirus, but he failed to do so. However, not sharing blame makes sense given that Trump has always blamed others and not himself. My guess is that Trump seldom uses shared blaming as a mechanism of moral disengagement because in doing so he admits that he too is to blame, and thus is at least partially responsible. The motive for not sharing blame with others is similar to that for his not sharing credit for his successes with others—he always wants to be *the* winner and never a loser or even associated with losing. This is part of his narcissism and consistent with his belief that he is never to admit wrongdoing or apologize, as they are signs of personal weakness.

They Made Me Do It (Displacement of Responsibility)

As with shared blaming, it is difficult to find examples of Trump using this mechanism of moral disengagement, and likely for the same reason, which is that in doing so he admits some responsibility. Also, by displacing responsibility onto someone of higher authority he recognizes that someone is above him, which is very difficult for him and other narcissists to do.

Although it is a challenge to find examples of Trump using displacement of responsibility, there is no lack of examples of Trump's supporters using this mechanism of moral disengagement. Many blamed Trump for their own failure to wear masks, while stating that they did not wear masks because Trump told them they need not do so. Many also blamed Trump for their storming of the Capitol. Again, they were following orders, as good authoritarians do.

It Could Have Been Worse (Advantageous Comparison)

As often modeled by Trump and many of his supporters, in use of this mechanism of moral disengagement immoral behavior can be viewed favorably, even as praiseworthy, when it is compared with other more negative outcomes. For example, in absolving himself of responsibility for taking few actions to curtail the spread of the virus, Trump argued that a worse outcome would have been slowing the economy if he had tried more to stop the spread.

Another example of Trump's use of advantageous comparisons is seen in one of the very rare instances in which he apologized for his behavior—for saying on a videotape that he liked grabbing women's vaginas. After apologizing (as it was clear that he could not use the common strategy of "deny, deny, deny" when assaulting women since his bragging about it was on videotape), he quickly attempted to minimize any harm in what he had said by stating that Bill Clinton "said far worse to me on the golf course."[61] (Months after videotape incident, Trump told others that it was not his voice.)

It Was for a Good Reason (Moral, Social, or Economic Justification)

Consistent with his self-centered moral reasoning, the moral justifications Trump uses to defend his actions and to disengage negative emotions are almost always driven by "winning." As Trump stated at one of his campaign rallies: "We love winners. We love winners. Winners are winners." … . "My whole life is about winning. I don't lose."[62] Multiple individuals in the Trump White House, including members of his cabinet noted previously, have asserted that most of Trump's behavior was driven by winning re-election. In "*The Room Where It Happened*," John Bolten, who served as one of Trump's national security advisors, stated: "I am hard-pressed to identify any significant Trump decision during my tenure that wasn't driven by re-election calculations."[63] Likewise, Dr. Fauci told others that Trump's leadership was "rudderless," his attention span was "like a minus number," and "His sole purpose is to get reelected."[64]

From Trump's perspective, nothing is wrong with lying, cheating, and bullying to win an election. Winning an election, regardless of what means, makes him "a winner," wealthier, and more powerful. His supporters also "win," with Trump ensuring the protection of MAGA values and individual rights, particularly their gun and religious rights, and their protection from Antifa, immigrants, socialists, and rioters (i.e., rioters not at the Capitol, but the ones in cities Trump called "rodent infested"). Thus, the means always justify the ends, even if individuals and democracy are harmed along the way.

Let's Call It Something Else That Sounds Better (Euphemistic Labeling)

Euphemistic labeling is used to sanitize or neutralize harmful behavior, and Trump is very good at it. His grabbing women by their vaginas is "locker room talk," a large concrete wall on the Mexican border is a "great, beautiful wall," White supremacists who marched in Charlottesville carrying Confederate flags are "very fine people," his phone call to Ukrainian President Volodymyr Zelensky that led to his second impeachment was a "perfect phone call," and his contracting the coronavirus was "a blessing from God." The euphemism "executive time" was created by the White House to describe a large block of time when Trump avoided meetings and briefings most mornings to send out tweets, watch *Fox News*, and call or text friends.[65] While Trump supporters were storming the Capitol, Trump was engaged in his executive time, watching what Congressman Andrew Clyde of Georgia called a "normal tourist visit."[66]

Euphemistic language serves not only to sanitize what many find unpleasant, but also to distort the truth. This is perhaps best seen in the euphemisms "fake news" and "alternative facts." In 2017, the American Dialect Society recognized "fake news" as the Word of the Year, and "alternative facts" as the Euphemism of the Year.[67]

Euphemisms often appear within the context of *convoluted language* —language that is twisted, overly complicated, distorted, and difficult to follow. In addition to sanitizing one's harmful behavior, convoluted language confuses others and thus it disguises or distorts the harmful behavior or its effects. As with other mechanisms of moral disengagement, euphemistic and convoluted language is used to convince others, and oneself, that a behavior is not bad or as bad as one might think; thus, mitigating or absolving one's responsibility.

Convoluted language is commonly heard when someone offers a long and illogical argument supporting their misbehavior. Trump rarely uses convoluted language as a mechanism of moral disengagement, as he tends to use more simple and direct language that denies responsibility, blames others, and distorts facts. Studies of his speeches and media interviews find that his language is more similar to that of fourth to fifth graders than of college graduates. This is not because he is incapable of more mature language, but because he prefers simple, direct, and anti-intellectual language that plays to his political base.[68] Nevertheless, one can find examples of Trump's use of convoluted language, such as when he denied that COVID-19 was a serious problem, dismissed the importance of wearing masks, and offered instead his own possible treatment during a press conference, as follows:

> I see disinfectant, where it knocks it out in a minute, one minute, and is there a way we can do something like that by injection inside, or almost a cleaning. Because you see it gets in the lungs and it does a tremendous number on the lungs, so it'd be interesting to check that. So you're going to have to use medical doctors, but it sounds interesting to me. So, we'll see. But the whole concept of the light, the way it kills it in one minute, that's pretty powerful.[69]

It Didn't Harm Anyone! (Disregard, Distortion, and Denial of Harmful Effects)

Many of the examples of Trump's use of denial presented in Chapter 3 on his lying consisted of him disregarding, distorting, or denying the significance of any harmful impact of his actions. His most common strategy for doing so is to simply go on the offensive and attack all critics of his behavior; thus, invalidating the source of such criticism. This is seen in Trump and others in the White House, and many Republicans in Congress, raging a deliberate campaign of smearing reporters and the media whenever they questioned or challenged Trump's decisions, behavior, and lying. Their reports were labeled "fake news" or "alternative facts." Fake news often became a more sinister "hoax." Whereas "fake news" and an "alternative fact" might be an unintended typo, a hoax implies malicious intent—a deliberate attempt by others to falsely accuse or mislead others. Trump used "hoax" over 300 times in speeches, rallies, and Tweets in 2019 and again in 2020. Each of those years, *Fox News* used it over 1,000 times, which included Sean Hannity stating that the Coronavirus crisis was greatly exaggerated and used by Democrats to "bludgeon Trump again with this new hoax."[70]

Disregarding, distorting, and denying the negative impact of his actions also were clearly seen in Trump's defense of his lack of action in curtailing the spread of the coronavirus. He stated that the virus was "totally harmless" in 99% of cases, the virus was "under control," it "will go away" … "like a miracle," it was "like a flu," that testing for the virus was "overrated," and wearing masks were not only ineffective but increased the risks of infection.[71]

As was discussed in the previous chapter, individuals with self-centered, hedonistic moral reasoning are more likely than others to lie, cheat, bully, and otherwise engage in antisocial and aggressive behavior. The same holds true about those who are lacking empathy, guilt, and shame, and those who are prone to the use of mechanisms of moral disengagement. When all three characteristics are present, a powerful combination exists for lying, cheating, and bullying, as well as narcissism. This is particularly true when the combination is formed at an early age and is positively reinforced throughout development in childhood, adolescence, and adulthood. As seen with Trump, the combination has been very effective in him getting things done. How Trump developed the combination of those traits is the focus of the next chapter.

Notes

1 Elise Viebeck, 2018. "Trump: 'I Think I Am a Great Moral Leader,'" *The Washington Post*, November 7. https://www.washingtonpost.com/politics/2018/live-updates/midterms/midterm-election-updates/trump-i-think-i-am-a-great-moral-leader/
2 Bob Woodward, 2020. *Rage*. New York: Simon & Schuster.
3 Jake Tapper, 2020. "Former White House Chief of Staff Tells Friends That Trump 'Is the Most Flawed Person' He's Ever Met." *CNN*, October 16. https://www.cnn.com/2020/10/16/politics/donald-trump-criticism-from-former-administration-officials/index.html
4 John Harwood, 2020. "Trump's Historical Place Defined by His Amorality," *CNN*, February 12. https://www.cnn.com/2020/02/12/politics/amorality-presidency-donald-trump/index.html
5 Ashley Parker and Josh Dawsey, 2022. "Trump's Cable Cabinet: New Texts Reveal the Influence of Fox Hosts on Previous White House." *The Washington Post*, January 9. https://www.washingtonpost.com/politics/trump-cable-cabinet/2022/01/09/96fac488-6fe6-11ec-b9fc-b394d592a7a6_story.html
6 Grace Panetta, 2020. "Hope Hicks Is Returning to The White House—Here Are 21 People Who Have Gone through the Revolving Door Between Fox and the Trump Administration," Business Insider, February 13. https://www.businessinsider.com/19-people-who-have-worked-at-fox-news-trump-administration-2019-5
7 Phillip Rucker and Josh Dawsey, 2019. "'We Fell in Love': Trump and Kim Shower Praise, Stroke Egos on Path to Nuclear Negotiations." *The Washington Post*, February 25. https://www.washingtonpost.com/politics/we-fell-in-love-trump-and-kim-shower-praise-stroke-egos-on-path-to-nuclear-negotiations/2019/02/24/46875188-3777-11e9-854a-7a14d7fec96a_story.html
8 This was response to Putin having commented that Trump was "Yarkii," which was translated to Trump to mean bright or brilliant, with Trump announcing that "Putin called me a genius!" Yarkii was misinterpreted, however, as it means colorful, not smart.
9 "Trump Defends Putin Praise: 'If He Says Great Things about Me,'" ABC News, https://www.youtube.com/watch?v=MQi5peFD7r8

10 Woodward, 244.
11 "Here Are Some of the People Trump Pardoned," 2021. *The New York Times*, January 26. https://www.nytimes.com/article/who-did-trump-pardon.html
12 Tara Paleri, 2022. "Trump Considered Blanket Pardons for Jan. 6 Rioters before He Left Office." *Politico,* February 02 https://www.politico.com/news/2022/02/02/trump-considered-blanket-pardons-for-jan-6-rioters-before-he-left-office-00004738
13 Mariana Alfaro, 2022. "Trump Vows Pardons, Government Apology to Capitol Rioters If Elected." *The Washington Post,* September 1. https://www.washingtonpost.com/national-security/2022/09/01/trump-jan-6-rioters-pardon/
14 Donald J. Trump and Bill Zanker, 2007. *Think Big and Kick Ass in Business and Life.* New York: HarperCollins, 190.
15 Laurence Leamer, 2018. "'Let's Make a Deal': Trump's Unlikely Truce at Mar-a-Lago.'" *Vanity Fair*, December 26. https://www.vanityfair.com/news/2018/12/lets-make-a-deal-trumps-unlikely-truce-at-mar-a-lago
16 James D. Zirin, 2019. *Plaintiff in Chief: A Portrait of Donald Trump in 3,5000 Lawsuits.* New York: All Points Books. xi. https://www.vanityfair.com/news/2018/12/lets-make-a-deal-trumps-unlikely-truce-at-mar-a-lago
17 Tom Porter, 2019. "Trump Tried to Block The $85 Billion AT&T-Time Warner Merger to Spite CNN, According to a Scathing New Profile of His Cozy Relationship with Fox News," *Business Insider*, March 4. https://www.businessinsider.com/trump-tried-to-block-the-att-time-warner-merger-to-spite-cnn-report-2019-3
18 Whereas Trump claimed he fired Mattis, Mattis insists that he resigned.
19 Emily Singer, 2021. "'Get Rid of Them All': Trump Issues Call to Punish GOP Members Who Don't Support Him." *The American Independent*, March 1. https://americanindependent.com/donald-trump-cpac-speech-republicans-impeachment-get-rid-of-them-all/
20 Eric Bradner, Kristen Holmes, and Kate Sullivan, 2023. "Trump Says He Won't Drop Out of 2024 Race if He's Indicted." *CNN*, March 4. https://www.cnn.com/2023/03/04/politics/trump-cpac-speech
21 George T. Conway III, 2019. "Unfit for Office." *The Atlantic*, October 3. https://www.theatlantic.com/ideas/archive/2019/10/george-conway-trump-unfit-office/599128/
22 Jeffrey Goldberg, "Trump: Americans Who Died in War Are 'Losers' and 'Suckers'," The Atlantic, September 3, 2020, https://www.theatlantic.com/politics/archive/2020/09/trump-americans-who-died-at-war-are-losers-and-suckers/615997/
23 Devan Cole and Tara Subramaniam, 2020. "Trump on Covid Death Toll: 'It Is What It Is,'" *CNN*, September 3. https://www.cnn.com/2020/08/04/politics/trump-covid-death-toll-is-what-it-is/index.html
24 Bob Woodward, 2018. *Fear: Trump in the White House.* New York: Simon & Schuster, 235.
25 Ibid.
26 Michael D'Antonio, 2016. *The Truth about Trump.* New York: Thomas Dunne Books, 1.
27 Tony Schwartz, 2020. "The Psychopath in Chief," *Gen*, May 28. https://gen.medium.com/the-psychopath-in-chief-aa10ab2165d9
28 Aaron Blake, 2016. "Here Are the Juiciest Colin Powell Comments about Trump and Clinton from His Hacked Emails," *The Washington Post*, September 14. https://www.washingtonpost.com/news/the-fix/wp/2016/09/14/here-are-the-juiciest-colin-powell-comments-about-trump-and-clinton-from-his-leaked-emails/

29 Woodward, 2018, 75.
30 Ibid., 146.
31 Ibid., 175.
32 D'Antonio, 54.
33 Woodward, 2018, 73.
34 Note that Bandura tends to limit this mechanism to attributing blame to the victim (the "The Victim Locus") but I include both the victim and others to whom blame is attributed.
35 Ashley Collman, 2020. "Trump's New Tactic for Reelection Is Blaming Governors for the Coronavirus Response," *Business Insider*, April 20. https://www.businessinsider.com/trump-coronavirus-blaming-governors-reelection-tactic-2020-4
36 Maegan Vazquez, 2019. "Trump's Ever-Shifting Shutdown Blame Game." *CNN*, January 3. https://www.cnn.com/2019/01/03/politics/government-shutdown-blame-game-donald-trump/index.html
37 Veronica Stracqualursi and Liz Stark, 2018. "Trump Claims Media to Blame for 'Anger' after Bombs Sent to CNN, Dems." CNN, October 25. https://www.cnn.com/2018/10/25/politics/trump-blames-media-for-anger-after-attacks/index.html
38 Binyamin Applelbaum, 2018. "Stock Market Rout Has Trump Fixated on Fed Chair Powell." *The New York Times*, December 23. https://www.nytimes.com/2018/12/23/us/politics/fed-chairman-trump-jerome-powell.html
39 Kaitlan Collins, Sarah Westwood, Jeremy Diamond and Jeff Zeleny, 2019. "Trump Campaign Fires Multiple Pollsters after Unflattering Numbers Leak." *CNN*, June 16. https://www.cnn.com/2019/06/16/politics/trump-fire-campaign-pollsters-numbers-leak/index.html
40 Maggie Haberman, 2022. *Confidence Man: The Making of Donald Trump and the Breaking of America*. New York: Penguin.Jonathan Lemire, 2022. *The Big Lie: Election Chaos, Political Opportunism, and the State of American Politics After 2020*. New York: Flatiron Books.
41 Ibid.
42 Jonathan Swan, 2021. "Scoop: Trump Falsely Blames Antifa for Capitol Insurrection." *AXIOS*, January 11. https://www.axios.com/2021/01/12/trump-falsely-blames-antifa-for-capitol-riot
43 Alexander Bolton, 2023. "Trump's Call to Defund DOJ, FBI Puts Senate, House GOP at Odds," *The Hill*, April 06. https://thehill.com/homenews/senate/3936557-trumps-call-to-defund-doj-fbi-puts-senate-house-gop-at-odds/
44 Yasmeen Abutaleb and Damian Paletta, 2021. *Nightmare Scenario: Inside the Trump Administration's Response to the Pandemic That Changed History*. New York: Harper, 299.
45 Daniel Dale, David Wright, Arman Azad, and Holmes Lybrand, "Fact Check: Trump Falsely Claims, Again, That Anybody Who Wants a Test Can Get One," *CNN*, May 11, 2020. https://www.cnn.com/2020/05/11/politics/trump-fact-check-may-11/index.html
46 Abutaleb and Paletta.
47 Ibid.
48 Ibid.
49 Woodward, 2020, 354.
50 Jennifer Steinhauer, 2020. "Trump Suggests Gold Star Families May Be to Blame for His Infection, *New York Times*," October 8. https://www.nytimes.com/2020/10/08/us/politics/trump-coronavirus-gold-star-families.html
51 Susan Page and Sarah Elbeshbishi, 2021. "Exclusive: Defeated and Impeached, Trump Still Commands the Loyalty of the GOP's Voters," *USA Today*,

February 22. https://www.usatoday.com/story/news/politics/2021/02/21/exclusive-trump-party-he-still-holds-loyalty-gop-voters/6765406002/

52 Holmes Lybrand, Tara Subramaniam and Janie Boschma, 2021. "Fact Check: Some Republicans Have Tried to Rewrite the History of January 6. Here's How." CNN, July 27. https://www.cnn.com/2021/07/27/politics/republicans-rewrite-january-6-history-fact-check/index.html

Arpan Rai, 2022. "Marjorie Taylor Greene Still Claims Antifa behind Jan 6 Despite 875 Arrests, 360 Convictions and House Probe," *Independent*, August 08. https://www.independent.co.uk/news/world/americas/us-politics/marjorie-taylor-greene-antifa-jan-6-riot-b2140383.html

53 Celine Castronuovo, 2021. "Poll: Majority of Republicans Blame Biden for Mob Storming the Capitol," *The Hill*, January 7. https://thehill.com/homenews/news/533171-poll-majority-of-republicans-blame-biden-for-mob-storming-the-capitol

54 Brian Resnick, 2018. "Donald Trump and the Disturbing Power of Dehumanizing Language," *Vox*, August 14. https://www.vox.com/science-and-health/2018/5/17/17364562/trump-dog-omarosa-dehumanization-psychologyPhilip Bump, 2018. "Trump's Long History of Referring to Nonwhite Groups He Sees as Dangerous as 'Animals'," *The Washington Post*, May 17. https://www.washingtonpost.com/news/politics/wp/2018/05/17/trumps-long-history-of-referring-to-nonwhite-criminals-as-animals/

55 Rebecca Morin, 2018. "Haley Breaks with Trump: 'In America, Our Political Opponents Are Not Evil'," *Politico*, October 19. https://www.politico.com/story/2018/10/19/haley-trump-not-evil-915174Catherine Lucey and Andrew Restuccia, 2020. "Trump Denounces Impeachment, Saying He 'Went Through Hell,'" *Wall Street Journal*, February 6. https://www.wsj.com/articles/president-trump-denounces-terrible-ordeal-of-impeachment-11581002046?emailToken=98a4d399f8ff72cb7ad43bd53ade903b7re4vonmJKcPPK29GKC4ZvoTTFoH9E-Pw3d6PLUHC1J1Yk76LBS5QDrgu2bDgVqzTmKKosZUxPD+tEzPN13GgkQlYDRx8JvKP987eerq0QTi82QZb3WBUI5Eml1jXv8H1&reflink=article_gmail_share

56 Ryan Nobles, 2021. "Marjorie Taylor Greene Compares House Mask Mandates to the Holocaust," *CNN*, May 22. https://www.cnn.com/2021/05/21/politics/marjorie-taylor-greene-mask-mandates-holocaust/index.html

57 Brian Resnick, 2018. "Psychologists Surveyed Hundreds of Alt-Right Supporters. The Results Are Unsettling," *Vox*, August 12. https://www.vox.com/science-and-health/2017/8/15/16144070/psychology-alt-right-unite-the-right

58 David Gergen, 2020. "In a Sad Week for America, Trump Has Fled from His Duty," CNN, May 31. https://www.cnn.com/2020/05/30/opinions/trump-twitter-minneapolis-george-floyd-gergen/index.html

59 Chris Cillizza, 2020. "Donald Trump Jr. Just Said Something Unreal about Democrats and the Coronavirus," *CNN*, February 28. https://www.cnn.com/2020/02/28/politics/donald-trump-jr-coronavirus-democrats/index.html

60 Christian Holub, 2017. "'Eric Trump: Democrats Are 'Not Even People.'' *Entertainment*, June 7. https://ew.com/tv/2017/06/07/eric-trump-democrats-not-people-chelsea-clinton/

61 Louis Nelson, "From 'Locker Room Talk' on, Trump Fends Off Misconduct Claims," *Politico*, December 12, 2017. https://www.politico.com/story/2017/12/12/trump-timeline-sexual-misconduct-allegations-defense-292146

62 Rick Reilly, 2019. *Commander in Cheat: How Golf Explains Trump*. New York: Hachette Books, 148.

63 John Bolton, 2020. *The Room Where It Happened: A White House Memoir*. New York: Simon & Schuster.

64 Woodward, 2020, 354.
65 David Smith, 2019. "'Executive Time': How, Exactly, Does Trump Spend 60% of His Day?" *The Guardian*, February 6. https://www.theguardian.com/us-news/2019/feb/07/executive-time-donald-trump-white-house
66 Brittany Shammas, 2021. "A GOP Congressman Compared Capitol Rioters to Tourists. Photos Show Him Barricading a Door." *The Washington Post*, May 18. https://www.washingtonpost.com/politics/2021/05/18/clyde-tourist-capitol-riot-photos/
67 Mark Abadi, 2018. "One of Trump's Favorite Phrases Was Named the 2017 Word of the Year." *Insider*, January 8. https://www.businessinsider.com/word-of-the-year-2017-fake-news-2018-1
68 Orly Kayam. "The Readability and Simplicity of Donald Trump's Language." *Political Studies Review*, 16, 1, 2017, 73–83. https://doi.org/10.1177/1478929917706844
69 Deb Riechmann, Kevin Freking, and Aamer Madhani, 2020. "Trump Suggested Studying Injections of Disinfectant to Treat Coronavirus, Then Said He Was Being Sarcastic. Here's Video and a Transcript," *Chicago Tribune*, April 24. https://www.chicagotribune.com/coronavirus/ct-nw-trump-white-house-sunlight-heat-fight-virus-20200424-7dnhtyxltvdazkp24mybuefmou-story.html
70 Brian Stelter, 2020. *Hoax: Donald Trump, Fox News, and the Dangerous Distortion of Truth* New York: Atria/One Signal.
71 Aaron Blake, 2020. "President Trump, Coronavirus Truther," *The Washington Post*, July 6. https://www.washingtonpost.com/politics/2020/07/06/trump-throws-caution-wind-coronavirus/Chris Cillizza, 2020. "Donald Trump Can't Face the Stubborn Reality: He Was Wrong About Coronavirus." *CNN*, March 31. https://www.cnn.com/2020/03/31/politics/donald-trump-coronavirus/index.html
    Amber Phillips, 2020. "What You Need to Know from Sunday's White House Coronavirus Briefing." April 15. *The Washington Post*, https://www.washingtonpost.com/politics/2020/04/05/sunday-white-house-coronaivirus-takeaways/dialogWoodward, 2020.
Top of Form
Bottom of Form
*In mid-March, Trump said this: "This is a very contagious virus. It's incredible. But it's something we have tremendous control of." We did not have "tremendous control" of the virus. See above.

There are plenty more examples, but you get the idea. It is beyond ridiculous for Trump to claim with a straight face that every "individual statement" he made about the virus was (or is) true. I don't care whether you love Trump or hate him, you simply cannot draw that conclusion based on the examples cited above. It's not logically possible.

Now, I get what Trump was doing then—and what he is doing now.

In January, February, and even earlier this month, he was downplaying the virus because a) he wanted it to be not that bad and b) he didn't want people to freak out, for fear that it would send the economy, on which he has based his entire campaign for a second term, to spiral downward.

"The statements I made are I want to keep the country calm, I don't want panic in the country," Trump explained to Acosta on Monday, adding: "I could cause panic much better than even you. I could do much—I would make you look like a minor league player."

Of course, Trump's attempts to undersell the virus to the public had real-world consequences—including a very slow start to testing for the virus in this country and our current shortages on masks and ventilators. (Doubt it? Read this Times piece: "The Lost Month: How a Failure Test Blinded the U.S. to COVID-19.")

What Trump is doing now is what he always does about everything: Attempting to rewrite history so that it looks like he was always the smartest guy in the room, the one person who saw this all coming from a mile away.

"I've always known this is a real—this is a pandemic," he said on March 17. "I felt it was a pandemic long before it was called a pandemic."

That statement is, of course, demonstrably untrue. But Trump doesn't care. Because his political career has proven to him that if he simply repeats the history he wants to be true, plenty of people will follow his lead. He'll blame Democrats or the media (or both) for twisting his words or making thing up. Remember that this is a man who said this out loud: "Stick with us. Don't believe the crap you see from these people, the fake news .... What you're seeing and what you're reading is not what's happening."

But the truth still matters. And the truth is that Trump repeatedly downplayed the threat coronavirus posed to the country, providing Americans with false hope when they needed candor and transparency most of all.

12 Development of a Liar, Cheat, Bully, and Narcissist

Making of a "King" and "Killer"

How did Trump become a pathological liar, cheat, bully, and narcissist? This chapter examines the most influential factors contributing to Trump's character development. As recognized by Trump, "racehorse" genes played a major role, but it is extremely doubtful if he would have become a billionaire and the person he is if he had not lived, and thrived, in environments in which his lying, cheating, bullying, and narcissism were modeled, reinforced, and avoided punishment. At an early age, his father told him he was a "king" and needed to become a "killer" in anything he did.[1] A blend of overly indulgent and authoritarian parenting at home and the authoritarian discipline at New York Military Academy (NYMA), where he spent nearly all his adolescence, helped achieve that goal. Before adulthood, the foundation had been established for him to become the king and killer his father, and Trump himself, desired.

In an article entitled *The Men Who Gave Trump His Brutal Worldview*, Trump's biographer Joe D'Antonio posits that five individuals had a major influence on Trump: his father, Norman Vincent Peale, Theodore Dobias, Roy Cohn, and Roger Stone.[2] As discussed later in this chapter, each helped shape Trump's moral character. Trump's father, Cohn, Dobias, and Stone taught him that "winning was everything," one wins by dominating others, and that fear is the key to successful domination. All four were classic authoritarians, with Cohn viewed by many as outright ruthless. Each was instrumental in developing Trump's self-centered and hedonistic moral reasoning; lack of empathy, guilt, and shame; and his proclivity for mechanisms of moral disengagement. Peale did not teach the same as the others; however, he helped foster Trump's belief that God loved winners, including rich and famous ones.

Although the influence of parenting and influential others on Trump's moral character are the focus of the chapter, Trump was not a passive learner: He sought and absorbed what he wanted and created environments that have fostered and reinforced his lying, cheating, bullying, and narcissism. As seen

DOI: 10.4324/9781003401278-12

later, in those environments he has used fearmongering as an effective tool for getting things done.

"Super Genius" and "Racehorse" Genes

As discussed in Chapter 2 and noted in other chapters, genetics plays a major role in moral behavior, with research indicating that it explains about two-thirds of the variance in aggressive antisocial behavior (e.g., bullying) and half in non-aggressive rule-breaking (e.g., lying and cheating).[3] Environmental effects account for the remaining variance. Genetically linked differences are found not only in those behaviors but also in the cognitive and emotional processes that underlie them, which include moral reasoning and the moral emotions of empathy, guilt, and shame.

For decades, Trump has attributed his success, personality traits, and being a "very stable genius" to "great genes." In an interview with Oprah Winfrey in 1988, Trump told her "You have to be born lucky in the sense that you have to have the right genes."[4] In an interview for *Playboy* in 1990, he ruled out learning as a factor in his behavior, stating: "I can be a killer and a nice guy. You have to be everything. You have to be strong. You have to be sweet. You have to be ruthless. *And I don't think any of it can be learned. Either you have it or you don't"* [italics added].[5] And as he once told his biographer, Michael D'Antonio, "I had it. I always had it."[6] and "I don't think people change very much."[7] As noted by D'Antonio, "he really believes in genetic gifts. He wants to assume that he can do something that others can't do simply because of who he is."[8]

On several occasions when explaining the role of genes in his success, Trump has used the analogy of breeding fast racehorses. In a 2010 interview with CNN, he touted his genetic superiority, stating: "Well, I think I was born with a drive for success because I have a certain gene. I'm a gene believer … hey, when you connect two racehorses you usually end up with a fast horse. I had a good gene pool from the stand point of that so I was pretty much driven."[9] In what many perceived as racist, he repeated his racehorse theory of success in a 2020 campaign rally in Bemidji, Minnesota to a nearly all-White crowd (in a nearly all-White state), praising them for sharing his racehorse genes: "You have good genes, you know that, right? You have good genes. A lot of it is about the genes, isn't it, don't you believe? The racehorse theory. You think we're so different? You have good genes in Minnesota."[10]

The product of two "racehorses," Trump attributed his mother as the source of his showmanship, noting in *The Art of the Deal* that "She always had a flair for the dramatic and the grand."[11] As asserted by Trump himself, he resembles his father the most and credits him for his intelligence and personality. Whereas he likely inherited antisocial behavior and lack of moral emotions from his father, he inherited personality traits associated with narcissism from both parents. Trump has described his mother as being obsessed with social status, his father with always winning, and both obsessed with wealth.[12] At an early age Trump had the same obsessions, believing he was superior to others. As noted by Trump's niece, Dr. Mary Trump, "by the time he was 12, the right side of his mouth was curled up in an almost perpetual sneer of self-conscious superiority, and Freddy [his brother] had dubbed him 'the Great I-Am,' echoing a passage from Exodus he learned in Sunday school in which God first reveals himself to Moses."[13]

In addition to inheriting personality predispositions and traits associated with antisocial behavior and narcissism, Trump also inherited physical features, particularly physical attractiveness, size, and athleticism, that made him a better showman. Those same features have often enhanced the effectiveness of his lying, cheating, and bullying, and have fostered his narcissism.

How genes are expressed in one's personality and behavior is highly influenced by the environment. Unrecognized by Trump, a thoroughbred racehorse doesn't become a winner without excellent training, and someone financing it. It is very likely that "TRUMP" would *not* be emblazoned on buildings, airplanes, baseball caps, and so forth if Trump had not been born to billionaire parents in America and instead born to poor parents, regardless of their genetics, living in what Trump calls the "shithole" countries of Africa[14] or if he had been born not in New York City but in Baltimore, which Trump described as a "disgusting, rat and rodent infested mess."[15] As seen in this chapter, at home and school as a child and early in his career as a young adult, Trump received excellent training and support in expressing the antisocial traits that he inherited.

Parenting the Future "Killer" and "King" with Uninvolved/ Overindulgent and Authoritarian Parenting

In *Too Much and Never Enough*, written by Trump's niece, Dr. Mary Trump, a clinical psychologist, her uncle's lack of moral character was seen at an early age. According to her, "Mary [Trump's mother] couldn't control him at all, and Donald disobeyed her at every turn. Any attempt at discipline by her was rebuffed. He talked back. He could never admit he was wrong; he contradicted her even when she was right; and he refused to back down. He tormented his little brother and stole his toys. He refused to do his chores and everything else he was told to do."[16] Trump's sister, Maryanne Trump Barry, agreed with her niece in describing her brother as "extremely rebellious" in his youth.[17] As noted by Dr. Trump, her rebellious uncle learned "to be tough at all costs, lying is okay, admitting you're wrong or apologizing is weakness" and that "there can be only one winner and everybody else is a loser."[18]

Such comments by family members are consistent with ones made by his biographers. For example, in *The Truth About Trump*, Michael D'Antonio writes: "Donald was to be both a killer and a king. .... Not surprisingly, he became an argumentative, bullying and physically aggressive little boy."[19] Such behavior was seen not only at home but also at school, with a teacher at the private elementary school he attended describing him as "headstrong," "determined," and "surly." Another of his teachers desribed him as a "a little shit" who constantly needed attention.[20] His disrespect and disobedience of rules at home and school was the primary reason his father sent him to live at a military school during the bulk of his adolescence.

Trump wrote many books about his business successes and about how great he is but wrote very little about his childhood, parents, and upbringing. What little we do know about Trump's upbringing comes mostly from books written by his biographers and his niece. Based on those sources, the parenting that Trump received can best be described as a combination of two of the four major styles of parenting described in Chapter 2 and mentioned in other chapters: *uninvolved* parenting (also called disengaged and neglectful) and *authoritarian* parenting. His parents also were overindulgent—a style that some researchers lump under the permissive style of parenting while others view as distinct. In the Trump household, "overindulgent" is more fitting than "permissive." The overindulgence most often occurred in combination with Trump's parents being uninvolved; thus, *uninvolved/overindulgent* best describes Trump's parenting.

In all biographies of Trump, his father is described as uninvolved—seldom tending to his children, as he was too busy building more wealth. Trump's niece, Dr. Mary Trump, described her grandfather (Fred) as a high-functioning sociopath characterized by "a lack of empathy, a facility for lying, and indifference to right and wrong, abusive behavior, and a lack of interest in the rights of others."[21] She further notes that due to her grandmother's illnesses and her grandfather's work and sociopathy, neither of Trump's parents was much involved, especially emotionally, in Trump's parenting. Trump admits such himself, writing in *The Art of the Deal* that his father spent very little time with his family, noting that "My father would come home every night at seven, have his dinner, read the newspaper, watch the news, and that was that." He added "And I'm as much of a rock as my father."[22] He further commented that what little relationship he had with his father was "almost businesslike."[23] According to his niece, a clinical psychologist, in becoming "a rock" like his father and lacking in moral emotions, Trump also became a sociopath, observing "Having been abandoned by his mother for at least a year, and having his father fail not only to meet his needs but to make him feel safe or loved, valued or mirrored, Donald suffered deprivations that would scar him for life."[24]

Buying their children whatever they want and sending them to the most elite private schools are ways that many uninvolved parents try to win their children's love and compensate for their own lack of emotional involvement and time spent together. As with Fred Trump (and his son, Donald), many parents simply do not have time to be directly involved. They are too busy striving to achieve what they perceive as more important goals in life, such as greater wealth, while leaving the parenting responsibilities to others. This includes not having time to respond to their children's social and emotional needs.

Despite being uninvolved in much of their children's upbringing, Trump's parents managed to overindulge them in the niceties of their wealth. In a chapter of *The Truth about Trump*, entitled "The Boy King," D'Antonio writes that Trump's father did not want to spoil his children, but nevertheless did so while imbuing them with a sense of entitlement. Whereas his father made his three sons earn spending money by doing chores around the house, collecting soda bottles, and delivering newspapers, he also drove them on their paper routes in his Cadillac when it rained. A chauffeur drove the children to school in either the Cadillac or the family's Rolls Royce. Whereas other kids in the neighborhood had Schwinn bikes, Trump was given a 10-speed Italian racer. With a cook and nannies, the Trump family's 23-room mansion was among the first to have a color television, intercom system, and a sprawling electric train set.[25]

As reported by the *New York Times*, Trump was a millionaire by the age of eight and over the years he received at least $413 million from his father's real estate empire.[26] To avoid estate taxes, during his lifetime Fred Trump gifted over $1 billion to his children.[27] Trump was born rich.

The uninvolved/overindulgent style of parenting characterized the Trump household, but so too did the authoritarian style, especially whenever the father was around. Fred Trump was a classic authoritarian in both his personality and parenting. He held high standards and behavioral expectations, and his children were to adhere to them. Although he spent little time with his children, he was the head of the household and other family members were not to question him. He demanded obedience. As noted previously, according to Trump's niece, her grandfather was a sociopath who failed to demonstrate warmth, empathy, and responsiveness to the needs of his children. Whether genetic or learned, a lack of emotions was common among Trump family members, especially the men: As observed by Trump's niece, "I never saw any man in my family cry or express affection for one another in anyway other than the handshake that opened and closed any encounter."[28]

It was overindulgent parenting that helped fulfill his father's desire for his son to become a king. And it was authoritarian parenting, which Trump experienced at home from his father and at NYMA (between the ages of 13 and 18) that helped Trump become the "killer" his father desired. As discussed previously in Chapter 2 and mentioned in other chapters, the authoritarian approach to parenting and school discipline is characterized by high behavioral expectations, demandingness, and adult control. Children are rewarded when they meet adult expectations and punished when they fail to do so. Punishment is often harsh and physical (which was not the case with Trump). However, punishment also can be more psychological, with the fear of withdrawal of parental love and rejection replacing physical harm as the method of psychological control. This was more Fred's style. Trump's niece explains that this is what led to her father, Donald's older brother Fred Trump, Jr., leaving the family business and eventually dying from an illness related to his alcoholism—he could never live up to his father's expectations.

As true with uninvolved parenting, authoritarian parenting is characterized by a lack of nurturing and responsiveness to children's social and emotional needs. It is likely that this characteristic of both uninvolved and authoritarian parenting had the greatest and most lasting impact on the development of Trump's character. This is particularly the case with respect to his bullying, as research indicates that bullies tend to come from homes where parenting is similar to the uninvolved and authoritarian styles.[29]

Interestingly, Trump does not exhibit other negative outcomes often associated with uninvolved and authoritarian parenting: increased risks of low self-esteem, poor social skills, low achievement, substance abuse, and delinquent behavior during adolescence.[30] In contrast, Trump thinks he is the greatest, possesses good social skills (but often fails to use them), is a successful businessman and a billionaire, does not drink alcohol or use illegal substances, and is not a juvenile delinquent. Not experiencing those negative outcomes can be attributed to other factors offsetting the effects of uninvolved and authoritarian parenting, and primary among them were the absence of the kind of neglect, abuse, and harshness found among many uninvolved (often neglectful) and authoritarian parents. Likewise, he was not exposed to role models of poor self-esteem, low achievement, poor social skills, substance abuse, and delinquent behavior. He did not grow up in a "shithole" and "rat-infested" city neighborhood. As a child and adolescent, he lived a rather sheltered life in which he was pampered and treated like a king, and more so than his two brothers. As noted by Trump's niece, whose father became an alcoholic, Fred treated his two sons differently. Because Fred viewed her father, Fred Jr., as lacking the ambition and killer instinct of Donald, Fred was more abusive toward Fred Jr.

Uninvolved and authoritarian parenting also fails to fully explain the severity of Trump's lying, cheating, bullying, and narcissism. That is, few children raised under those two parenting styles lie, cheat, and bully as much as Trump, and fewer feel great about themselves despite those behaviors. It is likely that his parent's overindulgence and his sense of entitlement fostered Trump's effectiveness and self-confidence in lying, cheating, and bullying, while buffering their negative effects. Genetics also certainly contributed. So too did environmental factors beyond parenting, as discussed next.

Outside of Home: Key Influencers

As noted previously, Trump's biographer Joe D'Antonio recognized five individuals as having the greatest influence on Trump's character: Fred Trump, Norman Vincent Peale, Theodore Dobias, Roy Cohn, and Roger Stone.[31] As discussed next, each helped shape Trump's moral character, but some had a much greater influence than the others.

Fred Trump: Beyond Parenting in Childhood and Adolescence

As discussed above, uninvolved/overindulgent and authoritarian parenting were clearly influential in Trump's development. His father's influence did not end there, however. As noted in earlier chapters (and particularly Chapter 5 on Trump's cheating), it was largely as an adult that Trump learned from his father how to lie, cheat, and bully as a real estate developer. When Trump began working with his father, his father taught him how to circumvent and manipulate government regulations, laws, and grants to his advantage and how political connections help. As documented by the *New York Times*, Trump and his father participated in various tax schemes that greatly increased both of their fortunes.[32] They included Fred and Mary Trump transferring over $1 billion in the form of gifts and inheritances to their children, on which they paid only about 5% in taxes and thus avoided the typical 55% tax rate on gifts and inheritances. The *Times* documented a total of 295 streams of revenue created by Fred over five decades, often in collaboration with his chosen son, to help make his son a billionaire (and his other children millionaires). As noted by the *Times*, Fred and his son "were both fluent in the language of half-truths and lies, interviews and records show. They both delighted in transgressing without getting caught. They were both wizards at manipulating the value of their assets, making them appear worth a lot or a little *depending* on their needs."

Norman Vincent Peale and the Power of Positive Thinking

Peale was the pastor of Marble Collegiate Church in Manhattan, which Trump's family attended when he was a child. He is well known for authoring *The Power of Positive Thinking*, which was published in 1952 and has sold over seven million copies . In his books, radio shows, and newspaper columns, Peale's message was to always feel self-confident, strive to win, persevere, overcome all obstacles to winning, and not feel guilty or remorseful as those feelings interfere with success. Many wealthy New Yorkers, including Trump's parents, were attracted to Peale's main teachings and particularly the message that they deserved to be rich and powerful. Richard Nixon attended the same church, and over 750 firms subscribed to Peale's *Guidepost* magazine which was read by their employees.

As noted by biographer Gwenda Blair, author of *The Trumps: Three Generations That Built an Empire*, Peale's philosophy and inspirational messages "fit perfectly into the Trump family culture of never hesitating to bend the rules, doing whatever it took to win, and never, ever giving up."[33] As also noted by Trump's niece, Dr. Mary Trump, Peale also "confirmed what Fred already thought: he was rich because he deserved to be."[34]

Peale's teachings promoted materialism and narcissistic self-perceptions of superiority and entitlement (i.e., God blessed the Trumps and others with richness). They supported Trump's self-centered and hedonistic moral reasoning, and his use of mechanisms of moral disengagement to absolve himself of responsibility for harm caused to others. To be fair, and as asserted by Dr. Peale's son, John Peale, a professor of ethics, his father's teachings about positive thinking were not only about justifying materialism; they also emphasized humility, empathy, and helping others through the power of Jesus Christ. But as noted by John Peale, "I never heard of anything that came out of Trump that had anything to do with that."[35] Indeed, in *The Art of the Deal*, Trump wrote "It's been said that I believe in the power of positive thinking. In fact, I believe in the power of negative thinking."[36]

Although Peale is often credited for influencing Trump's character, it is very doubtful if his influence was anywhere as great as that of the other four influencers cited by D'Antonio. This is for reasons other than Trump claiming that he believes more in the power of negative than positive thinking. Foremost among them is that he rarely attended Peale's church or any other church, especially as an adolescent (when he was at NYMA) and as an adult. While running for election in 2015, Trump claimed to be a "Presbyterian Protestant" and that he attended church "as often as I can, a lot," while mentioning Marble Collegiate.[37] Shortly after making those claims, Marble Collegiate (which is not Presbyterian but part of the Reformed Church in America denomination), released a statement that Trump was not an active member. As an adult, Trump rarely attended any church, having attended only 14 times during his presidency.[38]

Whatever influence Peale had, it was largely indirect, by way of Trump's father who was a great admirer of Peale and who attended church more often than his son.[39] Moreover, it was not of the same type as that of the other influencers: Peale did not share their (and Trump's) brutal worldview.

Theodore Dobias and New York Military Academy: Winning Was Everything

Concerned and annoyed with his son's disobedient behavior at home and at the local private elementary school he attended, Fred sent Donald off to NYMA, a boarding school. Trump lived there between the ages of 13 and 18, which is considered by many psychologists as the most impressionable years of a child's life. NYMA shared Fred's authoritarian style of parenting, or discipline, and the staff at NYMA shared Fred's authoritarian personality. At NYMA, there were rulers and then there were followers. The school's code of conduct strictly governed how cadets were to act, and dress. Rules were not to be questioned, nor were those who enforced them. Violations resulted in demerits, detentions, and often harsher discipline. As described by Trump, "In those days they'd smack the hell out of you. It was not like today where you smack somebody and you go to jail."[40] But while they would "smack the hell out of you" at NYMA for bad behavior, cadets also earned badges, honors, and promotions for good behavior. This was well-suited for Trump's self-centered and hedonistic moral reasoning of avoiding punishment and seeking rewards.

Aggression was modelled not only by adults in authority, but also by cadets themselves. Bullying, especially of underclassmen and weaker cadets, was the norm. Bullying, hazing, fist fights, and smacking cadets, were viewed as ways to toughen cadets up. Trump observed a major upside to being a bully (and one that suited his narcissistic personality quite well): Bullies not only have power and often get what they want, but they also can be popular—in the limelight and center stage (and dressed accordingly). He discovered that bullies even earn medals for loyalty, following orders, and leadership.

As a cadet in military uniform, Trump's authoritarian personality and sense of entitlement and superiority continued to grow. As described by D'Antonio, Trump "absorbed the sense of superiority that was preached at NYMA with the consistency of a drumbeat." "He believed he was the best." Trump told his biographer that he was "Always the best player. Not in only baseball, but every sport."[41] Being best didn't end with sports, as Trump also stated "I was an elite person. When I graduated, I was a very elite person."[42]

At NYMA, Trump was highly influenced by World War II veteran Sergeant Theodore Dobias, Trump's military instructor and baseball coach. Dobias served as a substitute father and was a lot like Fred Trump: he was authoritarian, harsh, and obsessed about winning. As noted by D'Antonio, Trump "came to regard Dobias as his first real role model, aside from his father."[43] As coach, Dobias strived to instill in his players that "winning wasn't everything, it was the only thing." Dobias told D'Antonio "Donald picked right up on this. He would tell his teammates, 'We're out here for a purpose. To win.' He always had to be number one, in everything. He was a conniver even then. A real pain in the ass. He would do anything to win."[44]

Dobias saw Trump as a "real pain in the ass" and Trump saw Dobias the same. Trump told D'Antonio that "He [Dobias] could be a fucking prick. He absolutely would rough you up. You had to learn to survive."[45] Trump learned to survive and flourish. He did so by being in a position of power, bullying and manipulating others, and not experiencing moral emotions of empathy, guilt, or shame. Reflecting back on his life at NYMA and revealing how manipulative he was at an early age, Trump bragged to his biographers Michael Kranish and Marc Fisher about manipulating Dobias: "I figured out what it would take to get Dobias on my side. I finessed him. It helped that I was a good athlete, since he was a baseball coach and I was the captain of the team. But I also learned how to play *him*."[46] Playing others was a skill he learned early, practiced, and perfected throughout adulthood, and one that made him more effective at lying, cheating, and bullying.

Roy Cohn: "Pure Evil"

As noted by biographer Glenda Blair, Trump "never had truly close friends."[47] In an interview with Blair, Trump's first-year roommate at

NYMA, Ted Levine, commented that Trump "wasn't that tight with anyone" adding that "People liked him, but he didn't bond with anyone …. It was like he had this defensive wall around him, and he wouldn't let anyone get close."[48] Trump's having no close friends is insightful, as close friendships are widely recognized by developmental psychologists as instrumental to healthy social, emotional, and moral development.[49] It is in the context of close friendships that other-oriented moral reasoning and emotions are developed and that one learns valuable interpersonal skills such as social perspective-taking, trust, mutual respect, and conflict resolution.

Widely recognized by Trump's biographers as the most influential person in Trump's life, for years Cohn was his close friend and personal attorney. Their friendship began in 1973, when Trump was 27, and lasted until Cohn's death in 1986. When the two met, Cohn was well known as a ruthless prosecutor who worked alongside Wisconsin Senator Joe McCarthy in the 1950s. McCarthy is infamous for accusing hundreds of individuals as being "Communist sympathizers." The accused included many well-known entertainers, members of the armed services, and even members of Congress. Whether innocent or guilty, careers were ruined. When the "Red Scare" ended, Cohn moved to New York City and became the lawyer and henchman for mob bosses and others looking for illegal or legally dubious ways to gain wealth and avoid prison. As when he was in Wisconsin, Cohn became a well-known character assassin. Jewish and a closet homosexual, he was notorious for his racist, anti-Semitic, and homophobic slurs; his vanity and showmanship; his exploitive political connections; his self-promotion via gossip columns; and his attraction to tall blond, wealthy, and younger men (gay or straight).[50] Cohn introduced Trump to the swanky clubs and the lifestyles of the rich, famous, and powerful in New York City. As remarked by Liz Smith, a journalist, popular gossip columnist, and talk show host for *Fox News*, "Trump lost his moral compass when he made an alliance with Roy Cohn."[51] And as commented by Victor A. Kovner, a lawyer who knew Cohn for years: "You knew when you were in Cohn's presence you were in the presence of pure evil."[52]

Trump recognized Cohn as his "best friend,"[53] describing him as "a total genius" who "would kill for somebody that he liked."[54] As confessed by Trump, "He was no Boy scout. He once told me that he'd spent more than two thirds of his adult life under indictment on one charge or another." Trump added, "That amazed me."[55] Trump called Cohn 15 to 20 times a day to help him in avoiding taxes and zoning variances, with shady deals, and bullying contractors and others who interfered with his getting things done.[56] Trump had already learned much about lying and cheating from his father, and what Cohn added to his arsenal for getting things done was bullying, including cold and callous character assassination, and doing so without experiencing any sense of guilt or shame.

As remarked by attorney and author, James Ziren, in *Plaintiff in Chief*:

"Cohn unveiled for Trump an attack-dog approach to the law, in which you take no prisoners, inflict needless expense on the opposing party. Admit nothing, deny everything; lie, dissemble, and prevaricate. Make false and scurrilous accusations to demonize your adversary. Drag it out as long as the courts will let you ... Seal the settlement papers so no one will know. Declare victory, bragging that you never settle —and go home."[57] As noted by Ziren, "in Trump's eyes, Cohn was a sorcerer who could beat the system, and Trump eagerly cast himself as a sorcerer's apprentice."[58]

Cohn was indicted multiple times for violating the law, including blackmail, extortion, and bribery. Eventually, he was disbarred from practicing law in New York for dishonesty, fraud, deceit, and misrepresentation. Although their close friendship had waned, Trump testified as a character witness during Cohn's disbarment hearings. Trump had little to do with Cohn when he died, at age 59, with complications due to AIDS and two months after being disbarred. As noted by Marie Brenner in *Vanity Fair*, "Donald found out about [Cohn's condition] and just dropped him like a hot potato, Cohn's personal secretary, Susan Bell, was quoted as saying."[59] Loyalty was not reciprocal.

Roger Stone: The Dirty Trickster

Trump's friendship with Roger Stone was not as close and enduring as with Cohn, and at times it was tumultuous. Nevertheless, Stone was influential in shaping Trump's lying, cheating, bullying, and narcissism. It was Cohn who first introduced Trump to Stone. Stone had a reputation as one of Richard Nixon's political dirty tricksters, and at the time was running the presidential-campaign organization for Ronald Reagan in several states, including New York. Trump contributed $200,000 to the campaign. Because $1,000 was the maximum contribution allowed by law, Trump bundled the $200,000 into 200 legal payments of $1,000, as advised by Stone. Impressed with Stone's advice, Trump became Stone's first client as a professional lobbyist, assisting him with such tasks as obtaining a government permit to dredge the channel to the Atlantic City marina to accommodate Trump's large yacht. Stone had set up shop as a lobbyist with Paul Manafort, who later became Trump's campaign manager.[60]

Over the years, Stone encouraged Trump to run for president, and he served in various capacities as Trump's campaign adviser or torch carrier. Throughout their friendship, Stone's advice to Trump was the same as that of Cohn's, "Attack, attack, attack—never defend" and "admit nothing, deny everything, launch counter attack."[61]

In the process of Mueller's Special Counsel investigation of Trump for Russia's interference in the 2016 election and for potential obstruction of justice, which led to Trump's first impeachment, Stone was convicted on seven counts of lying to Congress, tampering with witnesses, and obstructing

Congress's investigation. Stone's friend Paul Manafort also was convicted on the same charges, and for multimillion-dollar bank and tax fraud. Stone's 40-month prison sentence was commuted by Trump, and Manafort served less than two years of his seven and a half years prison sentence. On his last day in office, Trump repaid both friends for their loyalty and lying during Mueller's investigations: He pardoned both.[62]

Learning from Others That Life Is Mainly Combat: The Winner Dominates Others

D'Antonio credits Trump's mentors—his father, Peale, Dobias, Cohn, and Stone—for instilling in him a basic philosophy of living that is "fairly simple and severe" which is "Life is mainly combat; the law of the jungle rules; pretty much all that matters is winning or losing and rules are made to be broken."[63] And as asserted by Schwartz, Trump's winning is all about his need to dominate others, which supersedes Trump's "insatiable narcissistic hunger to be loved, accepted, admired, and praised."[64] What Trump's father, Dobias, Cohn, and Stone had in common were their authoritarian personalities and obsessions with winning, which translated into dominating and defeating others (and from Peale he heard that there's nothing wrong about winning). Trump watched and adopted that philosophy, while learning how to win by lying, cheating, and bullying, and feeling good about it.

Without inheriting his father's genes and especially his considerable wealth, it is much less likely that Trump would have turned out much like his father—a self-centered authoritarian obsessed about wealth. It is Cohn (and Stone), however, that Trump resembles the most when it comes to ruthless and pathological lying, cheating, and bullying, as well as narcissism. His father was no saint, but neither was he evil like Cohn. Much less is known about Dobias than the others, but it seems unfair to place his influence in the same category. To be sure, Dobias modeled bullying, helped foster a schoolwide atmosphere where bullying was the norm, and reinforced Trump's obsession about winning. However, there is no evidence that Dobias was a liar, cheat, and narcissist. Likewise, it is unlikely that those traits were encouraged by Dobias and other adults at NYMA. True, as an authoritarian, Dobias viewed dominating others favorably, but it is unlikely that he shared the brutal worldview of Fred Trump, Cohn, and Stone that "rules are made to be broken." As an instructor at NYMA, and having been a sergeant in the Army, Dobias believed the opposite—that rules were to be strictly followed. Also, unlike the others, Dobias served his country, both in the military (he was a World War II veteran) and as an educator. And he was far from being or desired to be a socialite. Dobias was tough and obsessed about winning but was not lacking in moral character as were the others. Dobias probably would have been appalled to have witnessed Trump violate his oath to protect the Constitution and doing so by inciting an insurrection.

It's What He Wanted, Sought, and Created

As recognized by modern-day theories of psychology, human behavior is influenced by the dynamic interaction of multiple individual and environmental factors. Individuals are not passive learners. In the process of directly observing and learning from others, we determine which behaviors, attitudes, values, and beliefs are internalized. Trump was no passive learner: He embraced what he wanted and applied it to business, politics, and life in general. He also actively sought and created environments conducive to the lying, cheating, bullying, and narcissistic behaviors that he observed and internalized. This included seeking and associating with others who displayed the same behaviors and valued dominating others. Whereas Trump did not choose his parents and teacher/coach (Dobias), he *chose* Roy Cohn as his attorney and friend, and he chose "pure evil."

The expression "birds of a feather flock together" rings true. Beginning in childhood and adolescence, and continuing into adulthood, individuals tend to be most attracted to those who are most similar to themselves.[65] This is seen in Trump not only choosing Cohn as his closest friend, but also in his hiring employees, lawyers, cabinet members, staff, and others who share his own views, and often his lying, cheating, bullying, and narcissism; firing those who dare to challenge him; surrounding himself with cheering MAGA supporters at campaign rallies; supporting only MAGA GOP candidates who pledge their loyalty; appearing primarily on Fox and other conservative media outlets that praise and rarely question him; posting on social media (and creating his own social media company) designed to reap praise and financial rewards; and viciously attacking those who question him. Just as the environment shaped Trump, so too has he shaped his environment—and the environment of millions of others.

Real Power Is Fear

Over five centuries ago, in *The Prince*, written by Niccoló Machiavelli, princes and other potential leaders were advised that although it was best to be both loved and feared, fear was more powerful and reliable.[66] Trump is likely one of the millions of business students and executives who read the book, as he has certainly followed Machiavelli's advice. When interviewed while running for president in 2016, Trump told Bob Woodward, author of *Fear: Trump in the White House,* that "Real power is—I don't even want to use the word—fear."[67] Trump learned early, and primarily from Cohn, that lying, cheating, and bullying strikes fear in others and thus is a powerful tool for dominating others. That bullying induces fear is self-evident, particularly with respect to physical bullying. Verbal and social bullying also induce fear, and often coexist with lying, as seen in a bully lying about the victim's character and spreading false rumors about the victim. Suing others, and threatening to do so, also causes fear, especially when one has the wealth and determination to prolong the lawsuit. Knowing that one cheats and has the resources to cheat on a large scale also creates fear. Even narcissism can trigger fear—as when one hears over and over how great and powerful the narcissist is.

Trump understands that lying induces fear more effectively and efficiently than either bullying or cheating. His fear-inducing firehose of lies arouses his base, many of whom are Evangelical Christians accustomed to motivation by fear. Trump has always played to their fears, knowing that their fears, such as their fear of hell, are great motivators. Trump is well aware that fear often causes rage and greater motivation for action. In a 2016 interview with Woodward, Trump conceded that "I bring rage out. I do bring rage out. I always have. I don't know if it's an asset or a liability. But whatever it is, I do."[68]

Knowing that fear and rage get things done, Trump capitalized on his position of authority and power as president (and ex-president), and on his wealth to control and manipulate the media. Trump had 80 million followers on Twitter, and created his own social media platform after he was banned from that social media platform. His campaign rallies have always been a firehose of lies and fearmongering. And, he has been very effective in using Fox and GOP supporters to reinforce and spew the same firehose. As noted by Steven Hassan in his book *The Cult of Trump*, "for both Trump and Fox, fear is a business strategy—it keeps people watching."[69]

Trump's fearmongering was on full display in his "Make America Great" 2016 campaign for president, in which he alarmed voters that Mexicans, many of whom were "animals" and "rapists," were invading our country; Muslims, many of whom were "terrorists," were a big threat and should be banned from entering the country; and that "Crooked" Hilary Clinton was a big liar and cheat (and he wasn't) who would ruin the economy, take away guns, and strip away religious rights. In stoking fear of increasing crime, he claimed that the murder rate in the United States was the highest in 45 years, when in reality it had declined 42% since 1993.[70]

Knowing that fearmongering helped get him elected in 2016, Trump continued his fearmongering throughout his presidency and magnified it during his "Keep America Great" campaign for reelection in 2020. With no evidence to support the charges, in one form or another Trump repeated over and over, and often over 100 times, that if Biden and the Democrats were elected, the economy would be in ruins with everyone's 401(k) taking a "big nosedive" of 50 to 70%; taxes would increase greatly; Second Amendment rights would be revoked; law enforcement would be dismantled, and crime would be "everywhere"; American health care, Medicare and Social Security destroyed ("Giving it, by the way, to illegal aliens who come into our country"); and democracy would be replaced by socialism. Invoking fear at one campaign rally in North Carolina and simultaneously portraying about half of Americans (i.e., those not voting for him) as evil, he warned his Evangelical base that if they did not vote for him their religious freedoms would be stripped, while stating that Democrats and the "the American-hating left" are "not big believers in religion" (at that time a Pew Poll showed that about three-fourths of Democrats said that religion was important in their lives and they were certain in their belief in God).[71] At other rallies, he foreboded that Biden and the Democrats "will try to plunge our country into a nightmare of gridlock, poverty, and chaos" with the county becoming "the next Venezuela." Worse than Venezuela, he warned voters that "[Democrats will] turn our entire country into one giant sanctuary for criminal aliens, setting loose tens of thousands of dangerous offenders and putting MS-13 gang members straight into your children's schools."[72] As was successful in his 2016 campaign, he invoked the fear of hell for those voting for Biden and Democrats and promised salvation and heaven for those voting for him and his fellow Republicans.

Trump is using the same winning strategy in his Make America Great and Glorious Again (MAGAGA) campaign for the 2024 presidential election. In a fall 2022 campaign rally for fellow Republicans, he predicted that over 10 million illegal immigrants would soon enter the country—over four times as many as in the previous year. Arousing his base, he falsely claimed that crime was at an all-time high, asserting that "Nobody's ever seen anything like what's happening now," that "Biden and the radical Democrats do nothing at all to stop the death and devastation caused by this invasion into our country," and that "We are a nation whose economy is collapsing into a cesspool of ruin." As in previous campaigns, he promised that he was elected the hell he was predicting could be avoided and "we will soon be a great nation again" as when he was president. In covering this campaign rally and his other rallies, reporter Issaac Arnsdorf of *The Washington Post* observed that "For many of his fans in the crowd, that message was exactly what they came to hear."[73]

Telling them exactly what they want to hear, Trump made similar fear-monger claims and threats at the March 2023 Conservative Political Action Conference (CPAC). He claimed that Biden was leading the nation into "oblivion" and other Republicans would not be able to correct course. Also reminiscent of his assertion "I alone can fix it" made at the GOP convention that preceded his 2020 re-election campaign, Trump asserted at CPAC that "I am the only candidate who can make this promise: I will prevent World War Three," and that if he did not prevail in 2024 our country "will be lost forever."[74]

As a perfect example of positive reinforcement of lying (as well as bullying, cheating, and narcissism) and helping Trump remain the "killer" and "king" that his father desired, Trump's speeches at CPAC and the campaign rally above were met with applause, standing ovations, and campaign contributions. The crowd roundly supported how Trump has got things done. In doing so, they also endorsed his teaching today's youth that morality doesn't matter, and that winning and losing does. As Trump once told Robert Woodward in one of their many interviews: "I don't care about my legacy. My legacy doesn't matter. If I lose, that will be my legacy. My people expect me to fight, and if I don't, I'll lose em."[75]

Notes

1 Michael Kranish and Marc Fisher, 2016. *Trump Revealed: The Definitive Biography of the 45th President.* New York: Scribner, 37.
2 Michael D'Antonio, 2016. "The Men Who Gave Trump His Brutal Worldview." *Politico,* March 29. https://www.politico.com/magazine/story/2016/03/2016-donald-trump-brutal-worldview-father-coach-213750/
3 Alexandra S. Burt, 2009. "Are There Meaningful Etiological Differences within Antisocial Behavior? Results of a Meta-Analysis." *Clinical Psychology Review* 29, no. 2: 163–178. https://doi.org/10.1016/j.cpr.2008.12.004
4 Donald Trump on the Role Genetics Play in Success, 1988. *The Oprah Winfrey Show.* April 25. https://www.oprah.com/own-oprahshow/donald-trump-on-the-role-genetics-play-in-success-video
5 Glenn Plaskin, 1990. "The Playboy Interview with Donald Trump." *Playboy,* March 1. https://www.playboy.com/read/playboy-interview-donald-trump-1990
6 Michael D'Antonio, 2016. *The Truth about Trump.* New York: Thomas Dunne Books, 326.
7 Ibid., 40.
8 Jonathan Chait, 2011. "Trump's Lifelong Obsession with His Superior DNA Is Being Put to the Test." *Intelligencer,* October 11. https://nymag.com/intelligencer/2020/10/donald-trump-genetic-delusions-and-covid-19.html
9 Phil Han, 2020. "Donald Trump: I have Genes for Success." *CNN,* February 11. http://www.cnn.com/2010/SHOWBIZ/02/11/donald.trump.marriage.apprentice/index.html
10 Brandon Tensley, 2020. "The Dark Subtext of Trump's 'Good Genes' Compliment." *CNN,* September 22. https://www.cnn.com/2020/09/22/politics/donald-trump-genes-historical-context-eugenics/index.html
11 Donald J. Trump, 1985. *The Art of the Deal.* New York: Ballantine Books, 79–80.
12 Ibid.
13 Mary L. Trump, 2020. *Too Much and Never Enough: How My Family Created the World's Most Dangerous Man.* New York: Simon & Schuster, 48.
14 Eli Watkins and Abby Phillip, 2018. "Trump Decries Immigrants From 'Shithole Countries' Coming to US." *CNN,* January 12. https://www.cnn.com/2018/01/11/politics/immigrants-shithole-countries-trump/index.html
15 Meridith McGraw, 2019. "President Trump Heads to Baltimore, a City He Called a 'Rodent Infested Mess.'" *ABC News,* September 12. https://abcnews.go.com/Politics/president-trump-heads-baltimore-city-called-rodent-infested/story?id=65570278
16 Mary Trump, 49.
17 Ibid., 40.
18 Ibid., 43.
19 D'Antonio, xvii.
20 Ibid., 34–35.
21 Mary Trump, 24.
22 Donald J. Trump, 96.
23 Ibid., 71.
24 Mary Trump, 26.
25 Kranish and Fisher.
26 David Barstow, Susanne Craig, and Russ Buettner, 2018. "11 Takeaways from the Time's Investigation into Trump's Wealth." *The New York Times.,* October 2. https://www.nytimes.com/2018/10/02/us/politics/donald-trump-wealth-fred-trump.html
27 James D. Zirin, 2019. *Plaintiff in Chief: A Portrait of Donald Trump in 3,5000 Lawsuits.* New York: All Points Books, 12.

28 Mary Trump, 44.
29 Khushmand Rajendran, Edyta Kruszewski, and Jeffery M. Halperin, 2016. "Parenting Style Influences Bullying: A Longitudinal Study Comparing Children with and without Behavioural Problems." *Journal of Child Psychology and Psychiatry* 57 no. 2: 188–198. https://doi.org/10.1111/jcpp.12433
30 Robert E. Larzelere, Amanda Sheffield Morris, and Amanda W. Harrist (Editors), 2013. *Authoritative Parenting: Synthesizing Nurturance and Discipline for Optimal Child Development.* Washington, DC: American Psychological Association.
31 Michael D'Antonio, 2016. "The Men Who Gave Trump His Brutal Worldview." *Politico*, March 29. https://www.politico.com/magazine/story/2016/03/2016-donald-trump-brutal-worldview-father-coach-213750/
32 David Barstow, Susanne Craif, and Russ Buettner, 2018. "Trump Engaged in Suspect Tax Schemes as He Reaped Riches from His Father." *New York Times*, October 2. https://www.nytimes.com/interactive/2018/10/02/us/politics/donald-trump-tax-schemes-fred-trump.html
33 Gwenda Blair, 2015. "How Norman Vincent Peale Taught Donald Trump to Worship Himself." *Politico*, October 6. https://www.politico.com/magazine/story/2015/10/donald-trump-2016-norman-vincent-peale-213220/
34 Mary Trump, 38.
35 Paul Schwartzman, 2016. "How Trump Got Religion—And Why His Legendary Minister's Son Now Rejects Him." *The Washington Post*, January 21. https://www.washingtonpost.com/lifestyle/how-trump-got-religion–and-why-his-legendary-ministers-son-now-rejects-him/2016/01/21/37bae16e-bb02-11e5-829c-26ffb874a18d_story.html
36 Donald J. Trump, 49.
37 Eugene Scott, 2015. "Church Says Donald Trump Is Not an 'Active Member'." *CNN*, August 28. https://www.cnn.com/2015/08/28/politics/donald-trump-church-member/index.html
38 Emily Singer, 2020, "Trump Has Attended Church 14 Times Since Taking Office—Including Photo-Ops." June 02. https://americanindependent.com/donald-trump-church-attendance-photo-ops-st-johns-religion-white-house/
39 In support of my position that Norma Vincent Peale was much less of an influence, I found that Trump made no reference to him in *The Art of the Deal*, while citing his father, Dobias, and Cohn as major influencers.
40 D'Antonio, *The Truth About Trump*, xvii.
41 Ibid., 46.
42 Ibid., 44.
43 Ibid., 44.
44 Ibid., 43.
45 Ibid., 42.
46 Kranish and Fisher, 40–41.
47 Gwenda Blair, 2000. *The Trumps: Three Generations That Built an Empire.* New York: Simon & Schuster, 237.
48 Blair, 237
49 Kenneth H. Rubin, William M. Bukowski, and Brett Laursen (Editors), 2009. *Handbook of Peer Interactions, Relationships, and Groups.* New York: Guilford.
50 D'Antonio, *The Truth about Trump.*
    Kranish and Fisher.
51 Marie Brenner, 2017. "How Donald Trump and Roy Cohn's Ruthless Symbiosis Changed America." *Vanity Fair*, June 28. https://www.vanityfair.com/news/2017/06/donald-trump-roy-cohn-relationship
52 Ibid.
53 Ibid.

54 D'Antonio, *The Truth about Trump*, 78.
55 Donald Trump, 99–100.
56 Brenner.
57 Zirin, 17.
58 Ziren, 14.
59 Ziren.
60 D'Antonio, *The Truth about Trump*.
61 Ibid., 243.
62 Maggie Haberman and Michael S. Schmidt, 2020. "Trump Gives Clemency to More Allies, Including Manafort, Stone and Charles Kushner." *The New York Times*, December 23. https://www.nytimes.com/2020/12/23/us/politics/trump-pardon-manafort-stone.html
63 Michael D'Antonio, *Politico*.
64 Tony Schwartz, 2020. "The Psychopath in Chief." *GEN*, May 28. https://gen.medium.com/the-psychopath-in-chief-aa10ab2165d9
65 Amy C. Hartl, Brett Laursen, & Antonius H. N. Cillessent, 2015. "A Survival Analysis of Adolescent Friendships: The Downside of Dissimilarity." *Psychological Science* 26, no. 8: 1304–1315. https://doi.org/10.1177/0956797615588
66 Machiavelli, Niccolò, 1469–1527. 1981. *The Prince*. New York: Penguin Books.
67 Bob Woodward, 2018. *Fear: Trump in the White House*. New York: Simon & Schuster, xiii.
68 Bob Woodward, *Rage*, 2020. New York: Simon & Schuster, 369.
69 Steven Hassan, 2019. *The Cult of Trump*. New York: Free Press, 121.
70 Michelle Ye Hee Lee, 2016. "Trump's false claim that the murder rate is the 'highest it's been in 45 years.'" *The Washington Post*, November 3. https://www.washingtonpost.com/news/fact-checker/wp/2016/11/03/trumps-false-claim-that-the-murder-rate-is-the-highest-its-been-in-45-years/
71 Detsy Klein, 2019. "Trump Says Democrats Are 'Not Big Believers in Religion' during North Carolina Rally." September 9. https://www.cnn.com/2019/09/09/politics/donald-trump-north-carolina-rally/index.html
72 Glenn Kessler, 2018. "A Witches' Brew of Over-the-Top Trump Attacks." *The Washington Post*, October 24. https://www.washingtonpost.com/politics/2018/10/24/president-trumps-witchs-brew-over-the-top-attacks/
73 Issaac Arnsdorf, 2022. "In Speeches, Trump Uses Dozens of Lies, Exaggerations to Draw Contrast with Biden." November 7. *The Washington Post*. https://www.washingtonpost.com/politics/2022/11/07/trump-falsehoods-lies-speeches/
74 Daniel Dale, 2023. "Fact Check. Trump Delivers Wildly Dishonest Speech at CPAC." CNN, March 5. https://www.cnn.com/2023/03/05/politics/fact-check-trump-cpac/index.html
75 Bob Woodward and Robert Costa, 2021. *Peril*. New York: Simon & Schuster, 153.

13 Implications and Recommendations

Firehose of Falsehoods versus Squirt Gun of Truth

For decades now, Trump's lying, cheating, bullying, and narcissism have been reinforced both externally and internally—they have made him wealthier, more famous, more dominating, and a greater narcissist. They have gone unpunished. This is likely to continue. For example, in April 2023, Trump was rewarded with $4 million from his MAGA followers in the first 24 hours after being indicted on 34 felonies[1]—reinforcement of lying, cheating, and bullying experienced by no other. As an indication of further reinforcement, and as discussed in Chapter 1, polls showed that after being indicted he continued to be popular among Republicans, with polls in May, June, and August 2023 reporting that about 70% of Republicans believing that he won the 2020 election and planning to vote for him in 2024.

In avoiding punishment, and with contributions from his supporters, Trump has amassed a huge war chest to defend against lawsuits and criminal investigations. However, as one might expect based on his history of lying and cheating, not all of that money goes where he promised. In tracing $250 million Trump raised shortly after the 2020 election to "Stop the Steal" and combat "election fraud," the House January 6 committee discovered that most of it went to other purposes, and as Trump saw fit. Funds went to his aides and assistants, including to Melania's fashion adviser and Trump's former golf caddie and deputy chief of staff, Dan Scavino. Scavino received a salary of almost $10,000 per month, while a company at his address, and with no website, received an additional $420,000 from the same fund.[2]

Children watch and learn from Trump, but so too do many MAGA Republicans imitate his lying, cheating, bullying, and narcissistic behaviors, with some doing so in an even more incendiary manner that pays handsomely. For example, Rep. Marjorie Taylor Greene of Georgia hauled in more than $3 million from MAGA Republicans in her first three months of 2022 (which is more than the average House member raises in two years).[3] This was shortly after the January 6 insurrection, which she supported, and her removal from Congressional committee assignments because of her racist, anti-Semitic, and anti-Muslim rhetoric and promotion of far-right

DOI: 10.4324/9781003401278-13

conspiracy theories and violence against Democratic leaders. Again, children watch and learn, learning that lying, cheating, bullying, and narcissism is the norm—it gets things done.

Sadly, preventing a new normal where lying, cheating, bullying, and narcissism are valued traits is not easy. With respect to extinguishing the firehose of falsehoods in America, the RAND study, which was discussed in Chapter 2 on lying, concluded "We are not optimistic about the effectiveness of traditional counterpropaganda efforts. Certainly, some effort must be made to point out falsehoods and inconsistencies, but the same psychological evidence that shows how falsehood and inconsistency gain traction also tells us that retractions and refutations are seldom effective."[4] RAND notes that this is especially true when the lie continues over a period of time, as people tend to forget which is the truth and which is a lie. As stated by RAND: "Put simply, our first suggestion is *don't expect to counter the firehose of falsehood with the squirt gun of truth.*" Applied to Trump's Big Lie, his telling it long before the election was held and repeating it over and over makes it very difficult for his followers to accept overwhelming evidence that he indeed lost the election. Such evidence includes even *Fox News* admitting, after losing a $787.5 million defamation suit, that the network repeatedly lied about the election. Trump's firehose of falsehoods also has convinced millions of Americans that either Trump is not a pathological liar, cheater, and bully (and criminal) or that those behaviors are well justified. A squirt gun of truth will not change their beliefs.

RAND makes several recommendations for countering the firehose of falsehood with more than a squirt gun of truth. Drawing from research in psychology, they offer three recommendations: (1) Warn viewers ahead of time or at the time of their initial exposure to disinformation about its source (e.g., the person or site tends to spread disinformation), the quality of the information, and the intent of spreading false information (i.e., to manipulate others); (2) Quickly challenge and correct the disinformation, while providing truthful information to replace the false information and attempting to counter the power of first impressions; (3) Repeat corrections, retractions, or refutations of the disinformation. Of these three recommendations, RAND suggests that the first, forewarning, is perhaps the most effective strategy. Each of those recommendations applies to the media, but perhaps more importantly they apply to parenting, and whether today's parents choose to raise another Donald J. Trump.

Raising Another Trump, or Not

Parents who admire Trump and desire that their children be like him simply need to replicate the factors that account for his lying, cheating, bullying, and narcissism, which were discussed in the previous chapter. Unfortunately for those parents, few have the "racehorse" genes that Trump believes are critical to his success. Even fewer are billionaires like Trump's parents. Nevertheless, there is much that parents can do to replicate, *or not*, Trump's development. As emphasized throughout this book, much of Trump's development and behavior can be explained by three basic principles of learning: modeling, positive reinforcement, and punishment, and by three social cognitive and emotional processes that underlie moral behavior: moral reasoning, moral emotions, and mechanisms of moral disengagement. If it is another Trump that parents desire, they can replicate those factors by (a) providing ample role models of lying, cheating, bullying, and narcissism; (b) ensuring that those behaviors are positively reinforced and not punished—that they get things done; (c) fostering the development of self-centered, hedonistic moral reasoning and a lack of moral emotions; and (d) promoting mechanisms of moral disengagement. Each of those goals is best achieved by adopting the parenting style of Trump's parents, which was a combination of over-indulgent/uninvolved and authoritarian parenting, as discussed in Chapter 2. This should be good news for those desiring another Trump.

The bad news for those not desiring another Trump is that raising a child to be a pathological liar, cheat, bully, and narcissist is much easier than raising one to be honest, kind, and humble. Achieving the latter requires greater parental involvement, skills, and patience ("racehorse" genes also help, but not those that Trump inherited). This is not as easy as most parenting guidebooks tout. Nevertheless, research on parenting shows that the authoritative parenting style stands out with respect to decreasing the odds of children turning out to be pathological liars, cheats, bullies, and narcissists, and instead honest, kind, and modest.

The focus of this chapter is on general parenting strategies, common among authoritative parents, that have been shown to be effective in pre-venting and correcting antisocial behavior, including lying, cheating, bullying, and narcissistic behaviors, and in promoting prosocial behavior and self-discipline. It is beyond the scope of this book to provide more specific rec-ommendations on lying, cheating, bullying, and narcissism. Plenty of books, websites, blogs, and other resources are available to parents, professionals, and others for that purpose.

Best Advice for Preventing and Correcting Lying, Cheating, Bullying and Narcissism and for Developing Self-Discipline: Authoritative Parenting

As described in Chapter 2, and discussed in other chapters, research has shown that authoritative parenting is the most effective style of parenting.[5] It stands in contrast to the uninvolved/overindulgent and authoritarian parenting ex-perienced by Trump. The long-term aim of authoritative parents is not to manage and control their children's behavior but for their children to manage their behavior themselves. More specifically, the aim is to develop social and emotional competencies that underlie self-discipline and are associated with prosocial behavior and the inhibition of antisocial behavior. Achieving this aim requires a healthy balance of *responsiveness* and *demandingness*—a balance found only in the authoritative style of parenting. Responsiveness is seen in parents' caring, warmth, and respect, and in addressing their children's basic psychological needs. As widely recognized by developmental psychologists, primary among those needs are autonomy, competence, and relatedness (relatedness includes feeling loved and experiencing social belonging).[6] In demonstrating responsiveness, authoritative parents provide the kind of guidance that helps meet those needs and develops the self-discipline associated with prosocial behavior and the inhibition of antisocial behavior.

As with authoritarian parents, authoritative parents are demanding. They have high behavioral expectations, closely monitor their children's behavior, and set and enforce fair rules and consequences. They differ from authoritarian parents, however, in that they are not overly controlling and harsh. Although they do not hesitate to correct their children's misbehavior, their methods are less harsh than those of authoritarian parents (e.g., they don't generally send their children to residential military school for being defiant). To be sure, mild forms of punishment are often used, such as taking away privileges, time-outs, and verbal reprimands, but guiding persuasion and reasoning are preferred. Additional, and more specific, characteristics of authoritative parenting follow.

Authoritative Parents Build and Maintain a Close Parent-Child Relationship and Encourage Their Children's Close Interpersonal Relationships with Others

Supported by attachment theory[7] and social control theory,[8] authoritative parents recognize the critical importance of social bonds, and especially the parent-child bond, which is seen in warmth, caring, support, and unconditional love. A strong parent-child bond is instrumental in the internalization of parental values and moral codes. It helps deter harmful and deviant behavior and promotes prosocial behavior (assuming, of course, that those are the behaviors the parent desires). Authoritative parents recognize the importance of their children having close interpersonal relationships with others, and thus promote friendships and positive peer relations. Close interpersonal relationships serve as a powerful self-sanction against lying, cheating, bullying, and other antisocial behaviors, as children do not want to disappoint others whom they are close to.

Authoritative Parents Model and Provide Additional Models of Desired Behaviors

Authoritative parents provide ample models of individuals who display the prosocial values, moral reasoning and emotions, and behaviors that they aim to develop in their own children. This includes models at home and in school, sports, social media, movies, videogames, books, and so forth. They also buffer their children's exposure to models of undesired behaviors. They recognize that although family members and peers (especially during adolescence) are typically the most influential role models, anyone can serve the same. Children are more likely to emulate others they like or who possess characteristics they desire (e.g., financial success, fame, power, physical attractiveness, athletic skills).

Authoritative Parents Are Attuned to Their Children's Individual Needs

They recognize that behavioral expectations, the amount of supervision and monitoring needed, and the use of discipline (i.e., type and frequency of use) should vary as a function of their child's age, personality, and behavior. Likewise, they recognize that their expectations will not always be met, and that occasional lying, cheating, bullying behaviors (e.g., teasing), and narcissistic behaviors (e.g., bragging, self-admiration) are developmentally normal, especially at some ages more so than others.

They recognize when a behavior is normal or abnormal, and when intervention, or greater intervention, is called for. They seek help from professionals when antisocial behavior, and especially a pattern (e.g., lying, cheating, stealing, vandalism, and bullying) is observed and resistant to common interventions. In addition to seeking assistance from mental health professionals, they seek assistance from their child's school. In preventing and correcting undesired behavior, they work together with mental health professionals, teachers, school staff, and others (e.g., relatives, caregivers, neighbors).

Authoritative Parents Monitor Their Children's Behavior, Responding Immediately to Instances of Lying, Cheating, Bullying, and Narcissistic Behavior

Unfortunately, far too often parents ignore those behaviors; thus, allowing them to be positively reinforced. For example, one study found that parents rarely address their children's lying, doing so only 3% of the time.[9] This led to their children lying more frequently in the future. When lying and other undesired behaviors are corrected only occasionally and are effective in achieving their goal, intermittent reinforcement occurs. This results in an increase in undesired behavior and greater resistance to correction. To reduce the likelihood of this occurring, authoritative parents do not ignore their children's lies (while also recognizing that many go undetected). They increase their monitoring when they discover, or suspect, an increase in lying.

Authoritative Parents Use Confrontative Control and Inductive Discipline, While Viewing Disciplinary Encounters as Educational Opportunities

In correcting misbehavior in a more educative than punitive manner, authoritative parents use what are referred to as *confrontative control* and *inductive discipline* (also called *induction*), as described next. Both practices, often used in combination, are supported by research showing that they foster internalization of the values of caring and concern about others and a sense of responsibility for one's own actions.[10] In the short-term, both are intended, and often effective, in bringing about willing compliance, as opposed to the grudging compliance or outright disobedience often found with coercive control. In the long-term, both foster the development of self-discipline, promoting prosocial behavior and deterring antisocial behavior.

Confrontative Control

Confrontative control is not to be confused with the coercive control common among authoritarian parents. As noted by Baumrind, "Confrontative control is demanding, firm, and goal-directed, whereas coercive control is intrusive, manipulative, punitive, autonomy undermining, and restrictive."[11] While clearly expressing their disappointment in their children's misbehavior, authoritative parents do not rely solely on punishment for correction. Instead, they rely more on persuasion and Socratic reasoning (e.g., "Help me understand why you didn't think about how your behavior affects others?"), without belaboring the point. They also provide guidance. Although their children are encouraged to express their own opinions and actively participate in responsible decision-making, harmful actions and their excuses are never accepted.

This does not mean that authoritative parents are too soft when it comes to discipline and refrain from the use of punitive consequences, or punishment. Consistent with high demandingness being a primary characteristic of authoritative parenting, they confront and correct their children's misbehavior immediately, and often with punitive consequences. However, the punitive consequences are not overly controlling or overly harsh. Few use corporal punishment (i.e., spankings), and when it is used it is mild, infrequent, and occurs in the context of a warm, caring, and supportive parent-child relationship.[12] Punishment fits the crime, with punitive consequences ranging from the use of mild verbal reprimands to the loss of privileges and preferred activities (e.g., loss of video time, driving privileges).

Finally, authoritative parents confront not only the lie, cheating, or bullying behavior but also immature moral reasoning and various mechanisms of moral disengagement commonly employed to avoid responsibility and punishment.

Inductive Discipline

Inductive discipline emphasizes the impact of children's behavior on others and relationships with others. For example, children are challenged to take the perspective of others who are lied to, cheated, or bullied, and to recognize the harm those behaviors cause others, as well as its impact on one's own reputation. An additional focus is on accepting responsibility for behavior and making restitution or "fixing" any damage caused (e.g., apologizing, reestablishing interpersonal relationships).

As with confrontative control, when correcting misbehavior, inductive discipline occurs in a calm, respectful, yet firm, manner. Parents are aware that they are modeling their own behavior to their children. Thus, they manage their emotions, and rarely yell or show anger. They understand that when yelling, empty threats, and emotional outbursts are common, children become accustomed to and tend to ignore them.

Authoritative Parents Reflect upon What Might Be Contributing to the Undesired Behavior: Where Feasible, They Address Those Factors When Correcting the Behavior and Preventing Its Reoccurrence

They consider the full range of factors that contribute to their children's dishonesty, aggression, narcissism, or other undesired behaviors. As discussed in previous chapters, contributing factors lie within children and within their environments. They include both the presence of risk factors (those that increase the risk of undesired behaviors) and the absence of protective factors (those that decrease the risk). Rarely does only one-factor account for behavior, as there are multiple pathways to all behavior.

Effective parents recognize that certain factors are much more malleable than others. They focus primarily on factors thought to be most influential and more malleable. Examples of such factors are parental pressure for high grades contributing to academic cheating; harsh and unfair rules contributing to lying; role models and peer influences contributing to bullying; and social media contributing to narcissistic behaviors. Authoritative parents understand that the presence of any one or combination of risk factors does not destine a child to lie, cheat, bully, or be a narcissist. Likewise, they understand that protective factors do not necessarily preclude lying, cheating, bullying, or narcissism. Risk and protective factors only increase, or decrease, the odds. Whether a given characteristic serves as a risk or protective factor depends on its presence (or absence), its strength, and other individual, environmental, and situational factors that promote or stifle behavior.[13] Rarely can a parent, or child, control all those factors, much less any one of them at all times.

Authoritative Parents Use Punitive Consequences, or Punishment, Strategically and Wisely to Decrease Undesired Behaviors

As defined in psychology, punishment consists of anything that decreases a behavior. This is contrary to what many parents have been led to believe, which is that punishment is always harmful and is the same as corporal punishment. To be sure, most psychologists and nearly all professional mental health organizations frown upon spanking children and strongly recommend against it. Nevertheless, about 20 states (mostly in the South, Midwest, and Southwest) allow schools to use spank students,[14] and about 80% of Republicans support spanking children.[15]

In viewing punishment and corporal punishment as one and the same and equally harmful, too often all forms of "punishment" are discouraged. This is a big mistake. In correcting misbehavior, punishment ranges from simply looking at a child or stating "Stop that please" to time out and corporal punishment. Note that those and other punitive consequences are not always effective in decreasing a behavior. It is only when they are effective that they truly constitute punishment. When used strategically and wisely, and as recommended in this chapter, punitive consequences *are* generally effective and thus constitute punishment, with decades of research supporting their utility and effectiveness in deterring and decreasing antisocial behavior.[16]

What has contributed to much of Trump's lying, cheating, and bullying is the *absence* of punitive consequences and especially those that are truly punishing. As described in the book *Untouchable: How Powerful People Get Away with It,* written by Elie Honig, a former federal and state prosecutor, Trump's extreme wealth (and power) has protected him from punishment. Indeed, in 2022, with donations from his MAGA supporters, Trump's political action committee (PAC), Save America, spent approximately $10 million, with most of it going to his own legal fees related to investigations and lawsuits against him and his company—expenses to spare him from punishment.[17]

There are times when all parents rely upon punitive consequences, hoping they will stop or decrease (i.e., punish) their children's misbehavior. This includes authoritative parents. Use of punitive consequences is a major part of the demandingness dimension to parenting, which characterizes both authoritative and authoritarian parents. However, authoritative parents differ greatly from authoritarian parents in their use of punitive consequences. As noted earlier, foremost among the differences is that authoritative parents use punitive consequences less frequently and less harshly. Perhaps more importantly, however, is that seldom do they need to use punitive consequences because they make greater use of more positive techniques that prevent behavior problems and develop their children's self-discipline. When used by authoritative parents, punitive consequences are much more effective than when used by authoritarian parents because they are more likely to be perceived by their children, and especially adolescents, as fair and not overly harsh; to be implemented judiciously; used in combination with more positive techniques for encouraging desired behavior; and used in context of confrontative control and not coercive control.[18]

Authoritative parents also use punitive consequences less often because they are aware of their limitations, and among them are the following (see Bear, 2020 for a discussion of each):

- *They often produce undesirable side effects,* such as children becoming angry, retaliating, or avoiding or disliking the person who renders the punishment. The effects are usually temporary, but when punishment is used frequently and is overly harsh the undesirable side effects are likely to be more lasting.

- *They teach children what not to do, rather than what they should do.* This limitation can be avoided by combining punitive consequences with other authoritative parenting techniques, especially inductive discipline.
- *Children simply learn "not to get caught."* Learning not to get caught reinforces self-centered, hedonistic moral reasoning. Not getting caught often entails lying. As discussed in Chapter 2, the harsher the expected punishment, the greater the likelihood of lying. Punishing children for lying may simply make them more skilled liars.
- *Children learn to punish others.* By observing his mentor Roy Cohn, Trump learned that lawsuits, verbal insults, and other punitive consequences are effective in manipulating and controlling others.
- *An emphasis on punitive consequences fails to address the multiple factors that likely contributed to the problem behavior.* Multiple individual and environmental factors determine behavior; punitive consequences seldom change them. For example, punishing a child for academic cheating does not change peer influences, parental pressure, lack of academic skills and motivation, or self-centered moral reasoning and beliefs that contributed to the cheating.
- *Their use is often reinforcing.* Three types of reinforcement might occur. Firstly, *negative reinforcement* occurs when the punitive consequences increase as a result of causing the removal or decrease in frequency of a behavior that is viewed as aversive by the person administering the punitive consequence. For example, a parent yells and screams to stop their adolescent's arguing, and it works. The parent's yelling and screaming is negatively reinforced and thus increase in frequency (while the adolescent's arguing is punished, and thus decreases, at least in the short-term). Secondly, *positive reinforcement* occurs when the person administering the punishment increases his or her use of the punishment, regardless of its effectiveness, as a result of others praising or rewarding the use of punishment. A perfect example is Trump being rewarded when he bullies and punishes others during campaign rallies—his fans love it, applaud, and later contribute more money to his campaign. Thirdly, *self-reinforcement* occurs, as in Trump admitting that punishing others makes him feel good.
- *In general, the frequent use of punitive consequences creates a negative environment.* Homes and schools are not positive places for either parents or children when anger, fear, and punitive consequences are ever-present.

Authoritative Use of Praise and Rewards Strategically and Wisely to Teach and Motivate Prosocial Behavior, Especially Behavior, Thoughts, and Emotions That Buffer Antisocial Behavior and Promote Prosocial Behavior

Observed behaviors are more likely to be emulated if they are observed to lead to rewards, and not punishment, and the observer expects to experience the same. Of course, whether the observer experiences reinforcement or punishment upon exhibiting the same behavior greatly determines if the behavior increases (i.e., is positively reinforced) or decreases (i.e., results in punishment). Types of rewards commonly associated with positive reinforcement are *tangible rewards* (e.g., money, properties, possessions) and *social rewards* (e.g., praise, fame, social status). Both types are powerful reinforcers of lying, cheating, bullying, and narcissism. Two other types of rewards are more common among children than adults and much less associated with lying, cheating, bullying, and narcissism: *token rewards* (e.g., stickers, points, and tickets exchangeable for tangible rewards) and *preferred activities or privileges* (e.g., listening to music, playing a video game). Each of those types of rewards, as age appropriate, can be used to decrease antisocial behaviors by reinforcing alternative prosocial behaviors such as honesty, kindness, and modesty.

Unquestionably, rewards are effective in teaching behavior, either prosocial or antisocial, and in strengthening existing behaviors. They provide valuable feedback and often reinforce the target behavior. Perhaps more importantly, their use often enhances the parent-child relationship, as well as the relationship between others who share in giving and receiving rewards. In turn, this helps prevent lying, cheating, bullying, and other undesired behaviors. Rewards also serve as a powerful technique for developing skills and cognitive processes that help prevent those behaviors. However, rewards are not very effective as an intervention strategy for correcting behaviors that are to be decreased or eliminated, rather than increased, and especially those that are not often detected when they occur. This is especially true with lying, as rewarding not lying is problematic. One could reward an alternative, or incompatible behavior, to lying, which is telling the truth, as recommended by most applied behavior analysts. However, although this might help, rarely is it sufficient, as intermittent reinforcement of lying is likely to continue.

In addition to the above limitation of using rewards as an intervention for lying, cheating, and bullying, the general use of praise and rewards, irrespective of the target behavior, is not without criticism. Most of the criticism is specific to the frequent use of tangible rewards, with the primary criticism being that tangible rewards harm intrinsic motivation and encourage extrinsic motivation. Intrinsic motivation is seen in children helping and not harming others because they value kindness and enjoy helping others. They also willingly follow rules out of respect for adults and an understanding and valuing of their purpose. In contrast, extrinsic motivation is seen when they comply with rules to gain external rewards or comply, and do so grudgingly, to avoid punishment. Extrinsic motivation tends to be self-centered and hedonistic, reflecting the kind of moral reasoning, as illustrated in Chapter 11, that characterizes Trump and other pathological liars, cheats, bullies, and narcissists, such as "Be nice to me and I'll be nice to you" and "Maximize rewards and avoid punishment."[19]

Research suggests that under certain conditions tangible rewards are likely to harm intrinsic motivation and encourage extrinsic motivation.[20] Two common conditions are (1) when individuals perceive the tangible rewards being used in a controlling or manipulating manner (e.g., perceived as "If you do this, you will be rewarded.") and (2) when social comparisons are made, especially publicly (e.g., "Maurice earned 5 points, and you earned only 3"). Under those conditions, intrinsic motivation is often stifled, whereas extrinsic motivation and self-centered moral reasoning are promoted. This is especially found among adolescents, who tend to resent adult control and social comparisons, and thus often resist or object to the manipulative use of tangible rewards.

The potentially negative effects on intrinsic motivation are avoided when tangible rewards are not used in a socially controlling or socially comparative manner. Research also suggests that the negative effects are avoided when tangible rewards are combined with other more positive techniques, as found among authoritative parents, for preventing and correcting misbehavior and developing self-discipline, which includes inductive discipline and demonstrating warmth and support.[21]

General Recommendations on the Use of Praise and Rewards

Recommendations follow on using praise and rewards in a wise and strategic manner that reinforces behavior while also promoting intrinsic motivation and self-discipline. They are adapted from other books and articles I have written on classroom management and school discipline.[22] Although written for teachers, administrators, school psychologists, and others working in the schools, they were drawn from research and theory on their use in the school, home, and other settings. As written here, they apply to all settings.

- Praise prosocial behavior (including other-oriented moral reasoning and moral emotions) often, and much more often than the occurrences of negative comments and punitive consequences when correcting misbehavior. For example, every time a child is corrected for any misbehavior, he or she is praised three times for good behavior (as well as for effort toward a behavioral goal). As noted earlier, praising and rewarding honesty, kindness, and modesty are unlikely to be sufficient in curtailing lying, cheating, bullying, and narcissism, but doing so almost always helps in increasing desired behaviors. This not only reinforces desired behaviors, including those that are alternatives to the targeted undesired behavior, but it also provides valuable feedback about the behavior and helps build and maintain positive interpersonal relationships. The child's fear of harming those relationships often deters lying, cheating, bullying, and narcissistic behaviors.
- Use praise more than rewards. Praise is easier to use than most rewards, occurs more naturally in most environments, and requires no cost and little time. Perhaps more importantly, praise is seldom viewed as controlling, manipulating, and undermining autonomy (which should be a greater concern with adolescents than younger children).

- Use tangible rewards as little as necessary. It makes little sense, and is potentially harmful, to use rewards when they are not needed. Thus, tangible rewards should primarily be used when teaching behavior that is new and difficult or when intrinsic motivation is lacking. Otherwise, sincere praise is typically sufficient for recognizing and reinforcing desired behaviors and tangible rewards should be used only occasionally and in a surprise manner.
- Praise and reward not only the specific behavior desired, but also the thoughts, emotions, and dispositions that underlie the behavior. In addition to praising and rewarding specific acts of honesty, kindness, and other prosocial behaviors, praise the underlying processes such as voicing other-oriented moral reasoning, inhibiting impulsivity, and managing one's emotions (e.g., anger, frustration). Also, praise general dispositions reflected in the behavior such as kindness, caring, honesty, trustworthiness, and integrity. When praising desired behaviors, their underlying processes, and dispositions, emphasize their value and usefulness, both presently and in the future. Where appropriate, also communicate that those values are self-chosen—that the child chose to act in an honest or kind way, and not because he or she simply wanted the reward or recognition. This promotes self-discipline, which consists of intrinsic motivation, mature moral reasoning, a moral identity, autonomy, self-esteem, and self-efficacy.
- Use different kinds of praise and rewards, and especially those that the child is likely to perceive favorably. Using the same praise and rewards repeatedly, and in the same manner, can cause those positive techniques to become stale and ineffective. Children appreciate surprise and creativity, and often find them more reinforcing. They also appreciate having a choice of rewards, which helps avoid perceptions of rewards being used to control their behavior; thus, fostering a sense of autonomy. Rewards should be individualized, based on the child's age, preferences, needs, and the frequency and intensity of any behavior targeted for change (e.g., more frequent and intense behavior problems often call for more frequent rewards for alternative behaviors).
- Communicate sincerity. The way someone is praised or rewarded often matters a lot. Children, and especially adolescents, recognize when others are not sincere, such as by giving "faint praise" or praising and rewarding in a non-caring, mechanical manner, as opposed to expressions of happiness and pride. In communicating sincerity, it often helps to praise privately. This is particularly important during adolescence, when many adolescents dislike being praised publicly.[23] This does not mean that public praise should be avoided, but that it should be used in combination with praise given privately, such as in private text messages, notes, and letters, or with the embrace of a hug.
- Avoid reinforcing undesired behavior. This might sound obvious, but rewarding undesired happens often. A common example is parents reinforcing their children's tantrums by giving them what they want to stop the

tantrum (instead of ignoring the tantrum, where feasible, or using time out). Parents also contribute to the reinforcement of lying, cheating, and bullying by not confronting those behaviors and thus allowing for either their external reinforcement or self-reinforcement (e.g., obtaining what is desired by lying, cheating, or bullying). They also reinforce the undesired behaviors by modeling the same and showing how they "get things done."

There Are Some Moral Exemplars, Even in Our Government

Fortunately, there are individuals, both Democrats and Republicans, of sound moral character in our government who serve as good role models for our children. Some even served during the Trump presidency. It is likely that their parents followed the recommendations above. Having been raised by a father who was a Marine and a stepfather who was a Navy Chief, I am pleased to say that foremost among those of moral character in the Trump White House were military leaders. This was seen in military generals and members of Trump's cabinet who either resigned or were fired upon disagreeing with Trump. They include National Security Adviser Lt. General HR McMaster, Secretary of Defense General Jim ("Mad Dog") Mattis, White House Chief of Staff General John Kelly, Secretary of the Navy Richard Spencer, and National Security Aide Lt Col Alexander Vindman. Although he managed to avoid being fired at the very end of Trump's presidency, General Mark Milley, Chairman of the Joint Chiefs of Staff, displayed the exemplary moral character credited by many as instrumental in avoiding an actual military coup recommended by several of Trump's advisers, and believed by many to have been attempted by Trump.[24]

Moral character also was seen in nearly 500 retired senior military officers, former Cabinet secretaries, service chiefs, and other government officials, both Republicans and Democrats, signing an open letter supporting Joe Biden for president, saying that Biden has "the character, principles, wisdom and leadership necessary to address a world on fire." Unlike Trump, these officials learned from their parents that moral character matters.

Although not in the military, there were many other life-long government officials in positions of national security who also served in the Trump administration and had the moral character to challenge Trump. Again, many were either fired or resigned under pressure. They included Mark Esper (Secretary of Defense), Dan Coats (Director of National Intelligence), John Bolton (National Security Advisor), James Comey (Director of FBI), Andrew McCabe (Acting Director of FBI), Jeff Sessions (Attorney General), Sally Yates (Acting Attorney General), and Rod Rosenstein (Deputy Attorney General). Likewise, there were a few (far too few) Republicans in Congress who put country over politics and challenged Trump on moral issues, knowing they would pay the price by becoming targets of his bullying and targets of scorn from fellow Republicans. Foremost among them were

Senators John McCain, Mitt Romney, and Ben Sasse. Worthy of Profiles in Courage recognition (or "Worthy of Roasting in Hell" from the perspective of Trumphites), Mitt Romney was the only Republican senator who voted in favor of Trump's first impeachment. Although a few other Republicans in Congress publicly challenged Trump's moral character, they did so only after it was clear to them that he lost the 2020 election. Six other senators joined Romney in voting to try Trump in his second impeachment: Richard Burr, Bill Cassidy, Susan Collins, Lisa Murkowski, Ben Sasse, and Patrick Toomey. Only ten of the 211 Republican members of the House of Representatives voted for his second impeachment. Showing the selfless moral courage and risking their re-elections were Jaime Herrera Beutler, Liz Cheney, Anthony Gonzalez, John Katko, Adam Kinzinger, Peter Meijer, Dan Newhouse, Tom Rice, Fred Upton, and David Valadao.

Finally, there were many other less-known individuals of moral character in government at the state level and in state and federal courts, Republicans and Democrats alike, who were instrumental in saving our democracy and modelling moral character. Perhaps foremost among them was Brad Raffensperger, Secretary of State in Georgia and a Republican, who repeatedly rejected attempts, including by Trump himself, to reverse the election results. In response to his service to the country (and to his integrity), he was roundly and publicly bullied by Trump and other Republicans in Georgia and throughout the nation, with his family receiving death threats.

Although perhaps just a squirt gun of truth compared to Trump's firehose of falsehoods, role models such as these, and authoritative parenting, are the greatest hope for preventing a generation of children from learning that the best way to get things done is by lying, cheating, and bullying, while feeling good about it.

Notes

1 Anisha Kohli, 2023. "Trump Campaign Says It Saw a Spike in Donations After Indictment." *Time,* April 15. https://time.com/6272256/trump-2024-indictment-donation-surge/
2 Greg Farrell and Bill Allison, 2022. "Trump 'Stop the Steal' Funds Were a 'Rip-Off.' Jan. 6 Committee Says." *Bloomberg,* December 23. https://www.bloomberg.com/news/articles/2022-12-23/jan-6-report-says-donald-trump-s-stop-the-steal-funds-diverted-in-rip-off#xj4y7vzkg?leadSource=uverify%20wall
3 Isaac Arnsdorf and Derek Willis, 2021. "How Josh Hawley and Marjorie Taylor Greene Juiced Their Fundraising Numbers." *ProPublica,* April 21. https://www.propublica.org/article/how-josh-hawley-and-marjorie-taylor-greene-juiced-their-fundraising-numbers
4 Christopher Paul and Miriam Matthews, 2023. *"The Russian 'Firehose of Falsehood' Propaganda Model: Why It Might Work and Options to Counter It."* Retrieved April 17 from https://www.rand.org/pubs/perspectives/PE198.html
5 Diana Baumrind, 2013. "Authoritative Parenting Revisited: History and Current Status," in *Authoritative Parenting: Synthesizing Nurturance and Discipline for Optimal Child Development,* edited by Robert E. Larzelere, Amanda S. Morris, and

Amanda. W. Harrist. Washington, DC: American Psychological Association, 89–112.

6 Ryan, R. M., & Deci, E. L., 2017. *Self-Determination Theory: Basic Psychological Needs in Motivation, Development, and Wellness.* New York: Guilford Press.

7 Mary D. S. Ainsworth, 1989. "Attachments Beyond Infancy." *American Psychologist*, 44 no. 4: 709–716. https://doi.org/10.1037/0003-066X.44.4.709

8 Travis Hirschi, 1969. *Causes of Delinquency.* Berkeley, CA: University of California Press.

9 Anne E. Wilson, Melissa D. Smith, and Hildy S. Ross, 2003. "The Nature and Effects of Young Children's Lies." *Social Development* 12 no. 1: 21–45. https://doi.org/10.1111/1467-9507.00220

10 Baumrind.

Nancy Eisenberg, Tracy L. Spinrad, and Ariel Knafo-Noam, 2015. "Prosocial Development," in *Handbook of Child Psychology and Developmental Science, Seventh Edition, Vol. 3. Socioemotional Processes,* edited by Michael E. Lamb and Richard M. Lerner. Hoboken, NJ: Wiley. https://doi.org/10.1002/978111 8963418.childpsy315

Martin L. Hoffman, 2000. *Empathy and Moral Development: Implications for Caring And Justic*e. Cambridge, MA: Cambridge University Press.

Robert E. Larzelere, Ronald B. Cox Jr., and Jelani Mandara, 2013. "Responding to Misbehavior in Young Children: How Authoritative Parents Enhance Reasoning with Firm Control" in *Authoritative Parenting: Synthesizing Nurturance and Discipline for Optimal Child Development,* edited by Robert E. Larzelere, Amanda S. Morris, and Amanda W. Harrist. Washington, DC: American Psychological Association, 11–34.

11 Baumrind 19.

12 Baurind.

13 National Research Council and Institute of Medicine, 2009. *Preventing Mental, Emotional, and Behavioral Disorders among Young People: Progress and Possibilities.* Washington, DC: The National Academies Press.

14 Robert Kennedy, 2021. "Corporal Punishment Is Still Legal in Many States." *Boarding School Review*, November 25. https://www.boardingschoolreview. com/blog/corporal-punishment-is-still-legal-in-many-states

15 Phillip Bump, 2016. "Ted Cruz Spanks His Daughter, and Republicans Are A-OK With That." *The Washington Post*, January 9. https://www.washingtonpost.com/news/the-fix/wp/2016/01/09/ted-cruz-spanks-his-daughter-and-republicans-are-a-ok-with-that/

16 Albert Bandura, 1986. *Social Foundations of Thought and Action: A Social Cognitive Theory.* Upper Saddle River, NJ: Prentice-Hall.

17 Maggie Haberman, 2023. "Trump Spent $10 Million from His PAC on His Legal Bills Last Year." *The New York Times*, February 2. https://www.nytimes.com/2023/02/21/us/politics/trump-campaign-spending-pac-lawyer-bills.html

18 George G. Bear, 2020. *Improving School Climate: Practical Strategies to Reduce Behavior Problems and Promote Social-Emotional Learning.* New York: Taylor & Francis.

19 Bear, G. G., 2010. *School Discipline and Self-Discipline: A Practical Guide to Promoting Prosocial Student Behavior.* New York: Guilford Press.

George G. Bear, Jessica Slaughter, Lindsey Mantz, and Elizabeth Farley-Ripple, 2017. "Rewards, Praise, and Punitive Consequences: Relations with Intrinsic and Extrinsic Motivation." *Teaching and Teacher Education*, 65: 10–20. https://doi.org/10.1016/j.tate.2017.03.001.

20 Ryan & Deci.

21 Bear et al.

22 Bear, 2020.

Bear, 2010.

George G. Bear (with Albert Cavalier and Maureen Manning), 2005. *Developing Self-Discipline and Preventing and Correcting Misbehavior.* Boston: Allyn & Bacon.

George G. Bear, Angela Stolys, and Fiona Lochman, 2022. "Positive Psychology and School Discipline: In Support of Positive Educational Processes," in *The Handbook of Positive Psychology in Schools (3rd edition)* edited by Kelly-Ann Allen, Michael J. Furlong, Dianne Vella-Brodrick, and Shannon Suldo. New York, NY: Taylor and Francis, 1–5.

George G. Bear, 2019. "Preventing and Correcting Misbehavior and Developing Self-Discipline: Helping Handout for Home," in *Helping Handouts: Supporting Students at School and Home* edited by George G. Bear and Kathleen M. Minke. Bethesda, MD: National Association of School Psychologists.

Bear, G. G., Homan, J., & Morales, S., 2019. Using Praise and Rewards Wisely: Helping Handout for School and Home. In G.G. Bear & K.M. Minke (Eds.), *Helping Handouts: Supporting Students at School and Home.* Bethesda, MD: National Association of School Psychologists, 1–5.

George G. Bear, 2015. "Preventive Classroom Management," in *Handbook of Classroom Management* (2nd edition) edited by Edmund T. Emmer and Edward. J. Sabornie New York: Routledge, 15–39.

23 Paul C. Burnett, 2002. "Teacher Praise and Feedback and Students' Perceptions of the Classroom Environment." *Educational Psychology* 22 no. 1: 5–16. https://doi.org/10.1080/01443410120101215

24 Yasmeen Abutaleb and Damian Paletta, 2021. *Nightmare Scenario: Inside the Trump Administration's Response to the Pandemic That Changed History.* New York: Harper Colling.

Michael Wolf, 2021. *Landslide: The Final Days of the Trump Presidency.* New York: Henry Holt and Company.

Carol Leonnig and Philip Rucker, 2021. *I Alone Can Fix It: Donald J. Trump's Catastrophic Final Year.* New York: Penguin Press.

Index

For Product Safety Concerns and Information please contact our EU
representative GPSR@taylorandfrancis.com
Taylor & Francis Verlag GmbH, Kaufingerstraße 24, 80331 München, Germany